ZAGAT
2014

Chicago
Restaurants

LOCAL EDITOR
Alice Van Housen

STAFF EDITOR
Emily Rothschild

Published and distributed by
Zagat Survey, LLC
76 Ninth Avenue
New York, NY 10011
T: 212.977.6000
E: feedback@zagat.com
www.zagat.com

ACKNOWLEDGMENTS

We're grateful to our local editor, Alice Van Housen, a freelance writer and editor. We also sincerely thank the thousands of people who participated in this survey – this guide is really "theirs."

We also thank Stefanie Tuder (editor), Andrew Murphy and Megan Steintrager, as well as the following members of our staff: Aynsley Karps (editor), Brian Albert, Sean Beachell, Maryanne Bertollo, Reni Chin, Larry Cohn, John Deiner, Nicole Diaz, Kelly Dobkin, Jeff Freier, Alison Gainor, Michelle Golden, Justin Hartung, Marc Henson, Anna Hyclak, Ryutaro Ishikane, Natalie Lebert, Mike Liao, Vivian Ma, Molly Moker, James Mulcahy, Polina Paley, Josh Siegel, Albry Smither, Amanda Spurlock, Chris Walsh, Jacqueline Wasilczyk, Art Yagci, Sharon Yates, Anna Zappia and Kyle Zolner.

ABOUT ZAGAT

In 1979, we asked friends to rate and review restaurants purely for fun. The term "user-generated content" had yet to be coined. That hobby grew into Zagat Survey; 34 years later, we have loyal surveyors around the globe and our content now includes nightlife, shopping, tourist attractions, golf and more. Along the way, we evolved from being a print publisher to a digital content provider. We also produce marketing tools for a wide range of corporate clients, and you can find us on Google+ and just about any other social media network.

The reviews in this guide are based on public opinion surveys. The ratings reflect the average scores given by the survey participants who voted on each establishment, while the text is based on quotes from the surveyors' comments. Ratings and reviews have been updated throughout this edition based on our most recent survey results. Phone numbers, addresses and other factual data were correct to the best of our knowledge when published in this guide.

JOIN IN

To improve our guides, we solicit your comments – positive or negative; it's vital that we hear your opinions. Just contact us at **nina-tim@zagat.com.**

Contents

Ratings & Symbols

Name	Symbols	Cuisine	Zagat Ratings			
			FOOD	DECOR	SERVICE	COST

Area, Address & Contact
Tim & Nina's ◗ *Pizza* ▽ 23 | 9 | 13 | $15
Hyde Park | 456 E. Chicago Ave. (Division St.) |
312-555-3867 | www.zagat.com

Review, surveyor comments in quotes
Hordes of "unkempt" U of C students have gone nuclear over this "low-budget" cafeteria-style "24/7 dive", which "single-handedly" started the "deep-dish sushi pizza craze" that's "sweeping the Windy City like a lake-effect tsunami"; try the "to-die-for" eel-pepperoni-wasabi-mozzarella or Osaka-Napolitano pies – but be patient, since "the service here blows hot and cold – mostly cold."

Ratings   **Food, Decor** & **Service** are rated on a 30-point scale.

26 – 30   extraordinary to perfection

21 – 25   very good to excellent

16 – 20   good to very good

11 – 15   fair to good

0 – 10   poor to fair

▽   low response | less reliable

Cost   The price of dinner with a drink and tip; lunch is usually 25% to 30% less. For unrated **newcomers,** the price range is as follows:

I $25 and below   E $41 to $65

M $26 to $40   VE $66 or above

Symbols   ◗   serves after 11 PM
　　　　　　 ⊠   closed on Sunday
　　　　　　 Ⓜ   closed on Monday
　　　　　　 ⊅   cash only

Maps   Index maps show restaurants with the highest Food ratings and other notable places in those areas.

Chicago at a Glance

WINNERS:

- **Katsu** (Food)
- **Shanghai Terrace** (Decor)
- **Next** (Service)
- **Alinea** (Most Popular)

SURVEY STATS:

- 1,147 restaurants covered
- 7,634 surveyors
- In our recent Dining Trends Survey, Chicago respondents report that they eat 2.3 dinners out per week, spending an average of $38.99 per person for dinner ($1.54 less than the national average).
- When presented with a choice of dining irritants, surveyors selected noise as the most irritating, with 71% of diners saying they avoid restaurants that are too loud.
- Sixty-two percent of Chicago participants typically make restaurant reservations online, and 51% will not wait more than 30 minutes at places that don't take reservations.
- The majority of surveyors (54%) feels that taking pictures of food in a restaurant is ok in moderation, while 57% say it's rude and inappropriate to text, e-mail, tweet or talk on mobile phones.

TRENDS: The burgeoning chicken craze grew wings with eateries like hipster magnet **Parson's Chicken & Fish,** Filipino-accented **Pecking Order** and the low-key **Dak Korean Chicken Wings,** plus the soon-to-be **Honey Butter Fried Chicken** and **Leghorn** from the **Old Town Social/Nellcôte** team. German grub is making an unexpected resurgence at spots like **Himmel's,** the returning **Prost!** and the soon-to-open **The Radler,** a Bavarian beer hall coming to Logan Square in tandem with **D.A.S.,** its luxe little sister, both offering seasonal German eats. The availability of kosher grub also got a surprise boost with the additions of **Hamachi Sushi Bar** and **Milt's Barbecue for the Perplexed,** which joined **County Barbeque, Sweet Baby Ray's, Urbanbelly** and a new French Market branch of **Lillie's Q** in enhancing the BBQ scene.

HOT NEIGHBORHOODS: West Loop (**Belly Q, Embeya, Grace, Little Goat Diner, OON, RM Champagne Salon, Sushi Dokku**); River North (**Bavette's Bar & Boeuf, Boarding House, Brindille, Siena Tavern, Tortoise Club**); Logan Square (**Fat Rice, Parson's Chicken & Fish, Table, Donkey & Stick**).

MOST SEARCHED ON ZAGAT.COM: Gibsons, NoMI Kitchen, Spiaggia, Publican, Everest, Sixteen, Catch 35, Hugo's Frog Bar & Chop House, Coco Pazzo, Next

Chicago, IL
September 4, 2013

Alice Van Housen

KEY NEWCOMERS

Google

W Devon Ave
Found
NORTH PARK
W Granville Ave
W Peterson Ave

N Lincoln Ave
N Pulaski Rd
N Kimball Ave
N Kedzie Ave

LAKEWOOD-BALMORAL
ANDERSONVILLE
W Foster Ave

Elizabeth
Himmel's
UPTOWN
W Lawrence Ave

ALBANY PARK
LINCOLN SQUARE
SHERIDAN PARK

W Montrose Ave
NORTH CENTER
BUENA PARK

e+o Food & Drink
W Irving Park Rd
N Lake Shore Dr

Leadbelly
IRVING PARK
WRIGLEYVILLE
41

Lake Michigan

AVONDALE
W Addison St
Sweet Baby Ray's

W Belmont Ave
LAKE VIEW

Fat Rice
Senza

N Milwaukee Ave
N Pulaski Rd
N Elston Ave
N Clybourn Ave
N Ashland Ave

Juno
Lincoln Park

LOGAN SQ
BUCKTOWN

N Clark St
N Lincoln Ave
N Lake Shore Dr

Parson's
Table, Donkey & Stick
LINCOLN PARK

PALMER SQ
W Armitage Ave

Trenchermen
WICKER PARK
N Halsted St

W North Ave
OLD TOWN
GOLD COAST

Mott Street
90
94

N Kedzie Ave
W Division St
NOBLE SQUARE

HUMBOLDT PARK
W Augusta Blvd
W Chicago Ave

N Central Park Ave
W Grand Ave
See Downtown Chicago below
Navy Pier

EAST GARFIELD PARK
Belly Q
W Lake St

N Pulaski Rd
W Madison St
NEAR WEST SIDE

FIFTH CITY
Dwight D. Eisenhower Expwy
41

290
County Barbeque
W Harrison St

DOWNTOWN CHICAGO

W Division St
GOLD COAST
Jellyfish
Del Frisco's

GOOSE ISLAND
N Orleans St
N Larrabee St
N Halsted St
W Oak St
Masaki Sushi
41

N LaSalle St
RUSH & DIVISION
STREETERVILLE

N Ogden Ave
W Chicago Ave
Boarding House
NEAR NORTH

RIVER WEST
Sumi Robata Bar
Restaurant Beatrix
American Junkie
N Michigan Ave
Tre Soldi

N Milwaukee Ave
N State St
Brindille
W Ohio St
Centro
E Ohio St

Kennedy Expwy
Bavette's Bar & Boeuf
RIVER NORTH
Lao 18

La Sirena Clandestina
Siena Tavern

NEAR WEST SIDE
Little Goat Diner
Grace
Tortoise Club
E Wacker Dr

Kabocha Japanese Brasserie
Oon
Embeya
Chicago River
W Wacker Dr

W Lake St
N State St

WEST LOOP
W Randolph St
E Randolph St
Millennium Park

90
94
W Washington St
THE LOOP
W Madison St
S Columbus Dr
Grant Park

S Halsted St
S Desplaines St
S Clinton St
S Canal St
S Wacker Dr
S Franklin St
S LaSalle St
Tesori

W Adams St
W Jackson Blvd

©2013 Google

Key Newcomers

Our editors' picks among this year's arrivals. See full list at p. 204.

BIG NAMES/ BIG TICKETS

Boarding House
Brindille
e+o Food & Drink
Elizabeth
Grace
Little Goat Diner
Masaki Sushi
Senza
Siena Tavern
Tre Soldi

ASIAN SPICE

Belly Q
Embeya
Jellyfish
Juno
Kabocha Japanese Brasserie
Lao 18
Mott Street
Oon
Sumi Robata Bar

DECADENT EATS

Bavette's
County Barbeque
Del Frisco's
Leadbelly
Sweet Baby Ray's
Tortoise Club

NEIGHBORHOOD STARS

Fat Rice
Found
Himmel's
Table, Donkey & Stick
Tesori

SCENES

American Junkie
Centro
La Sirena Clandestina
Parson's
Restaurant Beatrix
Trenchermen

WHAT'S NEXT

Burke's Bacon Bar: David Burke does pig-centric sammies in River North

Chicago Chop Shop: Steakhouse in an old Wicker Park auto body shop

Dillman's: Brendan Sodikoff (**Bavette's, Gilt**) keeps traditional Jewish fare alive at this River North revamp of **Steve's Deli**

Eataly: Mario Batali brings his Italian mecca to River North

Honey Butter Fried Chicken: Bird-focused eats take flight in Avondale

Leghorn: The **Old Town Social** team hatches this sandwich-focused chicken shop in a location still TBD

Madison Street Kitchen: Casual American fare in the West Loop

Maxim's: Revival of the storied Gold Coast supper club from Brendan Sodikoff

Nico: The Gold Coast's Thompson Hotel gains Paul Kahan's Italian seafooder

Old Crow: Massive Lakeview smokehouse with internationally accented eats

The Radler/D.A.S.: Casual and upscale German twins in Logan Square

Tanta: Globe-trotting chef Gastón Acurio introduces high-end Peruvian cooking to River North

Travelle: Mediterranean cuisine in River North's Langham Hotel

Most Popular

This list is plotted on the map at the back of this book.

1. Alinea | *American*
2. Gibsons | *Steak*
3. Frontera Grill | *Mexican*
4. Girl & The Goat | *American*
5. Topolobampo* | *Mexican*
6. Avec | *Mediterranean*
7. Lou Malnati's | *Pizza*
8. Blackbird | *American*
9. Joe's Sea/Steak | *Seafood/Steak*
10. Tru* | *French*
11. Morton's | *Steak*
12. Gene & Georgetti | *Steak*
13. Publican* | *American*
14. Next | *Eclectic*
15. Les Nomades | *French*
16. MK* | *American*
17. Purple Pig | *Mediterranean*
18. Hugo's | *Seafood/Steak*
19. L2O | *Seafood*
20. Spiaggia* | *Italian*
21. Capital Grille | *Steak*
22. Shaw's Crab House | *Seafood*
23. Everest | *French*
24. Giordano's* | *Pizza*
25. GT Fish & Oyster | *Seafood*
26. Hot Doug's* | *Hot Dogs*
27. Balena | *Italian*
28. Chicago Chop House | *Steak*
29. Coco Pazzo* | *Italian*
30. Café Spiaggia | *Italian*
31. Au Cheval | *American*
32. McCormick/Schmick's* | *Seafood*
33. Riccardo Trattoria* | *Italian*
34. Al's Beef | *Sandwiches*
35. Mastro's Steakhouse* | *Steak*
36. Original Gino's East | *Pizza*
37. Xoco | *Mexican*
38. Café des Architectes | *French*
39. RL* | *American*
40. RPM Italian* | *Italian*
41. Ann Sather | *American/Swedish*
42. Bavette's* | *American/Steak*
43. Schwa* | *American*
44. Wildfire* | *Steak*
45. Chicago Cut Steakhouse | *Steak*
46. Aviary | *Eclectic*
47. Harry Caray's* | *Italian/Steak*
48. Ruxbin* | *Eclectic*
49. Longman & Eagle | *American*
50. Sepia* | *American*

Many of the above restaurants are among the Chicago area's most expensive, but if popularity were calibrated to price, a number of other restaurants would surely join their ranks. To illustrate this, we have added two pages of Best Buys starting on page 16.

* Indicates a tie with restaurant above

Top Food

29 Katsu Japanese | *Japanese*
Vie | *American*
Next | *Eclectic*
Alinea | *American*

28 Ruxbin | *Eclectic*
Schwa | *American*
EL Ideas | *American*
Les Nomades | *French*
Riccardo Trattoria | *Italian*
Topolobampo | *Mexican*
Takashi | *American/French*
Avec | *Mediterranean*

27 Acadia | *American/Seafood*
Tru | *French*
Courtright's | *American*
Over Easy Café | *American*
Gaetano's | *Italian*
Girl & The Goat | *American*
MK | *American*
Arami | *Japanese*

Longman & Eagle | *American*
Mixteco Grill | *Mexican*
Joe's Sea/Steak | *Seafood/Steak*
Kuma's Corner | *Burgers*
Everest | *French*
Sai Café | *Japanese*
Frontera Grill | *Mexican*
Pelago Ristorante | *Italian*
Spacca Napoli Pizzeria | *Pizza*
Henri | *American*
Fontano's Subs | *Sandwiches*
Tallgrass* | *French*
Arun's | *Thai*
Blackbird | *American*
Green Zebra | *Vegetarian*
Hot Doug's | *Hot Dogs*
Xoco | *Mexican*
Nightwood | *American*

26 NoMI Kitchen | *American*
North Pond | *American*

Top Decor

28 Shanghai Terrace
Alinea
L2O

27 Courtright's
Sixteen*
Tru
North Pond
NoMI Kitchen
Aviary
Everest

Pump Room
26 Les Nomades
Spiaggia
Henri
RL
Next
Bedford
Lobby

25 Vie
Bavette's Bar & Boeuf

Top Service

29 Next
Alinea

28 Vie
Les Nomades
Tru

27 Courtright's
Tallgrass
L2O
Moto
Everest

Henri
Aviary*
26 Spiaggia
Arun's
EL Ideas
Topolobampo
MK
Seasons 52
NoMI Kitchen
Joe's Sea/Steak

Excludes places with low votes, unless otherwise indicated

TOPS BY CUISINE

AMERICAN (NEW)
29 Vie
Alinea
28 Schwa
EL Ideas
Takashi

AMERICAN (TRAD.)
25 Table Fifty-two
24 Hot Chocolate
Glenn's Diner
Bongo Room
Lou Mitchell's

BARBECUE
26 Smoque BBQ
23 Big Bricks
22 Smoke Daddy
Belly Q
Lillie's Q

BURGERS
27 Kuma's
26 Edzo's Burger Shop
25 Butcher/Burger
22 Burger Bar
DMK Burger Bar

CHINESE
26 Shanghai Terrace
25 Sun Wah BBQ
24 Yu's Mandarin
Lao Beijing
23 Phoenix

DINERS
24 Glenn's Diner
Lou Mitchell's
Chicago Diner
Manny's Cafe & Deli
22 Milk/Honey

ECLECTIC
29 Next
28 Ruxbin
26 Moto
Lula Cafe
Aviary

FRENCH
28 Les Nomades
Takashi
27 Tru
Everest
Tallgrass

GASTROPUB
27 Longman & Eagle
26 Purple Pig
Publican
25 Gilt Bar
Bristol

GREEK
26 Taxim
22 Avli
Santorini
Athenian Room
Greek Islands

HOT DOGS
27 Hot Doug's
25 Franks 'N' Dawgs
24 Gene/Jude's
22 Al's Beef
21 Superdawg

INDIAN
24 Cumin
22 Marigold
Bombay Spice Grill
Gaylord Indian
Hema's Kitchen

ITALIAN
28 Riccardo Trattoria
27 Gaetano's
Pelago Ristorante
26 Davanti
Rosal's Italian Kitchen*

JAPANESE
29 Katsu
27 Arami
Sai Café
26 Toro Sushi
Yoshi's Café

MEDITERRANEAN
28 Avec
26 Purple Pig
23 Pita Inn
Dawali
22 Naf Naf Grill

MEXICAN
28 Topolobampo
27 Mixteco Grill
Frontera Grill
Xoco
26 Big Star

MIDDLE EASTERN

25 Turquoise
24 Noon-O-Kabab
23 Pita Inn
    Sayat Nova
    Dawali

PIZZA

27 Spacca Napoli
25 Chicago Pizza/Oven
    Lou Malnati's
    Apart Pizza
    Piece

SANDWICHES

27 Fontano's Subs
26 Publican Meats
25 Big & Little's
24 Ricobene's
    Cafecito

SEAFOOD

27 Acadia
    Joe's Sea/Steak
26 L2O
25 GT Fish/Oyster
    Shaw's Crab

SMALL PLATES

28 Avec
27 Girl & The Goat

    Green Zebra
26 Davanti Enoteca
    Purple Pig

SPANISH/TAPAS

26 Mercat a la Planxa
25 Mesón Sabika
23 Emilio's Tapas
22 Tapas Gitana
    Cafe Ba-Ba-Reeba!

STEAKHOUSES

27 Joe's Sea/Steak
26 Chicago Cut Steak
    Mastro's Steak
    Gibsons
    Rosewood

THAI

27 Arun's
26 TAC Quick
24 Opart Thai
22 Joy's Noodles
21 Ruby of Siam

VEGETARIAN

27 Green Zebra
26 Mana Food Bar
24 Chicago Diner
    Karyn's/Green
23 Native Foods

TOPS BY SPECIAL FEATURE

BREAKFAST

27 Over Easy
26 NoMI Kitchen
    Lula
25 Lobby
    M Henry/Henrietta

BRUNCH

27 Over Easy
    Frontera Grill
    Nightwood
26 NoMI Kitchen
    North Pond

CHICAGO ICONS

25 Gene/Georgetti
24 Lou Mitchell's
    Manny's
22 Cape Cod
21 Superdawg

CHILD-FRIENDLY

27 Hot Doug's
26 Sweet Maple

    Smoque BBQ
25 Sapori Trattoria
    Chicago Pizza

CRAFT BEER

27 Kuma's
26 Publican
24 Hopleaf
23 Farmhouse
17 Goose Island

CRAFT COCKTAILS

27 Longman & Eagle
26 Aviary
    Perennial Virant
25 Sepia
19 Nellcôte

HOTEL DINING

27 Pelago (Raffaello Hotel)
26 NoMI Kitchen (Park Hyatt)
    Shanghai Terrace (Peninsula)
    Perennial Virant (Hotel Lincoln)
    Gibsons (Doubletree O'Hare)

LATE DINING

- 28 Avec
- 26 Purple Pig
  - Mastro's Steak
  - Big Star
- 19 Tempo

LIVE ENTERTAINMENT

- 26 Sabatino's
- 25 Shaw's Crab
- 22 Smoke Daddy
  - Uncommon Ground
  - Nacional 27

OUTDOORS

- 27 Longman & Eagle
  - Pelago Ristorante
  - Henri
  - Blackbird
  - Nightwood

ROMANTIC

- 27 Henri
- 26 North Pond
- 23 Le Colonial
- 19 Nellcôte
- ─ Brindille

SINGLES SCENES

- 26 Gibson's
- 21 Old Town Social
  - Tavern/Rush
- 20 Hub 51
  - SushiSamba

TRENDY

- 28 Ruxbin
  - Avec
- 27 Girl & The Goat
  - MK
  - Arami

VIEWS

- 27 Everest
- 26 NoMI Kitchen
  - North Pond
- 25 Sixteen
- 17 Signature Room

WINNING WINE LISTS

- 29 Next
  - Alinea
- 28 Les Nomades
  - Topolobampo
  - Takashi

TOPS BY OCCASION

Some best bets in a range of prices and cuisines for these occasions.

ANNIVERSARY WORTHY

- 29 Goosefoot ▽
  - Grace ▽
  - Alinea
- 28 Les Nomades
- 27 Everest

BACHELORETTE PARTY

- 25 Gilt Bar
- 22 Mercadito
  - Nacional 27
- 20 Paris Club
- 19 Nellcôte

BACHELOR PARTY

- 26 Gibsons
- 25 Keefer's
- 23 Chicago Chop
  - Gage
- 17 Alhambra

BRIDAL SHOWERS

- 27 MK
- 26 Naha
  - Mercat
- 23 Vivo
  - Lockwood

BRUNCH WITH PARENTS

- 26 NoMI Kitchen
  - North Pond
- 25 Sixteen
- 24 RL
- 23 Gage

BUSINESS DINNER

- 29 Next
  - Alinea
- 28 Les Nomades
  - Topolobampo
  - Takashi

GRADUATION

- 27 Acadia
- 25 Quince
  - La Petite Folie
- 22 Gioco
- ─ Found

GROUP DINNERS

- 24 Tango Sur
- 22 Santorini
  - Quartino
- 21 Carnivale
  - Club Lucky

HAPPY HOUR

25 Shaw's Crab
24 Trattoria No. 10
  Palm
20 Hub 51
19 McCormick/Schmick

MEET FOR A DRINK

27 Girl & The Goat
  MK
  Longman & Eagle
  Joe's Sea/Steak
  Henri

NEW YEAR'S EVE

26 L2O
  Shanghai Terrace
25 Sixteen
21 Pump Room
19 Nellcôte

PRIDE PARADE

26 Yoshi's Café
23 Angelina
21 Hearty
19 Hamburger Mary's
17 Jack's/Halsted

TOPS BY LOCATION

ANDERSONVILLE/ EDGEWATER

26 Anteprima
25 Apart Pizza Company
  M Henry/Henrietta
24 Hopleaf
  Big Jones

BUCKTOWN

28 Takashi
25 Bristol
24 Hot Chocolate
  Coast Sushi
23 Le Bouchon

CHINATOWN

24 Lao Beijing
23 Ba Le
  Phoenix
22 Three Happiness
20 Joy Yee/Shabu Shabu

EVANSTON

25 Quince
  Oceanique
24 Coast Sushi
  Campagnola
  Chef's Station

GOLD COAST

26 NoMI Kitchen
  Spiaggia
25 Café Spiaggia
  Merlo on Maple
  Table Fifty-Two

GREEKTOWN

24 Karyn's on Green
22 Santorini
21 Artopolis
  Parthenon
20 Roditys

LAKEVIEW

27 Mixteco Grill
26 Yoshi's Café
25 Chilam Balam
  HB Home Bistro
24 Tango Sur

LINCOLN PARK

29 Alinea
28 Riccardo Trattoria
27 Sai Café
26 North Pond
  Sprout

LINCOLN SQ./UPTOWN

26 Tweet
25 Sun Wah BBQ
  San Soo Gab San
  Bistro Campagne
  Tank Noodle

LITTLE ITALY

26 Sweet Maple Café
  Davanti
  Rosal's*
24 Chez Joël
  Tufano's

LOGAN SQUARE

27 Longman & Eagle
26 Lula Cafe
25 Urbanbelly
24 Owen & Engine
23 Revolution Brewing

LOOP

27 Everest
  Henri
24 Trattoria No. 10
  Palm
  Cafecito

OLD TOWN

24 Salpicón
Topo Gigio
23 Trattoria Roma
22 Twin Anchors
Bistrot Margot

RIVER NORTH

28 Topolobampo
27 Joe's Sea/Steak
Frontera Grill
Xoco
26 Naha

STREETERVILLE

28 Les Nomades
27 Tru

Pelago Ristorante
24 Niu
23 Gyu-Kaku

WEST LOOP

29 Next
28 Avec
27 Girl & The Goat
Blackbird
26 Moto

WICKER PARK

28 Schwa
26 Mana Food Bar
Big Star
Taxim
25 Mirai Sushi

TOPS BY DESTINATION

A selection of the best bets in a range of prices and cuisines near these points of interest.

ART INSTITUTE

23 Gage
22 Terzo Piano
Russian Tea
Atwood Cafe
15 Artist's Café

CHICAGO THEATRE

23 Catch 35
Vivere
19 Berghoff
Petterino's
Park Grill

GREEN CITY MARKET

26 North Pond
Perennial Virant
24 Salpicón
23 Bricks
20 Adobo

LINCOLN PARK/ZOO

19 R.J. Grunts
Stanley's
18 Potbelly Sandwich Shop
17 Orange
Five Guys

MAGNIFICENT MILE

26 Purple Pig
Gibsons
24 Café/Architectes
RL
23 Bandera

MERCHANDISE MART

26 Chicago Cut
24 Nick's Fish
Kinzie Chop
23 Hannah's Bretzel
22 Mercadito

MILLENNIUM PARK

27 Henri
26 Mercat
23 Gage
22 Terzo Piano
17 Tavern/Park

MUSEUM CAMPUS/
SOLDIER FIELD (BEARS)

24 Manny's
22 Chicago Firehouse
Gioco
19 Eleven City
18 Zapatista

NAVY PIER

23 Volare
22 Yolk
Harry Caray's
21 Riva
16 Billy Goat

RAVINIA

25 Froggy's
24 Abigail's
20 Bella Via
Isaac/Moishe DFV*
19 Curry Hut

SECOND CITY COMEDY

24 Salpicón
Topo Gigio
22 Bistrot Margot
21 Old Town Social
20 Adobo Grill

STEPPENWOLF THEATRE

26 Boka
24 Balena
21 Rustic House
20 Trattoria Gianni
Vinci

UNITED CENTER (HAWKS AND BULLS)

22 Belly Q
20 Carmichael's

16 Billy Goat
City Winery▽
─ Arrow/Ogden

U.S. CELLULAR FIELD (WHITE SOX)

27 Birrieria Zaragoza▽
24 Home Run Inn
23 Bruna's▽
22 Bacchanalia
Giordano's

WRIGLEY FIELD (CUBS)

24 Fish Bar
22 Uncommon Ground
DMK Burger Bar
19 Rockit
17 Goose Island

Best Buys

Top-rated restaurants $25 and under

1. Over Easy Café | *American*
2. Kuma's Corner | *Burgers*
3. Spacca Napoli Pizzeria | *Pizza*
4. Hot Doug's | *Hot Dogs*
5. Xoco | *Mexican*
6. Sweet Maple Café | *American*
7. Smoque BBQ | *BBQ*
8. Edzo's Burger Shop | *Burgers*
9. Big Star | *Mexican*
10. Tweet | *American*
11. TAC Quick | *Thai*
12. Wholly Frijoles | *Mexican*
13. Belly Shack | *Asian*
14. Franks 'N' Dawgs | *Hot Dogs*
15. Chicago Pizza | *Pizza*
16. Butcher/Burger | *Burgers*
17. Sun Wah BBQ | *Chinese*
18. Lou Malnati's | *Pizza*
19. San Soo Gab San | *Korean*
20. Urbanbelly | *Asian*

BEST BUYS BY NEIGHBORHOOD

EVANSTON
- 21 Hecky's BBQ
- Lulu's
- 20 Blind Faith
- Dixie Kitchen
- Lupita's

LAKEVIEW
- 24 Crisp
- Chicago Diner
- 23 Del Seoul
- Native Foods Café
- Southport

LINCOLN PARK
- 26 Edzo's
- 25 Franks 'N' Dawgs
- Chicago Pizza
- Butcher/Burger
- Lou Malnati's

LOGAN SQUARE
- 25 Urbanbelly
- 23 Revolution Brewing
- 90 Miles
- 22 Jam
- Margie's Candies

LOOP
- 24 Cafecito
- Lou Mitchell's
- Frontera Fresco
- 23 Hannah's Bretzel
- Wildberry

RIVER NORTH
- 27 Xoco
- 24 Mr. Beef
- 22 Pizzeria Due
- Bombay Spice Grill
- 21 25 Degrees

UPTOWN
- 26 Tweet
- 25 Sun Wah BBQ
- Tank Noodle
- 24 Pho 777
- 20 Demera

WICKER PARK
- 26 Big Star
- 25 Piece
- 24 Bongo Room
- 23 Birchwood Kitchen
- 22 Smoke Daddy

BEST BUYS BY CATEGORY

BRING THE KIDS

22	Three Happiness
20	Joy Yee's
19	Tempo
	Foodlife
18	Potbelly

BRING THE PARENTS

22	Ina's
21	Julius Meinl
	Ann Sather
	La Crêperie
18	Robinson's

BRUNCH

27	Over Easy Café
26	Sweet Maple
25	M Henry
24	Bongo Room
22	Toast

BYO

24	Crisp
23	Birchwood Kitchen
	Dawali
	Irazu
22	Bite Café

CHEAP DATE

27	Spacca Napoli
25	Chicago Pizza
	Piece
24	Crisp
23	Revolution Brewing

GLOBE-TROTTING

25	San Soo Gab San
24	Ricobene's
	Tre Kronor
23	Del Seoul
20	Andies

HEALTH CONSCIOUS

24	Chicago Diner
23	Native Foods Café
20	Andies
	Old Jerusalem Restaurant
17	Heartland Café

HOMETOWN CLASSICS

24	Mr. Beef
	Manny's
22	Al's Beef
21	Superdawg
16	Billy Goat Tavern

LATE DINING

23	Revolution Brewing
20	Bangers/Lace
	Twisted Spoke
19	Tempo
	Wiener's Circle

OFFBEAT

27	Hot Doug's
24	Lou Mitchell's
20	Bourgeois Pig
19	Hamburger Mary's
	Wiener's Circle

OFF THE RADAR

27	Birrieria Zaragoza▽
24	Vito/Nick's
	Gene/Jude's
21	Russell's BBQ
17	Heartland Café

SANDWICHES

27	Fontano's
25	Big/Little's
24	Cemitas Puebla
	Cafecito
23	Pita Inn

TOP CHEF BARGAINS

27	Xoco
25	Belly Shack
23	Tortas Frontera▽
22	Noodles/Takashi▽
19	Grahamwich

TRENDY

27	Hot Doug's
	Xoco
26	Big Star
25	Belly Shack
	Urbanbelly

RESTAURANT DIRECTORY

	FOOD	DECOR	SERVICE	COST

Abigail's 🛇Ⓜ *American*
24 | 20 | 21 | $41

Highland Park | Ravinia Business District | 493 Roger Williams Ave.
(St. Johns Ave.) | 847-780-4862 | www.abigails493.com

"Carefully orchestrated", "imaginative" New American fare,
"good wines by the glass, carafe or bottle" and "classic cocktails" lure "ladies who lunch" and "pre- or post-Ravinia"-goers to
this "quaint" North Shore "gem"; the "cramped" space often gets
"too noisy" and limited reservations (accepted only until 6 PM)
can mean "long waits", but moderate prices help ensure it's still
"deservedly crowded", so some simply suggest you "go early" or
"when you can sit outside."

Acadia Ⓜ *American/Seafood*
27 | 25 | 24 | VE

South Loop | 1639 S. Wabash Ave. (bet. 16th & 18th Sts.) |
312-360-9500 | www.acadiachicago.com

A "special-occasion place", this seafood-focused South Loop
New American impresses with Ryan McCaskey's "imaginative",
"delicious" prix-fixe meals presented "beautifully" in a "sleek,
modern" space with "natural accents"; "helpful" staffers "genuinely care", and while "expensive" prices match the "fine-dining"
cuisine, you can always "stop by the bar" for a more affordable
"spur-of-the-moment" meal.

Acre *American*
20 | 21 | 20 | $33

Andersonville | 5308 N. Clark St. (bet. Berwyn & Summerdale Aves.) |
773-334-7600 | www.acrerestaurant.com

"Creative", farm-focused American "comfort food" gets a boost
from an "extensive beer list", plus wine and house cocktails at this
"gentrified" Andersonville gastropub adjacent to Italian small-plates
sister Ombra; "professional" service, a "relaxed atmosphere" and
moderate prices also work in its favor, so even if it's "not worth a
long journey", it's still "nice to have in the neighborhood", and especially "excellent" for brunch.

Ada St. Ⓜ *American/Mediterranean*
▽ 24 | 21 | 22 | $53

Bucktown | 1664 N. Ada St. (Concord Pl.) | 773-697-7069 |
www.adastreetchicago.com

Beyond a "mysterious, nondescript entrance" lies this "sophisticated and hip" Bucktown hideaway from Michael Kornick and David
Morton (DMK Burger Bar, Fish Bar) that offers an "often-changing"
menu of "innovative" New American–Mediterranean small plates
showcasing "fresh, bright flavors"; "fancy, inventive" cocktails help
fuel a "vibrant scene" in the "cool" candlelit dining room, just don't
be surprised when it's "crowded on weekends."

Adelle's Ⓜ *American*
26 | 22 | 25 | $44

Wheaton | 535 W. Liberty Dr. (West St.) | 630-784-8015 |
www.adelles.com

"Top-notch", "imaginatively prepared" New American fare and
"friendly, warm" service are standouts at this moderate Wheaton
"jewel"; the modern, earth-toned space features fireplaces and an
"inviting" bar area, and there's live jazz on Thursdays.

		FOOD	DECOR	SERVICE	COST

Adobo Grill · *Mexican* — 20 | 19 | 21 | $33

Old Town | 1610 N. Wells St. (North Ave.) | 312-266-7999 |
www.adobogrill.com

A "step up" from many Mexican eateries, this "colorful", "lively" Old
Town cantina has a "diverse", "surprisingly creative" menu of "consistently good" eats that offer a "different take" on tradition; "excellent
margaritas", "knowledgeable" staffers and affordable tabs further explain why it's "popular", as does its "proximity to Second City."

Agami · *Japanese* — 24 | 21 | 22 | $42

Uptown | 4712 N. Broadway (Leland Ave.) | 773-506-1845 |
www.agamisushi.com

"Creative" "well-above-average sushi creations" are a "touch pricey,
but worth it" at this Uptown Japanese where the "large bar turns out
delicious cocktails" along with a "great selection of sake and Japanese
beers" and the "surreal decor" makes "you feel as though you are
eating in an aquarium"; "helpful" service is another plus, leading fans
to crown it a "godsend" to the "embattled neighborhood"; P.S. it's
"perfect for pre-Riviera concerts or a trip to the Green Mill for jazz."

NEW Ahjoomah's Apron ⑤Ⓜ *Korean* — - | - | - | I

Chinatown | 218 W. Cermak Rd. (Wentworth Ave.) | 312-326-2800 |
www.ahjoomahchicago.com

Affordable Korean standards (bibimbop, kalbi and bulgogi, soups,
stir-fries) mix things up in Chinatown at this affordable eatery; the
spare, ultramodern digs include bare tables and benches, industrial
lighting and food murals, and in place of alcohol, there are soft drinks,
Korean juice and barley tea.

Ai Sushi Lounge · *Japanese* — 21 | 21 | 19 | $42

River North | 358 W. Ontario St. (bet. Kingsbury & Orleans Sts.) |
312-335-9888 | www.aichicago.us

"Fresh", "authentic" sushi and sashimi, "creative" rolls and the "opportunity to eat fugu" (served seasonally) make this midpriced River
North Japanese "worth going"; "service can shift from mediocre to
great", but "trendy music, stylish people" and "contemporary loftlike" environs still help it reach "staple" status.

Akai Hana · *Japanese* — 21 | 14 | 18 | $29

Wilmette | 3223 W. Lake Ave. (Skokie Rd.) | 847-251-0384 |
www.akaihanasushi.com

"Cheap and cheerful", this Wilmette Japanese is "consistent" for
"reliably fresh" "sushi with minimal fuss" plus "solid tempura and
teriyakis"; so while it's "not innovative or startling" and its strip-mall
setting is "generic", service that "aims to please" helps compensate
and it remains a "popular" "local favorite."

Al Dente Ⓜ *American* — ▽ 23 | 16 | 23 | $36

Northwest Side | 3939 W. Irving Park Rd. (bet. Harding Ave. &
Pulaski Rd.) | 773-942-7771 | www.aldentechicago.com

Chef Javier Perez (ex MK, Spiaggia) uses Mexican and Italian influences in his "imaginative", "delicious" New American dishes at this

Irving Park BYO; the informal digs may not impress, but tabs are affordable, and hey, the decor is "not the reason to go" anyway.

Alhambra Palace Restaurant *Mideastern*　17 | 24 | 15 | $45

West Loop | 1240 W. Randolph St. (bet. Elizabeth St. & Racine Ave.) | 312-666-9555 | www.alhambrapalacerestaurant.com

Traditional Middle Eastern eats are on the menu but it's the "gorgeous" surrounds that leave the biggest impression at this "enormous" West Loop eye-popper rife with "rich colors and eye-catching elements" (including "entertaining belly dancers"); tabs aren't low, and not everyone's a fan of the cooking, but returnees say it "almost doesn't matter what the food tastes like when the space is this amazing."

Alinea Ⓜ *American*　29 | 28 | 29 | $273

Lincoln Park | 1723 N. Halsted St. (bet. North Ave. & Willow St.) | 312-867-0110 | www.alinea-restaurant.com

"Expect to be wowed" at Grant Achatz's "unrivaled" Lincoln Park New American, a "culinary experience of a lifetime" (and Chicago's Most Popular restaurant) where "transcendent flavors", "unforgettable, artistic presentation" and "mind-blowing technique" highlight a multicourse tasting menu that's akin to "going on a food safari"; "über-modern" decor is enhanced by "interactive, accommodating" staffers, and while you may need to "bring the Brink's truck" to pay, well, that might be the cost of "foodie heaven."

Allium *American*　▽ 23 | 23 | 22 | $56

Gold Coast | Four Seasons Hotel Chicago | 120 E. Delaware Pl., 7th fl. (bet. Michigan Ave. & Rush St.) | 312-799-4900 | www.alliumchicago.com

Chef Kevin Hickey's "creative, seasonal" fare is "comforting yet refined" at this "upscale" New American in the Gold Coast's Four Seasons where small and large plates share menu real estate with "elevated" Chicago favorites like "gourmet hot dogs"; the "attractive", richly colored modern space includes a lounge area and dining room, both of which are watched over by an "attentive" staff.

Al's Beef *Sandwiches*　22 | 9 | 16 | $11

Loop | 601 W. Adams St. (Jefferson St.) | 312-559-2333
River North | 169 W. Ontario St. (Wells St.) | 312-943-3222 ●
Wrigleyville | 3420 N. Clark St. (Sheffield Ave.) | 773-935-2333 ●
Roscoe Village | 2804 N. Western Ave. (Diversey Ave.) | 773-486-2333
NEW **Wicker Park** | 1300 N. Milwaukee Ave. (Paulina St.) | 773-663-4800
Chinatown | 5441 S. Wentworth Ave. (Garfield Blvd.) | 773-373-4700
Little Italy/University Village | 1079 W. Taylor St. (bet. May & Morgan Sts.) | 312-226-4017 ●◙⇥
Niles | 5948 W. Touhy Ave. (Lehigh Ave.) | 847-647-1577
Park Ridge | 1036 W. Higgins Rd. (bet. Cumberland Ave. & Dee Rd.) | 847-825-2345
Tinley Park | 7132 183rd St. (Harlem Ave.) | 708-444-2333
www.alsbeef.com
Additional locations throughout the Chicago area

Carnivores get their "fix" at this "classic" Chicago fast-foodery, a "tradition" for "wet, juicy", "drip-down-the-forearm" Italian beef plus "good, greasy fries", sausages and other low-priced eats; the "dive-ish" atmosphere comes with the territory, but service is "quick" and hey, "you don't go there for the decor."

American Girl Place Cafe *American*

13	22	20	$30

Streeterville | Water Tower Pl. | 835 N. Michigan Ave. (bet. Chestnut & Pearson Sts.) | 877-247-5223 | www.americangirlplace.com

"They certainly know how to treat a five year old" at this "delightful" "must-see" for "little ones" in Streeterville's Water Tower Place where "terrific" details like "matching dinnerware" for the dolls and "hair scrunchie" napkin rings make it "the place to go" when your children "need spoiling"; yes, the American offerings are "nothing great for adults" and it doesn't come cheap, but patient parents who appreciate the "organized dining experience" suggest just "soaking in" the "smiles" of the kids who "love every minute."

NEW American Junkie *American*

-	-	-	M

River North | 15 W. Illinois St. (bet. Dearborn & State Sts.) | 312-239-0995 | www.americanjunkiechi.com

Kendal Duque (formerly of Sepia) is cooking up refined American gastropub fare with artisanal ingredients at this River North hang where liquid refreshments include cocktails on tap and many draft brews; the huge bi-level industrial space features concrete floors, American flags, a phalanx of flat-screen TVs and a second floor with sofas, a dance floor, a retractable roof and bottle service.

Amuse *American*

-	-	-	M

Loop | Swissôtel Chicago | 323 E. Wacker Dr. (Columbus Dr.) | 312-565-0565 | www.swissotel.com

Dan McGee (he of the Frankfort namesake) mans the stoves at this New American in the Loop's Swissôtel lobby serving moderately priced creative snacks plus a drinks list showcasing craft cocktails and brown booze; the sleek open space is done in neutrals and modern lighting with a granite bar, communal high-tops and lounge groupings.

Andies *Mediterranean/Mideastern*

20	17	19	$24

Andersonville | 5253 N. Clark St. (Berwyn Ave.) | 773-784-8616
Lakeview | 1467 W. Montrose Ave. (Greenview Ave.) | 773-348-0654 M
www.andiesres.com

All the "simple", "authentic" Middle Eastern and Mediterranean dishes "you want and need", including "many vegetarian choices", are on the "huge menu" at these Andersonville and Lakeview "stand-bys" where an "unusually eclectic and interesting staff" provides "friendly" if occasionally "spotty service"; while "nothing fancy", they're "low-key" and "affordable", making them "reliable" "meeting places with friends."

NEW Andy's Thai Kitchen *Thai*

∇ 26	14	15	$24

Lakeview | 946 W. Wellington Ave. (Sheffield Ave.) | 773-549-7821 | www.andysthaikitchen.com

"Under the el tracks" in Lakeview sits this "tiny" cash-only BYO, a "real find" for "flavorful", "delicious" Thai plates, including many "adventurous" choices; the service might not rate as highly, and the interior's a bit "plain", but all is forgiven considering the "bargain prices."

Angelina Ristorante *Italian*   23 | 20 | 23 | $33

Lakeview | 3561 N. Broadway (Addison St.) | 773-935-5933 | www.angelinaristorante.com

"A little piece of Italy", this "quaint" Lakeview "delight" lures diners with "reliably solid" Italian dishes featuring a "wide variety of flavors and aromas", plus "reasonably priced wines" and "romantic", "calming" confines; "truly friendly" service and affordable tabs also make it good for "first dates, family dinners" or "girls' nights out"; P.S. weekend brunch – with "bottomless" champagne drinks and "spontaneous dancing from the flamboyant crowd" – is "legendary."

Anna Maria Pasteria *Italian*   ▽ 20 | 17 | 22 | $35

Ravenswood | 4400 N. Clark St. (Montrose Ave.) | 773-506-2662 | www.annamariapasteria.com

"Owned by sisters (one works in the kitchen and the other the dining room)", this "low-key" Ravenswood "gem" serves a "tasty" menu of "homestyle" Italian cooking in an "unassuming" setting; "knowledgeable service" and affordable bills are additional pluses.

Anna's Asian Bistro *Asian*   - | - | - | M

West Loop | 813 W. Lake St. (bet. Green & Halsted Sts.) | 312-733-8095 | www.annasbistro.com

The namesake Anna (former partner in Thalia Spice) and her chef mom are behind this mod West Loop BYO serving an exhaustive menu of sushi and mixed Asian fare (Chinese, Japanese, Thai, Vietnamese) plus lunch specials and weekend brunch; a Sputnik light fixture and recessed candle alcoves create romantic lighting amid exposed brick, wheel-inspired ceiling screens and black tablecloths.

Ann Sather *American/Swedish*   21 | 16 | 20 | $17

Andersonville | 5207 N. Clark St. (bet. Farragut & Foster Aves.) | 773-271-6677
Edgewater | 1147 W. Granville Ave. (B'way) | 773-274-0557
Lakeview | 909 W. Belmont Ave. (bet. Clark St. & Sheffield Ave.) | 773-348-2378
Ann Sather Café *American/Swedish*
Lakeview | 3415 N. Broadway (Roscoe St.) | 773-305-0024 | www.annsather.com

"Insanely good" cinnamon rolls "overflowing with glaze" are one of the "highlights" at these breakfast and brunch "classics", where "consistently good" Swedish-American "comfort food" comes in "large" portions; the "traditional" "old-school diner"-like environs can get "crowded" on weekends, but service stays generally "friendly", and affordable prices help seal the deal.

Anteprima *Italian*   26 | 21 | 23 | $42

Andersonville | 5316 N. Clark St. (bet. Berwyn & Summerdale Aves.) | 773-506-9990 | www.anteprimachicago.net

Acolytes "still dream" about the "market-driven" "authentic Italian cuisine" at this "lively" (some say "noisy") "little" Andersonville "storefront" where a "well-chosen" wine list complements the mid-priced menu; "accommodating" service and "cozy" environs complete with a "romantic outdoor patio" further leave regulars rhapsodizing "so sophisticated, so simple, so neighborhood fantastic."

The Anthem ◑ *Pub Food* | ▽ 18 | 17 | 22 | $21 |

Ukrainian Village | 1725 W. Division St. (Hermitage Ave.) | 773-697-4804 | www.theanthemchicago.com

Step back in time at this "unassuming" Ukrainian Village sports bar from the Bangers & Lace team, where the '70s vibe extends from the retro wood-paneled surrounds to the midpriced pub menu with nostalgic comfort-food classics like hamburger mac 'n' cheese and fish sticks plus salads, sandwiches and more; the many "big screens" are often tuned to the game, and front windows open in warm weather.

Antico Posto *Italian* | 23 | 20 | 22 | $33 |

Oak Brook | Oakbrook Center Mall | 118 Oakbrook Ctr. (Rte. 83) | 630-586-9200 | www.antico-posto.com

"Easy to like", this Oakbrook Center "oasis" is "reliable", delivering "well-prepared", "simple" Italian fare like "tasty brick-oven pizza" and "delicious ravioli" that "change with the seasons"; "good wine deals", "timely", "attentive" service and "value" prices also find favor, and if some say it's a bit "noisy from shopper victory talk", most maintain it's an overall "pleasant" pick.

Antique Taco Ⓜ *Mexican* | ▽ 23 | 20 | 18 | $17 |

Wicker Park | 1360 N. Milwaukee Ave. (Wolcott Ave.) | 773-687-8697 | www.antiquetaco.com

"Delicious" tacos with "interesting flavors" are the centerpiece of this Wicker Park taqueria offering a compact Mexican menu including house cocktails; the "cute" antique-enhanced space is counter-service only, and the "casual" vibe is matched by equally casual prices.

Apart Pizza Company *Pizza* | 25 | 11 | 20 | $15 |

Edgewater | 5624 N. Broadway St. (bet. Bryn Mawr & Hollywood Aves.) | 773-784-1550
Ravenswood | 2205 W. Montrose Ave. (Lincoln Ave.) | 773-588-1550 www.apartpizzacompany.com

The "incredible" pizzas are "creative", "flavorful" and topped by "quality" ingredients, but it's the "crisp" yet "chewy" thin crust that devotees agree really does set this Edgewater and Ravenswood duo "apart from the crowd"; service is "accommodating" and tabs "reasonable", but small, "bare-bones" settings with "lackluster" decor and limited seating make them "highly recommended for takeout and delivery."

Aquitaine *American/French* | ▽ 21 | 19 | 20 | $40 |

Lincoln Park | 2221 N. Lincoln Ave. (bet. Geneva Terr. & Orchard St.) | 773-698-8456 | www.aquitainerestaurant.com

"Well-seasoned" French–New American fare (including "to-die-for" duck confit mac 'n' cheese) at "reasonable prices" render this Lincoln Park "bistro in the heart of sports bar row" a "good neighborhood option"; "friendly" service and a "warm, intimate setting" also add appeal, so even if it's "not spectacular" it's still a "charming" choice.

Arami *Japanese* | 27 | 22 | 23 | $47 |

West Town | 1829 W. Chicago Ave. (bet. Wolcott Ave. & Wood St.) | 312-243-1535 | www.aramichicago.com

A "favorite for sushi", this "hip, urban" West Town storefront delivers "fresh, imaginative" rolls alongside other highly rated Japanese dishes including small plates, noodles and robata grill items; service is "helpful" in the "relaxing" "spa"-like setting done up in bamboo and exposed brick, and prices are moderate.

Aria *Asian* | 23 | 22 | 22 | $57 |

Loop | Fairmont Chicago Hotel | 200 N. Columbus Dr. (bet. Randolph St. & Wacker Dr.) | 312-444-9494 | www.ariachicago.com

Set in the Loop's Fairmont Hotel, this "upscale" sushi specialist "stands on its own" with "consistently delicious", "Asian-inspired" plates set down by "attentive" servers in a "quiet", "pretty space"; despite a few complaints that it's "a little overpriced", many rank it "worth the side trip" from "downtown traffic", especially for a "business lunch."

Arrow on Ogden *Pub Food* | - | - | - | I |

West Loop | 1659 W. Ogden Ave. (bet. Adams & Monroe Sts.) | 312-226-1888 | www.theogdenchicago.com

This sports bar near United Center serves a range of gourmet pub food (burgers, flatbreads, wings) accompanied by a large beer list and a few wines; the urban-industrial environs boast exposed brick, many TVs and a fireplace, and prices are budget-friendly.

NEW Artisan Table *American* | - | - | - | M |

Naperville | Chicago Marriott Naperville | 1801 Naper Blvd. (Diehl Rd.) | 630-505-4900 | www.marriott.com

At this modern New American in Naperville's Marriott Hotel, the three square midpriced meals are fashioned from local, organic and artisanal ingredients (including honey from a rooftop beehive); the earth-toned space has a modern, clean-lined hotel-dining vibe and a limited till-midnight menu at the cocktail lounge.

Artist's Cafe *Coffeehouse/Diner* | 15 | 15 | 15 | $24 |

Loop | Fine Arts Building | 412 S. Michigan Ave. (bet. Congress Pkwy. & Van Buren St.) | 312-939-7855
NEW **South Loop** | 1150 S. Wabash Ave. (bet. 11th St. & Roosevelt Rd.) | 312-583-9940
www.artists-cafe.com

Around for more than 50 years and named for the myriad creative types who've frequented it, this "cute, little" Loop coffeehouse (with a newer South Loop sequel) offers "generous" portions of classic diner eats plus some Greek-influenced plates too; a Michigan Avenue view from the Fine Arts Building doesn't hurt, and the 11 PM closing time is convenient for after-theater.

Art of Pizza *Pizza* | 23 | 9 | 16 | $14 |

Lakeview | 3033 N. Ashland Ave. (Nelson St.) | 773-327-5600 | www.theartofpizzainc.com

"Fresh ingredients", solid sauce and "lots of cheese" add up to "oh-so-good" pies (deep-dish, thin and stuffed crust) at this counter-service Lakeview pie purveyor that "also sells by the slice so you don't have to wait"; it may be "nothing to look at", but BYO keeps the tabs extra "reasonable" and service is "quick", making it a "darned good" option.

Artopolis ● Greek/Mediterranean | 21 | 20 | 18 | $21 |

Greektown | 306 S. Halsted St. (bet. Jackson Blvd. & Van Buren St.) | 312-559-9000 | www.artopolischicago.com

A "bright place for a light meal", this "cozy" Greektowner offering both counter and table service bakes up "beautiful breads" and "interesting savory pastries" to go with other "tasty", "affordable" Greek-Mediterranean bites; "too busy for the service to be perfect", it's still "quick" and easy for lunch or an "after-theater/concert snack."

Arun's Ⓜ Thai | 27 | 24 | 26 | $111 |

Northwest Side | 4156 N. Kedzie Ave. (Berteau Ave.) | 773-539-1909 | www.arunsthai.com

"Upscale Thai" is "taken to its apex" at this Northwest Side "must-visit", where chef-owner Arun Sampanthavivat prepares "out-of-this-world" prix fixe dishes elevated by presentations straight "out of a picture book"; the traditionally decorated space may not soar quite as high, and tabs are "pricey", but "excellent" service helps ensure an overall "fine-dining" experience.

A Tavola Ⓩ Italian | 26 | 21 | 26 | $49 |

Ukrainian Village | 2148 W. Chicago Ave. (bet. Hoyne Ave. & Leavitt St.) | 773-276-7567 | www.atavolachicago.com

All of the ingredients for a "great night out" can be found at this "small" Ukrainian Village Italian, from "wonderful comfort food", including some of the "best gnocchi in the city", to "knowledgeable" staffers who are "attentive, but not obtrusive"; if the dining room doesn't get the same high marks, there's always the "lovely" outdoor courtyard.

Athena Greek | 19 | 20 | 20 | $29 |

Greektown | 212 S. Halsted St. (Adams St.) | 312-655-0000 | www.athenarestaurantchicago.com

The "killer" patio provides "stellar views of the Chicago skyline" at this inviting Greektowner where the "classic" Hellenic dishes are also served in the spacious, fireplace-enhanced dining room; tabs are modest and service "organized", so even holdouts who feel the food is "nothing to die for" assure it's "awesome" on a "gorgeous night."

Athenian Room American/Greek | 22 | 12 | 19 | $19 |

Lincoln Park | 807 W. Webster Ave. (bet. Dayton & Halsted Sts.) | 773-348-5155

Situated "in the heart of Lincoln Park", this long-standing American-Greek is a "casual" "neighborhood standby" thanks to "basic" dishes "done right", including "delish" chicken and "incredible" "juice-soaked fries that are magically still crispy"; "quick", "friendly" servers contribute to the "laid-back atmosphere", and "large portions" and "low" prices make it an "insane bargain."

A Toda Madre 🗷 M *Mexican* `- | - | - | M`

Geneva | 416 W. State St. (bet. 4th & 5th Sts.) | 630-845-3015 | www.atmrestaurant.com

Located next door to sibling Bien Trucha, this affordable Geneva Mexican offers a modern, small plates–focused menu that makes it easy to "try several dishes"; the petite, wood-accented space has an open kitchen and casual feel, and many agree it's an overall "great addition to the dining scene."

Atwood Cafe *American* `22 | 24 | 22 | $41`

Loop | Hotel Burnham | 1 W. Washington St. (State St.) | 312-368-1900 | www.atwoodcafe.com

Set in the "landmark" Hotel Burnham, this "beautiful" Loop American appeals with "charmingly quirky" surroundings, "interesting" fare that's "innovative enough" for repeat visits and service that ensures you "don't feel rushed"; its locale makes it a "popular" "pre-theater spot", so it can get a "bit cozy (i.e. crowded)", but things calm down once the shows start.

Au Cheval ◗ *American* `25 | 21 | 20 | $35`

West Loop | 800 W. Randolph St. (Halsted St.) | 312-929-4580 | www.aucheval.tumblr.com

Brendan Sodikoff (Gilt Bar, Maude's Liquor Bar) "keeps the hits coming" with his West Loop "speakeasy diner" that offers "rich", "upscale" takes on classics like bologna sandwiches "piled high" and some of the "best burgers", all bolstered by an "impressive" beer list and updated cocktail classics; "mood lighting", "dark wood" and "comfortable" booths further the "cool" vibe, though no-reservations often mean an "inevitable wait."

Aurelio's Pizza *Pizza* `21 | 15 | 19 | $20`

Loop | Holiday Inn Chicago Downtown | 506 W. Harrison St. (Canal St.) | 312-994-2000

Addison | Centennial Plaza | 1455 W. Lake St. (Lombard Rd.) | 630-889-9560

Chicago Heights | 1545 S. Western Ave. (Illinois St.) | 708-481-5040

Homewood | 18162 Harwood Ave. (183rd St.) | 708-798-8050

South Holland | 601 E. 170th St. (Langley Ave.) | 708-333-0310

Palos Heights | 6543 W. 127th St. (Ridgeland Ave.) | 708-389-5170

Tinley Park | 15901 Oak Park Ave. (Rte. 6) | 708-429-4600

Downers Grove | 940 Warren Ave. (Highland Ave.) | 630-810-0078

Naperville | 931 W. 75th St. (Plainfield-Naperville Rd.) | 630-369-0077

Villa Park | 100 E. Roosevelt Rd. (Ardmore Ave.) | 630-629-3200 www.aureliospizza.com

Additional locations throughout the Chicago area

Fans who've been "going for decades" swear by the "crispy" thin-crust pies made with "tangy", "savory-sweet" sauce and "sufficient cheese and meat" at this homegrown pizza chain; if a few say it can be "hit-or-miss based on location", most "recommend" the Homewood

	FOOD	DECOR	SERVICE	COST

original, adding it has the "best" offerings; P.S. some locations are carryout and delivery only.

Autre Monde Café & Spirits M *Mediterranean*

▽ 26	20	24	$41

Berwyn | 6727 W. Roosevelt Rd. (bet. Eulicid & Oak Park Aves.) | 708-775-8122 | www.autremondecafe.net

They've "hit it right" at this Berwyn Mediterranean, a "sophisticated (but not pretentious) gem", where chefs Dan Pancake and Beth Partridge (both ex Spiaggia) make use of ingredients often sourced from their own Cakeridge Farms or the on-site greenhouse in "flavorful" dishes, boosted by "interesting" wines and "must"-try cocktails; "friendly" servers elevate the "warm, minimalist" space, so though it's a "little loud" for some, most say it's an overall "charmer."

Avec ● *Mediterranean*

28	23	24	$48

West Loop | 615 W. Randolph St. (bet. Desplaines & Jefferson Sts.) | 312-377-2002 | www.avecrestaurant.com

"Small plates at their best" can be found at this "energetic" West Loop Mediterranean, Blackbird's more "casual", less expensive sibling that's "still going strong" with "delicious" "elevated comfort food" (including "mandatory" chorizo-stuffed dates) dispensed by a "friendly, helpful" crew; the "teeny" space has a "festive", "lively" vibe, and while "social" communal seats "may not be for everyone" and "no reservations can mean a wait", it's still one of the "most consistently great" choices in town; P.S. it now serves brunch.

NEW The Avenue *American*

-	-	-	I

Wilmette | 1146 Wilmette Ave. (bet. Central Ave. & 11th St.) | 847-920-5962 | www.theavenuewilmette.com

A vast 9,000-sq.-ft. destination in Wilmette, this American entry serves traditional steaks, seafood and sandwiches along with brown spirits, craft pours and a moderately priced wine list; the affordable prices surprise in an upscale setting with fireplaces, white tablecloths, a walnut bar, a lounge and a family room with booths that becomes bar seating later on.

The Aviary M *Eclectic*

26	27	27	$60

West Loop | 955 W. Fulton Mkt. (Morgan St.) | 312-226-0868 | www.theaviary.com

Some of the "most interesting cocktails ever" come from Grant Achatz's "cool" West Loop lounge where the "expertly crafted" "over-the-top" drinks feature "playful, whimsical" touches and especially "inventive" presentations, and are offered alongside a recently retooled Eclectic menu (which may not be reflected in the Food score); "top-notch" service and "chic" banquette-enhanced digs also make it a place to "impress" – if you can "get over the sticker shock" that is.

Avli Restaurant *Greek*

22	20	22	$34

Winnetka | Laundry Mall | 566 Chestnut St. (Spruce St.) | 847-446-9300 | www.avli.us

"Authentic and robust" Hellenic cooking is "done with a little extra flair" at this "value" Greek in Winnetka, where "the menu goes way beyond tired standards" in delivering "traditional and contemporary" dishes; "gracious" service, an "extensive" wine list and a "comfortable" "relaxed room (no Greektown hoopla here)" further ensure it's a "go-to on the North Shore."

NEW ¡Ay Chiwowa! M *Mexican* — | — | — | I

River North | 311 W. Chicago Ave. (bet. Franklin & Orleans Sts.) | 312-643-3200 | www.aychiwowa.com

At the former Martini Ranch in River North, this Mexican bar from restaurant-and-club impresario Billy Dec and crew touts inexpensive street food and housemade and infused tequilas; in a graffitied space with plush booths and funky wallcoverings, live DJs and a 4 AM closing time (5 AM Saturday) keep the party going.

Bacchanalia ⊉ *Italian* 22 | 13 | 21 | $33

Southwest Side | 2413 S. Oakley Ave. (bet. 24th & 25th Sts.) | 773-254-6555 | www.bacchanaliainchicago.com

Situated in a little "pocket" of town called Heart of Italy, this "family-owned" "red-saucer" delivers "mounds of pasta" and other "huge" plates just like "nonna" used to make to "crowded tables" of regulars; the muraled decor "hasn't been updated" in years, but the "old-school" staff is "wonderful", and it's a "real bargain" to boot; P.S. "there's valet parking and an ATM inside" (it's cash-only).

Bacino's *Italian* 21 | 14 | 17 | $22

Lincoln Park | 2204 N. Lincoln Ave. (Webster Ave.) | 773-472-7400
West Loop | 118 S. Clinton St. (bet. Adams & Monroe Sts.) | 312-876-1188 🖾
www.bacinos.com

Bella Bacino's *Italian*

Loop | Club Quarters Wacker at Michigan | 75 E. Wacker Dr. (bet. Michigan & Wabash Aves.) | 312-263-2350
La Grange | 36 S. La Grange Rd. (Harris Ave.) | 708-352-8882 M
www.bellabacinos.com

"Extra-thin-crust" pies are offered alongside "pretty darn good stuffed 'zas" so "each team wins" at this "quaint" Italian foursome (the Bellas have fuller trattoria menus, the others are more pizza focused); some maintain they're merely "middle-of-the-road", but those who call them "solid" cite "helpful" service and affordable prices; P.S. the West Looper offers weekday lunch only.

BadHappy Poutine Shop *Eclectic* — | — | — | I

River North | 939 N. Orleans St. (Oak St.) | 312-890-2165 | www.badhappypoutineshop.com

As its name suggests, expect many cheekily named poutines at this inexpensive River North BYO where house-ground burgers, salads and shakes round out an Eclectic menu made from local ingredients when possible; order by checking off your picks on a sheet, then dine in the small open kitchen–enhanced space with a handful of tables and bar; P.S. a Sunday brunch (BYOV for Bloodies) lends further appeal.

The Bagel *Deli*

20 | 13 | 19 | $18

Lakeview | 3107 N. Broadway (Barry Ave.) | 773-477-0300
Skokie | Old Orchard Shopping Ctr. | 50 Old Orchard Ctr. (Skokie Blvd.) |
847-677-0100
www.bagelrestaurant.com

Everything you could want for a quick meal" can be found at this deli
duo dispensing "homestyle" Jewish "comfort food" like "delicious
corned beef", "cure-all" soups (with "matzo balls the size of planets")
and of course "perfectly satisfying bagels with all the trimmings";
sure, the "dinerlike" settings are "dated", but the "brisk" servers
"know how to take care of their customers' whims", and the portions
are "big", so "share and share nice."

Baker & Nosh *Bakery/Sandwiches*

- | - | - | I

Uptown | 1303 W. Wilson Ave. (Malden St.) | 773-989-7393 |
www.bakerandnosh.com

You can stock up on "well-done pastries and breads" at this Uptown
bakery/cafe also winning over fans with "delicious" sandwiches, pizzas and soup; "warm" wood-trimmed decor helps make it feel like a
"calm oasis" whether you're going for a quick "run-in" or settling in
"with a cup of coffee", and there's also garden seating.

Bakin' & Eggs *American*

20 | 18 | 18 | $17

Lakeview | 3120 N. Lincoln Ave. (bet. Ashland & Barry Aves.) |
773-525-7005 | www.bakinandeggschicago.com

"The flight of bacon trumps all else" (though the eggs are "tasty" too)
at this "bustling" Lakeview American watched over by a generally
"pleasant" crew; though the "eclectic", "shabby-chic" space is often
"packed", it's still a "comfortable" place for "families, friends or business meetings"; P.S. closes at 2 PM on weekdays, 3 PM on weekends.

Ba Le *Sandwiches/Vietnamese*

23 | 15 | 18 | $9

NEW **Loop** | 166 W Washington St (LaSalle Blvd.) | 312-346-3971
Uptown | 5014 N. Broadway (bet. Argyle & Winnemac Sts.) |
773-561-4424
Chinatown | 2141 S. Archer Ave. (bet. Cermark Rd. & Wentworth Ave.) |
312-528-6967 **M**
www.balesandwich.com

You can get your "banh mi fix" at this Chinatown and Uptown duo
(with a newer Loop third) where the "very good" sandwiches are offered in "many different" varieties and made to order on some of the
"world's freshest bread"; it also vends salads, soups, sweets and
smoothies, and if the counter-service digs aren't much, well what do
you expect when prices are this "amazing"; P.S. an Uptown bakery-
focused offshoot is in the works.

Balena *Italian*

24 | 23 | 23 | $53

Lincoln Park | 1633 N. Halsted St. (bet. North Ave. & Willow St.) |
312-867-3888 | www.balenachicago.com

Between the "consistently impressive" pizzas, "must-have" pastas,
"delicious" cocktails and "oustanding wine list", fans find lots to like
at this Lincoln Park 'in' spot where chef Chris Pandel's "inventive"

dishes offer an "original" take on Italian cuisine; the "sprawling", earth-toned space includes a brown leather and steel bar and can be a "bit of a scene", but service remains "helpful", and its location across from the Steppenwolf makes it an "excellent choice for pre- or post-theater dining."

Balsan *European*

23 | 23 | 22 | $54

Gold Coast | Waldorf-Astoria Chicago | 11 E. Walton St. (bet. Rush & State Sts.) | 312-646-1400 | www.waldorfastoriachicagohotel.com

"Informal" yet "posh", this "elegant but hardly stuffy" Euro cafe in the Gold Coast's Waldorf-Astoria presents charcuterie, tarte flambé and other "beautifully prepared" plates ("much better than hotel food") in a "lively", "stylish" room inspired by Paris in the '20s; it "can be as laid-back or fancy as you want to make it", and though the bites can get "pricey", the "Sunday supper is a steal."

Bandera *American*

23 | 21 | 21 | $35

Streeterville | 535 N. Michigan Ave., 2nd fl. (bet. Grand Ave. & Ohio St.) | 312-644-3524 | www.hillstone.com

A Southwestern "take on American favorites", including "top-notch rotisserie chicken", "skillet cornbread" and "huge salads", is on offer at this "comfortable" chain link with a "high-profile" Streeterville location "overlooking Michigan Avenue"; "polite" service, live jazz and "dim lighting in the evening" add to the "inviting" ambiance – just be prepared to "fight with the tourists" for a window seat.

Bangers & Lace ● *Pub Food*

20 | 22 | 18 | $24

Wicker Park | 1670 W. Division St. (Paulina St.) | 773-252-6499 | www.bangersandlacechicago.com

An "interesting menu" of "tasty upscale pub food" with an emphasis on sausages is buoyed by an "outstanding" brew selection that "always changes" at this lodgelike Wicker Park watering hole "run by colorful people who really know their beverages"; despite the potential "beer education", some sudsers find the service "aloof", but otherwise it's a fine "go-to" for "wasting away an afternoon, evening or both."

Banh Mi & Co. *Sandwiches/Vietnamese*

– | – | – | I

Lakeview | 3141 N. Broadway (bet. Belmont Ave. & Briar Pl.) | 773-868-9988

NEW **Lakeview** | 843 W. Belmont Ave. (Clark St.) | 773-281-1199

NEW **Roscoe Village** | 2057 W. Roscoe St. (Hoyne Ave.) | 773-360-7266 www.banhmiandco.com

At this Lakeview original and its Belmont Avenue & Roscoe Village sequels, "delectable" Vietnamese sandwiches made on house-baked bread help add a bit of "diversity" to the Chicago food scene; it also offers a few other dishes like noodles and salads, and the "minimal", "counter-service" environs are matched by "very reasonable" prices.

NEW Bar Pastoral *American*

– | – | – | I

Lakeview | 2947 N. Broadway (bet. Oakdale & Wellington Aves.) | 773-472-4781 | www.pastoralartisan.com

You can "get your wine and cheese on" at this boozy spin-off adjacent to Lakeview cheese shop Pastoral that serves American nibbles sourced from the store, either straight up or worked into affordable small plates by former *Top Chef*-testant Chrissy Camba (ex Vincent); quaffing options include vino by the glass, champagne on tap and craft beers, all enjoyed in a "cozy, intimate" space with tufted leather banquettes and light fixtures from vintage farm equipment.

Barrelhouse Flat ●☑ *American*

-	-	-	M

Lincoln Park | 2624 N. Lincoln Ave. (bet. Seminary & Sheffield Aves.) | 773-857-0421 | www.barrelhouseflat.com

Cocktails including house creations and punches by the pitcher or bowl feature "strong, cohesive bold flavors" and are paired with "refined" New American bar plates at this midpriced Lincoln Park hot spot that's open late; there's live piano music several nights a week in the convivial first floor bearing booths, barstools and Edison bulbs, and upstairs has an intimate lounge with plush seating, vintage-inspired wallpaper and a pool table.

Barrington Country Bistro ☑ *French*

24	20	22	$49

Barrington | Foundry Shopping Ctr. | 718 W. Northwest Hwy. (Hart Rd.) | 847-842-1300 | www.barringtoncountrybistro.com

"Tried-and-true", this "authentic", "first-rate" Barrington "standby" offers "excellent" "bistro cuisine" via "friendly, re-spectful" servers in a "charming" strip-mall space; it delivers a "real French experience" "without the 'tude" so most overlook tabs that are "high for the area."

Barrio Urban Taqueria *Mexican*

-	-	-	I

Lakeview | 714 W. Diversey Pkwy. (bet. Burling & Orchard Sts.) | 773-360-8316 | www.barriotaqueria.com

Expect "unusual taco filling choices" (everything from tongue to tilapia), "guacamole made tableside" and other "impressive" Mex favorites at this Lakeview taqueria also offering specialty drinks like "fantastic blood orange margaritas"; "reasonable prices" and casual surroundings decked out with arty red walls complete the picture.

Bar Toma *Italian/Pizza*

17	16	17	$36

Gold Coast | 110 E. Pearson St. (bet. Rush St. & Tower Ct.) | 312-266-3110 | www.bartomachicago.com

A "good quick-eats spot on the Magnificent Mile", this midrange Gold Coast Italian from Tony Mantuano (Spiaggia) offers a long list of "freshly baked" pizza "reminiscent of Italy", plus "interesting" small plates and "some good sandwich choices" too; critics complain it's just "ok" and say that you're "paying for location, location, location", but others find it an "inviting" pick "if you're shopping" nearby.

Basil Leaf Café *Italian*

19	17	19	$31

Lincoln Park | 2465 N. Clark St. (Roslyn Pl.) | 773-348-7243 | www.basilleaf.com

A "large selection" of "nicely prepared" pasta dishes is the "strength" of this "low-key" Northern Italian in Lincoln Park with a "cozy" feel for "not-too-noisy" lunches and dinners (especially weeknights); a few fault the "varied" menu as too "random", but the "friendly" "neighborhood" vibe and "reasonable prices" override that for regulars.

NEW Bavette's
Bar & Boeuf *American/Steak*

24 | 25 | 21 | $50

River North | 218 W. Kinzie St. (bet. Franklin & Wells Sts.) | 312-624-8154 | www.bavetteschicago.com

Part of Brendan Sodikoff's growing empire (Au Cheval, Gilt), this "cool", "trendy" River North chophouse is home to extravagant New American and Euro-inspired fare including prime dry-aged beef that has fans deeming it an "excellent choice for a steak and a martini"; the "classy", "dimly lit" dining room and basement 'parlor' are decked out with distressed wood and brick, ornate chandeliers and cushy leather booths that all further the "romantic" vibe and make it "good for a date."

The Bedford ●⊠ *American*

17 | 26 | 18 | $41

Wicker Park | 1612 W. Division St. (Ashland Ave.) | 773-235-8800 | www.bedfordchicago.com

Set in a refurbished bank, this "upscale" Wicker Park New American "wows" with one of the "most stylish" settings around, especially the "cool" vault area (the "real attraction"); the "hip, young crowd" also goes for "interesting" drinks, and if the fare is "not astounding" many barely notice since it's really "all about chilling and drinking" anyway.

Beer Bistro ● *American/Pub Food*

∇ 17 | 16 | 18 | $21

West Loop | 1061 W. Madison St. (bet. Aberdeen & Morgan Sts.) | 312-433-0013

Beer Bistro North ●⊟ *American/Pub Food*

Lincoln Park | 1415 W. Fullerton Ave. (bet. Janssen & Southport Aves.) | 773-525-2727
www.thebeerbistro.com

Beer lovers get their "drank" on at this "value"-priced West Loop and Lincoln Park duo where the"amazing" brew selection is offered alongside pub grub standards like wings and burgers; other pluses include "cool" digs and daily specials.

Bella Notte *Italian*

23 | 18 | 20 | $37

Noble Square | 1374 W. Grand Ave. (Noble St.) | 312-733-5136 | www.bellanottechicago.com

A "favorite of the locals" for "reliable, old-time" Southern Italian, this affordable Noble Square "standby" dishes up "terrific home-made cavatelli" and other "more than generous" specialties; "classic" surroundings and "professional" service also work in its favor, just be advised it can get hectic on UC game nights.

Bella Via *Italian*

20 | 18 | 22 | $32

Highland Park | 1899 Second St. (Elm Pl.) | 847-681-8300 | www.bellaviahp.com

Admirers appreciate the "generous" servings of "traditional" Italian fare and selections from the "large wine cellar" at this Highland

Parker where "reasonable prices" and "friendly" service in a "comfortable" setting add "family dining" appeal; a handful complaining of "high noise levels" and "pedestrian" offerings are outnumbered by satisfied regulars who "go over and over again."

NEW Belly Q *Asian/BBQ* | 22 | 23 | 20 | $42 |

West Loop | 1400 W. Randolph St. (Ogden Ave.) | 312-563-1010 | www.bellyqchicago.com

An Asian menu "designed for sharing" yields "delicious, flavorful" choices like BBQ meats, hot pots and more at this "group"-friendly West Loop hangout where some tabletop grills provide an "interactive experience"; the "industrial" concrete and wood space features a communal chef's table and karaoke lounge, and even if a few critics feel it's "nothing special", that doesn't lessen its "energetic" buzz.

Belly Shack ☑ *Asian* | 25 | 16 | 19 | $17 |

Humboldt Park | 1912 N. Western Ave. (Homer St.) | 773-252-1414 | www.bellyshack.com

"So inventive and it all works" say foodies who "crave" the "always tasty, never boring" fare at chef-owner Bill Kim's Humboldt Park "hipster" haven, offering a "limited" yet "extraordinary" menu of "solidly executed" Asian dishes with Nuevo Latino accents, capped off with "must"-try soft-serve; "affordable" tabs match the "über-casual" digs, and "BYO never hurts either."

NEW Benjamin Tapas ☑ *Spanish* | - | - | - | M |

Highland Park | 1849 Second St. (bet. Central Ave. & Elm Pl.) | 847-748-8737 | www.benjamintapas.com

Benjamin Brittsan closed Benjamin and replaced it with this Highland Park Spaniard serving tapas, paella, craft cocktails, sangria and a compact beer and wine selection; the redecorated space is more informal with added seating, and prices are moderate.

Benny's Chop House *Steak* | 25 | 24 | 25 | $66 |

River North | 444 N. Wabash Ave. (bet. Hubbard & Illinois Sts.) | 312-626-2444 | www.bennyschophouse.com

Regulars say you'll feel "well taken care of" at this River North haunt where "consistently excellent" chops are presented by a "hospitable" crew; "classic" steakhouse surrounds complete with frequent live piano mean you almost "expect the Rat Pack to walk in at any moment", and if prices aren't cheap, well that's the cost of "high-end" dining.

Bento Box ☑ *Asian* | ▽ 27 | 14 | 23 | $28 |

Bucktown | 2246 W. Armitage Ave. (bet. Leavitt St. & Oakley Ave.) | 773-278-3932 | www.artisancateringchicago.com

The chef is "always coming up with new things for the menu" at this dinner-only Bucktown BYO, an offshoot of a catering company where the highly rated Asian eats come in bento boxes; it's counter-service only, and the digs are "small", but that doesn't deter fans who deem it "worth seeking out."

Berghoff
Restaurant/Cafe ⓏⓈ *German*

19	19	18	$28

Loop | 17 W. Adams St. (bet. Dearborn & State Sts.) | 312-427-3170

Berghoff Cafe *Coffeehouse*

O'Hare Area | Terminal 1, Gate C30 | 10000 Bessie Coleman Dr. (Zemke Blvd.) | 773-601-9180

www.theberghoff.com

"Faithfully prepared" German "classics" like "schnitzel and co." "dominate" the midpriced menu at this redone Loop "landmark", a "sentimental favorite" where "honest, generous" eats and drinks take you "back in time" – and lure in plenty of "tourists" too; "charming" and "faithful to the original" in many ways (the house-label microbrew and "best homemade root beer" remain), it's bittersweet for those who "hope the old Berghoffs will magically reappear" and note the "staff clearly isn't from Bavaria anymore"; P.S. the downstairs cafe and airport spin-off are also "reliable" for "hearty sandwiches."

Bien Trucha ⓈⓂ *Mexican*

▽ 29	20	25	$35

Geneva | 410 W. State St. (bet. 4th & 5th Sts.) | 630-232-2665 | www.bientrucha.com

Enthusiasts "create food memories" at this wallet-friendly Geneva "favorite" tended by "attentive" staffers who deliver "inventive, skillfully prepared" drinks and "authentic" Mexican fare highlighting "perfect levels of spice and acidity"; the "tiny" light-toned space gets "packed" quickly, so "get there before it opens" or you may "wait for hours."

Big & Little's Ⓢ⊅ *Seafood*

25	9	18	$14

Near North | 860 N. Orleans St. (bet. Chestnut & Locust Sts.) | 312-943-0000 | www.bigandlittleschicago.com

"Delightfully indulgent meals" can be had at this "basic, no-frills" River North operation where "delicious, unpretentious seafood", like tilapia tacos and some of the "best" fish 'n' chips, is supplemented by plenty for landlubbers too (burgers, hot dogs, "to-die-for" duck-fat fries); it's counter-service only, but staffers work "fast", so it remains a "go-to" for economical eats – just "bring cash" as it doesn't take cards (there's also an on-site ATM).

Big Bowl *Asian*

20	18	20	$25

River North | The Shops at North Bridge Block 125 | 60 E. Ohio St. (Rush St.) | 312-951-1888

Gold Coast | 6 E. Cedar St. (State St.) | 312-640-8888

Lincolnshire | Citypark at Lincolnshire | 215 Parkway Dr. (Milwaukee Ave.) | 847-808-8880

Schaumburg | 1950 E. Higgins Rd. (Frontage Rd.) | 847-517-8881

www.bigbowl.com

A "consistent" option for "quick", "tasty" Asian eats with an "emphasis on more healthy choices", "local ingredients" and "gourmet flourishes", this "create-your-own" stir-fry chain offers a "large menu variety", "homemade drinks" (including "fresh ginger ale") and "right-on" service; though it's too "Americanized" for some, most agree it's a "cheap and cheerful" choice.

Big Bricks ● *BBQ/Pizza*   23 | 16 | 17 | $22

North Center/St. Ben's | 3832 N. Lincoln Ave. (Berenice Ave.) | 773-525-5022 | www.bigbrickschicago.com

Bricks *BBQ/Pizza*

Lincoln Park | 1909 N. Lincoln Ave. (Wisconsin St.) | 312-255-0851 | www.brickschicago.com

You'll find a "plethora" of "delicious" thin-crust pizzas with "some of the best" toppings around at this Lincoln Park hangout and its newer North Center sequel that also adds a host of BBQ offerings (brisket, pulled pork, ribs) to its budget-friendly roster; the original's "hole-in-the-wall" digs have somewhat of a "basement atmosphere", while the newer sib is larger and more spacious, and both count a "good beer selection" and "low-key" vibe as other assets.

Big Jones *Southern*   24 | 21 | 22 | $33

Andersonville | 5347 N. Clark St. (bet. Balmoral & Summerdale Aves.) | 773-275-5725 | www.bigjoneschicago.com

"When you miss NOLA" or long for "a night out in Charleston", fans suggest this midpriced Andersonville "destination" for a "genuine, quality Southern food experience" (especially at the "don't-miss brunch") courtesy of a "surprising" menu featuring both "locally sourced" products and ingredients that are somewhat "unheard of" in Chicago; "helpful" servers, "warm, welcoming" surroundings and a landscaped outdoor patio also make for a "memorable" experience.

Big Star ●⚏ *Mexican*   26 | 19 | 17 | $19

Wicker Park | 1531 N. Damen Ave. (Wicker Park Ave.) | 773-235-4039 | www.bigstarchicago.com

"Hipsters" pile into Paul Kahan's "affordable" Wicker Park Mexican for "flavorful" tacos "like you've never tasted" plus "delicious", "strong" margaritas, "solid" beers and a "top-notch bourbon selection"; it's cash-only and the "modern garage-type" space can seem "acoustically tragic", but it's still "always packed", especially on the happening patio ("if you can grab a spot, never leave"); P.S. "ridiculous waits" may be remediated by a recent expansion.

Bijan's Bistro ● *American*   20 | 18 | 18 | $30

River North | 663 N. State St. (Erie St.) | 312-202-1904 | www.bijansbistrochicago.com

Staying "a step above regular bar fare", with some "French touches" and "comforting" breakfast plates (the "best" steak and eggs), this "pleasant" River North New American is "popular" among pub-"hoppers" of all stripes (even "Kanye and Kardashians"); though a few knock it as a "schizoid mix of bistro and sports bar" and add the menu "needs some updating", its late hours earn it a "gold star for availability" when the "hunger monster calls."

Billy Goat Tavern *Burgers*   16 | 12 | 15 | $14

Loop | 330 S. Wells St. (Van Buren St.) | 312-554-0297 🖪
NEW Loop | 60 E. Lake St. (bet. Garland Ct. & Wabash Ave.)
River North | Shop The Showrooms | 222 W. Merchandise Mart Plaza
(Wells St.) | 312-464-1045
River North | 430 N. Lower Michigan Ave. (Ohio St.) |
312-222-1525 ◑⊟
Streeterville | Navy Pier | 700 E. Grand Ave. (Streeter Dr.) |
312-670-8789
O'Hare Area | Terminal 1, Gate C19 - Food Court |
10000 Bessie Coleman Dr. (Zemke Blvd.) | 773-462-9368
West Loop | 1535 W. Madison St. (Ogden Ave.) | 312-733-9132 ⊟
Mt. Prospect | 164 Randhurst Village Dr. (Perimeter Dr.) | 847-870-0123
www.billygoattavern.com

Those "longing for good old grease" hit these "classic" Chicago
"hamburger joints" to relive the famous *SNL* skit over "cheezborg-
ers" and "no fries, chips" served with the "expected rude service";
many gripe they're "tired" and "overhyped", but concede the "underground" original on Lower Michigan Avenue is an "institution"
that's "worth the trip."

NEW Billy Sunday ● *American*   - | - | - | M

Logan Square | 3143 W. Logan Blvd. (bet. Kedzie & Milwaukee Aves.) |
773-661-2485 | www.billy-sunday.com

From Yusho's Matthias Merges, this midpriced, cocktail-centric
Logan Square spot serves up state-of-the-art tipples, mixed with
vintage spirits, housemade bitters and specialty ice, alongside
cheffy, tweaked gastropub fare including an eclectic mix of snacks,
'things in jars' and desserts; upholstered banquettes, antique artwork and cabinets lined with vintage glassware and rare liquors
create a chic tavern vibe.

Bin 36 *American*   21 | 21 | 21 | $41

River North | 339 N. Dearborn St. (bet. Kinzie St. & Wacker Dr.) |
312-755-9463 | www.bin36.com

An "inspired wine list" (including "flights up the wazoo") is
matched with "incredible cheese" and other "well-prepared"
New American plates at this "reasonably priced" River North
"meeting spot"; "knowledgeable staffers" offering "pairing sug-
gestions" add to a "convivial atmosphere" in the "contemporary,
open" space, and diners can buy bottles of their favorites from
the adjoining shop.

Birchwood Kitchen Ⓜ *Sandwiches*   23 | 19 | 21 | $16

Wicker Park | 2211 W. North Ave. (bet. Bell Ave. & Leavitt St.) |
773-276-2100 | www.birchwoodkitchen.com

"You can always depend on something delicious" at this counter-
service Wicker Park BYO where "quality" offerings like "savory"
brunch dishes, "terrific" burgers and "creative" sandwiches in "well-
thought-out combinations" highlight "top-shelf" local ingredients;
the "cozy" space comes with a "sunny patio" and "welcoming" staffers "remember your name", so it's a "regular stop" for many.

	FOOD	DECOR	SERVICE	COST

Birrieria Zaragoza *Mexican* ▽ 27 | 11 | 23 | $15

Southwest Side | 4852 S. Pulaski Rd. (49th St.) | 773-523-3700 | www.birrieriazaragoza.com

"Who knew you could do such wonderful things with goat" marvel fans at this simple Southwest Side Mexican, an "amazing hole-in-the-wall" that offers the "delicious" meat in tacos, quesadillas and by itself; "run by the nicest family" it feels just "like being at the Zaragoza home", just be aware it's counter-service only and closes at 7 PM.

Bistro Bordeaux *French* 23 | 21 | 22 | $48

Evanston | 618 Church St. (bet. Chicago & Orrington Aves.) | 847-424-1483 | www.lebistrobordeaux.com

For "a slice of the Left Bank" on the North Shore, Francophiles favor this "tiny, charming" "date-night" destination serving a "simple menu of beautifully prepared" "bistro faves" accompanied by "lovely wines"; "friendly, convivial" service sans the "Parisian disdain" and "medium" prices help loyalists overlook "close quarters" that can get "noisy."

Bistro Campagne *French* 25 | 23 | 22 | $43

Lincoln Square | 4518 N. Lincoln Ave. (bet. Sunnyside & Wilson Aves.) | 773-271-6100 | www.bistrocampagne.com

"Consistently solid, traditional French food in an adorable, comfortable setting" sums up this "upscale" Lincoln Square bistro specializing in "authentic" seasonal "country" cooking bolstered by "great Belgian beers" and "an excellent, reasonably priced wine list"; "hospitable" service and "cozy" wood-accented environs complete with an "enchanting" outside garden also help make it a "mainstay."

NEW Bistro Dre Ⓜ *American/Vegetarian* - | - | - | M
(fka Flour & Water)

Lakeview | 2965 N. Lincoln Ave. (Wellington Ave.) | 773-697-9067 | www.bistrodre.com

New American shared plates with a vegetarian slant are the focus of the moderately priced menu at this Lakeview BYO bistro; the cozy surroundings features a red-and-white color scheme, wood and chalkboard accents, a tin ceiling, and funky artwork and curios.

Bistronomic *French* 23 | 20 | 21 | $48

Gold Coast | 840 N. Wabash Ave. (bet. Chestnut & Pearson Sts.) | 312-944-8400 | www.bistronomic.net

Martial Noguier "still rocks" at this Gold Coast French where his menu goes "well beyond the obvious standards", featuring "flavorful" "small, medium and large plates", many with "nouveau" touches, all served in a dining room with an "authentic bistro feel" and enhanced by a "secluded" outdoor patio; sure, some dishes are "better than others", but service is "responsive", and while tabs aren't cheap, the "somewhat glitzy" clientele says it's "priced right."

	FOOD	DECOR	SERVICE	COST

Bistrot Margot *French*
22 | 20 | 21 | $39

Old Town | 1437 N. Wells St. (bet. North Ave. & Schiller St.) | 312-587-3660 | www.bistrotmargot.com

Offering a bit of "Paris on Wells", this Old Town "mainstay" delivers "simple", "authentic French" fare in a "charming", "classic bistro" setting; "reasonable" prices and "friendly" servers are other pluses, so even if some sniff it's "not spectacular", most agree it's "reliable" for "romance" or "an easy night out" "with family or friends."

Bistrot Zinc *French*
21 | 22 | 22 | $40

Gold Coast | 1131 N. State St. (bet. Cedar & Elm Sts.) | 312-337-1131 | www.bistrotzinc.com

"Wonderfully unintimidating", this "high-energy" Gold Coast boîte featuring front windows that open on a warm day and a "beautiful" zinc bar is "like being in Paris" with its "authentic" French "comfort food" and "true bistro feel"; "friendly" servers contribute to the "warm, cozy neighborhood vibe", and prices are "modest", so though "nothing exciting", it's "reliable" for a "bit of Rive Gauche in Chicago."

Bistro Voltaire ⧄ *French*
22 | 22 | 23 | $44

Near North | 226 W. Chicago Ave. (bet. Franklin & Wells Sts.) | 312-265-0911 | www.bistrovoltaire.com

"The food is pure French bistro" at this authentic" Near North eatery where "well-prepared" plates highlighting "delicate, refined" flavors are served alongside an "interesting selection of wines" in "cozy, upscale-comfortable" surroundings; "prices are reasonable" and service "friendly", so though "tables are tight" and the quarters are "small", supporters say it's easy to "feel right at home."

Bite Cafe ◑ *American*
22 | 13 | 18 | $20

Ukrainian Village | 1039 N. Western Ave. (Cortez St.) | 773-395-2483 | www.bitecafechicago.com

"Solid" and "remarkably affordable", this "funky" Ukrainian Village BYO adjacent to nightclub sibling Empty Bottle dispenses "tasty, mildly inventive" American "comfort food", offering "a selection not found everywhere" including a number of vegetarian choices; the basic, brick-accented surroundings may lag behind, but service is "fast", so many insist it's still an all-around "enjoyable" "neighborhood joint."

Blackbird ⧄ *American*
27 | 23 | 25 | $69

West Loop | 619 W. Randolph St. (bet. Desplaines & Jefferson Sts.) | 312-715-0708 | www.blackbirdrestaurant.com

"Interesting", "sophisticated" New American dishes are "beautifully presented" by "attentive" staffers at this "well-established" West Loop "classic" from Paul Kahan and crew; the "sleek, modern" space can get "a bit loud", and it's certainly not cheap, but many still consider it a "top" place to "impress" and just right for a "special occasion."

		FOOD	DECOR	SERVICE	COST

NEW BlackFinn
American Grille ● *American*
— | — | — | M

Mt. Prospect | 157 Randhurst Village Dr. (Perimeter Dr.) | 847-398-5501 | www.blackfinnamericangrille.com

Part of a small national chain, this "upscale" sports bar and grill in Mt. Prospect offers a "wide variety" of modern American "comfort food", plus late-night snacks and weekend brunch; the spacious wood-paneled tavern setting includes a handsome bar and multiple TV screens; P.S. a River North branch is in the works.

Blind Faith Café Ⓜ *Vegetarian*
20 | 16 | 19 | $24

Evanston | 525 Dempster St. (bet. Chicago & Hinman Aves.) | 847-328-6875 | www.blindfaithcafe.com

"One of the first meat-free zones" in town, this "down-to-earth" Evanston "institution" is "veggie heaven", serving "imaginative" "no-guilt" dishes so "tasty" you won't be "nervous about taking your non-vegetarian parents"; "accommodating" servers elevate the "simple" "hole-in-the-wall" space, and if a few find it more "expensive" than its competitors, they concede it's "worth the extra money."

Blokes & Birds ●Ⓜ *British*
18 | 20 | 19 | $31

Lakeview | 3343 N. Clark St. (bet. Buckingham Pl. & Roscoe St.) | 773-472-5252 | www.blokesandbirdschicago.com

"Interesting craft cocktails" and an "extensive beer list" pair with "contemporary English comfort food" at this "upscale" Lakeview pub in a bi-level, wood-accented space featuring two fireplaces and a pool table; "friendly" servers contribute to the "casual" vibe, so even if budgeters believe it's "a bit expensive for what it is", most maintain it's "a great addition to the sometimes-too-sporty neighborhood."

The Bluebird ● *American*
22 | 22 | 21 | $37

Bucktown | 1749 N. Damen Ave. (Willow St.) | 773-486-2473 | www.bluebirdchicago.com

"Tasty" New American small plates "perfect for sharing" backed by an "endless" beer selection and "interesting" wines bring attention to this "cozy" Bucktown "gem"; toss in affordable tabs, and it's often "singing on the weekends with lively crowds."

Bluegrass Ⓜ *American*
21 | 17 | 21 | $33

Highland Park | 1636 Old Deerfield Rd. (Richfield Ave.) | 847-831-0595 | www.bluegrasshp.com

Southern-influenced American fare is the draw at this midpriced Highland Park "joint" where "inventive" offerings plus "tried-but-true" classics make for a "fine all around menu" "with many winners"; "eager-to-please" staffers and a "warm", wood-accented space are other reasons it "can get crowded."

NEW Boarding House ● *American*
▽ 22 | 28 | 22 | $64

River North | 720 N. Wells St. (Superior St.) | 312-280-0720 | www.boardinghousechicago.com

Master sommelier and former host of *Check, Please* Alpana Singh is behind this tri-level River North showplace where a "cool", "stunning" space dramatically decorated with massive sculptures of wine bottles and glasses provides the backdrop for "creative" New American plates and an "awesome" vino selection with labels from "all over the world"; tabs aren't inexpensive, but that doesn't stop fans from vowing to "definitely return."

NEW Bobby's Deerfield *American*   ▽ | 17 | 15 | 15 | $32 |

Deerfield | 695 Deerfield Rd. (Waukegan Rd.) | 847-607-9104 | www.bobbysdeerfield.com

The Cafe Lucci team (brothers Bobby and Augie Arifi) is behind this upscale Deerfield New American serving a wide-ranging, midpriced menu along with a "surprisingly good" wine list plus craft brews and signature cocktails; the open space has high ceilings, funky globe lights and a modern urban vibe, and if a few early testers find it just "fair", others insist it's a "nice addition to the area."

Bob Chinn's Crab House *Seafood* | 23 | 14 | 19 | $42 |

Wheeling | 393 S. Milwaukee Ave. (bet. Jeffery & Mors Aves.) | 847-520-3633 | www.bobchinns.com

"If you're craving fresh shellfish", this "hectic", "high-energy" Wheeling "landmark" is "the place" say finatics touting the "huge selection" of seafood, including "out-of-this-world" crab, plus "deliciously lethal" garlic rolls and "famous mai tais"; the "huge", "warehouse"-like space is often "packed", and service can be a little too "fast" ("turnover is the name of the game"), but the ambiance is "upbeat" and tabs are "middle of the road."

Bob San *Japanese*   ▽ | 23 | 17 | 20 | $39 |

Wicker Park | 1805-1809 W. Division St. (bet. Honroe & Wood Sts.) | 773-235-8888 | www.bob-san.com

This spacious Wicker Park Japanese "gets it just right", offering "high-quality" "sushi standards" "without ridiculous prices"; service is solid, and since the menu is "large enough to suit everyone", it's "good for groups."

NEW Bodega ⚫ *Mexican* | - | - | - | I |

Lincoln Park | 1964 N. Sheffield Ave. (Armitage Ave.) | 773-348-0121 | www.chicagobodega.com

The longtime Twisted Lizard space in Lincoln Park now houses this casual eatery cooking modern Mexican grub including sandwiches and a hefty list of gourmet tacos plus many margaritas, adult milkshakes and creative cocktails mixed with housemade syrups; the art-filled space remains much the same, and prices won't break the bank.

Boka *American* | 26 | 24 | 25 | $69 |

Lincoln Park | 1729 N. Halsted St. (Willow St.) | 312-337-6070 | www.bokachicago.com

Chef Giuseppe Tentori's "sophisticated", "inventive" menu includes "well-cooked", often "exceptional" small and large plates at this Lincoln Park New American; the "knowledgeable" staff also delivers drinks from a "fablously stocked" bar, and the "beautiful" modern space and "wonderful" patio have a "calm, relaxing" vibe – which comes in handy once the check comes.

	FOOD	DECOR	SERVICE	COST

Bombay Spice Grill *Indian* | 22 | 21 | 22 | $24 |

River North | 450 N. Clark St. (bet. Hubbard & Illinois Sts.) |
312-477-7657 | www.bombayspice.com

You'll find a "healthy twist" on Indian at this affordable River North
chain link where the "delicious" fare, including "create-your-own" options, are all made with olive oil instead of the more traditional butter/
ghee; "helpful" servers and a "beautiful" space add to the allure.

Bongo Room *American* | 24 | 17 | 19 | $19 |

Andersonville | 5022 N. Clark St. (bet. Ainslie St. & Winnemac Ave.) |
773-728-7900

Wicker Park | 1470 N. Milwaukee Ave. (Honore St.) | 773-489-0690

South Loop | 1152 S. Wabash Ave. (Roosevelt Rd.) | 312-291-0100
www.thebongoroom.com

A "crazy good" menu of "decadent" daytime grub including "to-die-
for" pancakes draws hordes to these "reliable" American "breakfast
and brunch joints"; service is "pleasant" enough, and though you
should "prepare for a long wait" (unless you "show up right when the
doors open"), "large" portions and small bills help ensure they're
"worth going to."

Bourgeois Pig *Coffeehouse/Sandwiches* | 20 | 18 | 16 | $13 |

Lincoln Park | 738 W. Fullerton Ave. (bet. Burling & Halsted Sts.) |
773-883-5282 | www.bpigcafe.com

A "vestige of the old Lincoln Park", this "charming" cafe set inside an
old row house "with creaky wooden floors and perfectly worn furniture" offers a "massive menu" of "tasty", "inventive" sandwiches
(many with "clever" "literary names"), "yummy pastries" and a "wide
variety of fresh teas"; "lots of cozy nooks" and "cushy couches" further make it "everything a coffee shop should be."

Branch 27 ❶ *American* | 19 | 18 | 20 | $33 |

Noble Square | 1371 W. Chicago Ave. (Noble St.) | 312-850-2700 |
www.branch27.com

Expect "solidly good" cooking "with just enough creativity to keep it
interesting" at this "reasonably priced" Noble Square New American;
"excellent brew selections" contribute to the "gastropub vibe", while
generally strong service helps make it an overall "pleasant" choice.

Brasserie by LM *French* ▽ | 18 | 21 | 21 | $26 |

South Loop | Essex Inn | 800 S. Michigan Ave. (bet. 8th & 9th Sts.) |
312-431-1788 | www.brasseriebylm.com

Inside the South Loop's Essex Inn sits this midpriced brasserie, where
"well-prepared" French classics (onion soup, steak frites, croque
monsieur) are served in a mod space with "huge" floor-to-ceiling
windows "overlooking Grant Park"; weekend brunch and daily bar
specials further the appeal as does a seasonal patio.

NEW Brasserie 54 by LM ❶ *French* | - | - | - | M |

Andersonville | 5420 N. Clark St. (bet. Balmoral & Catalpa Aves.) |
773-334-9463 | www.brasserie54.com

The LM crew moves into Andersonville with this casual French brasserie featuring midpriced Gallic classics and a chef's prix fixe option,

plus a compact wine list and craft cocktails (celery martini, anyone?); the space features the group's familiar brown-and-orange color palette, multiple seating options and blackboard menus.

Brazzaz *Brazilian/Steak*
22 | 20 | 23 | $58

River North | 539 N. Dearborn St. (Grand Ave.) | 312-595-9000 | www.brazzaz.com

"Bring your appetite" to this all-you-can-eat River North Brazilian for the "bottomless" "gourmet salad bar" and "never-ending meat parade" delivered by service "with flair"; it's not cheap, but the "warm" wood-accented space has an "overall nice feel", so fans say you might "want to stay forever" – just "let your belt out a few notches" first.

Bread & Wine ⊠ Ⅿ *American*
∇ 20 | 17 | 21 | $34

Irving Park | 3732 W. Irving Park Rd. (bet. Hamlin & Ridgeway Aves.) | 773-866-5266 | www.breadandwinechicago.com

At this "affordable" Irving Park New American, local ingredients are crafted into "interesting" small and large plates offered alongside cheese and charcuterie plus "tasty" cocktails, craft beers and a "good wine list"; "chic" touches like white counters, molded chairs and abstract light fixtures stand out in the concrete and raw wood space, and there's also an open kitchen and a display area featuring gourmet foods.

Briciola Ⅿ *Italian*
- | - | - | M

Ukrainian Village | 937 N. Damen Ave. (bet. Lowa & Walton Sts.) | 773-772-0889 | www.briciolachicago.com

BYO to this midpriced Ukrainian Village trattoria where Italian classics are joined by seasonally inspired entrees with a more modern appeal; the petite space has an open kitchen and mottled yellow walls dotted with baroque mirrors and black-and-white photographs from the old country, and there's patio seating too.

Bridge Bar Chicago *American*
- | - | - | M

River North | 315 N. LaSalle St. (bet. Kinzie St. & Wacker Dr.) | 312-822-0100 | www.bridgebarchicago.com

Creative American food and even more creative drinks (spotlighting interesting ingredients like candied bacon) is the concept at this midpriced River North 'cocktail kitchen' above Fulton's on the River; beer is also a focus, though it's outshone by an extensive brown booze selection, which you can sip in the funky, sprawling setting with massive columns and industrial ductwork.

Bridge
House Tavern ●⊠Ⅿ *American*
18 | 20 | 19 | $30

River North | Quaker Tower | 321 N. Clark St. (bet. Carroll Ave. & Wacker Dr.) | 312-644-0283 | www.bridgehousetavern.com

A "great place to enjoy the river view", this moderate River North tavern offers "wonderful" "waterside seating", "decent" American pub fare and "friendly" service; the "quaint" amber-hued dining room has "people-watching" appeal, but patio tables are the bigger draw given the "impressive scenery."

	FOOD	DECOR	SERVICE	COST

NEW Brindille 🗷 *French* — | — | — | E

River North | 534 N. Clark St. (bet. Grand Ave. & Ohio St.) |
312-595-1616 | www.brindille-chicago.com

French fine dining from Carrie Nahabedian and the Naha team regales River North at this luxury dinner-only destination with both à la carte and tasting menu options (and plenty of wine, champagne, craft cocktails, absinthe and fromage); the sophisticated, urban Paris-inspired setting is done in earth tones with soft lighting and forest murals that echo the name of the restaurant (translation: twig).

Brio — | — | — | M
Tuscan Grille *Italian*

Lombard | The Shops on Butterfield | 330 Yorktown Shopping Ctr. (Yorktown Mall Dr.) | 630-424-1515 | www.brioitalian.com

"You wouldn't mistake it for an authentic local Italian place", but this "relaxed" Lombard chain link in the Shops on Butterfield still "holds its own" with a "wide range" of "decent quality" dishes at "reasonable prices", plus happy-hour specials and "one of the best kids' menus"; service is "accommodating" too, so even if foes find it merely "adequate", most agree it's "never a disappointment."

The Bristol *American* 25 | 21 | 22 | $42

Bucktown | 2152 N. Damen Ave. (bet. Shakespeare & Webster Aves.) |
773-862-5555 | www.thebristolchicago.com

A "locavore heaven" rave raters of this "buzzy" Bucktown New American where chef-owner Chris Pandel's "thoughtful use of interesting ingredients" results in "consistently creative" "farm-to-table" fare, including "life-changing" raviolo, "freaking awesome" duck-fat fries and "unusual meats" that "make for a fun adventure" in the "rustic" gastropub environs; not everyone's into the "new togetherness" (aka communal tables), but "friendly, knowledgeable" servers add to the "alluring", "peppy" vibe, and with moderate prices, many confer it with "must-stop" status.

Broadway Cellars *American* 22 | 19 | 23 | $34

Edgewater | 5900 N. Broadway (Rosedale Ave.) | 773-944-1208 |
www.broadwaycellars.net

"One of the best values" around promise patrons of this "friendly" Edgewater New American offering "creative", "flavorful" meals; "attentive" servers give the bistro environs a "wonderfully warm" feel so locals say each visit is "like coming home."

Browntrout 🅼 *American* 24 | 19 | 22 | $42

North Center/St. Ben's | 4111 N. Lincoln Ave. (bet. Belle Plaine & Warner Aves.) | 773-472-4111 | www.browntroutchicago.com

They "use local ingredients creatively" at this "exciting" North Center New American that reels in diners with "surprising, inspiring" small and large plates and "well-chosen" wines via "patient", "knowledgeable" servers; if "decor is a bit low-budget" for some, others find the "casual" space "comfie", and while prices inspire further disagreement ("reasonable" vs. "high"), most say it's "definitely worth the try."

Bruna's Ristorante *Italian*

▽ 23 | 14 | 23 | $36

Southwest Side | 2424 S. Oakley Ave. (24th Pl.) | 773-254-5550 | www.brunasristorante.com

Set in a "quiet" Southwest Side locale, this circa-1933 "landmark" ladles "large portions" of "traditional" Italian fare "made the way it should be made"; the "tiny" "old-school" digs are "nothing to look at", but tabs are moderate and "you're treated like family", so it's "still a great haunt", especially when you need a "comfort-food blanket."

Brunch *American/Sandwiches*

16 | 16 | 15 | $18

River North | 644 N. Orleans St. (bet. Erie & Ontario Sts.) | 312-265-1411 | www.brunchit.com

Hearty American breakfast, brunch and lunch fare is served at this big, bustling casual-chic River North BYO specializing in signature skillets, sandwiches and salads; the loftlike setting features rustic wood pillars, oversized drum light fixtures, a diner counter, a separate coffee bar and, most unusually, a working shoe-shine booth.

🆕 Bub City ◗ *BBQ*

- | - | - | M

River North | 435 N. Clark St. (bet. Hubbard & Illinois Sts.) | 312-610-4200 | www.bubcitychicago.com

From the Melman scions (Paris Club, Hub 51, RPM Italian) comes this River North revival of the early-'90s party spot, a sprawling, pseudo country-western bar serving "good but not great barbecue" plus raw bar items, classic cocktails and a solid whiskey selection; the wood and brick digs sport an American flag made of beer cans and a stage for live music, and given the affordable tabs it can get "quite packed."

Bullhead Cantina ◗Ⓜ⇪ *Mexican*

- | - | - | I

Humboldt Park | 1143 N. California Ave. (bet. Division St. & Haddon Ave.) | 773-772-8895 | www.bullheadcantina.com

The "great variety of tacos" gets top billing at this budget-friendly Humboldt Park cantina where farm-fresh ingredients and handmade tortillas elevate the Mexican fare (fill-ins include burgers, salads and quesadillas), plus "good specials" on craft cocktails, brews and brown booze; the low-lit room is decorated with funky signage and Americana, and diners should bring cash or hit the in-house ATM.

Burger Bar *Burgers*

22 | 15 | 18 | $21

Lincoln Park | 1578 N. Clybourn Ave. (bet. Dayton & Halsted Sts.) | 312-255-0055 | www.burgerbarchicago.com

"Juicy, flavorful" gourmet burgers are the thing at this Lincoln Park joint where the "many options" include build-your-own and preset choices plus sides, shakes, "heavenly" mac 'n' cheese bar offerings and a "huge" beer list; service is "attentive" in the "lively" wood-and-brick warehouse chic space, and it all comes at a "good price."

Burger Joint *Burgers*

▽ 16 | 14 | 17 | $13

River North | 675 N. Franklin St. (bet. Erie & Huron Sts.) | 312-440-8600 | www.burgerjoint675franklin.com

Not your usual burger joint, this River North quick-serve specializes in burgers, gyros and burgers topped with gyros, plus dogs and a bevy of fry flavors (including renditions made with feta and Merkts cheddar), along with cookies and shakes; the funky setting is done up with rustic woodwork and photo murals of Chicago's skyline and El trains – which seem to come to life when the real thing rumbles by; P.S. night owls can nosh until 5 AM Fridays and Saturdays.

Burger Point *Burgers*

| – | – | – | I |

South Loop | 1900 S. State St. (bet. Archer Ave. & Cullerton St.) | 312-842-1900 | www.theburgerpoint.com

At this BYO counter-serve in the South Loop, all-natural meats are house ground and topped with a dizzying number of gourmet garnishes and ordered via iPads; while it "may look like a fast-food joint", each burger is "prepared to order", and enthusiasts say it serves some of the "best burgers" around.

Butcher & The Burger *Burgers*

| 25 | 17 | 20 | $17 |

Lincoln Park | 1021 W. Armitage Ave. (Kenmore Ave.) | 773-697-3735 | www.butcherandtheburger.com

Chef-owner Allen Sternweiler (ex Duchamp, Allen's) "wows" with "ah-mazing" "build-your-own burgers" featuring "awfully good customizing options", from the "unsurpassed rubs and variety of meat" to the "non-soggy" buns, plus "fries to die for" and a "nice selection of sodas" at this retro-looking counter-service BYO in Lincoln Park; thriftsters say it "could benefit from a bit of a lower price point", but converts only "wish it had more seating"; P.S. there are also breakfast burgers, beignets and butcher-shop take-out options.

Butch McGuire's Tavern ● *American*

| 18 | 19 | 19 | $24 |

Near North | 20 W. Division St. (Dearborn St.) | 312-787-4318 | www.butchmcguires.com

"Don't let the nightlife posture fool you", because though this inexpensive Near North "watering hole" "landmark" (since 1961) turns into a "boisterous" "pickup" scene at night, by day it's a suitable "lunch place for families" with solid American eats ferried by "friendly" servers; loyalists also note its "famous" "holiday display" makes it a "Christmastime tradition."

Butterfly Sushi Bar & Thai Cuisine *Japanese/Thai*

| 20 | 16 | 19 | $26 |

Noble Square | 1156 W. Grand Ave. (bet. May St. & Racine Ave.) | 312-563-5555
West Loop | 1131 W. Madison St. (bet. Aberdeen St. & Racine Ave.) | 312-997-9988
West Town | 1421 W. Chicago Ave. (bet. Bishop & Noble Sts.) | 312-492-9955
www.butterflysushibar.com

A "broad menu with lots of options", including "inventive" sushi and "satisfying" Thai specialties all "at a decent price", makes this Asian BYO trio a "consistent" "go-to"; service can sometimes feel "rushed", and even if some say "you won't be wowed", they concede you also "won't be disappointed."

	FOOD	DECOR	SERVICE	COST

Café Absinthe ☒ *American/French* ▽ 21 18 19 $44
Bucktown | 1954 W. North Ave. (Damen Ave.) | 773-278-4488 | www.cafe-absinthe.com

"Clever and tasty" seasonal American-French fare in an "intimate" setting is the draw of this longtime Bucktown bistro; if some complain the "close" seating is "not conversation-friendly", loyalists point instead to moderate tabs and say "well-meaning" staffers contribute to the overall "good vibe."

Cafe Ba-Ba-Reeba! *Spanish* 22 20 20 $33
Lincoln Park | 2024 N. Halsted St. (bet. Armitage & Dickens Aves.) | 773-935-5000 | www.cafebabareeba.com

A "Chicago classic" that's "been around forever" (or since 1985), this "lively", "always reliable" Lincoln Park Spaniard "never fails to please" with its "vast menu" of "interesting", "authentic" small plates, plus "delish" paella and "the best" sangria, all at "approachable" prices; "snappy" servers "keep a steady pace of food coming" in the "cozy" dining room and "beautiful" patio, and it's versatile enough for both "groups of friends or romantic dates."

Cafe Central ☒ *French* 22 19 23 $39
Highland Park | 455 Central Ave. (bet. Linden Ave. & Sheridan Rd.) | 847-266-7878 | www.cafecentral.net

The "classic bistro menu brings comfort" and the "noisy", "busy atmosphere" brings "great people-watching" at this "casual" Highland Park French putting out "well-prepared" dishes; despite "tight quarters", "friendly" staffers "make diners feel comfortable", and while it may be "nothing fancy", "reasonable prices" further ensure it comes "recommended."

Cafecito *Coffeehouse/Cuban* 24 13 20 $13
Loop | 26 E. Congress Pkwy. (Wasabash Ave.) | 312-922-2233
NEW Loop | 7 N. Wells St. (bet. Madison & Washington Sts.) | 312-263-4750
www.cafecitochicago.com

"Perfectly pressed, crunchy" Cuban sandwiches get heaps of praise at this Loop coffeehouse (with a newer Wells Street sib) also vending lots of other sammies plus "really good" salads, platters and more; counter-service staffers work "quickly", and "cheap" tabs provide another reason to go.

Café des Architectes *French* 24 25 24 $57
Gold Coast | Sofitel Chicago Water Tower | 20 E. Chestnut St. (Wabash Ave.) | 312-324-4063 | www.cafedesarchitectes.com

"Imaginative", "gourmet" dishes are fit for "the serious diner" at this New French in the Gold Coast's Sofitel Chicago Water Tower, where service is "attentive" "without being fussy", and the "beautiful" "modern" room has a "casual elegance"; it's also known for its "especially good" breakfast, and while tabs aren't low, that just makes it "special"-occasion worthy.

	FOOD	DECOR	SERVICE	COST

Café Iberico ● *Spanish*   22 | 16 | 19 | $30

River North | 737 N. LaSalle Dr. (bet. Chicago Ave. & Superior St.) | 312-573-1510 | www.cafeiberico.com

"Every day is a party" at this "bustling, boisterous" River North "tapas standard", "a favorite for large groups" seeking a "wide selection" of "well-crafted" "authentic" Spanish plates bolstered by "amazing sangria"; sure, the "huge" "community center"–like space "lacks decor", service can be "slow" and a no-reservations policy (except for parties of six or more) often results in "long waits" (especially on weekends), but "affordable" tabs still ensure it's a "must."

Cafe Laguardia *Cuban/Mexican*   19 | 19 | 19 | $29

Bucktown | 2111 W. Armitage Ave. (Hoyne Ave.) | 773-862-5996 | www.cafelaguardia.com

Be "transported to Havana" at this "casual", "reasonably priced" Bucktown "break from Chicago" featuring "well-seasoned" "authentic" Cuban-Mexican dishes ferried by "caring" servers who "go that extra mile"; the funky space includes a lounge area "full of charm and character", and live music some nights provides an opportunity to "salsa the night away."

Cafe Lucci *Italian*   24 | 19 | 22 | $38

Glenview | 609 Milwaukee Ave. (Central Rd.) | 847-729-2268 | www.cafelucci.com

"Gourmet" "old-school Italian" cooking highlighting "some interesting combinations" pairs with "a wine list to excite anyone's palate" at this "small" Glenview "gem"; "elegant decor", "friendly, efficient" servers and moderate prices also help explain why it "draws a big crowd."

Café Selmarie *American*   21 | 17 | 19 | $25

Lincoln Square | 4729 N. Lincoln Ave. (bet. Lawrence & Leland Aves.) | 773-989-5595 | www.cafeselmarie.com

"Go for brunch, stay for lunch" (or dinner) say fans of this "no-fuss, no-attitude" Lincoln Square "fixture" known for "homestyle" American cooking including "out-of-this-world" pastries and "to-die-for" desserts from its "top-notch bakery"; "cozy" confines and solid service make it a "pleasant" choice when you want to "eat with a friend and just be", so if it's "pricey" for the category, most insist it's "worth the splurge"; P.S. "on a nice day", try brunch on the "wonderful" patio.

Café Spiaggia *Italian*   25 | 23 | 24 | $56

Gold Coast | 980 N. Michigan Ave., 2nd fl. (Oak St.) | 312-280-2750 | www.cafespiaggia.com

A "more economical", "less formal" "alternative" to next-door sibling Spiaggia, this Gold Coast Italian "doesn't skimp on taste", sending out "luscious", often "creative" fare set down by "informed" staffers; windows in the "lovely" space afford "beautiful" city views, and while tables can sometimes feel a "bit tight", and bills aren't low, that doesn't stop many from "going back time and again."

	FOOD	DECOR	SERVICE	COST

Café Touché ⓜ *French*
23 | 21 | 22 | $38

Edison Park | 6731 N. Northwest Hwy. (Oshkosh Ave.) | 773-775-0909 | www.cafetouche.com

Locals choose this "secret little" Edison Park bistro for "delightful" "French country food" backed by a "good wine list"; the wood and brick-lined space can get "a bit loud", but the patio provides an escape, and "reasonable" prices are another mark in its favor.

Caffe Rom *Coffeehouse*
22 | 23 | 25 | $11

Loop | Prudential Plaza | 180 N. Stetson Ave. (bet. Lake & Randolph Sts.) | 312-948-8888 🖃

Loop | The Shoreham | 400 E. South Water St. (bet. Lower Wacker Dr. & Randolph St.) | 312-981-7766

Loop | Hyatt Ctr. | 71 S. Wacker Dr. (bet. Arcade Pl. & Monroe St.) | 312-379-0291 🖃

www.cafferom.com

Fans say you can find "some of the best coffee and espresso drinks in the Loop" at this Italian-style cafe trio also offering "tasty breakfast treats" and more "wholesome" "light" bites like sandwiches and panini; a "welcoming", "European feel" elevates the "bright, modern" surrounds, and "exemplary", "engaging" service is the cherry on top, making it a "great alternative to the big chains."

Calo Ristorante ➊ *Italian*
21 | 19 | 21 | $28

Andersonville | 5343 N. Clark St. (bet. Balmoral & Summerdale Aves.) | 773-271-7782 | www.calorestaurant.com

An Andersonville "institution" since 1963, this "old-time" Italian delivers "large quantities" of "quality" fare, including "traditional pastas", all at "reasonable prices"; the "comfortable" room features front windows that open in summer, and service is "always great."

Campagnola ⓜ *Italian*
24 | 20 | 23 | $43

Evanston | 815 Chicago Ave. (Washington St.) | 847-475-6100 | www.campagnolarestaurant.com

"Casual Italian gets a serious upgrade" at this "consistent" Evanston "gem" where the "authentic" fare features "first-rate, fresh ingredients straightforwardly and thoughtfully prepared"; "pleasant" servers work the "comfortable" rustic environs, which along with "reasonable prices" help make it a "neighborhood go-to."

Cantina Laredo *Mexican*
18 | 23 | 19 | $32

River North | 508 N. State St. (Illinois St.) | 312-955-0014 | www.cantinalaredo.com

Set in a "huge" "modern" space featuring fireplaces and a floating staircase, this midpriced River North chain link offers "average to good" Mexican eats that don't quite live up to the "beautiful" setting; still, service is "attentive" and the "cool vibe" attracts a "lively" crowd.

🆕 Cantina Pasadita 🖃ⓜ *Mexican*
– | – | – | M

Avondale | 2958 W. Irving Park Rd. (Sacramento Ave.) | 773-463-8226 | www.cantinapasadita.com

A 'bar & grill' Mexican dining experience can be had at this Avondale eatery featuring grub like Angus beef and 'quesadilla burgers' alongside margaritas, rum-spiked horchata and more; the striking setting has comfy booths, a stone fireplace, sports on TV and outdoor dining.

Cape Cod *Seafood*   22 | 22 | 23 | $59

Streeterville | Drake Hotel | 140 E. Walton St. (Michigan Ave.) | 312-787-2200 | www.thedrakehotel.com

"What a trip down memory lane" wax nostalgics of this "venerable" dining room in Streeterville's Drake Hotel, a circa-1933 "oldie but goodie" known for "classic" New England seafood, "lovely cocktails" and "old-school top-notch" service that beckons "back to a time when dining was elegant and people dressed for dinner"; while complainers find it a bit "tired" and "stuffy" and bemoan "expense-account" prices, it remains a "comfortable tradition, like going home" for many.

The Capital Grille *Steak*   24 | 21 | 24 | $68

Streeterville | 633 N. St. Clair St. (Ontario St.) | 312-337-9400
Rosemont | 5340 N. River Rd. (bet. Foster Ave. & Technology Blvd.) | 847-671-8125
Lombard | 87 Yorktown Shopping Ctr. (Highland Ave.) | 630-627-9800
www.thecapitalgrille.com

A "solid" "steak and martini" kind of place, this "refined" chophouse chain with an "old-school" atmosphere turns out "excellent" beef and sides plus a "good selection for non-meat eaters" too; an "incredible" wine list and service that "makes you feel special" up its appeal, and if it's "not the cheapest place in town", at least it's "consistent."

Caravan *Mediterranean/Mideastern*   - | - | - | I

Uptown | 4810 N. Broadway (Rosemont Ave.) | 773-271-6022 | www.caravanrestaurantchicago.com

The antithesis of your neighborhood falafel shack, this Uptown arrival offers midpriced Middle Eastern and Med fare; the swanky, opulent setting, done up with chandeliers and disco balls, includes two bars, plush gold-patterned chairs and funky settees, and weekend nights heat up with DJs.

Carlos & Carlos Ⓜ *Italian*   ▽ 25 | 23 | 25 | $58

Arlington Heights | 27 W. Campbell St. (bet. Dunton & Vail Aves.) | 847-259-2600 | www.carlosandcarloschicago.com

This Arlington Heights "keeper" dispenses "inventive" Northern Italian cooking at "value" prices that extend to the "aggressively priced" wine list; bistro-style surroundings and an outdoor patio complete the picture.

Carlucci *Italian*   22 | 21 | 23 | $46

Rosemont | Riverway Complex | 6111 N. River Rd. (Higgins Rd.) | 847-518-0990 | www.carluccirosemont.com

The "combination of good food and good service" makes this "bustling", "slightly upscale" Rosemont Italian set in Tuscan-style digs a "safe bet" for "business crowds" and travelers just in from O'Hare; if it seems "overpriced" to some, others say it's an "always consistent" "meeting spot."

Carmichael's
Chicago Steak House *Steak*

| 20 | 20 | 22 | $47 |

West Loop | 1052 W. Monroe St. (bet. Aberdeen & Morgan Sts.) | 312-433-0025 | www.carmichaelsteakhouse.com

"Take your man" to this West Loop chophouse for "steaks and martinis without the attitude" suggest diners who find the staff "friendly" and the location "easy"; the clubby space has an "old-time" feel, and though it's not cheap many say it's "reasonable for the genre."

Carmine's *Italian*

| 21 | 19 | 21 | $41 |

Gold Coast | 1043 N. Rush St. (bet. Bellevue Pl. & Cedar St.) | 312-988-7676 | www.rosebudrestaurants.com

Relive "the glory days of the Rush Street supper club scene" at this "lively" Gold Coaster from the Rosebud team where "mammoth portions" of "traditional" Italian eats come via servers who "complement the food"; tabs are "reasonable", if "somewhat inflated because of the location", and critics complaining it's "overhyped" and "overcrowded" are countered by others opining about its "access" to "exceptional people-watching."

Carnivale *Nuevo Latino*

| 21 | 25 | 20 | $44 |

West Loop | 702 W. Fulton Mkt. (Union Ave.) | 312-850-5005 | www.carnivalechicago.com

"Festive", "loud" and "happening" sums up this "huge" West Loop "social arena" that "lives up to its name" thanks to "vibrant" decor ("colors explode at you"), "fabulous" drinks and Nuevo Latino dishes so "flavorful" some have a "foodgasm"; inside has a "lively" atmosphere and prices are "reasonable" , so even if a few sniff it's just "so-so", most agree it's "perfect for large groups."

NEW Carriage House ●◙Ⓜ *Southern*

| ▽ 21 | 18 | 20 | $43 |

Wicker Park | 1700 W. Division St. (Paulina St.) | 773-384-9700 | www.carriagehousechicago.com

"Delicious, hearty Southern food" is what it's about at this Lowcountry concept in Wicker Park from Mark Steuer and The Bedford team; the midpriced offerings are served alongside signature craft cocktails and punches in a funky-rustic space with homey whitewashed wood, leather banquettes and communal seating, and there's a sheltered front porch with rocking chairs.

Carson's *BBQ*

| 21 | 15 | 19 | $33 |

River North | 612 N. Wells St. (Ontario St.) | 312-280-9200
Deerfield | 200 Waukegan Rd. (Oakmont Dr.) | 847-374-8500
www.ribs.com

"Bring it on" say fans of the "delectable" ribs rubbed with "smoky, sweet" sauce, "mounds" of complimentary chicken liver pâté and other "classic" BBQ offerings (the stuff of "cardiologists' nightmares") served by "accommodating" staffers at this circa-1977 River North original and its Deerfield double; there's "not a great deal of atmosphere", and some find it "a bit pricey" "compared to the competition", but it's still "quite popular", nonetheless.

	FOOD	DECOR	SERVICE	COST

Catch 35 *Seafood*

23	22	22	$49

Loop | Leo Burnett Bldg. | 35 W. Wacker Dr. (bet. Dearborn & State Sts.) | 312-346-3500
Naperville | 35 S. Washington St. (bet. Benton & Van Buren Aves.) | 630-717-3500
www.catch35.com

Afishionados catch "amazingly fresh" seafood at this "high-end" Loop and Naperville twosome turning out "solid", "well-executed" fare, including some dishes with "interesting" "Asian flair"; "elegant" decor and a "knowledgeable staff" are other pluses, so though "not for the faint of wallet", it's a "nice change of pace from all the beeferies"; P.S. Downtown has a "great piano bar."

Cellar at
The Stained Glass *Eclectic*

22	19	21	$38

Evanston | 820 Clark St. (bet. Benson & Sherman Aves.) | 847-864-8678 | www.thecellarevanston.com

There's "never a dull bite" say fans of this "lively" Evanston hangout tended by "friendly" staffers where the "imaginative" Eclectic small plates are "big on flavor" and the "excellent" wine list is accompanied by an even "better beer selection"; prices are more "accessible" than its nearby Stained Glass sib, and though it can still be a "bit of a splurge" for some, it remains a "popular" "drop-in place" (though no reservations may result in a wait).

Cemitas Puebla *Mexican*

24	6	18	$11

Humboldt Park | 3619 W. North Ave. (bet. Central Park & Monticello Aves.) | 773-772-8435 | www.cemitaspuebla.com

"Some of the best streetlike Mexican food" hails from this bargain-priced Humboldt Park "hole-in-the-wall" famous for its "phenomenal" namesake *cemitas* (sandwiches); a "friendly" staff that "treats you like family" provides another reason to brave the "dingy, dive"-like digs and somewhat "desolate" location.

NEW Central Standard *American/Eclectic*

–	–	–	M

River North | 169 W. Kinzie St. (bet. LaSalle & Wells Sts.) | 312-527-9409 | www.centralstandardchicago.com

This midpriced River North tavern serves an eclectic mash of American cuisines sourced locally and based on state-by-state inspiration, along with 40-odd draft beers and regional cocktails; the setting combines rustic Americana (reclaimed barn wood, Route 66 memorabilia) and industrial chic (ductwork, light bulbs encaged in wire, granite pillars), with a variety of seating and two bars.

NEW Centro Ristorante ● *Italian*

–	–	–	M

Near North | 6 W. Hubbard St. (State St.) | 312-988-7775 | www.rosebudrestaurants.com

The return of this Rosebud family concept in Near North (last seen in the early '90s) marks a comeback for 'neoclassic' Italian dining, with many items served in communal copper dishes; the swanky supper club setting has walls decorated with paintings, and prices are moderate.

	FOOD	DECOR	SERVICE	COST

Ceres' Table ☒ *American*
24 | 16 | 21 | $44

Uptown | 4882 N. Clark St. (bet. Ainslie St. & Lawrence Ave.) | 773-878-4882 | www.cerestable.com

Set in an "unlikely location" on a "nondescript block", this Uptown New American is the "definition of a hidden gem" cheer fans who say chef-owner Giuseppe Scurato's "creativity shines" in the "delicious" seasonal fare that's further lifted by "varied, well-priced" wines; the "sleek, bordering on stark" decor "leaves something to be desired", but "warm, welcoming" service and an "excellent price point for the quality" make it "worth knowing and worth visiting."

Chalkboard *American*
23 | 21 | 22 | $43

Lakeview | 4343 N. Lincoln Ave. (bet. Montrose & Pensacola Aves.) | 773-477-7144 | www.chalkboardrestaurant.com

An "interesting and varied" selection of seasonally inspired dishes is displayed on the chalkboard menu at this moderate Lakeview New American where "standards" like "excellent" fried chicken are offered alongside a few more "adventurous" picks; a "wonderful" selection of wines, "upscale" service and "intimate", "cozy" surrounds all extend the appeal.

Chef's Station ⓜ *American*
24 | 20 | 22 | $55

Evanston | Davis Street Metro Station | 915 Davis St. (Church St.) | 847-570-9821 | www.chefs-station.com

At once "civilized", "quirky" and "charming", this "casual" "fine-dining" destination "hidden away" in an Evanston Metro station crafts "consistently good", "occasionally brilliant" New American fare in an "unpretentious, comfortable-arty setting" that's "quiet and amenable to conversation"; if a few holdouts find it "overpriced", "excellent wine choices", "friendly" service and an "atmosphere that works for family or friends" have many fans vowing a "return trip."

Chens *Asian*
▽ 20 | 19 | 21 | $23

Wrigleyville | 3506 N. Clark St. (Cornelia Ave.) | 773-549-9100 | www.chenschicago.com

The "appealing mix" of "quality Chinese", Thai and sushi "in a classy setting" makes this "inexpensive" Wrigleyville waystation "a welcome change" from the neighborhood "norm"; "energetic, personable" service adds further appeal, so even if it's "not the best food in town", it's "consistently good" "for a quick bite before a ball game" and a "go-to" for "delivery so fast, you'd swear they have a truck circling the block."

Chez Joël ⓜ *French*
24 | 22 | 24 | $47

Little Italy/University Village | 1119 W. Taylor St. (May St.) | 312-226-6479 | www.chezjoelbistro.com

A "definite go-to" featuring "high-quality" "French comfort food", this "comfortable" "Little Italy charmer" also wields a "nice wine list with a variety of grapes and prices"; throw in that it "feels like Paris" and tabs are "small for what you get", and loyalists say it's "what a bistro should be."

Chez Moi ☒ *French*
FOOD	DECOR	SERVICE	COST
-	-	-	E

Lincoln Park | 2100 N. Halsted St. (Dickens Ave.) | 773-871-2100 | www.chezmoichicago.com

The "moi" in the name of this Lincoln Park French refers to chef-owner Dominique Tougne (of defunct Bistro 110) who prepares "beautifully served" bistro classics that remind of being "back in France"; the space features warm woods, floral paintings and a soft glow emanating from wire-wrapped chandeliers, and while entrees are somewhat spendy, the rest of the menu has plenty of lower-priced offerings; P.S. reservations are for large parties only.

NEW Chez Simo Bistro ☒ *French*
FOOD	DECOR	SERVICE	COST
-	-	-	M

Lincoln Square | 1968 W. Lawrence Ave. (Damen Ave.) | 773-334-7466 | www.chezsimobistro.com

Classic French bistro fare at moderate prices goes with your choice of BYO wine at this brick-walled Lincoln Square respite filled with bright booths and decorated with iconic photos and advertising posters.

Chicago Chop House *Steak*
FOOD	DECOR	SERVICE	COST
23	20	23	$74

River North | 60 W. Ontario St. (bet. Clark & Dearborn Sts.) | 312-787-7100 | www.chicagochophouse.com

You can fill your "hankering for some beef" at this "classic" River North chophouse, where "well-prepared" steaks are served in a dark wood–accented space "converted from a vintage Chicago two-flat" and decorated with photos of local celebs; "great old-school service" is another reason to go, and while it's not cheap, it is "steady."

Chicago Curry House *Indian/Nepalese*
FOOD	DECOR	SERVICE	COST
20	15	18	$31

South Loop | 899 S. Plymouth Ct. (9th St.) | 312-362-9999 | www.curryhouseonline.com

For "something different", South Loopers visit this Indian-Nepalese offering a "huge" menu of "usual and unusual" dishes ("try the momo"); servers are "helpful" and the atmosphere "pleasant", so even if the space doesn't quite match, most appreciate the "inexpensive" prices fit for "lovers of deals"

Chicago Cut Steakhouse ● *Steak*
FOOD	DECOR	SERVICE	COST
26	24	25	$72

River North | 300 N. LaSalle St. (bet. Kinzie St. & Wacker Dr.) | 312-329-1800 | www.chicagocutsteakhouse.com

Returnees say this River North steakhouse "gets it right every time", turning out "excellent" chops offered alongside a serious iPad wine list large enough to "get lost in"; service is "knowledgeable", and its "right-on-the-river" locale helps lend a "very Chicago" vibe, so many shrug off "pricey" tabs and sometimes "noisy" conditions, finding the overall experience "worth it."

Chicago Diner *Diner/Vegetarian*
FOOD	DECOR	SERVICE	COST
24	16	22	$18

Lakeview | 3411 N. Halsted St. (Roscoe St.) | 773-935-6696
NEW Logan Square | 2333 N. Milwaukee Ave. (California Ave.) | 773-252-3211
www.veggiediner.com

A "vegetarian paradise", this "hippie-inspired" Lakeview diner (with a newer Logan Square spin-off) has "stayed true to its mission" for

FOOD DECOR SERVICE COST

nearly 30 years, providing "interesting", eco-conscious eats (many of which are vegan too) "cooked just right", plus "rich, flavorful" "milk-free milkshakes" (a "must-try"); there's a "cute staff" and the "divey" diner atmosphere befits the budget prices, so "long lines" are the "only downside" for most.

Chicago Firehouse *American* 22 | 22 | 21 | $50

South Loop | 1401 S. Michigan Ave. (14th St.) | 312-786-1401 | www.chicagofirehouse.com

A "pioneer of the South Loop renaissance", this revived "landmark with lots of history" does "delicious", "hearty" Traditional American food in a "charming" setting complete with the "old firehouse pole in the bar"; if a few hotheads assert it's merely "ordinary", it's still a "dependable" option especially given its "excellent wine-by-the-glass selection", "pleasing" service and "beautiful summer patio."

Chicago Pizza & Oven Grinder Co. ⊭ *Pizza* 25 | 19 | 22 | $24

Lincoln Park | 2121 N. Clark St. (bet. Dickens & Webster Aves.) | 773-248-2570 | www.chicagopizzaandovengrinder.com

The "upside-down pizza in a bowl" pot pies turn guests "giddy" at this cash-only "Lincoln Park institution", a "wood lodge look-alike" that also excels with "Italian grinders" and "amazing salads"; it's "not for the faint of heart" given the "long waits" (no reservations), quirky "seating system" (the host "somehow remembers your face") and "cramped" tables, but it's an affordable "treat" for something "different", especially with "out-of-towners" in tow.

Chicago Prime Steakhouse *Steak* ▽ 25 | 23 | 23 | $75

Schaumburg | 1444 E. Algonquin Rd. (bet. Meacham Rd. & Thorntree Ln.) | 847-969-9900 | www.chicagoprimesteakhouse.com

"Simply the best" cheer suburbanites of this Schaumburg steak-house where "consistently good" fare, including the fortune 500 platter (lobster tails, oysters, crab cake, etc.), is served in a dark wood–accented space enhanced by a fireplace; strong service is an-other reason it comes "highly recommended", and there's a year-round patio with fireside seating too.

Chicago Q *BBQ* 21 | 22 | 21 | $36

Gold Coast | 1160 N. Dearborn St. (bet. Division & Elm Sts.) | 312-642-1160 | www.chicagoqrestaurant.com

"Chicago modern meets Southern BBQ" at pitmaster Lee Ann Whippen's "cool" Gold Coast contender where diners with "an empty stomach and posh clothing" feast on "upscale" 'cue including "outta control" smoked ribs, "delicious" Kobe brisket and "rustic" sides set down by "friendly" servers in a "rocking, jam-packed" room; bean counters find prices "high" for what's on offer, but most don't mind since it's "total comfort-food heaven."

Chief O'Neill's ● *Irish* 18 | 21 | 19 | $25

Northwest Side | 3471 N. Elston Ave. (Albany Ave.) | 773-583-3066 | www.chiefoneillspub.com

A "warm Irish pub atmosphere" brings Northwest Siders to this "woody" bi-level bar where the eats are not always "exciting" but boast "occasional flashes of fried-food brilliance"; with solid service, frequent live music and a "fantastic outdoor area", it's the "perfect place to raise your glass after a hard week."

Chilam Balam 🖻 🎹 ⌖ *Mexican* — 25 | 16 | 20 | $34

Lakeview | 3023 N. Broadway (bet. Barry & Wellington Aves.) | 773-296-6901 | www.chilambalamchicago.com

"World-class", "super-seasonal" Mexican small plates wow guests at this "tiny" cash-only Lakeview "treasure" where the "basement atmosphere" is trumped by "penthouse food" and "BYO adds an extra draw" (though there's margarita mix and "luscious" virgin sangria); "insane waits" are downsides and the "reasonable" prices can "add up", but most agree it's "definitely worth it."

Chilapan 🖻 *Mexican* — ▽ 25 | 16 | 23 | $27

Logan Square | 2459 W. Armitage Ave. (bet. Bingham St. & Campbell Ave.) | 773-697-4597 | www.tenangrypitbulls.com

"Authentic, upscale" "Mexican comfort food" – including "life-changing queso" – is "the stuff dreams are made of" at this "small, family-owned" BYO "gem" in Logan Square; service is "warm and friendly", so even if the setting doesn't rate that highly, it's enough for a "relaxed" meal.

🆕 Chuck's Manufacturing *American* — - | - | - | M

Loop | Hard Rock Hotel | 224 N. Michigan Ave. (bet. Lake St. & Wacker Pl.) | 312-334-6700 | www.chucksmanufacturing.com

Named for the owner's erstwhile family biz, this Loop lair in the Hard Rock Hotel (formerly home of China Grill) serves a midpriced menu of updated American comfort food for lunch, after-work and dinner and features a bar highlighting signature cocktails and over 100 vodkas; the colorful ultramodern environs include space-age furnishings, an eye-catching DJ setup and a massive video wall, plus tables conveniently outfitted with WiFi and electrical outlets.

Cité *American* — 19 | 24 | 19 | $72

Streeterville | Lake Point Tower | 505 N. Lake Shore Dr. (Streeter Dr.) | 312-644-4050 | www.citechicago.com

"Amazing views of the city" from the 70th floor of the Lake Point Tower lure diners to this elegant Streeterville New American where "romantic" environs trump the "fine" fare and service; still, the "fantastic" panoramic vistas make it "worth going" for "drinks at the bar around sunset", "an anniversary or a birthday" or when "you're in trouble with the wife" – just "bring a fat wallet."

City Farms Market & Grill 🎹 *Sandwiches* — - | - | - | I

Lakeview | 1467 W. Irving Park Rd. (bet. Greenview & Janssen Aves.) | 773-883-2767 | www.cityfarmsgrill.com

The brainchild of an ex-banker, this unfettered, farm-to-fork North Center sandwich slinger offers modern handhelds (and updated morning eats) in a space with an open kitchen and communal wood table seating; suppers and a companion food truck are also in the works.

City Tavern *American*   ▽ 16 | 17 | 18 | $43

South Loop | 1416 S. Michigan Ave. (bet. 14th & 16th Sts.) |
312-663-1278 | www.citytavernchicago.com

An 18th century–inspired tavern, this South Loop haunt has a mid-priced menu of New American gastropub fare, tankards of beer (the list nears 100) and vintage cocktails; the onetime Grace O'Malley's space has time-traveled backwards and now boasts federal blue walls, Windsor chairs and period-style chandeliers to transporting effect.

NEW City Winery *Mediterranean*   ▽ 16 | 24 | 18 | $38

West Loop | 1200 W. Randolph St. (bet. Elizabeth St. & Racine Ave.) |
312-733-9463 | www.citywinery.com

This "trendy" New York import in the West Loop is a multifaceted amalgam of all things wine, from sampling from the "excellent" selection (plus beer too) to making it (down to designing your own label), and also doubles as a live entertainment venue and a moderately priced Med restaurant (with a klezmer brunch as one twist); the massive 30,000-sq.-ft. space includes an open dining room, a garden courtyard and, yes, plenty of barrels.

The Clubhouse *American*   22 | 22 | 22 | $38

Oak Brook | Oakbrook Center Mall | 298 Oakbrook Ctr. (22nd St.) |
630-472-0600 | www.theclubhouse.com

There's "something for everybody" at this "casual" American in Oak Brook mall where "well-prepared" "comfort food" comes in "hearty" portions "big enough to share"; "a lot of after-work action" takes place at the "busy" bar, while the quieter upstairs dining room is more "special-occasion" worthy, and affordable tabs help make it an overall "reliable" pick.

Club Lucky *Italian*   21 | 17 | 20 | $31

Bucktown | 1824 W. Wabansia Ave. (Honore St.) | 773-227-2300 |
www.clubluckychicago.com

Smells of "traditional" "homestyle Italian cooking" "waft for blocks" from this "'faux old-school" Bucktown "supper club" where there are "no surprises", just "huge portions", "solid" eats and "killer martinis"; "reasonable costs", "friendly" servers and a vibrant atmosphere" further explain why it's "managed to remain hip and fun" since its 1990 inception.

Coalfire Pizza Ⓜ *Pizza*   24 | 14 | 20 | $22

Noble Square | 1321 W. Grand Ave. (Ogden Ave.) | 312-226-2625 |
www.coalfirechicago.com

"Rich sauces", "fresh ingredients" and "light", "crispy" crusts charred "with a bit of black" "all come together" in the "sublime" pizzas at this "unpretentious" Noble Square pie house; "friendly" service "warms up the uninspired setting" and so regulars are left wishing it "would become a chain."

Coast Sushi Bar ⚫ *Japanese*   24 | 20 | 21 | $34

Bucktown | 2045 N. Damen Ave. (bet. Dickens & McLean Aves.) |
773-235-5775 | www.coastsushibar.com

(continued)

Coast Sushi & Sashimi *Japanese*
Evanston | 2545 Prairie Ave. (bet. Central & Harrison Sts.) | 847-328-2221 | www.coastsushi.net

Southcoast *Japanese*
South Loop | 1700 S. Michigan Ave. (bet. 16th & 18th Sts.) | 312-662-1700 | www.southcoastsushi.com

"You can rely on" this South Loop Japanese and its Bucktown BYO twin (with an Evanston triplet) for "high-quality" sushi, "imaginative" rolls and "delicious entrees" in "modern" environs; service also gets high marks and tabs are "good", so they're often "hopping."

Coco Pazzo *Italian*
25 | 23 | 23 | $52

River North | 300 W. Hubbard St. (Franklin St.) | 312-836-0900 | www.cocopazzochicago.com

"Outstanding Italian food" including Tuscan "classics" and "seasonal offerings" in a lovely and civilized setting" combine with "attentive service" to make this high-end, "sophisticated" River North ristorante "a triple win" "perfect for a date-night, business meeting or family event"; a "well-dressed crowd" populates the "white tablecloth setting" where the "conversation level is perfect", and with a "great wine list", it's an all-around "classy" contender.

Coco Pazzo Café *Italian*
22 | 21 | 22 | $41

Streeterville | 636 N. St Clair St. (Ontario St.) | 312-664-2777 | www.cocopazzochicago.com

The "informal" "junior version of Coco Pazzo", this longtime Streeterville "favorite" maintains its "go-to" status with "thoughtfully prepared" Northern Italian fare, "helpful" service and "fair prices"; inside features a "relaxed country atmosphere" and outside offers prime "people-watching", so "plan ahead" because it's often "busy."

Convito Café & Market *French/Italian*
20 | 18 | 19 | $38

Wilmette | Plaza del Lago | 1515 Sheridan Rd. (Westerfield Dr.) | 847-251-3654 | www.convitocafeandmarket.com

Set in the back of the market, this affordable Wilmette cafe appeals with "trusty salads", pastas and other "well-prepared" French-Italian fare; a "wonderful selection of wine" leads to lingering in the "cozy" confines, so though it's "nothing exceptional", it's still a "local go-to."

Coobah Ⓜ *Filipino/Nuevo Latino*
23 | 20 | 19 | $33

Lakeview | 3423 N. Southport Ave. (Newport Ave.) | 773-528-2220 | www.coobah.com

"Flavorful, exciting" Filipino–Nuevo Latino "fusion food" in "sexy", "exotic" environs provide a "wonderful escape" from the "blahs" at this "affordable" Lakeview haunt; a few warn of "tables crammed next to each other", but fans focus instead on the "great" drinks and "fun atmosphere" that "adds to the experience."

Cooper's Hawk
Winery & Restaurant ◗ *American*
21 | 21 | 21 | $36

Wheeling | 583 N. Milwaukee Ave. (Wolf Rd.) | 847-215-1200

(continued)

(continued)

Cooper's Hawk Winery & Restaurant

Arlington Heights | 798 W. Algonquin Rd. (Golf Rd.) | 847-981-0900
South Barrington | The Arboretum of South Barrington | 100 W. Higgins Rd.
(bet. Bartlett & New Sutton Rds.) | 847-836-9463
Burr Ridge | Burr Ridge Village Ctr. | 510 Village Center Dr. (Bridewell Dr.) |
630-887-0123
Orland Park | 15690 S. Harlem Ave. (157th St.) | 708-633-0200
Naperville | 1740 Freedom Dr. (Independence Ave.) | 630-245-8000
www.coopershawkwinery.com

Diners "unwind" at this "happening" American chain, a "gathering
place for family and friends" with its "strong" menu of "wholesome"
"comfort food", "interesting variety" of wines made on-site and
"prompt", "consistent" service; judges who "just don't get it" complain of "noisy", "conversation-challenged" digs and say it's "overpriced for the quality", but most find the tabs "reasonable" and like
that there's "something for everyone in the group."

NEW Copper House *American*

North Center/St. Ben's | 4337 N. Lincoln Ave. (Pensacola Ave.) |
773-935-2255 | www.copperhousechicago.com

Classic American pub grub is the name of the game at this North
Center neighborhood tavern (formerly the long-standing Jury's)
rebooted with an expanded, yet still affordable, menu of burgers,
sammies, entrees and craft suds; the digs have been renovated and
seating options include a warm weather sidewalk patio and beer
garden, but sports fans never fear, there are still plenty of TVs.

NEW Cottage on Dixie *American/Eclectic*

| – | – | – | E |

Homewood | 18849 Dixie Hwy. (bet. Terrace Rd. & Idlewild Ln.) |
708-798-2263 | www.thecottageondixie.com

Upscale, farm-to-table New American lunches and dinners plus
global monthly specials join a sommelier-curated wine list, craft
cocktails and small-batch infused sodas at this fine-dining destination in Homewood; the striking setting houses an exposed-beam
ceiling, massive stone pillars, seasonal outdoor seats and a fireplace
lounge serving a separate snack menu.

NEW County Barbeque Ⓜ *BBQ*

Little Italy/University Village | 1352 W. Taylor St. (Loomis St.) |
248-943-1098 | www.countybarbeque.com

The DMK team (Ada Street, DMK Burger Bar, Fish Bar) is behind this
Little Italy BBQ bastion, where the budget-friendly menu spotlights
house-smoked meats in different regional styles, plus bacon bar
offerings and updates of classic sides; the bar pours whiskey, craft
beers and cocktails, and the dark wood–paneled space is decorated
with American flags and buffalo plaid.

Courtright's Ⓜ *American*

| 27 | 27 | 27 | $69 |

Willow Springs | 8989 S. Archer Ave. (Willow Springs Rd.) |
708-839-8000 | www.courtrights.com

"Delicious" dishes and a "beautiful location" in the Willow Springs
forest preserve help put this fine-dining American on the map; ser-

vice gets high marks too, and while tabs are costly, at least you're assured a "memorable meal."

NEW Covo Gyro

	FOOD	DECOR	SERVICE	COST
	-	-	-	M

Market *Greek/Sandwiches*

Wicker Park | 1482 N. Milwaukee Ave. (Honore St.) | 312-626-2660 | www.covogyro.com

This affordable quick-serve gyro house (the name is Greek for 'carve') in Wicker Park offers three all-natural meat options for the signature sandwich, served on housemade grilled pitas with topping choices, feta fries with seasonal dips and entree salads, plus microbrews and Greek wine; the design is a nod to the old meat-packing district with repurposed cooler doors, barn wood and white tile.

Cozy Noodles & Rice *Thai*

FOOD	DECOR	SERVICE	COST
21	19	20	$14

Lakeview | 3456 N. Sheffield Ave. (Clark St.) | 773-327-0100 | www.cozychicago.com

"Delicious Thai dishes" at "super-cheap" prices leave enthusiasts saying this tiny Lakeview BYO "rocks"; "whimsical" and "quirky" toy store decor lends "charm" and service is "friendly" too, but with limited seating many opt for "very fast takeout."

Crêperie Saint-Germain M *French*

	FOOD	DECOR	SERVICE	COST
	-	-	-	I

Evanston | 1512 Sherman Ave. (bet. Grove & Lake Sts.) | 847-859-2647 | www.creperiestgermain.com

Crêpes sweet and savory, salads and hors d'oeuvres including classic onion soup and duck terrine come out of the kitchen at this midpriced French beneath a striped awning in Evanston; a massive map of the Paris Metro monopolizes one wall in the casual cafe setting with warm wood, butcher block tables and hanging window frames.

Crisp *Korean*

FOOD	DECOR	SERVICE	COST
24	12	18	$13

Lakeview | 2940 N. Broadway St. (bet. Oakdale & Wellington Aves.) | 773-697-7610 | www.crisponline.com

"Decadent", "sinfully good" Korean "crispy fried chicken in spicy and savory flavors" stars at this "reasonably priced" Lakeview BYO where diners opting for other options like burritos and "tasty" rice bowls often find themselves "jealous for the rest of the meal"; the counter-service space offers "no real frills but no snobbery either", so many join the ranks of "satisfied diners with greasy fingers and smudged faces."

NEW Crosby's Kitchen *American*

	FOOD	DECOR	SERVICE	COST
▽	19	22	19	$27

Lakeview | 3455 N. Southport Ave. (Cornelia Ave.) | 773-883-2525 | www.crosbychicago.com

A "great addition to the neighborhood" say fans of this "homey" Lakeview American that turns out "solid" comfort-food favorites including "tender, flavorful" rotisserie meats along with a compact wine list and craft brews; touches like an afternoon kids eat free program and stroller valet help make it "family-friendly", but with warm woodwork, "massive" booths and a lively bar area it's "sophisticated" enough to be "adult-friendly" too.

Cumin *Indian/Nepalese*   24 | 18 | 18 | $28

Wicker Park | 1414 N. Milwaukee Ave. (bet. Evergreen & Wolcott Aves.) | 773-342-1414 | www.cumin-chicago.com

"The smell of spices will draw you in" and the "delicious" fare will "keep you there" assure acolytes of this "casual yet modern" Wicker Park Indian-Nepalese offering "interesting" dishes filled with "exciting flavors"; toss in "friendly" service and "value" tabs and most "can't wait to go back."

Curry Hut   19 | 13 | 18 | $25
Restaurant *Indian/Nepalese*

Highwood | 410 Sheridan Rd. (bet. Bank Ln. & Highwood Ave.) | 847-432-2889 | www.curryhutrestaurant.com

Tasters "try new things" at this "value" Indian-Nepalese in Highwood offering "complex curries", "great veggie dishes" and other "solid" fare; the confines are "nothing fancy", but "servers are helpful", so if some shrug it "should be better", others find it a "nice change of pace."

Cyrano's Farm Kitchen 🗷 *French*   19 | 18 | 19 | $39
(fka Cyrano's Bistrot & Wine Bar)

River North | 546 N. Wells St. (bet. Grand Ave. & Ohio St.) | 312-467-0546

You'll feel like you're in a "country bistro" at this River North eatery serving farm-focused Gallic fare; dining in the rustic space with ceiling beams and vintage chandeliers feels "like being in a French village", and prices are moderate.

NEW Dak Korean   - | - | - | I
Chicken Wings 🅼 *Korean*

Edgewater | 1104 W. Granville Ave. (Winthrop Ave.) | 773-754-0255 | www.dakwings.com

Edgewater locals chow down on jumbo double-fried chicken wings at this casual, budget-friendly Korean whose chalkboard menu includes rice bowls, dumplings and classic entrees along with imported soft drinks; bare tables with aluminum chairs dot the modern space, but takeout is a popular option.

NEW Da Lobsta *Seafood*   - | - | - | I

Gold Coast | 12 E. Cedar St. (bet. Lake Shore Dr. & State St.) | 312-929-2423 | www.dalobstachicago.com

Expect a "simple but creative menu" of globally influenced lobster rolls plus soup, salad, mac 'n' cheese and more at this sea shanty–inspired Gold Coast seafooder; it's counter-service only, making it "good for a quick, casual lunch", simple dinner or take-out meal.

D & J Bistro 🅼 *French*   24 | 19 | 24 | $43

Lake Zurich | First Bank Plaza Ctr. | 466 S. Rand Rd./Rte. 12 (Rte. 22) | 847-438-8001 | www.dj-bistro.com

"Still going strong after many years", this "true suburban gem" set in an "unlikely" Lake Zurich strip mall earns "bravos" for its "excellent" French bistro "classics" bolstered by a "fresh" wine list in "cozy" environs elevated by a "warm, friendly" staff; it also provides a "strong value", so while food is "better than the ambiance", unswerving supporters agree it's "aging gracefully."

Dan McGee ▣ *American*

▽ | 26 | 21 | 25 | $44

Frankfort | 9975 W. Lincoln Hwy. (Locust St.) | 815-469-7750 | www.danmcgees.com

For a "bit of Downtown Chicago in Frankfort", fans hit up this "small, intimate" New American where "creative" chef-owner Dan McGee prepares "delicious" "gourmet" dishes; service scores strong marks, and while prices aren't low, they're not terribly expensive either.

Davanti Enoteca *Italian*

26 | 22 | 22 | $39

Little Italy/University Village | 1359 W. Taylor St. (Loomis St.) | 312-226-5550

NEW **Western Springs** | 800 Hillgrove Ave. (Wolf Rd.) | 708-783-1060 www.davantiwesternsprings.com

"Inventive" takes on "rustic" Italian cuisine, including small plates with "enormous taste" and "lick-the-bowl" pastas, come via restaurateur Scott Harris (Mia Francesca, The Purple Pig) at this "laid-back" Little Italy enoteca (with a newer Western Springs double); no-reservations mean there's "typically a wait", but the "knowledgeable" staff aptly handles the "crowds", so customers call it "casual dining at its best."

David Burke's Primehouse *Steak*

25 | 22 | 24 | $73

River North | James Chicago Hotel | 616 N. Rush St. (Ontario St.) | 312-660-6000 | www.davidburkesprimehouse.com

"Delight" in "dry-aged perfection" at this chophouse in River North's James Hotel where "showman" David Burke delivers "humongous" steaks complemented by a "supporting cast" of "imaginative" eats like pretzel-crusted crab cakes and "the best starter popovers" in a "beautiful" room that's "upscale without being too highfalutin"; add in carefully "choreographed" service and it all "comes at a price" – though the prix fixe lunch is an "awesome deal" and the "weekend brunch can't be beat."

Davis Street Fishmarket *Seafood*

19 | 16 | 17 | $35

Evanston | 501 Davis St. (Hinman Ave.) | 847-869-3474 | www.davisstreetfishmarket.com

"Satisfied" fans cast their votes for the "comfortable, casual fish dining done well" at this midpriced Evanston old-timer with "a bit of a New Orleans theme" to its "solid" seafood; the service swings from "very good" to "lacking" and some anglers say it's "just meh", but most reckon "there's a reason you have to get here early to get in."

Dawali *Mediterranean/Mideastern*

23 | 14 | 20 | $16

Lincoln Park | 1625 N. Halsted St. (North Ave.) | 312-944-5800
Albany Park | 4911 N. Kedzie Ave. (Ainslie St.) | 773-267-4200
www.dawalikitchen.com

"Solid", "full-of-flavor" fare like "excellent baklava and falafel" earn respect for these Mediterranean–Middle Eastern sibs;

Lincoln Park is BYO and convenient to nearby theaters, while the Albany Park locale is alcohol-free, and if neither gets high praise for its decor, with wallet-friendly bills fans say they're still "really worth" visiting.

Deca Restaurant + Bar *French*

`21` `21` `22` `$51`

Streeterville | Ritz-Carlton Chicago | 160 E. Pearson St., 12th fl. (bet. Michigan Ave. & Mies van der Rohe Way) | 312-573-5160 | www.decarestaurant.com

Just off the 12th-floor lobby of the Streeterville Ritz-Carlton, this French brasserie provides a "lovely" art deco–inspired setting for a "wide range of fresh, well-prepared" fare (including "decadent desserts") to go along with the "obliging", "friendly" service and pleasant "people-watching"; few fault the fare as "middling" for hotel prices, but it couldn't be more convenient for pre-theater dining or breaks from "exercising your card at Water Tower Place"; P.S. there's seasonal noshing and sipping with a view at The Dec rooftop.

De Cero ⊠ Ⓜ *Mexican*

`20` `18` `18` `$35`

West Loop | 814 W. Randolph St. (bet. Green & Halsted Sts.) | 312-455-8114 | www.decerotaqueria.com

Order the "mix and match" taco platter and "you can't go wrong" at this "trendy" yet "authentic" West Loop taqueria where the "broad" menu of "gourmet" Mex eats gets a boost from "killer margaritas"; the "casual" space has a "cantina-meets-warehouse" feel, and if a few find it "pricey" for the genre and "don't see the big deal", more claim the "flavorful food" will "keep you coming back."

Dee's *Asian*

▽ `19` `17` `18` `$29`

Lincoln Park | 1114 W. Armitage Ave. (Seminary Ave.) | 773-477-1500 | www.deesrestaurant.com

A "reasonable mix" of sushi and "basic but satisfying" Mandarin and Sichuan specialties comes "recommended" at this affordable Lincoln Park longtimer; the "owner's personal attention" and a "lovely" out-door patio further qualify it for "neighborhood favorite" status.

Deleece *Eclectic*

`21` `18` `20` `$35`

Lakeview | 3747 N. Southport Ave. (bet. Grace St. & Waveland Ave.) | 773-325-1710 | www.deleece.com

Enthusiasts say "every 'hood" should have a "charming little place" like this Lakeview "gem" where "well-made" Eclectic fare is served in a "cozy, casual" indoor/outdoor space; moderate tabs and "friendly" servers help seal the deal for a "family gathering, group of friends" or even "date night."

NEW Del Frisco's Double Eagle Steakhouse *Steak*

▽ `27` `26` `24` `$81`

Gold Coast | 58 E. Oak St. (bet. Michigan Ave. & Rush St.) | 312-888-2499 | www.delfriscos.com

Part of a small national chain, this massive Gold Coast steakhouse offers a "top-notch" dining experience, from the "perfectly cooked", "tender" filets and "extensive" wine list to the "beautiful" setting with plush furnishings, a sweeping marble staircase and Oak Street views; service earns high marks too, and while prices are unsurprisingly expensive, fans who appreciate the "great energy" find it "a nice change from the old standards."

Del Rio 🗷 Ⓜ *Italian*   20 | 16 | 20 | $41

Highwood | 228 Green Bay Rd. (Mears Pl.) | 847-432-4608 | www.delriorestaurant.biz

"Time stands still" at this "family-run", "red-sauce Italian" that's been in Highwood "forever" (or at least since 1923), and that's fine with fans who say it's a "joy" to revisit for "properly priced", "classic" cooking, "old-school" service and "strong drinks" mixed by "great bartenders"; foodies who feel the fare is "not the draw" nod to "one of the most extensive and best" wine selections around and advise you "ask them about the cellar list they keep at the bar."

Del Seoul *Korean*   23 | 11 | 17 | $13

Lakeview | 2568 N. Clark St. (Wrightwood Ave.) | 773-248-4227 | www.delseoul.com

Eaters have "endless love" for the Asian-Mexican "mash-up" tacos (a "cultural fusion that works") at this "cheap", "quick-serve" Korean in Lakeview where revamped banh mi and more traditional specialties also "earn their place" on the "small menu"; the surroundings are "bare and bland" and the seating "isn't the most comfortable", but Seoul-searchers say you're here for the "amazing" food, "not the decor."

Demera Ethiopian *Ethiopian*   20 | 16 | 17 | $25

Uptown | 4801 N. Broadway (Lawrence Ave.) | 773-334-8787 | www.demeraethiopianrestaurant.com

Fans swear "you can smell the sauces" cooking all the way from the Lawrence El stop at this "inexpensive" Uptown Ethiopian that offers a "nice variety" of "spicy meats" and veggie options served up in "generous portions" and followed by coffee from house-roasted beans; "so-so service and decor" don't deter pros who point to the "pleasant" outdoor seating and "fun atmosphere" (with occasional live music).

Depot Nuevo *Nuevo Latino*   18 | 20 | 20 | $31

Wilmette | 1139 Wilmette Ave. (bet. Central & Lake Aves.) | 847-251-3111 | www.depotnuevo.com

A "fun, inventive" take on Nuevo Latino eats, "creative", "delicious" cocktails and service "friendly to everyone from families to dates" all result in "lively" "crowds" at this affordable Wilmette spot in a converted train station; even if a few deem it "nothing too impressive", the "year-round covered porch" is still a draw; P.S. no reservations on weekends.

Devon Seafood Grill *Seafood*   21 | 21 | 21 | $47

River North | 39 E. Chicago Ave. (Wabash Ave.) | 312-440-8660

(continued)

(continued)

NEW Devon Seafood + Steak *Seafood/Steakhouse*

Oakbrook Terrace | JRC Plaza East | 17W400 22nd St. (Maple Pl.) | 630-516-0180
www.devonseafood.com

"Not just your basic seafood place" is how fans describe this "upscale" River North chain link (with a newer Oakbrook twin) where the fin fare is "prepared in delicious ways" and boosted by a "solid wine list"; generally "attentive service" also works in its favor, and "fantastic happy-hour specials" help explain the lively "bar scene."

Dimo's Pizza ● *Pizza*   22 | 14 | 20 | $9

Lakeview | 3463 N. Clark St. (Sheffield Ave.) | 773-525-4580 | www.dimospizza.com

"Awesomely weird" (some say "ingenious") toppings like "steak and fries, mac 'n' cheese, etc." are "like every kid's dream" at this Lakeview pizzeria BYO; there's "not much ambiance" and late-night eaters should expect imbibers "coming from nearby bars", but service "moves quickly", so when you want to "experiment with funky" combinations, it fits the "inexpensive" bill.

Dining Room at Kendall College ☒ *French*   ▽ 23 | 20 | 21 | $41

Near West | Kendall College | 900 N. North Branch St. (Halsted St.) | 312-752-2328 | www.kendall.edu

There's "something so charming" about this Near West "learning" ground turned "pleasant surprise", where Kendall College students prepare and "earnestly" (if "nervously") serve the New French "fine-dining" fare in modern digs where "big windows" provide "great views"; even supporters who say it's "nothing amazing" note "nothing beats the value."

Dinotto Ristorante *Italian*   21 | 18 | 20 | $38

Old Town | 215 W. North Ave. (bet. Wells & Wieland Sts.) | 312-202-0302 | www.dinotto.com

This "cozy" Old Town "hideaway around the corner from Second City" ranks as "reliable" for "very good", "reasonably priced" Italian fare, "consistent" service and "great patio dining"; so if it's "not unique", it's still a "perfect neighborhood" spot – and "nice place to take a lady for dinner."

DiSotto Enoteca ● *Italian*   ▽ 23 | 21 | 21 | $37

Streeterville | Mia Francesca | 200 E. Chestnut St. (bet. DeWitt Pl. & Michigan Ave.) | 312-482-8727 | www.disottoenoteca.com

A "welcome addition" from Scott Harris (Davanti Enoteca, Mia Francesca, The Purple Pig), this "casual" Streeterville Italian under Francesca's on Chestnut offers "delicious, well-prepared" small plates to go with a large vino list; the "comfortable" "wine cellar"–like setting is elevated by "friendly", "knowledgeable" staffers and prices are affordable too, so it's a "fine option" for a "perfect first date."

	FOOD	DECOR	SERVICE	COST

Ditka's *Steak* — | 22 | 21 | 22 | $50 |

Gold Coast | Tremont Hotel | 100 E. Chestnut St. (Ernst Ct.) | 312-587-8989
Oakbrook Terrace | 2 Mid America Plaza (22nd St.) | 630-572-2200
www.ditkasrestaurants.com

"Da coach gets it done" cheer fans of these "iconic" Gold Coast and Oakbrook Terrace steakhouses where you may "run into football legends" or Mike himself while feasting on "surprisingly good" fare including "Chicago-sized" cuts, "succulent" pork chops and "not-to-be-missed pot roast nachos" via "consistent" servers; if some say it's "kinda pricey", others find tabs "relatively reasonable", especially when considered part of a "sporting museum entrance fee" given all the "Bears memorabilia"; P.S. Downtown is "the place for game day."

Dixie Kitchen & Bait Shop *Cajun/Southern* — | 20 | 17 | 18 | $22 |

Evanston | 825 Church St. (bet. Benson & Sherman Aves.) |
847-733-9030 | www.dixiekitchenchicago.com

Fans get their Cajun and Southern food "fix" at this "consistently good" joint where the "Louisiana-style" menu includes eats like fried chicken, gumbo and "fine fried green tomatoes"; "interesting trinkets" fill the "casual" space, giving it a "funky" vibe, and "reasonable prices" help seal the deal.

DMK Burger Bar *Burgers* — | 22 | 16 | 19 | $21 |

Lakeview | 2954 N. Sheffield Ave. (Wellington Ave.) | 773-360-8686 ◗
Lombard | 2370 Fountain Square Dr. (Butterfield Rd.) | 630-705-9020
www.dmkburgerbar.com

"Eclectic gourmet burgers", including options for non-beef eaters, and "damn fine sides" like "addictive" "grown-up french fries" are "complemented incredibly well by a drink menu" feauring milk-shakes, "well-made" craft cocktails and an "outstanding selection of microbrews" at the Lakeview original and Lombard spin-off from restaurateurs David Morton and Michael Kornick; a no-reservations policy often results in "long waits" and it's "loud" ("bring your earplugs"), but the "young and trendy" don't mind, especially because "service moves quickly" and "the price is right."

NEW Dryhop Brewers ◗ *European* — | - | - | - | M |

Lakeview | 3155 N. Broadway (bet. Belmont Ave & Briar Pl.) |
773-857-3155 | www.dryhopchicago.com

This Lakeview gastropub serves seasonal house-brewed suds paired with a midpriced Euro-style menu of small plates, and also pours growlers to go; the space has an oak bar, a half-dozen beer tanks, butcher block tables and flannel-upholstered booths.

Due Lire Ⓜ *Italian* — | 23 | 17 | 23 | $31 |

Lincoln Square | 4520 N. Lincoln Ave. (bet. Sunnyside & Wilson Aves.) |
773-275-7878 | www.due-lire.com

"Cozy" and "convivial (i.e. loud)", this "lovely", "little" Lincoln Square "storefront" "gem" serves "simple", "tasty" Italian fare including "handmade pastas with delicious fresh sauces" alongside a "wine list to match"; "friendly" service and midscale prices help keep it a neighborhood "go-to."

Duke of Perth ● *Scottish*

20 | 18 | 21 | $22

Lakeview | 2913 N. Clark St. (Bet. Oakdale Ave. & Surf St.) | 773-477-1741 | www.dukeofperth.com

"All that's missing is the dark and stormy night" at this "authentic" Scottish pub in Lakeview offering "flavorful, non-greasy pub grub" and a "tremendous selection of whiskeys and beers" in "cozy" surrounds where "the lack of TVs (and subsequent lack of bros) make it even better"; add in "rational prices" and "friendly" service and it's a "serious watering hole" "destination", especially when the back patio is open.

NEW Duran European Sandwiches & Café *European/Sandwiches*

- | - | - | I

West Loop | 529 N. Milwaukee Ave. (bet. Green & Halsted Sts.) | 312-666-6007 | www.duraneurosandwich.com

The first American outpost of a Vienna-based chain, this inexpensive West Loop cafe offers a long list of artful open-faced sandwiches in miniature along with pastries from breakfast through (very) late lunch; there's also teas, juices and La Colombe coffee, all dispensed in a casual, modern space hung with a curated art collection.

NEW e+o Food & Drink *American*

- | - | - | M

Mt. Prospect | 125 Randhurst Village Dr. (Elmhurst Rd.) | 847-398-3636 | www.eofoodanddrink.com

There's "lots of creativity" on the midpriced menu at this Mt. Prospect New American, where chef-owner Rodelio Aglibot's globally accented offerings include everything from small plates, pizza and grilled meats to shellfish bar items and sushi; specialty cocktails, craft beers and a compact wine list extend the appeal, as does the "trendy" setting including banquettes, a fire pit–enhanced patio and bar area with communal tables.

Edelweiss *German*

22 | 21 | 22 | $29

Norridge | 7650 W. Irving Park Rd. (Overhill Ave.) | 708-452-6040 | www.edelweissdining.com

"You'll waddle out" of this "authentic" German joint in Norridge after chowing down on "surprisingly good" sausages and schnitzels, throwing back Bavarian brews and listening to the live "oompah band"; the service earns high marks and the setting brings back "memories of the old country", so even those wondering if "maybe the beer makes everyone like the so-so specialties" still agree you'll leave "one happy camper."

Eduardo's Enoteca *Italian*

∇ 23 | 19 | 22 | $31

Gold Coast | 1212 N. Dearborn St. (bet. Division & Goethe Sts.) | 312-337-4490 | www.eduardosenoteca.com

In an "almost total reinvention", the same owners turned what was once the casual Edwardo's Natural Pizza into a more upscale Gold Coast offshoot, where a "polished" staff serves "delish" Italian dishes, "interesting", affordable small plates and "boutique" bottles; exposed rafters highlight the space's heritage as an old theater, and low lights make this wine bar a "charming date spot."

Edwardo's Natural Pizza *Pizza*

| 19 | 10 | 15 | $19 |

Lincoln Park | 2662 N. Halsted St. (bet. Diversey Pkwy. & Wrightwood Ave.) | 773-871-3400
Hyde Park | 1321 E. 57th St. (bet. Kenwood & Kimbark Aves.) | 773-241-7960
Skokie | 9300 Skokie Blvd. (Gross Point Rd.) | 847-674-0008
Oak Park | 6831 North Ave. (Grove Ave.) | 708-524-2400
www.edwardos.com

"Classic" deep-dish and "solid" thin-crust pies crafted with "emphasis on fresh, natural ingredients" please patrons of this "reliable, not awesome" series of "casual" city and suburban pizza parlors; decor ranges from recently updated to "hole-in-the-wall", but "great prices" help.

Edzo's Burger Shop Ⓜ *Burgers*

| 26 | 13 | 20 | $12 |

NEW Lincoln Park | 2218 N. Lincoln Ave. (Webster Ave.) | 773-697-9909 Ⓢ
Evanston | 1571 Sherman Ave. (bet. Davis & Grove Sts.) | 847-864-3396
www.edzos.com

"Simply awesome" "top-of-the-line" burgers with "tons of options for customization", plus a "fantastic selection" of "imaginative" "to-die-for" fries and "transcendent" "thick malts in terrific flavors" earn "wows" at this counter-service Evanston joint (with a Lincoln Park sequel); so even with "nonexistent" decor, "short hours" (the newer sib is open later) and "crazy long lines", it's still "really hard to complain."

Eggy's *Diner*

| - | - | - | M |

Streeterville | 333 E. Benton Pl. (Field Blvd.) | 773-234-3449 | www.eggysdiner.com

Redefining classic American diner fare with seasonal, locally sourced ingredients and many "creative" dishes, this East Lakeshore BYO offers all-day breakfast and lunch items and family-style dinners; the open, industrial space taps into nostalgia with counter seating and a soda fountain, and prices are predictably affordable.

NEW 8,000 Miles Ⓜ *Chinese/Japanese*

| - | - | - | M |

Roselle | 107 Main St. (Prospect St.) | 630-283-0053 | www.8000milesrestaurant.com

Chinese and Japanese meals comprising sushi, classic dishes (kung pao, general tso's), small plates, noodles and more are on offer at this midpriced eatery in Northwest Suburban Roselle; the rustic-industrial space features distressed wood, modern seating and a bar with signature cocktails.

EJ's Place *Italian/Steak*

| 20 | 16 | 20 | $57 |

Skokie | 10027 Skokie Blvd. (Old Orchard Rd.) | 847-933-9800 | www.ejsplaceskokie.com

"Meat and potatoes fare" with an "Italian slant" is on offer at this Skokie steakhouse from the Gene & Georgetti crew, where "knotty pine paneling" creates a "rustic" "Wisconsin cabin" feel; portions are "huge", so those who find prices "steep" are advised to "try splitting an entree – it works much better."

	FOOD	DECOR	SERVICE	COST

Eleven City Diner *Diner* `19` `18` `19` `$21`
South Loop | 1112 S. Wabash Ave. (bet. 11th St. & Roosevelt Rd.) | 312-212-1112

NEW **Eleven Lincoln Park** *Diner*
Lincoln Park | 2013 N. Clark St. (Armitage Ave.) | 773-244-1112
www.elevencitydiner.com

"Stacked sandwiches", "soothing" matzo ball soup and other "traditional" "Jewish deli" standards bring noshers to this "solid" South Looper (with a Lincoln Park sequel) in a "diner"-meets–"art deco"–styled space complete with a soda fountain; service gets mixed marks ("fun" vs. "difficult") and some find "big bills" surprising for the genre, but devotees kvell it's "well worth the price for the level of quality."

NEW **El Hefe** ● *Mexican* `-` `-` `-` `I`
Near North | 15 W. Hubbard St. (bet. Dearborn & State Sts.) | 312-548-6841 | www.elhefechicago.com

Mexican meets gastropub meets sports bar at this funky, affordable Near North 'super macho taqueria' from an Arizona-based mini-chain, serving up beef cheek and duck tacos, tortas and burgers; skull-themed decor, multiple margarita variations and table taps pouring pay-as-you-go beers create a party atmosphere.

EL Ideas Ⓢ Ⓜ *American* `28` `20` `26` `$189`
Pilsen | 2419 W. 14th St. (bet. 15th St. & Ogden Ave.) | 312-226-8144 | www.elideas.com

"Genius" chef Phillip Foss has "reinvented fine dining" at this Pilsen New American where he prepares an "original", "standout" tasting menu in "intimate" (read: tiny) digs with decor so simple it has a "kind of pop-up feel"; the open kitchen "allows you to interact with the chef", so "real foodies" shrug off big-ticket prices since it's "more like an experience" than a meal – just "bring some nice wine" as it's BYO.

NEW **Elizabeth** Ⓢ Ⓜ *American* `-` `-` `-` `VE`
Lincoln Square | 4835 N. Western Ave. (bet. Gunnison St. & Lawrence Ave.) | 773-681-0651 | www.elizabeth-restaurant.com

At this Lincoln Square New American, forager/underground chef Iliana Regan serves a fine-dining take on 'new gatherer cuisine' (farm-to-table, nose-to-tail and root-to-branch) in an "innovative" tasting menu reserved online through a ticketing system; the setting evokes a funky cottage with white, wood and metal surfaces, mismatched chairs and animal figurines, and though it's pricey, early adopters say it's one of "Chicago's most creative and artistic new restaurants."

NEW **Embeya** *Asian* ▽ `22` `26` `22` `$57`
West Loop | 564 W. Randolph St. (bet. Clinton & Jefferson Sts.) | 312-612-5640 | www.embeya.com

Chef Thai Dang (ex L2O, Ria) does high-end, progressive Asian plates to "delicious" effect at this sceney West Looper turning out shareable small and large plates; the "sleek, sexy" 7,000-sq.-ft.

space is decorated with striking wood accents and a resin flower light sculpture, and though it's on the pricey side, those who've been say it's a "dining experience to remember."

Emilio's Tapas *Spanish*

23 | 19 | 21 | $35

Hillside | 4100 Roosevelt Rd. (bet. Center St. & Mannheim Rd.) | 708-547-7177

Emilio's Tapas Sol y Nieve *Spanish*

Streeterville | 215 E. Ohio St. (Fairbanks Ct.) | 312-467-7177 www.emiliostapas.com

A "favorite" for "tip-top tapas", these "reasonable priced" Hillside and Streeterville sibs offer a "good diversity" of "well-made", "flavorful" Spanish dishes that are "both traditional and innovative"; "warm" servers and "informal" Iberian-themed digs replete with "in-demand" outdoor seating further explain why they're "go-tos."

Emperor's Choice *Chinese*

∇ 22 | 13 | 20 | $27

Chinatown | 2238 S. Wentworth Ave. (bet. Alexander St. & 22nd Pl.) | 312-225-8800 | www.emperorschoicechicago.com

"An enduring Chinatown choice" with an "interesting, authentic menu" spotlighting "creative seafood", this Cantonese longtimer also caters to guests with its "caring ownership and experienced servers"; though the decor doesn't earn raves despite white table-cloths and a fish tank, and a few find it a tad "pricey" for the area, fans assure it's "always a step above the many others."

NEW Endgrain Ⓜ *American/Bakery*

- | - | - | M

Roscoe Village | 1851 W. Addison St. (Wolcott Ave.) | 773-687-8191 | www.endgrainrestaurant.com

A veteran of Nightwood and Girl & The Goat is behind this Roscoe Village New American offering gourmet donuts and coffee in the morning followed by bar snacks and seriously comforting cooking, plus a separate dinner menu and a changing beer and wine list; end-grain and reclaimed wood are on display throughout the space, and diners can choose from seating at long banquettes, communal tables and utilitarian barstools.

NEW En Hakkore Ⓢ *Eclectic/Korean*

- | - | - | I

Bucktown | 1840 N. Damen Ave. (bet. Churchill & Moffat Sts.) | 773-772-9880

This hip, counter-serve Eclectic in Bucktown combines budget-friendly Korean classics with tacos, sandwiches, sushi and soft drinks; the funky setting features regular and communal tables, chandeliers from repurposed materials and antique books on the walls.

NEW Enso Sushi & Bar *Japanese*

- | - | - | M

Bucktown | 1613 N. Damen Ave. (North Ave.) | 773-878-8998 | www.ensochicago.com

Housemade noodles, grilled skewers, fusion-y riffs on traditional fare and build-your-own maki, plus Asian-accented cocktails are what you'll find at this midpriced Japanese in Bucktown; the low-lit space has a stylized cavern feel and is furnished with bare wood tables.

Epic Burger *Burgers*

19 | 14 | 16 | $13

Loop | University of Columbia | 517 S. State St. (bet. Congress Pkwy. & Harrison St.) | 312-913-1373

NEW River North | 407 N. Clark St. (Kinzie St.) | 312-239-0110 Ⓢ

Streeterville | 227 E. Ontario St. (bet. St. Clair St. & Fairbanks Ct.) | 312-257-3260

Gold Coast | 40 E. Pearson St. (Wabash Ave.) | 312-257-3262

Lincoln Park | 1000 W. North Ave. (Sheffield Ave.) | 312-440-9700

Near South Side | 550 W. Adams St. (bet. Clinton & Jefferson Sts.) | 312-382-0400 Ⓢ

Skokie | Westfield Old Orchard | 4999 Old Orchard Ctr. (Skokie Blvd.) | 847-933-9013
www.epicburger.com

Hamburger hounds "heart" this quickly growing "high-end fast-food" mini-chain (with locations in the city and Skokie) for its all-natural beef patties served "with various toppings" like a cage-free fried egg or Wisconsin aged cheddar; "fresh-cut" fries and "fabulous" milkshakes compensate for the "utilitarian" "counter-service" settings, and while a frugal few contend they "could eat at a sit-down for the cost", most say "the price is right."

Epic Restaurant Ⓢ *American*

▽ 20 | 24 | 20 | $57

River North | 112 W. Hubbard St. (bet. Clark & LaSalle Sts.) | 312-222-4940 | www.epicrestaurantchicago.com

A winding staircase separates a second-floor dining room with soaring windows from a stylish first-floor lounge (with a different menu) at this swanky River North haunt offering "beautifully presented" upscale New American eats backed by specialty cocktails and a "well-rounded" wine list; there's also a vast rooftop in season.

Erie Cafe *Steak*

22 | 18 | 22 | $53

River North | 536 W. Erie St. (Larrabee St.) | 312-266-2300 | www.eriecafe.com

A "solid contender in the steakhouse sweepstakes", this "oldie" in an "obscure" part of River North offers "a good hunk o' meat without the pretension" (and some say "even better" fish) served by a staff that "treats you like family"; it's not cheap, but the "lawyer crowd" in the cedar-lined "Sinatra-style" quarters and the "friendly regulars" in the bar don't seem to mind – plus there's "wonderful" riverside seating in summer.

Estate Ultra Bar ● *American*

- | - | - | M

River West | 1177 N. Elston Ave. (Division St.) | 312-582-4777 | www.estateultrabar.com

This swanky River West lounge serves midpriced American shared plates, salads and sandwiches paired with signature cocktails, 20-ish draft brews and a compact wine list; inside the wood-clad bunker, multiple environments add a range of options, from the spacious bar with TVs to plush lounge areas, refined dining tables, patios and a roof deck, with design highlights that include Sputnik light fixtures, mosaic tile and a fireplace.

	FOOD	DECOR	SERVICE	COST

Ethiopian Diamond *Ethiopian*   22 | 15 | 20 | $24

Edgewater | 6120 N. Broadway (bet. Glenlake & Hood Aves.) |
773-338-6100

Ethiopian Diamond II *Ethiopian*

Rogers Park | 7537 N. Clark St. (bet. Howard St. & Rogers Ave.) |
773-764-2200
www.ethiopiandiamondcuisine.com

Those who have a "yen" for Ethiopian cooking find it's "worth the trek"
to this "authentic" twosome, where the flavors are "tangy", the honey
wine is "housemade" and "helpful" servers come to your aid "if you
don't know the cuisine"; the "large" space "handles a party very well",
and there is live "music to dine by" some Fridays and Saturdays.

Everest 🗷Ⓜ️ *French*   27 | 27 | 27 | $117

Loop | One Financial Pl. | 440 S. LaSalle St., 40th fl. (Congress Pkwy.) |
312-663-8920 | www.everestrestaurant.com

"Incredible" views of the city are just one of the draws at this "high-
class", high-elevation Loop dining room atop the Chicago Stock
Exchange, where chef Jean Joho prepares "sublime" Alsatian-
influenced French prix fixe menus augmented by a "wine list that includes wonderful offerings not found elsewhere"; the "gorgeous"
room is matched by top service – no surprise it's a "favorite for cel-
ebrating the biggest events."

Exchequer *American*   20 | 15 | 19 | $21

Loop | 226 S. Wabash Ave. (bet. Adams St. & Jackson Blvd.) |
312-939-5633 | www.exchequerpub.com

"Huge burgers" are among the inexpensive "bar food" "cooked up
well" at this "ageless" Loop pub that's "not much to look at" but "has a
certain character"; "attentive" staffers help make it a "local spot" for
an "informal meal", or to "enjoy a drink, watch a game and unwind."

Farmhouse ❶ *American*   23 | 22 | 22 | $34

Near North | 228 W. Chicago Ave. (bet. Franklin & Wells Sts.) |
312-280-4960 | www.farmhousechicago.com
NEW **Evanston** | 703 Church St. (bet. Orington & Sherman Aves.) |
847-492-9700 | www.farmhouseevanston.com

"Homey" New American dishes (the "best cheese curds ever",
"tasty" short ribs) meet an "incredible" Midwestern beer list at
this midpriced "farm-to-table tavern" in Near North (with an
Evanston spin-off) that also keeps it local with Michigan wine on
tap and housemade sodas; salvaged decor across two stories and
occasional live music add to the "welcoming", "convivial" vibe.

FatDuck   ▽ 20 | 15 | 18 | $22

Tavern & Grill ❶ *American*
(fka Duckfat Tavern & Grill)

Forest Park | 7218 Madison St. (Elgin Ave.) | 708-488-1493 |
www.fatduckgrill.com

The signature duckfat fries are "the obvious highlight" and the
burger is "pretty good" too at this Forest Park pub serving "hearty",
low-cost American eats in digs with a "laid-back neighborhood" at-

mosphere; though some pooh-pooh it as "pedestrian", the patio's a sure bet for "a few pints in the sun."

NEW Fat Rice 🗷 Ⓜ *Eclectic* | - | - | - | M |

Logan Square | 2957 W. Diversey Ave. (Sacramento Ave.) | 773-661-9170 | www.eatfatrice.com

From the X-Marx supper club team comes this midpriced Logan Square Eclectic purveying "complexly" flavored comfort foods from China, India, Africa and the Caribbean accompanied by European wines, a handful of beers and crafty cocktails; the rustic-modern space has communal tables and a dining bar overlooking the open kitchen, and since it's tiny you might want to "get there early."

NEW Fat Sandwich Company ⬤ *Sandwiches* | - | - | - | I |

Lincoln Park | 2273 N. Lincoln Ave. (bet. Belden & Webster Aves.) | 773-880-1200 | www.fatsandwichcompany.com

Issuing from downstate Champaign, this counter-serve sandwich shop lets Lincoln Parkers compile their own unabashedly gluttonous creation or stick with preconceived, wallet-friendly belly bombs (e.g. a cheesesteak with chicken fingers, gyro meat, mozzarella sticks and tzatziki); the storefront space is no-frills, but it stays open late.

NEW Fatty's Burgers & More Ⓜ *Burgers* | - | - | - | I |

Lincoln Park | 2665 N. Clark St. (Drummond Pl.) | 773-248-3288
Evanston | 1903 Church St. (Dodge Ave.) | 847-475-5220
www.fattysburgerschicago.com

Thirteen varieties of creatively topped jumbo burgers take 'two hands to operate' at these outposts of a Texas-based chain; fresh-cut fries and nonalcoholic drinks round out a short menu in the casual corner storefront, with bare tables and a sporty theme throughout.

Fat Willy's Rib Shack *BBQ* | 20 | 13 | 18 | $22 |

Logan Square | 2416 W. Schubert Ave. (bet. Artesian & Western Aves.) | 773-782-1800 | www.fatwillysribshack.com

Customers "crave" the "just-right", "fall-off-the-bone" ribs and other "satisfying" BBQ eats at this "crowded", "real-deal" Southern smoke joint in Logan Square; a few gripe that delivery can be a "letdown", but more wager it's "worth checking out for a true 'cue experience."

Feast *American* | 21 | 18 | 20 | $27 |

Bucktown | 1616 N. Damen Ave. (bet. Concord Pl. & North Ave.) | 773-772-7100 | www.feastrestaurant.com

Fans say "you know you'll get a fine meal" at this "reasonably priced" Bucktown "standby", where the "something-for-everyone" New American menu features "tasty" "comfort-food" options; service is "accommodating", and the "relaxed yet bustling" digs include a patio.

NEW Ferris & Jack ⬤ *American* | - | - | - | M |

Near North | MileNorth | 166 E. Superior St. (Michigan Ave.) | 312-787-6000 | www.milenorthhotel.com

Set in Streeterville's MileNorth Hotel, this venue sends out American comfort food paired with classic and specialty cocktails, limited beer and wine lists and soda fountain creations; the comfortable setting in soothing neutrals, wood paneling and soft lighting has an upscale-casual feel, and bills are moderate.

The Fifty/50 ◑ *American*   18 | 13 | 15 | $20

Wicker Park | 2047 W. Division St. (bet. Damen & Hoyne Aves.) | 773-489-5050 | www.thefifty50.com

When the goal is "good-quality bar food" while "watching the game", this Wicker Park American scores with "some of the best wings in town" and flat-screens in all three levels (the "decor is sports"); the servers are "young and fun", just don't go in expecting "too much."

Filini *Italian*   ▽ 22 | 27 | 22 | $42

Loop | Radisson Blu Aqua Hotel | 221 N. Columbus Dr. (Wacker Dr.) | 312-477-0234 | www.filinichicago.com

This "beautiful" bi-level Italian with a "clever design" inside the Loop's curvaceous Radisson Blu Aqua Hotel dishes up hearty, mid-priced fare bolstered by a Boot-based wine list and a "friendly" crew in tux jackets and jeans; downstairs, the "trendy" bar with a separate menu and "crispy" thin-crust pizza is a destination on its own.

Fireside Restaurant &   20 | 19 | 19 | $24
Lounge ◑ *American*

Andersonville | 5739 N. Ravenswood Ave. (bet. Rosehill Dr. & Olive Ave.) | 773-561-7433 | www.firesidechicago.com

A "fireplace adds warmth" to this "dependable" Andersonville resto-pub with "surprisingly good" American fare (that "runs the gamut from pizza to fish"), a "huge" beer selection and somewhat of a "sports-bar" feel; it can get "noisy" at times, but service is "friendly" and the back patio (heated and enclosed in winter) "feels like the deck of a country club."

Fish Bar *Seafood*   24 | 18 | 21 | $30

Lakeview | 2956 N. Sheffield Ave. (Wellington Ave.) | 773-687-8177 | www.fishbarchicago.com

Adjoining Lakeview's DMK Burger Bar, this "popular" "hybrid between a clam shack and New Orleans po' boy house" lures with "delicious", "thoughtfully sourced" seafood, "lots of good beer" and a "relaxed", "unpretentious" atmosphere; a "small" space and "limited seating" mean there's often a "wait for a table" and you may need to shell out a bit to "fill up", "but it's seafood in Chicago, so what are you going to do?"; P.S. reservations taken for parties of three-four only.

Five Guys *Burgers*   17 | 10 | 15 | $13

Lincoln Park | 2140 N. Clybourn Ave. (bet. Magnolia & Southport Aves.) | 773-883-6038
Lincoln Park | 2368 N. Clark St. (Fullerton Pkwy.) | 773-883-8930
Rogers Park | 6477 N. Sheridan Rd. (Arthur Ave.) | 773-262-9810
NEW **Hyde Park** | 1456 E. 53rd St. (bet. Blackstone & Harper Aves.) | 773-363-6090
NEW **South Loop** | 1146 S. Wabash Ave. (bet. 11th St. & Roosevelt Rd.) | 312-431-8140

(continued)

(continued)
Five Guys

NEW **Evanston** | 816 Church St. (bet. Benson & Sherman Aves.) | 847-491-6921
NEW **Park Ridge** | 25 S. Northwest Hwy. (bet. Euclid & Prospect Aves.) | 847-292-1841
NEW **Berwyn** | 7150 Cermak Rd. (bet. Harlem & Maple Aves.) | 708-484-9940
Naperville | 22 E. Chicago Ave. (Washington St.) | 630-355-1850
Oak Park | 1115 W. Lake St. (bet. Harlem Ave. & Marion St.) | 708-358-0856
www.fiveguys.com
Additional locations throughout the Chicago area

"Honest", "juicy" burgers "with the right amount of grease", plus "mountains" of "heavenly fries" and "free peanuts while you wait" is "a formula that leaves patrons coming back for more" at this "cheerful", fast-growing chain; if faultfinders "don't see the fascination", those "addicted" to "all the free topping choices" simply insist "it works."

Fleming's Prime Steakhouse & Wine Bar *Steak*

| 20 | 21 | 21 | $61 |

Near North | 25 E. Ohio St. (bet. State & Wabash Sts.) | 312-329-9463
Lincolnshire | Lincolnshire Commons | 960 Milwaukee Ave. (Aptakisic Rd.) | 847-793-0333
www.flemingssteakhouse.com

The "name says it" at this often "jam-packed" chophouse chain known for "well-prepared" steaks and a "fabulous" wine list with 100 by the glass; "knowledgeable" staffers and "reasonably priced" specials also up the appeal, so even if it's "not a standout", it's "not bad" either.

Flight ☒ *Eclectic*

| 22 | 19 | 19 | $36 |

Glenview | The Glen Town Center | 1820 Tower Dr. (bet. Aviator Ln. & Navy Blvd.) | 847-729-9463 | www.flightwinebar.com

Whether it's the "wonderful wine flights" or "opportunity to try a little of this and a little of that", this Eclectic small-plater "in the heart of the Glen" fits the midpriced bill when you want to sample "something new"; service is "fast" and the modern space pleasant, if a "tad crowded", so many agree it's "just different enough" to please.

Flo Ⓜ *Southwestern*

| 20 | 13 | 19 | $20 |

Noble Square | 1434 W. Chicago Ave. (bet. Bishop St. & Greenview Ave.) | 312-243-0477 | www.flochicago.com

Fans find this Southwestern joint in Noble Square a "cool drink of water", thanks to "creative" fare and a "knock-your-boots-off" brunch with "incomparable" Bloody Marys; the "no-frills" setting is matched by wallet-friendly tabs and boosted by a "courteous" staff.

NEW Flour & Stone *Pizza*

| - | - | - | I |

Streeterville | 355 E. Ohio St. (bet. Fairbanks & McClurg Cts.) | 312-822-8998 | www.flourandstone.com

This Streeterville pizzeria fires up thin-crust, Brooklyn-style pies in red or white varieties; the bi-level space has a raw and industrial vibe, and has lots of windows for checking out the local action.

	FOOD	DECOR	SERVICE	COST

The Florentine *Italian*

| 20 | 21 | 21 | $47 |

Loop | JW Marriott Chicago | 151 W. Adams St. (bet. LaSalle & Wells Sts.) | 312-660-8866 | www.the-florentine.net

"Delicious" "contemporary" Italian cuisine paired with an "impressive" wine list draws the "expense-account" set to this "sleek, giant" venue inside the Loop's JW Marriott Chicago; tables "spaced far apart" make for "gracious" "fine dining", and that plus a "ready-to-please" staff further make it a "hot spot" for "business" meals.

Fogo de Chão *Brazilian/Steak*

| 24 | 20 | 23 | $64 |

River North | 661 N. La Salle Dr. (Erie St.) | 312-932-9330 | www.fogodechao.com

"Carnivores rejoice" at this all-you-can-eat Brazilian churrascaria chain, where the "variety" of "delicious" "prime meats" offered is plentiful enough to "make a T. rex blush", and the salad bar "impresses" too; there's also "attentive" service and upscale surrounds, and while it is "expensive", at least it's "impossible to leave hungry."

Fontano's Subs *Sandwiches*

| 27 | 9 | 19 | $10 |

Loop | 332 S. Michigan Ave. (bet. Jackson Blvd. & Van Buren St.) | 312-663-3061

Little Italy/University Village | 1058 W. Polk St. (bet. Aberdeen & Carpenter Sts.) | 312-421-4474 🛇

Hinsdale | 9 S. Lincoln St. (Chicago Ave.) | 630-789-0891

Naperville | 1767 W. Ogden Ave. (Aurora Ave.) | 630-717-7821

Naperville | 2879 W. 95th St. (Cedar Glade Rd.) | 630-305-8010

NEW Beverly | 2151W. 95th St. (Hamilton Ave.) | 773-881-7821 www.fontanossubs.com

"It's all in the bread" (and "finest deli meats") at this Chicago chain cranking out "awesome" subs "the way they should be" ("no wimpy" items); "you know it's good because all the cops eat here", but many get it to go since "it's a slice of life, not a fine-dining atmosphere."

Foodlife *Eclectic*

| 19 | 14 | 14 | $18 |

Streeterville | Water Tower Pl. | 835 N. Michigan Ave. (bet. Chestnut & Pearson Sts.) | 312-335-3663 | www.foodlifechicago.com

Foodease *Eclectic*

Streeterville | Water Tower Pl. | 835 N. Michigan Ave. (bet. Chestnut & Pearson Sts.) | 312-335-3663 | www.foodeasechicago.com

You'll find "something for everyone in the group" at this "reliable" Water Tower Place food court, the "ultimate cafeteria experience" with "plenty" of different stations offering a "wide variety" of choices "from stir-fry to Chinese, to Tex-Mex, BBQ" and more; the Foodlife side is much larger, and is "a good place to sit down" during a "day of shopping", while the smaller Foodease part adds offerings like a salad bar, sandwich counter and "quality" prepared items for a "quick" meal.

NEW Found Restaurant & Social House 🅼 *American*

| - | - | - | M |

Evanston | 1631 Chicago Ave. (bet. Church & Davis Sts.) | 847-868-8945 | www.foundkitchen.com

Owner Amy Morton (daughter of steakhouse founder Arnie Morton) teams up with chef Nicole Pederson (C-House) at this Evanston

New American, a "welcome addition" to the dining scene with French- and Midwestern-accented dishes plus local beers and creative cocktails; the funky space is divided into four separate areas (dining hall, kitchen counter, library and map room) and decorated with vintage-inspired decor and found objects; P.S. no reservations.

Fountainhead ● *American*

FOOD	DECOR	SERVICE	COST
20	21	19	$28

Ravenswood | 1970 W. Montrose Ave. (Damen Ave.) | 773-697-8204 | www.fountainheadchicago.com

"Unpretentious" yet "not too lowbrow", this "packed" Ravenswood pub with "damn near the best beer list in the city" goes "beyond typical bar food" with dishes ranging from a "simple" burger to more "extravagant" duck confit pasta; guests also go for the whiskey selection and "love the feel" of the mahogany bar and rooftop garden.

Francesca's Amici *Italian*

FOOD	DECOR	SERVICE	COST
22	19	21	$36

Elmhurst | 174 N. York St. (bet. 2nd & 3rd Sts.) | 630-279-7970

Francesca's Bryn Mawr *Italian*
Edgewater | 1039 W. Bryn Mawr Ave. (Kenmore Ave.) | 773-506-9261

Francesca's by the River *Italian*
St. Charles | 200 S. Second St. (bet. Illinois & Indiana Sts.) | 630-587-8221

Francesca's Fiore *Italian*
Forest Park | 7407 Madison St. (bet. Burkhardt Ct. & Circle Ave.) | 708-771-3063

Francesca's Forno *Italian*
Wicker Park | 1576 N. Milwaukee Ave. (Damen Ave.) | 773-770-0184

Francesca's Intimo *Italian*
Lake Forest | 293 E. Illinois Rd. (bet. Bank Ln. & Western Ave.) | 847-735-9235

Francesca's North *Italian*
Northbrook | Northbrook Shopping Plaza | 1145 Church St. (bet. Keystone Ave. & Shermer Rd.) | 847-559-0260

Francesca's on Chestnut *Italian*
Streeterville | Seneca Hotel | 200 E. Chestnut St. (Mies van der Rohe Way) | 312-482-8800

Francesca's on Taylor *Italian*
Little Italy/University Village | 1400 W. Taylor St. (Loomis St.) | 312-829-2828

La Sorella di Francesca *Italian*
Naperville | 18 W. Jefferson Ave. (bet. Main & Washington Sts.) | 630-961-2706
www.miafrancesca.com
Additional locations throughout the Chicago area

"Reliably solid" for Italian fare "done right", this Chicago-based chain (with a few out-of-state sibs) is a "family favorite" thanks to an "affordable" menu that "continues to change", highlighting "well-prepared" standards alongside some "unexpected dishes"; if doubters dub it merely "fair" and complain some locales are "too noisy", fans single out "prompt", "pleasant" service and say it's "always a good option."

	FOOD	DECOR	SERVICE	COST

Francesco's Hole in the Wall *Italian* | 22 | 15 | 21 | $35 |

Northbrook | 254 Skokie Blvd. (bet. Dundee & Lake Cook Rds.) |
847-272-0155 | www.francescosholeinthewall.com
The pasta is "always al dente" at this "tiny", "real-deal" Northbrook
Italian known for its "handwritten menus" of "well-prepared", midpriced dishes proffered by a "friendly" staff; though "not fancy", it's
a "longtime favorite" as evidenced by the "noisy", "jammed" dining
room and "long waits" (no reservations).

Frankie's Scaloppine & | 18 | 17 | 20 | $27 |
5th Floor Pizzeria *Italian/Pizza*

Gold Coast | 900 North Michigan Shops | 900 N. Michigan Ave.
(bet. Delaware Pl. & Walton St.) | 312-266-2500 |
www.frankieschicago.com
"Pizzas and pastas are tasty with enough variety to satisfy a group
of picky eaters" at this "cozy" Italian spot to "rest your tired feet"
located on the fifth floor of the 900 North Michigan Shops; even
"locals" "love the view", "reasonable prices" and "friendly" service.

Franks 'N' Dawgs ⓜ *Hot Dogs* | 25 | 12 | 19 | $14 |

Lincoln Park | 1863 N. Clybourn Ave. (bet. Kenmore & Sheffield Aves.) |
312-281-5187 | www.franksndawgs.com
An "oustanding dawg shack", this Lincoln Park BYO offers a "mega
selection" of gourmet hot dogs and sausages that come with "some
of the most interesting and delicious toppings ever", and are accompanied by "sinfully rich" sides, like "don't-miss" truffle fries; inside is
"not fancy", but the staff is "friendly", and there's a seasonal patio.

Fred's *American* | 20 | 22 | 20 | $45 |

Gold Coast | Barneys New York | 15 E. Oak St. (Rush St.) |
312-596-1111 | www.barneys.com
It's "quite the scene" for "people-watching" at this "swanky" Gold
Coaster that's "hidden" on the top floor of Barneys and "good look-
ing, like most of the diners"; even if opinions vary over the New
American fare – "fabulous" vs. "overpriced" – it still comes "alive at
lunch" and the terrace is "unbeatable on a gorgeous summer night."

🆕 freestyle food + drink ❶ *American* | – | – | – | M |
(fka Argent Restaurant & Raw Bar)

River North | Dana Hotel & Spa | 660 N. State St. (Erie St.) |
312-202-6050 | www.freestylefoodanddrink.com
Set in River North's Dana Hotel, this all-day New American offers an
internationally accented menu covering many bases including sushi,
share plates and mains; soaring windows and natural wood set an
earthy-elegant tone, while arching black banquettes and a steel
staircase leading to a mezzanine raw bar add modern appeal.

Froggy's French Cafe ⓢ *French* | 25 | 20 | 24 | $50 |

Highwood | 306 Green Bay Rd. (Highwood Ave.) | 847-433-7080 |
www.froggysrestaurant.com
A "hidden jewel", this Highwood bistro turns out "succulent" French
fare blending classic and modern styles while also offering a "good

selection of wine" and "attentive" service; if the brick-lined setting strikes some as "a bit faded", tabs are "reasonable" (thanks in part to a "great" prix fixe) and devotees still "love it" over "30 years later."

Frog n Snail ☑ *American/French* ▽ 20 | 18 | 18 | $44

Lakeview | 3124 N. Broadway St. (bet. Decon & Rosemont Aves.) | 773-661-9166 | www.frognsnail.com

Dale Levitski (Sprout) puts his spin on bistro fare at this midpriced American-French in Lakeview where "fresh and local ingredients" feature in both his classic dishes (including frogs' legs and escargot, of course) and more inventive plates; the space is awash in rustic wood and cool stone with a crêpes-and-coffee bar in the front.

Frontera Fresco *Mexican* 24 | 13 | 15 | $16

Loop | Macy's | 111 N. State St. (bet. Randolph & Washington Sts.) | 312-781-4483 ☑

Skokie | Old Orchard | 4909 Old Orchard Ctr. (Lamon Ave.) | 847-329-2638

www.fronterafresco.com

"A way to get a taste of chef Rick Bayless' creations" "without the prices", this Loop quick-serve in the Macy's food court (with a Skokie sib) offers tacos, tortas and other "quality" Mexican fare that's "way better than any cafeteria has any right to be"; groupies who "go to the mall just to come" also say "don't miss the fresh lime-based drinks."

Frontera Grill ☑☑ *Mexican* 27 | 22 | 24 | $45

River North | 445 N. Clark St. (bet. Hubbard & Illinois Sts.) | 312-661-1434 | www.fronterakitchens.com

Still "hip", "always packed" and "innovative" after more than 25 years, Rick Bayless' "top-notch" River North Mexican draws 'em in with "perfectly constructed" "gourmet" dishes elevated by "creative and novel" flavor combinations and further boosted by "powerful but re-fined" margaritas; "helpful" staffers work the colorful, art-enhanced digs, and even if reservations are tough to come by and "you could have a birthday waiting for a table", it remains a "perennial favorite" that fans say "belongs on eveyone's bucket list."

Frontier ● *American* 22 | 20 | 18 | $35

Noble Square | 1072 N. Milwaukee Ave. (bet. Noble & Thomas Sts.) | 773-772-4322 | www.thefrontierchicago.com

You can eat just about "any part of any animal" at this midpriced Noble Square gastropub where a "wild-game concept" plays out in "rustic, lodgy" environs; on the down side, it can be "really crowded" and "crazy loud" with "spotty service", but a "diverse" American menu including lots of oysters adds to reasons it's "very enjoyable", "if you get a seat"; P.S. there's a seasonal beer garden.

Fulton's on the River ☑ *Seafood/Steak* 18 | 20 | 18 | $46

River North | 315 N. LaSalle Dr. (Carroll Ave.) | 312-822-0100 | www.fultonsontheriver.com

"Location, location, location" is the reason to visit this "solid" River North steak and seafood spin-off of Disney's Orlando riverboat ver-sion, where the patio provides "awesome" views, the "slabs of beef"

| | FOOD | DECOR | SERVICE | COST |

are "big" and the "dynamite" deviled eggs are "topped with a generous helping of caviar"; still, sticklers say it's "a bit overpriced" for food that "doesn't quite measure up" to the setting and service.

Gaetano's 🅂 *Italian* | 27 | 21 | 24 | $58 |

Forest Park | 7636 Madison St. (bet. Ashland & Lathrop Aves.) | 708-366-4010 | www.gaetanos.us

"Prepare for an experience" at this smallish Forest Park Italian, where the "talented" chef delivers "completely unexpected", praiseworthy dishes available à la carte or in "unbelievable" tasting menus; service earns strong marks too in the upscale-casual space, and while tabs aren't cheap, fans still consider it "affordable" given the quality.

The Gage ◐ *American* | 23 | 22 | 21 | $40 |

Loop | 24 S. Michigan Ave. (bet. Madison & Monroe Sts.) | 312-372-4243 | www.thegagechicago.com

"In a row of ordinary eateries", this "über-hip" gastropub is an "upscale surprise", "really delivering" with "adventurous" New American eats and a "phenomenal beer selection" in "just plain cool" Loop digs featuring an "excellent view of Millenium Park"; enthusiasts justify the "packed and loud" conditions as "part of its charm" and give "attentive" service props too, so most excuse prices that may be a "tad high" for the genre; P.S. "if you value your hearing, wait for summer and eat outdoors."

Gale Street Inn *American* | 21 | 16 | 21 | $31 |

Jefferson Park | 4914 N. Milwaukee Ave. (Gale St.) | 773-725-1300 | www.galestreet.com

"Fall-off-the-bone", "perfectly tender" ribs and other "consistently good" Traditional American fare in "generous portions" have made this moderate Jefferson Park "supper club type of joint" a "Chicago tradition" since 1963; "friendly" service lends a "welcoming" vibe, so even those who find the "old-school" decor "lacking" say "don't let that stop you."

🆕 Gari Sushi & Asian Bistro *Japanese* | – | – | – | M |

East Village | 2020 W. Chicago Ave. (Damen Ave.) | 773-486-1118 | www.garisushitogo.com

Named for the ubiquitous ginger sushi condiment, this Ukrainian Village Asian bistro majors in artfully plated maki, yakitori, curries and noodle dishes, all at affordable prices; the sparsely furnished space is decorated with anime and miniature ships, and BYO is another plus.

🆕 Gather *American* | – | – | – | M |

Lincoln Square | 4539 N. Lincoln Ave. (bet. Sunnyside & Wilson Aves.) | 773-506-9300 | www.gatherchicago.com

A Trotter's and Cibo Matto alum is cooking moderately priced New American fare with artisanal ingredients paired with an extensive, approachable wine list, microbrews and craft cocktails at this Lincoln Square storefront; the quaint exterior gives way to a casually refined interior with a bar, two large communal tables, optical wall treatments and an open kitchen with a granite dining counter.

	FOOD	DECOR	SERVICE	COST

Gaylord Fine Indian Cuisine *Indian* — 22 | 19 | 20 | $34

Gold Coast | 100 E. Walton St. (bet. Michigan Ave. & Rush St.) | 312-664-1700
Schaumburg | 555 Mall Dr. (bet. Higgins Rd. & Kimberly Dr.) | 847-619-3300
www.gaylordil.com

"Complex, aromatic and flavorful" Indian "classics" delivered by "amicable" servers make for "happy" campers at this "authentic", moderately priced twosome; the newer Gold Coast location is more "upscale" than the Schaumburg branch, and both offer a lunch buffet.

NEW g.e.b. *American* — - | - | - | E

West Loop | 841 W. Randolph St. (bet. Green & Peoria Sts.) | 312-888-2258 | www.gebistro.com

Graham Elliot Bowles' "low-key" West Loop New American has a rocker-meets-religion theme and a midpriced menu (printed on vintage LPs) of "intriguing" dishes, most featuring just three components, plus craft cocktails too; the heavily styled space is frocked with pews, an amp-turned–host stand, a stained-glass private-dining 'confessional' and a cobbled patio dotted with cherry-red seats.

Geja's Cafe *Fondue* — 22 | 23 | 22 | $53

Lincoln Park | 340 W. Armitage Ave. (bet. Orleans & Sedgwick Sts.) | 773-281-9101 | www.gejascafe.com

"Perfect for a first date", this "pricey" Lincoln Park "throwback" provides an "intimate setting with dark lights, heavy curtains" and "guitar serenades" as a backdrop for "tasty" fondues of cheese, beef, seafood and chocolate; an "extensive wine list" and "attentive" service stoke the "romantic" vibe, though neatniks warn the "haze of candles and cooking oil" means "dry cleaning is required"; P.S. no kids under 10.

Gemini Bistro Ⓜ *American* — 21 | 20 | 22 | $45

Lincoln Park | 2075 N. Lincoln Ave. (Dickens Ave.) | 773-525-2522 | www.geminibistrochicago.com

Chef Jason Paskewitz's "approachable" New American fare with French-Med inflections is "designed to please" at this Lincoln Park bistro where a "friendly" staff and simple, "classy" decor including a big marble bar add to the "warm atmosphere"; some call it "solid but not stellar" but given the fair prices and "interesting" bites, locals deem it "worth going back to."

Gene & Georgetti Ⓩ *Steak* — 25 | 18 | 23 | $61

River North | 500 N. Franklin St. (Illinois St.) | 312-527-3718 | www.geneandgeorgetti.com

A "real Chicago steakhouse", this circa-1941 River North "classic" comes complete with "perfectly marbled, seared and seasoned steaks" and "old-school", "throwback" surroundings that make you "feel like you've gone back in time" (especially if served by staffers "older than the business"); true, tabs aren't low, and decor may be a touch "faded", but still most agree it's a "landmark for a reason."

| | | FOOD | DECOR | SERVICE | COST |

Gene & Jude's Red Hot Stand ●◐🖬 *Hot Dogs* | 24 | 8 | 20 | $8 |

O'Hare Area | 2720 River Rd. (Grand Ave.) | 708-452-7634 |
www.geneandjudes.com

A "very old-school", "super-affordable" O'Hare Area "institution" since 1950, this pup-house puts out "meaty, squeak-on-your-teeth" hot dogs, plus "fresh-cut fries, tamales and drinks, period!" handed out by "great characters" in "dive" digs (stand-up only); "yes, the line really is that long", but it "moves fast", so dogged diners swear "they still get it right every time, whether it's noon or 2 AM" (closes at 1 AM Sunday–Thursday); P.S. "do not ask for ketchup if you know what's good for you."

Gibsons Bar & Steakhouse *Steak* | 26 | 22 | 25 | $67 |

Gold Coast | 1028 N. Rush St. (Bellevue Pl.) | 312-266-8999 ●
Rosemont | Doubletree O'Hare | 5464 N. River Rd. (bet. Balmoral & Bryn Mawr Aves.) | 847-928-9900 ●
Oak Brook | 2105 S. Spring Rd. (22nd St.) | 630-954-0000
www.gibsonssteakhouse.com

A "big-time steakhouse for big-time folks", this Gold Coast "staple" and its suburban spin-offs deliver "cooked-to-perfection" chops, equally "excellent" seafood and drinks and "absurdly large desserts"; "professional, accommodating" staffers lend more appeal, while an "energetic" atmosphere (especially at the flagship, which can get "crowded" and "noisy") means it's tops for "people-watching."

Gilt Bar ●🗷🅼 *American* | 25 | 25 | 22 | $44 |

River North | 230 W. Kinzie St. (bet. Franklin & Wells Sts.) |
312-464-9544 | www.giltbarchicago.com

A "good variety" of "tasty" New American small plates pairs with "delicious" drinks from an "excellent" bar at this "hot" River North gastropub from Brendan Sodikoff (Au Cheval, Maude's Liquor Bar, Bavette's); the "dark", stylish space features ornate chandeliers and leather booths, and though prices aren't low, it's still a prime pick for "after work", for "date night" or when out "with friends."

🆕 Gino's East Sports Bar ● *Pizza* | – | – | – | I |

Printer's Row | 521 S. Dearborn St. (bet. Congress Pkwy. & Harrison St.) |
312-939-1818 | www.ginoseast.com

This Gino's East spin-off on Printers Row is a tad more upscale than your average neighborhood sports bar, with a wallet-friendly menu of deep-dish 'zas, gastropubby bar bites and "great local beers on tap"; the space flaunts an architectural feel with pillars and suspended grids, antique brick and wood, canning jar lights and retro barstools.

Gioco *Italian* | 22 | 22 | 22 | $43 |

South Loop | 1312 S. Wabash Ave. (13th St.) | 312-939-3870 |
www.giocorestaurant.com

"Solid" Northern Italian fare "true to the authentic flavors of Italy" does it for diners who recommend the "perfectly cooked pastas with complex and satisfying sauces" at this "rustic" South Looper set in a circa-1890 building; "friendly service", a "thoughtful wine list" and moderate tabs also help ensure it's a "keeper."

	FOOD	DECOR	SERVICE	COST

Giordano's *Pizza* `22` `16` `18` `$22`
Loop | Prudential Plaza Millennium Park | 135 E. Lake St. (Beaubien Ct.) | 312-616-1200
Loop | 223 W. Jackson Blvd. (bet. Franklin & Wells Sts.) | 312-583-9400
River North | 730 N. Rush St. (Superior St.) | 312-951-0747
Lakeview | 1040 W. Belmont Ave. (Kenmore Ave.) | 773-327-1200
Logan Square | 2855 N. Milwaukee Ave. (Wolfram St.) | 773-862-4200
Northwest Side | 5927 W. Irving Park Rd. (Mason Ave.) | 773-736-5553
Hyde Park | 5311 S. Blackstone Ave. (bet. 53rd & 54th Sts.) | 773-947-0200
Southwest Side | 5159 S. Pulaski Rd. (Archer Ave.) | 773-582-7676 ◑
Southwest Side | 6314 S. Cicero Ave. (63rd St.) | 773-585-6100 ◑
Greektown | 815 W. Van Buren St. (Halsted St.) | 312-421-1221
www.giordanos.com
Additional locations throughout the Chicago area
Enthusiasts will "never look at pizza the same again" after sampling the "epic" stuffed deep-dish pies made with "crispy", "buttery, melt-in-your-mouth crust" and "gooey" cheese at these "dependable" Chicagoland parlors; service gets mixed marks ("very good" vs. "just ok"), and no one's raving about the decor, but with "big" portions (especially the "gigantor personal pie") and "easy-on-your-budget" tabs, it remains a "favorite" of many – just "expect a long wait"; P.S. some serve alcohol, some are BYO.

Girl & The Goat *American* `27` `24` `25` `$58`
West Loop | 809 W. Randolph St. (bet. Green & Halsted Sts.) | 312-492-6262 | www.girlandthegoat.com
"Believe the hype" say fans of this spendy West Loop "blockbuster" where "genius" Stephanie Izard takes diners on a New American "culinary adventure" courtesy of "mind blowingly interesting" small plates including "brilliant" nose-to-tail creations ("how is it possible for pig face to be so delicious?"); the "warm", "casual" digs have a "lively" (some say "noisy") buzz and service is "knowledgeable", so many are left with but "one wish" – to be able to "get in more often."

Glenn's Diner & Seafood House *Diner* `24` `16` `21` `$31`
Ravenswood | 1820 W. Montrose Ave. (Honore St.) | 773-506-1720 | www.glennsdiner.com
Regulars rave "about half the ocean's on the menu" at this "crowded" Ravenswood eatery that's "quietly serving up" "an incredible selection" of "superbly prepared" seafood alongside Traditional American diner fare and "one-price-fits-all wines" (there's also a "bustling brunch with fabulous Bloody Marys"); "accommodating" service helps many overlook "tightly spaced tables" and a "nondescript setting", especially since some speculate "in another location the food would be 30% more"; P.S. Tuesday's "all-you-can-eat king crab leg is the bomb."

Glenview House ◑ *American* `19` `20` `21` `$29`
Glenview | 1843 Glenview Rd. (Railroad Ave.) | 847-724-0692 | www.theglenviewhouse.com
The "solid" menu featuring some "interesting" "twists" ("like pot roast nachos") attracts diners "young and old" to this Glenview

American, while "bourbons galore" and more than 100 beers add "hangout" appeal; set in a renovated 18th-century house, it has an "inviting" main downstairs area and an upstairs whiskey bar (typically open Friday–Saturday only), featuring a "cozy fireplace", and that plus "friendly" service help explain why it often gets "packed."

NEW Glunz Tavern M Hot Dogs — | — | — | I

Old Town | 1202 N. Wells St. (Division St.) | 312-642-3000 | www.glunztavern.com

A variety of jumbo wieners are paired with comfort-food toppings, exotic dipping sauces and classic sides at this gourmet dog BYO in Wicker Park; diminutive digs with brick and distressed wood, meat hooks and taxidermy fit the funky nabe perfectly; P.S. cash-only.

Goosefoot ⊠ M American ▽ 29 | 24 | 26 | $126

Lincoln Square | 2656 W. Lawrence Ave. (Washtenaw Ave.) | 773-942-7547 | www.goosefoot.net

Dining is an "event" at this big-ticket New American in Lincoln Square where Chris Nugent's "finely thought out" tasting menus yield "creative, beautiful and delicious" plates in a simple, upscale-casual space; it's BYO, but the "helpful" staff will assist in "selecting the wine before coming" – just note the tiny surrounds mean scoring reservations can be "very difficult."

Goose Island Brewing Co. Pub Food 17 | 16 | 17 | $23

Wrigleyville | 3535 N. Clark St. (bet. Addison St. & Sheffield Ave.) | 773-832-9040

Lincoln Park | 1800 N. Clybourn Ave. (bet. Willow & Wisconsin Sts.) | 312-915-0071

www.gooseisland.com

Quaffers honk approval for the "terrific" beer selection at these brewpub twins, where "well-priced" "standard bar fare" meets "some surprisingly upscale options", and service is "friendly"; Lincoln Park offers weekend brewery tours, while fans flock to Wrigleyville "before and after Cubs games" or to watch on the many TVs.

NEW Grace American ▽ 29 | 27 | 29 | $239

West Loop | 652 W. Randolph St. (Desplaines St.) | 312-234-9494 | www.grace-restaurant.com

Superlatives abound ("superb", "fabulous") at this "fine-dining" destination in the West Loop where chef-owner Curtis Duffy (ex Avenues, Alinea) prepares two "unforgettable" contemporary American tasting menus (omnivore and vegetable-focused) featuring "complex yet pure flavors" and "stunning" presentations; the space has a "minimalist elegance" with soothing neutrals, plush leather chairs, abstract art and a see-and-be-scene cocktail lounge, and service is "impeccable", so "huge" bills aren't unexpected.

Grafton Pub & Grill ● Pub Food ▽ 22 | 22 | 20 | $21

Lincoln Square | 4530 N. Lincoln Ave. (bet. Sunnyside & Wilson Aves.) | 773-271-9000 | www.thegrafton.com

A "classic Irish" pub setting provides the backdrop for a "great beer selection" and solid bar eats like "wonderful burgers" at this affordable Lincoln Square hangout; "friendly" staffers contribute to an atmosphere that "makes you want to pop in on a cold winter evening and stay indefinitely", and concertgoers advise checking it out "before a show" at nearby Old Town School of Folk Music.

Graham Elliot *American* 24 | 22 | 22 | $163

River North | 217 W. Huron St. (bet. Franklin & Wells Sts.) | 312-624-9975 | www.grahamelliot.com

A "culinary adventure" awaits at Graham Elliot Bowles' River North New American where "unique" tasting menus yield "inventive", sometimes "wonderful" dishes elevated by "classy" presentations; "knowledgeable" staffers add to the experience, and if the "relaxed" vibe seems at odds with the "fine-dining" fare (and big ticket pricing), that's simply a part of the "quirky" experience.

Grahamwich *Sandwiches* 19 | 15 | 16 | $16

River North | 615 N. State St. (bet. Ohio & Ontario Sts.) | 312-265-0434 | www.grahamwich.com

Graham Elliot Bowles' "take on the sandwich joint" is this "cool, little" River North operation vending "solid" sammies in "interesting combos", including an especially "tasty" grilled cheese; there are also a handful of salads and snacks plus "ridiculously good" soft serve, so the "small" space, "limited" seats and more "expensive" tabs are easier to take.

Grange Hall Burger Bar Ⓢ Ⓜ *American/Burgers* ∇ 22 | 21 | 21 | $22

West Loop | 844 W. Randolph St. (bet. Green & Peoria Sts.) | 312-491-0844 | www.grangehallburgerbar.com

"Very good" burgers made with grass-fed beef and topped with a variety of local cheeses and other "fresh ingredients" are the draw at this West Loop joint also serving snacks, sides and housemade pies and ice creams plus cocktails, beer, wine and breakfast too (weekends only); inside has "community tables" and a rustic "country farm"-like atmosphere with cowbells and antique linens, and prices are equally casual.

NEW Grass Fed *Steak* - | - | - | M

Bucktown | 1721 N. Damen Ave. (bet. Wabansia Ave. & Willow St.) | 773-342-6000 | www.grassfedbucktown.com

This Bucktown chophouse offers a modern menu including the requisite steak (grass-fed, of course) and a handful of vegetarian options, plus craft beers and cocktails made with house-infused spirits; it offers lunch, brunch and an affordable prix fixe dinner too, all served in contemporary surrounds that eschew the standard earth tones for a fresh white-and-green color scheme and soft light from dangling lanterns.

Greek Islands *Greek* 22 | 19 | 21 | $30

Greektown | 200 S. Halsted St. (Adams St.) | 312-782-9855 ◐

Lombard | 300 E. 22nd St. (bet. Northlake Rd. & St. Regis Dr.) | 630-932-4545

www.greekislands.net

Hellenophiles hail these "welcoming" Greektown and Lombard "go-tos" for "authentic", "down-to-earth Greek comfort food" (including "flaming cheese") "consistently well prepared" "in the traditional way"; generally "efficient service" and "reasonable prices" are other pluses, so it's often "packed" and also "perfect for family dining."

Green Zebra *Vegetarian* | 27 | 23 | 24 | $49 |

Noble Square | 1460 W. Chicago Ave. (Greenview Ave.) | 312-243-7100 | www.greenzebrachicago.com

"Exciting" meat-free dishes impress "even confirmed carnivores" at this Noble Square destination, where Shawn McClain's "upscale", "inventive" small plates make it the "best vegetarian in town"; a "knowledgeable" staff elevates the sage-colored space, and notable cocktails plus "interesting" wines are further enticements.

Grill on the Alley *American* | 20 | 20 | 22 | $48 |

Streeterville | Westin Michigan Ave. | 909 N. Michigan Ave. (Delaware Pl.) | 312-255-9009 | www.thegrill.com

"Solid" "standard American fare" awaits at this Beverly Hills spin-off in Streeterville's Westin Michigan Avenue where "reliable steaks" and other "enjoyable" dishes mean you may "not have a gastronomique festivale of an experience but you won't go away hungry"; it's not cheap, but service is "attentive", and a "low-key" vibe makes it a "quiet place to meet friends or business associates."

GT Fish & Oyster *Seafood* | 25 | 23 | 23 | $55 |

River North | 531 N. Wells St. (Grand Ave.) | 312-929-3501 | www.gtoyster.com

"Creative and tasty seafood small plates" are what you'll find at this River North hot spot, where chef Giuseppe Tentori "always excels" in his "inventive" interpretations of "classic dishes", and the bar "dreams up" some of the "best new drinks in town"; the nautical-themed space has a "modern feel", and the staff is "accommodating", so the only downfall is that it can be "hard to get a reservation."

NEW Guildhall *American* | – | – | – | E |

Glencoe | 649 Vernon Ave. (Hazel Ave.) | 847-835-8100 | www.guildhallrestaurant.com

This take on upscale, seasonal New American dining featuring local ingredients graces North Suburban Glencoe courtesy of chef Christian Ragano (ex Tru, NoMI Kitchen) and longtime Chicago restaurateur Phil Marienthal; the bar offers traditional and modern cocktails and generous wine and craft beer selections, while the space is a study in modern elegance from 555 International.

Gyu-Kaku *Japanese* | 23 | 18 | 20 | $33 |

Streeterville | 210 E. Ohio St. (bet. Fairbanks Ct. & St. Clair St.) | 312-266-8929 | www.gyu-kaku.com

If you want to "try something new" and like to "play with your food", fans suggest this Streeterville link of an international Japanese yaki-niku chain for "mouthwatering appetizers" and "nicely spiced meat and vegetables" that you cook yourself on in-table grills amid industrial, wood-accented stylings; "friendly" service "helps explain the procedure" and "the price is right", so it's a "great destination for a group dining experience."

Hackney's *Burgers*

18 | 15 | 19 | $22

Printer's Row | 733 S. Dearborn St. (bet. Harrison & Polk Sts.) | 312-461-1116
Glenview | 1241 Harms Rd. (bet. Ferndale Rd. & Lake Ave.) | 847-724-5577
Glenview | 1514 E. Lake Ave. (bet. Huntington Dr. & Waukegan Rd.) | 847-724-7171
Lake Zurich | 880 N. Old Rand Rd. (Rand Rd.) | 847-438-2103
Palos Park | 9550 W. 123rd St. (96th Ave.) | 708-448-8300
www.hackneys.net

"When you're craving a burger" that "soaks through the dark rye", "drips down your arm" and is accompanied by the "cardiac indulgence" of "don't-miss" onion rings, plus "interesting beers on tap" and "mean martinis" too, fans suggest these "reasonably priced" "local institutions"; complainers citing "dated", "divey" decor and fare that's "only average" are drowned out by diehards deeming them the "real deal" and "better than" newer joints "by a country mile."

Hai Yen *Vietnamese*

∇ 25 | 11 | 16 | $20

Uptown | 1055 W. Argyle St. (bet. Kenmore & Winthrop Aves.) | 773-561-4077 | www.haiyenrestaurant.com

Regulars at this Uptown Vietnamese say "if you're bold and move beyond pho, you will be rewarded" by some of the "best authentic" eats "outside of Hanoi"; the simple digs may not get the same high praise, but at least tabs are "value"-priced; P.S. closed on Wednesdays.

Half Shell ⊭ *Seafood*

22 | 9 | 17 | $34

Lakeview | 676 W. Diversey Pkwy. (Orchard St.) | 773-549-1773 | www.halfshellchicago.com

"Crab legs are the big draw" of this cash-only Lakeview "dungeon" where finatics who "don't care about the atmosphere" fill up on "huge portions" of "well-prepared" seafood at prices much "lower" than found elsewhere; sure, the "basement locale" is "divey" and service can be "rough", but it's all "part of the charm" for "an experience" that's considered "well worth" it; P.S. no reservations.

NEW Hamachi Sushi Bar *Japanese/Kosher*

– | – | – | M

West Rogers Park | 2801 W. Howard St. (California Ave.) | 773-293-6904 | www.hamachichicago.com

Certified kosher sushi with a massive, midpriced list of maki – along with starters, Japanese sandwiches and more – are served at this West Rogers Park storefront; the sleek interior has a small sushi bar, and given the limited seating, takeout is popular.

Hamburger Mary's *Burgers*

19 | 18 | 22 | $19

Andersonville | 5400 N. Clark St. (Balmoral Ave.) | 773-784-6969 | www.hamburgermaryschicago.com

"A spectacle of a dining experience" say fans of this "playful", "funky" Andersonville "must" dishing "inventive" (some say "crazy") "giant hamburgers", plus other "reliable comfort food" all "served up with a little sass" by the staff; it's nothing "fancy", but returners call it "fun at all times" – including when a "stiletto lands on the table with the bill"; P.S. the adjacent Rec Room sports bar serves the full menu.

Hannah's Bretzel *Sandwiches*

23 | 15 | 17 | $13

Loop | 131 S. Dearborn St. (bet. Adams St. & Marble Pl.) | 312-621-1111
Loop | 180 W. Washington St. (bet. La Salle & Wells Sts.) | 312-621-1111 🖾
Loop | Illinois Ctr. | 233 N. Michigan Ave. (South Water St.) | 312-621-1111 🖾
River North | 400 N. LaSalle St. (bet. Hubbard & Kinzie Sts.) | 312-621-1111
NEW **West Loop** | 555 W. Monroe St. (Clinton St.) | 312-621-1111
www.hannahsbretzel.com

"Delicious pretzel bread", "exciting flavor combinations" and "fresh, healthy options" add up to "addicting", "mouthwatering" sammies at these quick-serves where "quality" organic ingredients keep them "a step ahead of the competition" and justify "higher than average costs"; the spaces differ by locale (Washington Street has very limited seating and Dearborn is "roomy"), but "don't let the long lines fool you", because "friendly" service at each "gets you in and out quickly."

Han 202 Ⓜ *Asian*

25 | 22 | 23 | $32

Bridgeport | 605 W. 31st St. (bet. Lowe Ave. & Wallace St.) | 312-949-1314 | www.han202.com

"Unusual but delicious" say fans of this Bridgeport BYO, a "hidden gem" known for an "innovative", "well-presented" prix fixe menu of Asian dishes set down by "friendly" staffers in "serene", "conversation-friendly" digs; since tabs are "unbelievably inexpensive", many say it's one of the "best deals in town."

Harry Caray's *Italian/Steak*

22 | 21 | 22 | $45

(aka Harry Caray's Italian Steakhouse)

River North | 33 W. Kinzie St. (Dearborn Pkwy.) | 312-828-0966 ◗
Rosemont | O'Hare International Ctr., Holiday Inn | 10233 W. Higgins Rd. (Mannheim Rd.) | 847-699-1200
Lombard | Westin Lombard | 70 Yorktown Ctr. (Grace St.) | 630-953-3400

Harry Caray's Seventh Inning Stretch *American*

Southwest Side | Midway Int'l Airport | 5757 S. Cicero Ave. (bet. 55th & 63rd Sts.) | 773-948-6300
www.harrycarays.com

Diners who "like steak and sports memorabilia" find this midpriced trio (with a Midway sib) a "true Chicago treat", with "surprisingly good" chops plus "solid Italian staples" and "ample drinks" in "old-fashioned" surroundings displaying a "massive collection" of "interesting" baseball paraphernalia; foes crying foul over "predictable" eats and "tourist trap" vibes are outmatched by fans insisting the "laid-back" setting and "crowd-watching" capabilities are "endlessly entertaining"; P.S. there's also a more casual Navy Pier tavern offshoot.

Harry Caray's Tavern *American*

20 | 22 | 20 | $42

River North | Navy Pier | 700 E. Grand Ave. (Streeter Dr.) | 312-527-9700 | www.harrycaraystavern.com

"Consistently good" American standards (burgers, salads, pasta) offered at "reasonable" prices make this more casual River sib to the Harry Caray steakhouses the "valedictorian in a wasteland of subpar" Navy Pier dining options; critics complain it's a "tourist trap", but its "sports bar" vibe appeals to others who find it a "comfortable" choice, especially for "people-watching" on the patio.

🆕 Harvest Room *American* `-` `-` `-` `M`

Palos Heights | 7164 W. 127th St. (Harlem Ave.) | 708-671-8905 | www.harvestroomrestaurant.com

Open all-day, this Palos Heights New American uses local and organic products in its midpriced homestyle cooking, including some vegan and gluten-free options too; there's also a juice/smoothie bar, sophisticated tea program and thoughtful wine list, and it's all dispensed in a modern black-and-white space warmed by rustic, farm-inspired touches like a weathervane mural and china cabinet.

🆕 Hash House a Go Go *American* `▽ 21` `19` `22` `$26`

Gold Coast | 1212 N. State Pkwy. (bet. Division & Goethe Sts.) | 312-202-0994 | www.hashhouseagogo.com

"You won't leave hungry" from this affordable Gold Coast American, part of a small national chain known for "huge" portions of "inventive diner-style" "comfort food", like "bacon-infused waffles", plus cocktails and beer; the agricultural-inspired digs, decorated with farmer photos and corrugated metal, feature classic booths and barstools plus a garage door facade that opens to alfresco seating.

🆕 Haute & the Dog ∌ *Hot Dogs* `-` `-` `-` `I`

Wicker Park | 1252 N. Damen Ave. (Potomac Ave.) | 312-720-8185 | www.hauteanddog.com

A variety of gourmet wieners are paired with comfort-food toppings, exotic dipping sauces, classic sides and cut-to-order pickles at this Wicker Park hot dog BYO; diminutive digs with brick and distressed wood, meat hooks and taxidermy fit the funky neighborhood perfectly – just hit the ATM first as it's cash-only.

HB Home Bistro Ⓜ *American* `25` `21` `24` `$36`

Lakeview | 3404 N. Halsted St. (Roscoe St.) | 773-661-0299 | www.homebistrochicago.com

"Connoisseurs delight" in the "sublime" New American bistro fare at Joncarl Lachman's small Lakeview "gem" – "one of the most affordable upscale restaurants around" thanks to a BYO policy and an "amazing" Wednesday prix fixe; with a "cozy" atmosphere and service that's "charming" and "relaxed", you'll feel "like you're family – but one of those cool families."

Heartland Cafe ● *Eclectic/Vegetarian* `17` `17` `18` `$19`

Rogers Park | Heartland Bldg. | 7000 N. Glenwood Ave. (Lunt Ave.) | 773-465-8005 | www.heartlandcafe.com

"Real hippies" favor this "longtime" veggie "institution" in Rogers Park for "healthy", affordable Eclectic eats including "some decent carnivore options" in a "down-home" setting "with authentic character"; malingerers who say "meh", however, are "baffled" by the "mystique", citing occasionally "dodgy service", and musing its "few" nearby "competitors" may account for its popularity; P.S. you can "sit outside and enjoy the sunshine."

		FOOD	DECOR	SERVICE	COST

Hearty Ⓜ *American* — 21 | 18 | 19 | $38

Lakeview | 3819 N. Broadway (bet. Grace St. & Sheridan Rd.) | 773-868-9866 | www.heartychicago.com

Former Food Network stars the Hearty Boys "definitely bring it" at this "inventive", midpriced New American in Lakeview, serving "rich" yet "refined" comfort food with a "modern" Southern accent; "easygoing" if a bit "slick", it comes through with "solid" service and "consistent" cooking that devotees say "has yet to disappoint."

Heaven on Seven *Cajun/Creole* — 22 | 17 | 19 | $26

Loop | Garland Bldg. | 111 N. Wabash Ave., 7th fl. (bet. Randolph & Washington Sts.) | 312-263-6443 🗷 ⇗
River North | AMC Loews | 600 N. Michigan Ave., 2nd fl. (bet. Ohio & Ontario Sts.) | 312-280-7774
Naperville | 224 S. Main St. (bet. Jackson & Jefferson Aves.) | 630-717-0777
www.heavenonseven.com

For a "N'Awlins fix" of Cajun–Creole "delights", fans hit this "festive", "kitschy" mini-chain that "maintains its kick" with "toothsome" fare (plus a "wall of hot sauces") and "killer cocktails" like "spicy Bloody Marys", all ferried by generally "professional" servers; while some score it simply a "solid approximation" of the "real deal", most appreciate the "reasonable prices" and are especially loyal to the cash-only Loop original with a "lunch counter vibe" (it's not open for dinner).

Hecky's Barbecue *BBQ* — 21 | 4 | 14 | $17

Evanston | 1902 Green Bay Rd. (Emerson St.) | 847-492-1182 | www.heckys.com

The "sauce is the secret" at this "iconic" Evanston BBQ joint, a "long-time favorite" for "smoky, crunchy rib tips", "massive turkey legs" and "standout" sides, all at "reasonable" tabs; it's takeout only, so no matter that its "divey" ambiance "leaves something to be desired", since only those looking to "see a Chicago Bear" find reason to linger.

Hema's Kitchen *Indian* — 22 | 13 | 17 | $26

Lincoln Park | 2411 N. Clark St. (bet. Arlington Pl. & Fullerton Pkwy.) | 773-529-1705
West Rogers Park | 2439 W. Devon Ave. (bet. Artesian & Campbell Aves.) | 773-338-1627
www.hemaskitchen.com

"Solid", "authentic" Indian cooking including "stellar vegetarian standards" "satisfies" at these Lincoln Park and West Rogers Park BYOs where the "variety" of offerings is reminiscent of dining with "your grandma making sure you don't lose weight"; sure, the decor "could use some sprucing up", but service is "earnest" and prices "affordable", so most "will definitely come back."

Henri *American* — 27 | 26 | 27 | $69

Loop | 18 S. Michigan Ave. (Monroe St.) | 312-578-0763 | www.henrichicago.com

A "sophisticated" set frequents this upscale Loop New American for "delicious" dishes enhanced by "fabulous French flavors" and staffers who "go out of their way" to make you "feel welcome"; crystal chandeliers and leather and mohair upholstery help set an "elegant" but "unpretentious" tone in the white-tablecloth setting, so it all adds up to a "fine-dining" experience – with fine-dining prices to match.

NEW Himmel's European/Pizza (fka Pizza D.O.C.)

FOOD	DECOR	SERVICE	COST
-	-	-	M

Lincoln Square | 2251 W. Lawrence Ave. (bet. Bell & Oakley Aves.) | 773-784-8777 | www.himmelschicago.com

Lincoln Square's Pizza D.O.C. has been reborn as this European-accented offering adding German fare like schnitzels to the former menu of pastas, salads and pizzas from the wood-burning oven; the casual space remains recognizable, with exposed-brick walls, and prices are still generally affordable too.

Home Run Inn Pizza Pizza

FOOD	DECOR	SERVICE	COST
24	18	22	$19

Southwest Side | 4254 W. 31st St. (bet. Kildare & Tripp Aves.) | 773-247-9696 ◗
Southwest Side | 6221 S. Archer Ave. (Moody Ave.) | 773-581-9696
Addison | 1480 W. Lake St. (Foxdale Dr.) | 630-775-9696
Bolingbrook | 1280 W. Boughton Rd. (Weber Rd.) | 630-679-9966
Westmont | 605 N. Cass Ave (Ogden Ave.) | 630-789-0096
www.homeruninnpizza.com

Outlying areas lay claim to these "time-enduring" pie parlors that "pay homage to the past" with "addicting" "old-style" "thin pizza" "with a sweet crispy crust" "loaded" with so many ingredients "it's almost not thin anymore"; prized as much for being "neighborhood anchors" (some for "generations") as for their "reasonable prices", they hit a home run as fan "favorites."

Homestead ◗ American

FOOD	DECOR	SERVICE	COST
-	-	-	M

Ukrainian Village | Roots Handmade Pizza | 1924 W. Chicago Ave., 2nd fl. (Winchester Ave.) | 773-645-4949 | www.homesteadontheroof.com

Accessed through Roots Handmade Pizza, this hidden rooftop in Ukrainian Village serves farm-to-table New American dishes, many made with ingredients from the on-site garden; you can sit outside on the deck or indoors amid reclaimed materials, birch bark wall coverings and a tufted leather bar that pours elaborate craft cocktails alongside a hefty beer list; P.S. it has seasonal hours, so call before going.

Honey 1 BBQ Ⓜ BBQ

FOOD	DECOR	SERVICE	COST
21	8	18	$16

Bucktown | 2241 N. Western Ave. (bet. Belden Ave. & Lyndale St.) | 773-227-5130 | www.honey1bbq.com

"Your mouth waters from the smell of the meat slow cooking" attest admirers of this Bucktown BYO "cranking out" "authentic" BBQ offerings like "standout" ribs "smoked to perfection" via "friendly" staffers; it's "not a romantic spot for a first date", but the "no-frills" setting matches the budget-friendly tabs.

Hop Häus ◗ Burgers

FOOD	DECOR	SERVICE	COST
▽ 20	16	18	$20

Rogers Park | 7545 N. Clark St. (Howard St.) | 773-262-3783 | www.thehophaus.com

You can "watch the game or try some new brews" at this midpriced Rogers Park hang where a "nice selection" of beer is offered alongside a long list of burgers, including some made with "exotic" meat ("ostrich sliders, anyone?") plus other "pub-style fare"; inside has "multiple TVs", and while it's nothing fancy, it does work for a "casual" meal.

Hopleaf *Belgian*

FOOD	DECOR	SERVICE	COST
24	19	19	$29

Andersonville | 5148 N. Clark St. (Foster Ave.) | 773-334-9851 | www.hopleaf.com

"Hopsheads" say "one of the finest selections of beer in the world" can be found at this affordable Andersonville gastropub (21-plus only) where the "incredible" brews are joined by Belgian-focused eats like mussels and a "can't-miss" duck Reuben; a major expansion has resulted in "tons of seating" and a "cool vibe" that help make it a "great place to catch up with friends."

Hot Doug's 🗷🍽 *Hot Dogs*

FOOD	DECOR	SERVICE	COST
27	14	20	$14

Avondale | 3324 N. California Ave. (Roscoe St.) | 773-279-9550 | www.hotdougs.com

Fans say you "won't find a better hot dog place" than Doug Sohn's "distinctive" Avondale joint, where the "unbelieveable" pups go well "beyond the standard" with "tons of options" including "exotic and innovative sausages" plus "sinful" Friday and Saturday–only duck fat fries; there's often a "long wait", and because the "simple" space is "small" you may have to "brave the lines" outside, but given the "extremely tasty" payoff many still insist it's a "Chicago must-do."

NEW Howells & Hood ● *American*

FOOD	DECOR	SERVICE	COST
-	-	-	M

Streeterville | Tribune Tower | 435 N. Michigan Ave. (bet. Illinois & Water Sts.) | 312-262-5310 | www.howellsandhood.com

Taking its name from the architects of its Tribune Tower home, this midpriced gastropub purveys 100-plus draft beers, wines on tap and locally sourced New American eats; the massive setting boasts three copper-topped bars, Travertine walls, plush seating, multiple TVs and a spacious patio with heated umbrellas and fire tables.

Hubbard Inn 🗷 *Continental*

FOOD	DECOR	SERVICE	COST
20	22	18	$37

River North | 110 W. Hubbard St. (bet. Clark & LaSalle Sts.) | 312-222-1331 | www.hubbardinn.com

You can "spend time wandering around just looking" at the "interesting" art and "beautiful people" that fill this multilevel River North haunt serving a moderately priced Continental menu of "surprisingly good" share plates plus craft brews and "fantastic cocktails"; "happy servers" contribute to an overall "warm", "lively" atmosphere, but since it can get "noisy", some leave it to "the younger set."

Hub 51 ● *American/Eclectic*

FOOD	DECOR	SERVICE	COST
20	20	19	$35

River North | 51 W. Hubbard St. (Dearborn Pkwy.) | 312-828-0051 | www.hub51chicago.com

The "see-and-be-seen set" pack this "trendy" River North American-Eclectic serving "diverse" "upgraded bar food" (sushi, burgers, tacos) in addition to a "fantastic" brunch; "informed" staffers tend the "modern" space where "twentysomething scenesters" "tweet", "watch a game" or enjoy a "night on the town" that continues on to the "hopping" club Sub 51 downstairs.

Hugo's Frog Bar & Chop House ❶ *Seafood/Steak*

	FOOD	DECOR	SERVICE	COST
	24	21	23	$55

Des Plaines | Rivers Casino | 3000 S. River Rd. (Devon Ave.) | 847-768-5200

Hugo's Frog Bar & Fish House ❶ *Seafood/Steak*

Gold Coast | 1024 N. Rush St. (bet. Bellevue Pl. & Oak St.) | 312-640-0999
Naperville | Main Street Promenade Bldg. | 55 S. Main St. (Van Buren Ave.) | 630-548-3764
www.hugosfrogbar.com

A mix of "tourists", "business groups" and "locals" "hops" to this Gold Coast haunt and its suburban sequels for a "variety" of "upscale" menu items, from "fresh seafood" to "top-quality" steaks (supplied by Gibsons) to "very good" frogs' legs, of course; service is "attentive", and though a few complain about the "high price point", it's still often "crowded", especially the Rush Street flagship, which can get "crazy busy"; P.S. the Rivers Casino outpost is 21 and older only.

Ina's *American*

	FOOD	DECOR	SERVICE	COST
	22	18	20	$20

West Loop | 1235 W. Randolph St. (bet. Elizabeth St. & Willard Ct.) | 312-226-8227 | www.breakfastqueen.com

"Breakfast heaven" say fans of Ina Pinkney's West Loop New American that delivers "good old-fashioned comfort food" (offered at lunch too) via "warm" staffers known to "treat you like a relative who is actually liked"; the "simple" space "lined with salt and pepper shakers" is complemented by a "welcoming" vibe, and affordable prices are another reason it comes "highly recommended."

India House *Indian*

	FOOD	DECOR	SERVICE	COST
	22	18	19	$31

River North | 59 W. Grand Ave. (bet. Clark St. & Dearborn Pkwy.) | 312-645-9500
Buffalo Grove | Buffalo Grove Town Ctr. | 228-230 McHenry Rd. (bet. Old Checker Rd. & Townplace Pkwy.) | 847-520-5569
Hoffman Estates | 721 W. Golf Rd. (Higgins Rd.) | 847-278-0760
www.indiahousechicago.com

A "tremendous" selection of Indian dishes at "reasonable prices" has fans branding this chain a "solid performer", especially since the "large portions will keep you full"; "helpful" staffers and "tasteful" digs further the appeal, and the few who find tabs "a bit expensive" concede the lunch buffet is a "huge plus."

Indian Garden *Indian*

	FOOD	DECOR	SERVICE	COST
	20	20	18	$30

Streeterville | 247 E. Ontario St. (bet. Fairbanks Ct. & St. Clair St.) | 312-280-4910 | www.indiangardenchicago.com

An "extensive" menu of "solid" Indian dishes can be found at this midpriced Streeterville subcontinental that also offers a lunch buffet with a "good variety of dishes"; the second-floor space has large windows, and since it's "generally quiet" you can "avoid having to scream."

Indie Burger *Burgers*

	FOOD	DECOR	SERVICE	COST
	-	-	-	I

Lakeview | 1034 W. Belmont Ave. (Kenmore Ave.) | 773-857-7777 | www.indieburger.com

Organic, free-range and local ingredients are used in the budget-friendly burgers, sandwiches and salads at this funky Lakeview corner store; patrons order at the counter and camp out at booths and tables in a space decorated with farm-centric artwork and music posters.

Indie Cafe *Japanese/Thai* ▽ 24 | 20 | 22 | $22

Edgewater | 5951 N. Broadway (bet. Elmdale & Thorndale Aves.) | 773-561-5111 | www.indiecafe.us

"Gorgeous" presentations stand out at this "consistent" Edgewater "go-to" bringing together "quality" Thai and Japanese (including "excellent" sushi) in a simple, "unassuming" setting; customers also commend the "prompt" service and "outrageously affordable" tabs.

Ing ☒Ⓜ *American* 23 | 21 | 22 | $90

West Loop | 951 W. Fulton Mkt. (bet. Morgan & Sangamon Sts.) | 855-834-6464 | www.ingrestaurant.com

A "flavor tripping menu" awaits at this expensive West Loop New American from Homaro Cantu (Moto) where the "extremely creative" molecular gastronomy fare is offered in two multicourse tasting menus via "attentive" servers; the high-ceilinged space has red walls that contribute a "cool" feel to match the food.

Inovasi ☒ *American* 25 | 23 | 24 | $45

Lake Bluff | 28 E. Center Ave. (Scranton Ave.) | 847-295-1000 | www.inovasi.us

"Lake Bluff is on the inventive fine-dining map" thanks to this "refreshing" New American "foodie find" where "passionate" chef John des Rosiers turns out "innovative, delicious" small plates made with "sustainable" ingredients, including "über-local" produce from the rooftop garden; items are "expertly served" in a "bistro" setting, and while tabs aren't low, they're considered "reasonable" given the "quality."

Irazu ☒⇪ *Costa Rican* 23 | 12 | 19 | $17

Bucktown | 1865 N. Milwaukee Ave. (Moffat St.) | 773-252-5687 | www.irazuchicago.com

"Fantastic" "traditional" Costa Rican food offered at "cheap" prices makes this "vegetarian-friendly" Bucktown BYO a "favorite"; an "unimpressive" building is bettered by the "cantinalike" atmosphere, a "warm" staff and "improved outdoor seating" – just note no reservations and cash-only; P.S. "try the oatmeal shake", it's "the best."

NEW Isabel's Restaurant *Diner/Italian* - | - | - | M

Lincoln Park | 501 W. Diversey Pkwy. (Pine Grove Ave.) | 773-281-8950 | www.isabelsrestaurant.com

This Italian-leaning diner in Lincoln Park uses local ingredients in its from-scratch comfort food, which includes American-style breakfasts, sandwiches and burgers plus hand-rolled pastas and more; the informal space has a basic bar, booths, a small counter and Boot-centric food photos, and prices are affordable.

Itto Sushi ❶☒ *Japanese* 25 | 17 | 24 | $33

Lincoln Park | 2616 N. Halsted St. (Wrightwood Ave.) | 773-871-1800 | www.ittosushi.com

A "total real-deal that predates the sushi craze", this circa-1982 Lincoln Park Japanese proffers plates so "well prepared" that fans advise you "forget the trendy spots"; "entertaining chefs" engage with a "good local crowd" ("regulars, expats") in the simple space, and with patio seating and late service (till midnight), it's an "all-time fave."

Jack's on Halsted ● *American* | 17 | 15 | 17 | $38 |

Lakeview | 3201 N. Halsted St. (Belmont Ave.) | 773-244-9191 | www.jacksonhalsted.com

Loyalists find this "useful" Lakeview New American to be "one of the few good restaurants" in the area, citing a "fun" atmosphere, "thoughtful menu" and "well-priced wine list"; the vibe is "casual" and prices are moderate, so even if it's "not exceptional", it is "reliable."

Jake Melnick's Corner Tap ● *Pub Food* | 19 | 18 | 20 | $26 |

Gold Coast | 41 E. Superior St. (Wabash Ave.) | 312-266-0400 | www.jakemelnicks.com

"Above-average" bar food and "tons of beers" does it for those who tap this "dependable" Gold Coast pub; many TVs make it a "safe choice for watching sports", and with solid service and "reasonable prices", it also draws those simply looking for a "comfy place to hang out."

J. Alexander's *American* | 20 | 19 | 21 | $33 |

Lincoln Park | 1832 N. Clybourn Ave. (bet. Willow & Wisconsin Sts.) | 773-435-1018
Northbrook | 4077 Lake Cook Rd. (Pointe Dr.) | 847-564-3093
Oak Brook | 1410 16th St. (bet. Castle & Oak Brook Club Drs.) | 630-573-8180
www.jalexanders.com

Chain-averse "foodies make an exception" for these "well-managed" "meeting spots" that "aim to please" with "quick", "consistent" service and a "large, diverse" American menu of "reliable food at decent prices"; still, foes find them "average" and say "the only thing not mediocre is the bill at the end of the meal", while also conceding they "work when you need to sit down with a bunch of friends."

Jam ⊅ *American* | 22 | 21 | 21 | $20 |

Logan Square | 3057 W. Logan Blvd. (bet. Milwaukee & Sacramento Aves.) | 773-292-6011 | www.jamrestaurant.com

Breakfast gets taken to a "whole new level" courtesy of "creative" New American dishes at this daytime-only Logan Square BYO; the space has an upscale diner feel, and bills are affordable.

Jane's Ⓜ *American/Eclectic* | 21 | 19 | 20 | $32 |

Bucktown | 1655 W. Cortland St. (Paulina St.) | 773-862-5263 | www.janesrestaurant.com

The "chef strives to make every dish original and usually succeeds" at this "quaint" New American–Eclectic in a "tucked-away" Bucktown locale; service that warrants no complaints, moderate prices and cozy, "relaxed" surrounds "convince" most it's an overall "charming place."

Japonais *Japanese* | 24 | 25 | 20 | $58 |

River North | 600 W. Chicago Ave. (Larrabee St.) | 312-822-9600 | www.japonaischicago.com

Since "everything is so good" regulars say it can be "hard to choose what to order" at this "trendy" River North Japanese where "exotic" sushi rolls and other "interesting" eats are accompanied by "fancy" cocktails; the "beautiful" "modern" surroundings include a riverside terrace and hip downstairs bar, and though you "will pay", it still works for "date night, work dinners or entertaining out-of-towners."

NEW Jellyfish ● _Asian_

| - | - | - | M |

River North | 1009 N. Rush St., 2nd fl. (bet. Bellevue Pl. & Oak St.) | 312-660-3111 | www.jellyfishchicago.com

Tucked above the Gold Coast shopping district, this swanky Asian resto-lounge mixes midpriced small plates with sushi, noodles and entrees alongside sake, Asian beers and signature cocktails; the shimmering Miami-inspired setting features bright-blue accents, white-on-white seating and a year-round atrium, and it's open late on weekends.

Jerry's ● _Sandwiches_

| 20 | 16 | 16 | $19 |

Wicker Park | 1938 W. Division St. (bet. Damen & Wolcott Aves.) | 773-235-1006 | www.jerryssandwiches.com

"A sandwich for everyone" appears to be the motto of this Wicker Park deli offering what seems like the "largest menu of all time", with "over 100" "creative" sammies, plus salads, sides and more served alongside milkshakes, craft beers and wines by the glass; there's also a "nice outdoor area to people-watch", so even if service can tend toward "inconsistent", it's still a "charming" "hangout."

Jerry's Restaurant _American_

| 22 | 18 | 20 | $42 |

Winnetka | 507 Chestnut St. (bet. Elm & Oak Sts.) | 847-441-0134 | www.jerrys-restaurant.com

A suburban "gem" up Winnetka way, this "interesting" American offers a "delicious" if slightly expensive menu of "quality" fare that makes it a "special-occasion favorite", especially for "ladies who lunch"; it can get "noisy", so those in the know "ask to sit in the side room" when they want to "get away from the crowd at the bar."

Jilly's Cafe ⓜ _American/French_

| 21 | 16 | 21 | $44 |

Evanston | 2614 Green Bay Rd. (bet. Central & Livingston Sts.) | 847-869-7636 | www.jillyscafe.com

An "unexpected find in Evanston" say fans of this longtime New American–New French proffering "solid" dishes in an "unassuming" space with a "pleasant adult atmosphere"; "personable" service and "good prices" help make up for a "small" room that can feel "cluttered", and insiders advise "the best deal is the champagne brunch."

Jin Ju ⓜ _Korean_

| ∇ 24 | 19 | 23 | $28 |

Andersonville | 5203 N. Clark St. (bet. Farragut & Foster Aves.) | 773-334-6377 | www.jinjurestaurant.com

"Knowledgeable" staffers and "excellent" plates make this midpriced Andersonville "surprise" a "perfect place to introduce someone to Korean food"; devotees also "can't say enough good things about the soju martinis", so even if the decor doesn't win over quite as many, it still "won't disappoint."

Jin Thai *Thai*

| - | - | - | M |

Edgewater | 5458 N. Broadway (Catalpa Ave.) | 773-681-0555 | www.jinthaicuisine.com

Thai classics, whole snapper and a handful of Asian staples (sweet and sour, ginger and teriyaki dishes) mix on the menu at this Edgewater corner storefront, where dessert also gets more attention than your standard Thai spot; you can BYO or indulge in some interesting juices (longan, lemongrass, fresh coconut) in a spare setting of blond wood floors, gray walls, black tables and chairs and a stand of bamboo.

Joe's Seafood, Prime Steak & Stone Crab *Seafood/Steak*

| 27 | 22 | 26 | $66 |

River North | 60 E. Grand Ave. (Rush St.) | 312-379-5637 | www.joes.net

"If you can't get to Miami Beach", fans recommend this River North echo of the famed Florida original, where steaks are "cooked just right" and the "high-quality" seafood includes "not-to-be-missed" stone crab; it's all served by "charming, unpretentious" staffers in "bustling" dark wood–accented digs, and if the "special-occasion" tabs make some "crabby", well you can always go when "someone else is paying."

John's Place Ⓜ *American*

| 17 | 15 | 18 | $23 |

Lincoln Park | 1200 W. Webster Ave. (Racine Ave.) | 773-525-6670
Roscoe Village | 2132 W. Roscoe St. (Hamilton Ave.) | 773-244-6430
www.johnsplace.com

"Kudos to John" praise patrons of this "steady" Lincoln Park original and its Roscoe Village sequel where affordable American eats and "accommodating" staffers make them ripe for "family dining"; even doubters who dub them merely "fair" concede they're "good places to be relaxed with kids."

Joy's Noodles & Rice *Thai*

| 22 | 15 | 21 | $16 |

Lakeview | 3257 N. Broadway St. (bet. Aldine & Melrose Aves.) | 773-327-8330 | www.joysnoodlesandrice.com

"Meals are always inexpensive" at this "reliable" Lakeview BYO, a "favorite local haunt" for "solid" noodles and other "consistently tasty" Thai plates; the no-frills storefront space is helmed by an "attentive" crew, and consensus is it's a "staple for good reason."

Joy Yee's Noodle Shop *Asian*

| 20 | 12 | 16 | $18 |

NEW Lakeview | 1465 W. Irving Park Rd. (bet. Greenview & Janssen Aves.) | 773-281-2318
Chinatown | 2139 S. China Pl. (Princetown Ave.) | 312-328-0001
South Loop | 1335 S. Halsted St. (bet. Liberty & Maxwell Sts.) | 312-997-2128
Evanston | 521 Davis St. (bet. Chicago & Hinman Aves.) | 847-733-1900
Naperville | Iroquois Shopping Ctr. | 1163 E. Ogden Ave. (Iroquois Ave.) | 630-579-6800

Joy Yee Plus Shabu Shabu *Asian*

Chinatown | 2159 S. China Pl. (Princeton Ave.) | 312-842-8928 | www.joyyee.com

"It can take a half hour" to read through the "dizzying array" of Asian dishes offered at these BYO noodleries turning out "huge portions" of "well-crafted" plates served alongside "flavorful" fresh fruit smoothies and teas; many get "crowded" and "noisy", and what's "amazingly fast service" to some means feeling "rushed out" to others, but given the "great prices for the amount of food you get" ("share or plan to tote home mega leftovers"), most agree you "can't go wrong"; P.S. the Chinatown Shabu Shabu also serves sushi.

NEW J. Rocco Italian Table & Bar *Italian*   - | - | - | M

River North | 749 N. Clark St. (bet. Chicago Ave. & Superior St.) | 312-475-0271 | www.jroccoitalian.com

Longtime Chicago chef Steve Chiappetti (of the storied Chiappetti Meats family) takes his talents to River North with an approachable eatery where rustic Italian fare from seasonal ingredients is paired with a compact wine list, signature grappas and herbal martinis; the bi-level space has an in-house hydroponic garden and offers multiple seating options, including dining tables, a bar, one family-style table for 12 and a patio.

Julius Meinl *Austrian*   21 | 19 | 19 | $16

Lakeview | 3601 N. Southport Ave. (Addison St.) | 773-868-1857
Lincoln Square | 4363 N. Lincoln Ave. (bet. Montrose & Pensacola Aves.) | 773-868-1876
Ravenswood | 4115 N. Ravenswood Ave. (bet. Belle Plaine & Berteau Aves.) | 773-883-1862
www.meinl.com

"Quainlicious" ("quaint" plus "delicious") proclaim patrons of these coffeehouse twins in Lakeview and Lincoln Square (with a Ravenswood triplet) offering a mix of Austrian fare and cafe standards including "truly authentic" Viennese pastries, "well-proportioned" sammies and "imaginative, filling" breakfast items; "gracious" service and "calming" settings with a "European vibe" also win favor, and there's live music Fridays and Saturday nights.

NEW Juno ☑ *Japanese*   - | - | - | M

Lincoln Park | 2638 N. Lincoln Ave. (Wrightwood Ave.) | 872-206-8662 | www.junosushi.com

B.K. Park (ex Arami) and Jason Chan (ex Urban Union) pair up at this intimate Lincoln Park Japanese offering midpriced, contemporary takes on sushi and cooked cuisine with an interesting cocktails and sake selection; the small front room with red-and-black lacquer surfaces, globe light fixtures and some avant-garde mural and blackboard art gives way to a back room with a large sushi bar and omakase table.

NEW Kabocha Japanese Brasserie ☑ *Japanese*   - | - | - | E

West Loop | 952 W. Lake St. (Morgan St.) | 312-666-6214 | www.kabochachicago.com

Shin Thompson of the former Bonsoiree is behind this upscale West Loop New Japanese brasserie where a selection of raw and cooked dishes joins former Bonsoiree favorites; it's all served in a spartanchic, white-and-neutral dining room with an open kitchen, seafood aquarium, marble bar and private kaiseki table à deux.

	FOOD	DECOR	SERVICE	COST

NEW Kai Zan *Japanese*

- | - | - | M

Humboldt Park | 2557 W. Chicago Ave. (Rockwell St.) |
773-278-5776 | www.eatatkaizan.com

Fans say the kitchen "does great work" at this midpriced Humboldt Park BYO from a pair of sushi chef brothers who craft creative modern Japanese dishes – everything from teppenyaki to individually tailored omakase tasting menus; the low-lit space decorated with driftwood and fish netting houses a sushi bar and has booth seating.

Kamehachi *Japanese*

22 | 17 | 19 | $37

Loop | 311 S. Wacker Dr. (bet. Jackson Blvd. & Van Buren St.) |
312-765-8700 🛇

River North | Westin River North | 320 N. Dearborn St. (bet. Carroll Ave. & Wacker Dr.) | 312-744-1900

Old Town | 1531 N. Wells St. (bet. North Ave. & Schiller St.) |
312-664-3663 ☾

Northbrook | Village Green Shopping Ctr. | 1320 Shermer Rd.
(bet. Church St. & Meadow Rd.) | 847-562-0064
www.kamehachi.com

A "longtime anchor of the sushi scene", this relocated Old Town original (now "roomier") and its sister in Northbrook (with a Loop cafe sib and sushi bar spin-off in River North's Westin Chicago lobby) offer "authentic", "traditional" fare lifted by "innovative specials", "good sake" and "craft beer selections"; if "the service doesn't measure up to the food", prices are fairly "reasonable" and it's an overall "reliable" pick.

Karma *Asian*

∇ 23 | 26 | 22 | $41

Mundelein | Doubletree Libertyville-Mundelein | 510 E. Rte. 83
(Lake St.) | 847-970-6900 | www.karmachicago.com

"Beautiful decor" – including a "cool" pond in the dining room – "sets the mood" for "flavorful" Asian fusion fare at this "gem" in Mundelein's Doubletree Hotel; "low noise makes it conversation-friendly" and tabs are moderate, so devotees dub it "amazing for the suburbs."

Karyn's Cooked *Vegan/Vegetarian*

19 | 16 | 17 | $29

River North | 738 N. Wells St. (Superior St.) | 312-587-1050

Karyn's Fresh Corner *Vegan/Vegetarian*

Lincoln Park | 1901 N. Halsted St. (bet. Armitage Ave. & Willow St.) |
312-255-1590
www.karynraw.com

An "interesting dining adventure awaits" at this River North and Lincoln Park duo, the former mainly vegan, the latter raw, where those "in the mood" to go veggie are "not let down" by the "innovative" fare; still, doubters declare "nothing on the menu stands out", and what's "reasonable" to some is "pricey" to others, but supporters are soothed by the solid "customer service" and laid-back atmosphere.

Karyn's on Green Ⓜ *American/Vegan*

24 | 25 | 22 | $36

Greektown | 130 S. Green St. (bet. Adams & Monroe Sts.) |
312-226-6155 | www.karynsongreen.com

More "formal" than siblings Karyn's Cooked and Karyn's Fresh, this Greektown New American offers an "outstanding selection" of vegan dishes paired with organic wines, craft beers and a "large" cocktail menu; white walls and wood accents help create an "up-scale", "somewhat romantic" atmosphere, and affordable prices are another reason it's "date"-friendly.

Katsu Japanese ⓜ *Japanese*

29 | 19 | 24 | $61

Northwest Side | 2651 W. Peterson Ave. (bet. Talman & Washtenaw Aves.) | 773-784-3383

"If you crave real Japanese sushi" (and "not Westernized maki rolls") fans say "don't miss" this Northwest Side stalwart where chef-owner Katsu Imamura makes use of "excellent-quality" ingredients in his "expertly prepared" fare ("one word: omakase"), earning it top Food honors in Chicago; "friendly" staffers work the minimalist space, and "expensive" tabs aren't a surprise given the highly rated offerings.

Kaufman's Bagel & Delicatessen *Bakery/Deli*

▽ 23 | 14 | 16 | $15

Skokie | 4905 W. Dempster St. (bet. Bronx Ave. & Niles Center Rd.) | 847-677-6190 | www.kaufmansdeli.com

"Finally reopened" after a fire, this Skokie deli, a "mainstay" since 1955, offers the same "wide selection" of sandwiches ("to-die-for" pastrami) plus some of the "best bagels" and other bakery items that first put it on the map; prices are "reasonable", and since the space is counter-service only and has limited seats, many take it to go.

Keefer's ⓩ *Steak*

25 | 22 | 25 | $59

River North | 20 W. Kinzie St. (Dearborn St.) | 312-467-9525 | www.keefersrestaurant.com

A "reliable restaurant that doesn't rest on its laurels" is how fans describe this "first-class" (and "premium"-priced) River Norther offering "delicious" steakhouse fare plus an eclectic mix of apps and sides that go well beyond the "usual"; service rates highly, and the spacious modern setting is "sophisticated" enough for "business lunches and dinners" with a "comfortable", "people-watching" bar area too.

Kiki's Bistro ⓩ *French*

25 | 22 | 24 | $48

Near North | 900 N. Franklin St. (Locust St.) | 312-335-5454 | www.kikisbistro.com

An "old standby" that "refuses to bend to current trends", this "welcoming" Near North bistro appeals with "well-prepared" French fare and "high-quality wine" served by "friendly" staffers who "treat you as family"; the "cozy", "charming" space has a "happy buzz" and tabs are moderate, so Kiki-philes wanting an "escape from the city hustle bustle" return "again and again."

Kinzie Chophouse *Steak*

24 | 20 | 23 | $46

River North | 400 N. Wells St. (Kinzie St.) | 312-822-0191 | www.kinziechophouse.com

A River North "staple" "with a real Chicago feel", this chophouse offers "consistently good" fare and "generous drinks" from an "attentive" staff that "tries hard" and "knows its stuff"; the spacious dining room "never lacks for charm and ambiance" and prices are "fair", so even if it's "not spectacular", it's still a "favorite."

Kitsch'n on Roscoe *Eclectic*   ▽ 20 | 18 | 20 | $19
Roscoe Village | 2005 W. Roscoe St. (bet. Damen & Seeley Aves.) | 773-248-7372 | www.kitschn.com

"Updated comfort food" stars at this Roscoe Village Eclectic where the appropriately "kitschy" decor (lava lamps, vintage lunchboxes, action figures) "takes you back to a simpler time"; "friendly service" and affordable tabs also ensure it's a "classic"; P.S. it closes at 3 PM.

NEW Kizin Creole Kitchen *Creole/Haitian*   – | – | – | I
West Rogers Park | 2311 W. Howard St. (bet. Ridge & Western Aves.) | 773-961-7275 | www.kizincreole.com

This Rogers Park Haitian specializes in traditional fare served along with exotic juices and soft drinks (including Haitian Kola, a type of cream soda); the casual digs celebrate the art of the Caribbean, and a BYO policy makes already inexpensive tabs even more affordable.

Koda Bistro Ⓜ *French*   ▽ 23 | 20 | 20 | $46
Far South Side | 10352 S. Western Ave. (104th St.) | 773-445-5632 | www.kodabistro.com

Returnees say the classic French fare is something to "brag about" at this Far South Side bistro where the moderate menu includes small and large plates; "warm" service and a "welcoming environment" help cement its status as a "neighborhood jewel."

Koi *Asian*   17 | 17 | 17 | $32
Evanston | 624 Davis St. (bet. Chicago & Orrington Aves.) | 847-866-6969 | www.koievanston.com

Sushi, Chinese and Thai food make up the "wide-ranging" menu at this Evanston Asian, where "well-executed" rolls and some "unique" dishes come via "friendly" servers in a "bright, airy" space that becomes "cozy" during winter when the fireplace is lit; still, holdouts hint it's "pricer than others" nearby and sometimes "hit-or-miss."

Kuma's Corner ❶ *Burgers*   27 | 17 | 18 | $22
Avondale | 2900 W. Belmont Ave. (Francisco Ave.) | 773-604-8769 | www.kumascorner.com

NEW Kuma's Too ❶ *Burgers*
Lakeview | 666 W. Diversey Pkwy. (bet. Clark & Orchard Sts.) | 773-472-2666

"All hail" this "legendary" Avondale "dive" (with a newer Lakeview double) where "gigantic, inventive" burgers "named after Judas Priest, Slayer and Metallica" come in "unusual" yet "well-balanced" combinations alongside "excellent beers on tap", "good whiskeys" and a side of "loud heavy metal blasting"; yes, service can be a "bit lacking", and "boy should you expect a wait", but fans say "who cares" when the "payoff" is that "rockin'."

Kuni's *Japanese*   ▽ 23 | 17 | 22 | $33
Evanston | 511-A Main St. (bet. Chicago & Hinman Aves.) | 847-328-2004 | www.kunisushi.com

Some of the "freshest fish around" features in the "traditional sushi" served alongside other "excellent Japanese dishes" at this "old-school" Evanston "standard-bearer" that's "still more interested in quality than trendiness"; sure, there's "zero decor", but with "extremely reasonable" tabs and "attentive service", it's still considered a "favorite."

La Bocca della Verità *Italian*

▽ 22 | 16 | 20 | $30

Lincoln Square | 4618 N. Lincoln Ave. (Eastwood Ave.) | 773-784-6222 | www.laboccachicago.com

"Outstanding pastas" and other "authentic" Italian dishes ("not the Americanized versions") pair with a "wide assortment of wines" at this "reasonably priced" Lincoln Square "gem"; "service is leisurely" in the "charming" space, and "sidewalk seating provides for a perfect meal on a warm afternoon."

Labriola Bakery Café & Neopolitan Pizzeria *Italian/Pizza*

24 | 18 | 21 | $18

Oak Brook | 3021 Butterfield Rd. (Meyers Rd.) | 630-574-2008 | www.labriolabaking.com

The "broad" Italian-focused menu includes everything from "well-done" pizzas, "fantastic soups and sandwiches" and a burger to "boast" of to "delicious" baked goods including "out-of-this-world" bread at this Oak Brook cafe; "great service" and affordable tabs further make it solid for "any meal", but insiders acquainted with the "horrible lunch cram go at a different time."

La Casa de Isaac *Mexican*

20 | 15 | 20 | $26

Highland Park | 431 Temple Ave. (bet. Lauretta Pl. & Waukegan Ave.) | 847-433-5550 | www.lacasadeisaac.com

La Casa de Isaac & Moishe *Mexican*

Highland Park | 2014 First St. (bet. Elm Pl. & Green Bay Rd.) | 847-433-7400 | www.isaacandmoisherestaurant.com

Isaac & Moishe DFV *Mexican*

Highwood | 311 Waukegan Ave. (bet. Temple & Walker Aves.) | 847-433-0557 | www.isaacandmoishedeli.com

"Not your run-of-the-mill Mexican eatery" say admirers of this mid-priced Highland Park duo (with a Highwood deli sib) where the "solid", "well-prepared" fare comes with a few "interesting" "twists" and the margaritas are "outstanding"; the bright decor is "evocative of Mexico" and service is "cordial", so though "crowds can be tough", most give it a hearty *"bueno"*; P.S. it closes early Friday afternoons through sundown Saturday for Shabbat.

La Crêperie Ⓜ *Crêpes/French*

21 | 17 | 19 | $25

Lakeview | 2845 N. Clark St (bet. Broadway & Surf St.) | 773-528-9050 | www.lacreperieusa.com

The 40-year longevity "speaks to customer approval" of this "intimate" and "enduring" Lakeview kitchen offering "reasonably priced" "classic French crêpes with high-quality ingredients" ("chocolate, chicken, whatever they are serving") plus a "good wine list to accompany them"; "decor needs updating", but service is "friendly" and it "feels like a true Paris cafe" with a "gorgeous" garden "oasis in the spring/summer/fall."

	FOOD	DECOR	SERVICE	COST

Lady Gregory's ● *American/Irish*   20 | 20 | 20 | $26

Andersonville | 5260 N. Clark St. (Berwyn Ave.) | 773-271-5050 |
www.ladygregorys.com

"Soul-warming" Irish and American pub grub, an "excellent" beer
selection and a "whiskey list as long as the River Shannon" are offered in "warm", "homey" environs complete with a sizable patio at
this "upscale" Andersonville bar; service is "helpful" and tabs moderate, so the few who find it "formulaic" are overruled by those insisting "you won't find another like it."

La Gondola *Italian*   20 | 11 | 19 | $28

Lakeview | 1258 W. Belmont St. (Lakewood Ave.) | 773-935-9011
Lakeview | Wellington Plaza | 2914 N. Ashland Ave. (Wellington Ave.) |
773-248-4433
www.lagondolachicago.com

"Homestyle" cooking at "value" prices is the calling card of these
"red-sauce joints" in Lakeview known for "comforting pastas"
and other Italian "basics" served by "friendly" staffers; the
"quaint" original in Wellington Plaza is "tiny", while the BYO
spin-off has more seats, and if the surroundings don't appeal, both
are "recommended for carryout."

NEW La Grande Vie *American*   - | - | - | M

Streeterville | 215 E. Chestnut St., 2nd fl. (bet. Dewitt Pl. &
Mies van der Rohe Way) | 312-643-1111 | www.lgvchicago.com

The mix of American- and French-inspired fare at this midpriced
Streeterville eatery and lounge encompasses small plates, sandwiches, flatbreads, mains and more; signature cocktails and fine
wines are on offer too, as is a champagne brunch, all served in a
modern second-floor space accented with brushed metal and photographs of the city.

La Lagartija Taqueria ⬛ *Mexican*   - | - | - | I

West Loop | 132 S. Ashland Ave. (bet. Adams & Monroe Sts.) |
312-733-7772 | www.lalagartijataqueria.com

Laura Cid-Perea, tres leches queen and founder of Pilsen's former
Bombon Bakery, is co-owner of this "friendly" lizard-themed West
Loop taqueria where the budget-minded menu majors in "excellent"
tacos (including the requisite al pastor, breakfast and build-your-
own options) and minors in everything else casual Mex – from burritos and quesadillas to desserts; it now offers full bar service with a
focus on, of course, margaritas.

La Madia *Italian/Pizza*   23 | 21 | 21 | $30

River North | 59 W. Grand Ave. (bet. Clark St. & Dearborn Pkwy.) |
312-329-0400 | www.dinelamadia.com

"Delicious wood-fired pizza" "featuring a good selection of ingredients" is served alongside "interesting salads" and other "well-
thought-out" offerings plus a "wine list that works" at this "trendy"
yet "classy" River North Italian; "knowledgeable" service is another
feature, and "honest prices" make it "one of the better, affordable
options" in the area.

		FOOD	DECOR	SERVICE	COST

Lao Beijing *Chinese*   24 | 12 | 15 | $23

Chinatown | Chinatown Mall | 2138 S. Archer Ave. (Cermak Rd.) |
312-881-0168

Lao Shanghai *Chinese*

Chinatown | 2163 S. China Pl. (Princeton Ave.) | 312-808-0830

Lao Sze Chuan *Chinese*

Chinatown | 2172 S. Archer Ave. (Princeton Ave.) | 312-326-5040 ◗
Downers Grove | 1331 W. Ogden Ave. (Oakwood Ave.) |
630-663-0303

Lao You Ju ◗ *Chinese*

Chinatown | Richmond Ctr. | 2002 S. Wentworth Ave. (bet. Archer Ave. &
Cullerton St.) | 312-225-7818
www.tonygourmetgroup.com

"Local foodies" "travel to the Far East" courtesy of Tony Hu's "high-
quality" Chinese cuisine at these "cheap" "favorites" known for "en-
cyclopedialike menus" and "beautifully spiced", "intensely" flavored
dishes (including some so "hot" they'll "melt your socks off"); sure,
"the service is iffy" and "the decor is nonexistent", "but so what" ask
fans who advise you simply "close your eyes and savor the tastes";
P.S. clubby You Ju is more posh and modern than its predecessors.

NEW Lao 18 *Chinese*   - | - | - | M

River North | 18 W. Hubbard St. (bet. Dearborn & State Sts.) |
312-955-8018 | www.lao18.com

Set in an eight thousand sq.-ft. space in River North, this latest addition from Tony Hu offers midpriced Chinese cooking and dim sum
in a dining room, bar, lounge and patio; the chic setting is decorated
with cream-hued booths, bare wood tables, ornate metalwork and a
volcanic mural behind the bar, which shakes up exotic cocktails, some
involving ancient Chinese spirits.

Lao Hunan *Chinese*   ▽ 25 | 13 | 17 | $22

Chinatown | 2230 S. Wentworth Ave. (bet. Alexander St. & 22nd Pl.) |
312-842-7888 | www.tonygourmetgroup.com

Tony Hu's Chinatown "empire" includes this "amazing addition" where
the "incredible" renditions of "true Hunan dishes" are "different
than standard Chinese" offerings – and "not for the timid" (a "high
tolerance for spicy food" is helpful); the no-frills "Mao-themed" decor extends to the "kitschy" Red Army uniforms worn by the "welcoming" staff, and with affordable tabs, most rank it "definitely
worth a visit."

NEW Lao Ma La ◗ *Chinese*   - | - | - | I

Chinatown | Chinatown Square | 2017 S. Wells St. (bet. Cullerton St. &
Princeton Ave.) | 312-225-8989 | www.tonygourmetgroup.com

Tony Hu's Chinatown empire continues to grow with this affordable
stop whose menu is less focused on one region and instead celebrates all that is spicy in Chinese cuisine; beer, wine, sake and signature cocktails are on offer too in the former Lure Izakaya space
that's been given a decorative face-lift with a new color scheme,
though the wood banquettes, open kitchen and stylized hanging
umbrellas remain intact.

		FOOD	DECOR	SERVICE	COST

NEW Lao Yunnan *Chinese*
- | - | - | I

Chinatown | 2109 S. China Pl. (bet. Princeton Ave. & Wells St.) | 312-326-9966 | www.tonygourmetgroup.com

Empire-builder Tony Hu is behind this Chinatown eatery that highlights the bright, herbaceous cuisine of China's Yunnan Province, along with an obscure sub-cuisine called Dian, on an inexpensive menu featuring everything from hot pots to rice noodles to vegetarian feasts (but no alcohol); the traditional setting features Chinese lanterns, rattan chairs and tabletops embedded with white stones.

La Parrilla Colombian Steak House Ⓜ *Colombian/Steak*
- | - | - | M

Northwest Side | 6427 W. Irving Park Rd. (bet. Narragansett & Natchez Aves.) | 773-777-7720

You can fuel up on grilled churrascaria meats, empanadas, arepas, sandwiches and traditional Colombian entrees (the menu bears QR codes linking to food and travel info) at this Northwest Side steakhouse; the small, casual digs, done up in red and gold, include a bar dispensing signature cocktails, and there are beer towers on the cherry-stained tables.

La Petite Folie Ⓜ *French*
25 | 22 | 24 | $51

Hyde Park | Hyde Park Shopping Ctr. | 1504 E. 55th St. (Lake Park Blvd.) | 773-493-1394 | www.lapetitefolie.com

One of the "best choices" for "fine dining" in Hyde Park, this "charming" bistro offers "always great" "classic" French dishes and wines in a "quiet" white-tablecloth dining room; service gets strong marks too, so even if tabs are a touch high, locals agree it's a "real gem."

La Sardine ⓧ *French*
24 | 22 | 23 | $46

West Loop | 111 N. Carpenter St. (bet. Randolph St. & Washington Blvd.) | 312-421-2800 | www.lasardine.com

"Consistently first-rate bistro food with a distinctly French feel" can be found at this "moderate" West Loop Parisian, where the menu boasts "ample" portions of "comfort food your *grand-mère* would make", including "to-die-for" soufflés; "no-pretense" service and a "warm", "crowded" space that is "larger and easier to navigate" than sister restaurant Le Bouchon further lead fans to "highly recommend it."

La Scarola *Italian*
26 | 16 | 21 | $39

River West | 721 W. Grand Ave. (bet. Halsted St. & Union Ave.) | 312-243-1740 | www.lascarola.com

A "very small but high-powered place", this River West "hole-in-the-wall" "transports you back in time" to "grandma's Sunday afternoon Italian" meal with "plentiful" portions of "authentic and amazing" fare via "old-school" servers you can "laugh and have fun with"; tabs that "won't break the budget" are another reason it can get "crowded" and "loud", so "reservations are a must" – though "even with one, you could be waiting for a while."

	FOOD	DECOR	SERVICE	COST

NEW La Sirena Clandestina ● *South American*

▽ 24 | 21 | 22 | $48

West Loop | 954 W. Fulton Mkt. (bet. Morgan & Sangamon Sts.) | 312-226-5300 | www.lasirenachicago.com

"Thank you, John Manion" cheer fans of his moderate West Loop haunt where the solid South American dishes (including late-night snacks) come with a New American accent and get a boost from "amazingly awesome" cocktails; the intimate, "bustling" space is filled with rustic brick, ductwork and funky furnishings, and it's all watched over by a "friendly" crew.

Las Tablas *Colombian/Steak*

23 | 20 | 17 | $30

Lakeview | 2942 N. Lincoln Ave. (bet. George St. & Southport Ave.) | 773-871-2414

Northwest Side | 4920 W. Irving Park Rd. (Laporte Ave.) | 773-202-0999 www.lastablas.com

For some of the "best Colombian food around", diners visit these steakhouse "alternatives" in Northwest Side and Lakeview offering "tender" cuts and other "wonderfully spiced fare" that "you can smell from a block away"; service is "friendly", and with "high-energy vibes" they're good "with friends" for a "satisfying night out."

La Tasca *Spanish*

21 | 19 | 19 | $37

Arlington Heights | 25 W. Davis St. (Vail Ave.) | 847-398-2400 | www.latascatapas.com

A "great variety" of "authentic" tapas offers "so many tastes in one evening" at this midpriced Arlington Heights Spaniard in a festive "hustle-and-bustle"-filled dining room with colorful murals; it can get "a little loud on the weekends" and service swings from "good" to "slow", but those who appreciate the "citylike ambiance" and "excellent", if "potent" sangria consider it a "fave."

Lawry's The Prime Rib *American/Steak*

23 | 21 | 22 | $57

River North | 100 E. Ontario St. (Rush St.) | 312-787-5000 | www.lawrysonline.com

A "history-filled temple to prime rib", this "classic" River North link of the Beverly Hills–based chophouse chain offers its "excellent" namesake dish "served old-world style" "right from a roasting cart" in portions ranging from "manageable to football-player sized"; "accommodating" staffers are "on-point" in the "comfortable" former McCormick mansion setting, so despite a few grumbles about tabs "a bit on the expensive side", most rank it a "stop not to be missed."

NEW Leadbelly Ⓜ *Burgers*

‑ | ‑ | ‑ | I

Northwest Side | 5739 W. Irving Park Rd. (bet. Mango & Menard Aves.) | 773-283-7880 | www.leadbellyburgers.com

Wallet-friendly burgers and a touch of the blues are offered at this Portage Park rock 'n' roll-themed spot that grinds its meat, bakes its buns, hand-cuts its fries (available several ways) and makes its sauces from scratch; shakes and a rotating trio of craft beers are also on hand in the casual setting with musicians' portraits and music videos setting the tone.

Le Bouchon ⊠ *French*
23 | 19 | 20 | $43

Bucktown | 1958 N. Damen Ave. (bet. Armitage Ave. & Homer St.) | 773-862-6600 | www.lebouchonofchicago.com

"As close to a Parisian bistro as you can get in Chicago", this "fairly priced" Bucktown boîte on "Rue Damen" serves "tasty", "traditional" dishes in a "cozy" space; all in all it has "real French character without the server attitude", so though "tables are a bit cramped and it can get a little noisy", most swear that's "a small price to pay", especially if you go on Tuesday for the "pretty awesome" prix fixe.

Le Colonial *Vietnamese*
23 | 24 | 22 | $50

Gold Coast | 937 N. Rush St. (bet. Oak & Walton Sts.) | 312-255-0088 | www.lecolonialchicago.com

You'll feel like you're "back in the colonial era" at this "upscale" Gold Coast Vietnamese where an "intriguing" French-accented menu is served in a "chic" space with ceiling fans, bamboo and palms; "pleasant" staffers add more appeal, while "original" cocktails and an upstairs lounge and balcony further the "cool."

Les Nomades ⊠ Ⓜ *French*
28 | 26 | 28 | $126

Streeterville | 222 E. Ontario St. (bet. Fairbanks Ct. & St. Clair St.) | 312-649-9010 | www.lesnomades.net

"One of the last classic French white-tablecloth occasion restaurants", this Streeterville destination set in an "elegant" townhouse dispenses chef Roland Liccioni's "perfectly executed" plates paired with an "amazing wine list"; maybe it "costs a fortune", but "impeccable" service helps, and anyway, devotees swear it's "as good as it is expensive"; P.S. jackets required.

Le Vichyssois Ⓜ *French*
▽ 25 | 18 | 25 | $58

Lakemoor | 220 Rand Rd. (bet. Hollywood Terr. & Willow Rd.) | 815-385-8221 | www.levichyssois.com

"Always top-notch" laud loyalists of chef-owner Bernard Cretier's "classic French" cooking at this circa-1976 Lakemoor longtimer; "knowledgeable, efficient" staffers tend to guests in an antiquey country home setting that some find a bit "dated", but most still call it a "consistent", "well-worth-it" "favorite."

Libertad Ⓜ *Nuevo Latino*
▽ 25 | 18 | 24 | $36

Skokie | 7931 Lincoln Ave. (Oakton St.) | 847-674-8100 | www.libertad7931.com

A "revelation" swoon fans of the "flavorful" Nuevo Latino small plates at this "little" Skokie "hideaway"; "service could not be more attentive" and tabs are affordable, so even if the spare setting doesn't impress, its "booming business" reflects its "special-gem" status.

Lillie's Q *BBQ/Southern*
22 | 18 | 19 | $27

Bucktown | 1856 W. North Ave. (Wolcott Ave.) | 773-772-5500 | 🆕 **West Loop** | 131 N. Clinton St. (Randolph St.) | 773-772-5500 ⊠ | www.lilliesq.com

Reopened after a fire, Charlie McKenna's Bucktown 'cue joint (with a West Loop sib) remains a "meat lover's" "heaven" with "luscious" pulled pork, "scarf"-worthy ribs and other "Southern favorites", plus 'moonshine' cocktails and an "awesome beer selection", all served in rustic, wood-accented digs; service gets mixed marks ("terrific" vs. "unreliable"), the "no-reservations policy is annoying" and a few find it just "so-so", but with moderate prices most agree it's still a "solid choice."

NEW Little Goat

Bread ● *Bakery/Sandwiches*   - | - | - | I

West Loop | 820 W. Randolph St. (Green St.) | 312-888-3455 | www.littlegoatchicago.com

Stephanie Izard's Randolph Street takeover continues with this dedicated bakery adjacent to her same-name West Loop diner, where the budget-friendly menu is comprised of fresh breads, sweet pastries, bagels and a handful of soups, salads and sandwiches; the funky, rustic-modern surroundings are accented by a marble counter and distressed wood bread bins, a view of the baking action, a retail area with artisanal products and, naturally, goat references everywhere.

NEW Little Goat Diner ● *Diner*   ∇ 22 | 22 | 21 | $28

West Loop | 820 W. Randolph St. (Green St.) | 312-888-3455 | www.littlegoatchicago.com

"Not your typical diner", Stephanie Izard's "fancy greasy-spoon" follow-up to Girl & The Goat offers "reimagined comfort food" from a "huge" menu (you'll need "10-15 minutes to absorb all of the choices") full of "unusual flavor combinations" and "interesting twists"; a "hip, funky" vibe pervades the often "packed" space where diners can settle into tufted leather booths or snag a stool by the open kitchen, and there's also an attached bakery.

NEW Little Market

Brasserie *American*   - | - | - | M

Gold Coast | The Talbott Hotel | 10 E. Delaware Pl. (bet. Rush & State Sts.) | 312-640-8141 | www.littlemarketbrasserie.com

In the heart of the Gold Coast, The Talbott Hotel houses this modern brasserie from the Mercadito group showcasing Ryan Poli's New American small plates and midpriced entrees, along with classic breakfast and brunch fare, housemade sodas and a notable craft cocktail program; the smart decor is an updated nod to Parisian tradition with black-and-white subway tiles, antique framed mirrors and an outdoor cafe.

Lloyd's Chicago ⊠ *American*   16 | 16 | 19 | $30

Loop | Charter One | 1 S. Wacker Dr. (Madison St.) | 312-407-6900 | www.lloydschicago.com

A "convenient" Loop locale coupled with solid service and a varied menu of American standards make this midpriced option "dependable" for a "business lunch" or "pre-opera dinner"; though critics find it merely "average", its spacious white-tablecloth dining room is often still "crowded", and occasionally a "madhouse"; P.S. closed Saturdays unless the Lyric's in session.

| | FOOD | DECOR | SERVICE | COST |

NEW LM Bistro *French* — — — M
River North | Hotel Felix | 111 W. Huron St. (Clark St.) |
312-202-9900 | www.lmrestaurant.com
The team behind the now-closed LM has taken over the former Elate
space in River North's Hotel Felix, revamping it into this midpriced
French serving hearty bistro classics for three squares; the modern
loft space has been redecorated in warm amber and earth tones,
with new bentwood chairs pulling up to the bare wood tables, and
seasonal outdoor dining.

The Lobby *American* — 25 26 25 $57
River North | Peninsula Chicago | 108 E. Superior St., 5th fl.
(bet. Michigan Ave. & Rush St.) | 312-573-6760 | www.peninsula.com
The "expansive", "airy" setting featuring floor-to-ceiling windows
makes it hard to "concentrate on your meal" say wowed diners at this
"upscale" American in River North's Peninsula Hotel that delivers
"top-notch" fare, including a "fabulous brunch" and "popular high
tea"; toss in "attentive" service, and it's no surprise that those on a
"tight budget" should "bring an expense account."

NEW The Local ● *American* — — — M
Gold Coast | Hilton Suites Chicago/Magnificent Mile |
198 E. Delaware Pl. (Mies van der Rohe Way) | 312-280-8887 |
www.thelocalchicago.com
Chicago Cut Steakhouse spawned this midpriced American comfort-
food concept with primo ingredients (emphasis on local) showing
up in dishes like prime beef meatloaf, mac 'n' cheese carbonara,
roasted chicken pot pies and apple brown Betty; additional assets
are breakfast, bar service with iPad wine list and the handsome
architectural setting of polished wood and vintage Americana.

NEW Local Root *American/Sandwiches* — — — M
Streeterville | 601 N. McClurg Ct. (Ohio St.) | 312-643-1145 |
www.localrootchicago.com
Locally sourced ingredients star at this organic-leaning Streeterville
New American where daytime counter service transitions to table
service by night, with the sandwich-focused lunch menu following
suit and adding charcuterie and small plates at dinner; it also has
coffee, house-brand soda and wine, all offered in a modern space
with reclaimed wood and an open 'zero waste' kitchen.

Lockwood *American* 23 22 22 $53
Loop | Palmer House Hilton | 17 E. Monroe St (bet. State St. &
Wabash Ave.) | 312-917-3404 | www.lockwoodrestaurant.com
Set in the "famed" Palmer House Hotel lobby, this "upscale" Loop
New American is a "sight to be seen" with its "modern" elegant
stylings (especially after a recent half-million renovation including
updated furnishings and decor) that set the stage for "solid" sometimes "imaginative" fare backed by wines "uniformly good both in
selection and price"; service is generally "courteous", and though its
"location can make it rather pricey", you can't beat its "good proximity to downtown theaters."

	FOOD	DECOR	SERVICE	COST

Longman & Eagle ● *American* 27 | 21 | 23 | $42

Logan Square | 2657 N. Kedzie Ave. (Schubert Ave.) | 773-276-7110 | www.longmananddeagle.com

"Expect the hipsters" at this "in-demand" Logan Square New American where a "clear affection for niche ingredients" results in "exciting", "absolutely delicious" fare, including an "especially decadent" brunch; a "ridiculous" whiskey list and "killer" cocktails are other reasons to go, but "come early or plan on waiting" as it doesn't take reservations; P.S. if you overindulge, you can get a room upstairs and "sleep it off while your liver mends."

Los Nopales Ⓜ *Mexican* 23 | 15 | 19 | $23

Lincoln Square | 4544 N. Western Ave. (bet. Sunnyside & Wilson Aves.) | 773-334-3149 | www.losnopalesrestaurant.com

"Authentic" "homestyle" Mexican *comida* at "reasonable prices" have many swearing they'll "come back again and again" to this Lincoln Square BYO (modest corkage); "accommodating" service helps distract from the bare-bones setting, so those complaining it's "not noteworthy" are drowned out by fans deeming it a "go-to spot."

Lou Malnati's Pizzeria *Pizza* 25 | 16 | 20 | $22

River North | 439 N. Wells St. (Hubbard St.) | 312-828-9800
Lincoln Park | 958 W. Wrightwood Ave. (Lincoln Ave.) | 773-832-4030
Far South Side | 3859 W. Ogden Ave. (Cermak Rd.) | 773-762-0800
South Loop | 805 S. State St. (8th St.) | 312-786-1000
Evanston | 1850 Sherman Ave. (University Pl.) | 847-328-5400
Lincolnwood | 6649 N. Lincoln Ave. (Prairie Rd.) | 847-673-0800
Buffalo Grove | 85 S. Buffalo Grove Rd. (Lake Cook Rd.) | 847-215-7100
Elk Grove Village | 1050 E. Higgins Rd. (bet. Joey Dr. & Martin Ln.) | 847-439-2000
Schaumburg | 1 S. Roselle Rd. (Schaumburg Rd.) | 847-985-1525
Naperville | 131 W. Jefferson Ave. (bet. Main & Webster Sts.) | 630-717-0700
www.loumalnatis.com
Additional locations throughout the Chicago area

For "real Chicago pizza", fans hit up this "top-notch" chain "staple" that "sets the standard" with its "deep-dish butter crust" pies made "just right" with the "perfect" ratio of cheese to sauce – and its "crisp" thin-crust pies and "big", "not-to-be-missed" salads are a hit too; service is generally solid (if occasionally "slow"), and if the decor is considered just "fine", well you "don't go for the ambiance."

Lou Mitchell's *Diner* 24 | 14 | 20 | $17

Loop | 565 W. Jackson Blvd. (Jefferson St.) | 312-939-3111 | www.loumitchellsrestaurant.com

Eaters advise "come hungry" to this Loop "king of breakfast", a "quintessential" "Chicago icon" since 1923 where "oversized" portions of "hearty", "high-quality" diner fare like "lighter than air scrambled eggs" and "amazing French toast" are served morning through afternoon via "friendly" staffers who "have been working there for 20 years or more"; "you'll rub elbows with workers from the stock exchange and other executives" in the "crowded" "old-time" environs, but "get there early to avoid the lines" – though late-risers are "treated to donut holes and Milk Duds" while they wait.

Lovells of Lake Forest *American*   22 | 24 | 23 | $53

Lake Forest | 915 S. Waukegan Rd. (bet. Everett Rd. & Gloucester Crossing) | 847-234-8013 | www.lovellsoflakeforest.com

The "beautiful, quaint house setting" decorated with "out-of-this-world (literally) artifacts" from the chef-owner's father, Apollo 13 astronaut Jim Lovell, provides the backdrop for a "wonderful selection" of "tasty" New American plates at this pricey Lake Forester; "standout" service contributes to a "soothing ambiance", and if a few snipe you're "paying for a famous name", more find it a "magical place to dine"; P.S. try the downstairs Captain's Quarters "for a more casual evening with some additional bar food selections" and live music Friday and Saturday nights.

NEW L'Patron ≠ *Mexican*   - | - | - | I

Logan Square | 2815 W Diversey Ave (bet. California Ave. & Mozart St.) | 773-252-6335

Budget-friendly Mexican courtesy of a former Topolobampo chef is the draw at this tiny Logan Square taco/torta/burrito house touting fresh ingredients and seasonal salsas; it's hard to miss the lime-green exterior, which gives way to a bright and casual counter-seating space that's open late on weekends.

L2O *Seafood*   26 | 28 | 27 | $182

Lincoln Park | The Belden-Stratford | 2300 N. Lincoln Park W. (Belden Ave.) | 773-868-0002 | www.l2orestaurant.com

"Imaginative, exquisitely executed" tasting menus evoke "oohs and aahs" at this "fine-dining" seafood specialist in Lincoln Park; the "classy", "calming" space is tended by an "attentive, knowledgeable" staff, so those deep-pocketed enough to weather "aftershocks of the bill" declare it "money well spent."

Lucky's Sandwich Company ● *Deli/Sandwiches*   ▽ 18 | 12 | 16 | $15

Lakeview | 3472 N. Clark St. (Sheffield Ave.) | 773-549-0665
Pilsen | 717 Maxwell St. (Halsted St.) | 312-733-5700
www.luckysandwich.com

The "delicious" subs at these sandwich shops have the "unique" feature of being "packed with fries", along with tomatoes and coleslaw, and come in "huge" proportions that amount to a "whole meal in between two slices of bread"; add "decent drink specials" and you know "you'll get your money's worth", with appealing "old baseball/Cubs" memorabilia on the walls and a "helpful" staff sealing the deal.

Lula Cafe *Eclectic*   26 | 20 | 23 | $30

Logan Square | 2537 N. Kedzie Blvd. (bet. Fullerton Ave. & Logan Blvd.) | 773-489-9554 | www.lulacafe.com

"Classic dishes with a twist" feature on the somewhat "small" farm-to-table menu at this midpriced Logan Square Eclectic where the "interesting" and "divine" fare is often reminiscent of a *Top Chef* episode; "funky" staffers (think "tattoos and rad beards") enhance the "cool, unassuming" space, and though seating can be a bit "tight", especially during the "excellent brunch", there's always the patio.

LuLu's Dim Sum & Then Sum *Asian*   21 | 15 | 20 | $21

Evanston | 804 Davis St. (Sherman Ave.) | 847-869-4343 | www.lulusdimsum.com

"Big portions" of "deeply flavored", occasionally "inventive" dim sum, noodles and more make for a "solid, filling meal" at this "kid-friendly" Evanston Asian; "busy but efficient" staffers tend the "spunky, quirky" storefront space, and though it's probably "not the most authentic" option, it's "affordable" with a number of all-you-can-eat specials ("flavorful great deals").

Lupita's Ⓜ *Mexican*   20 | 15 | 21 | $24

Evanston | 700 Main St (Custer Ave.) | 847-328-2255 | www.lupitasmexicanrestaurant.com

You'll "never leave hungry" at this "family-friendly" Evanston Mexican offering a "mostly standard menu" of "delicious" fare via "caring" staffers in a "cheerful room" decorated with pictures and artwork; occasional weekend guitar music is another plus, and though a few deem it "pedestrian", it's still a "favorite with locals."

LuxBar ❶ *American*   19 | 18 | 20 | $34

Gold Coast | 18 E. Bellevue Pl. (Rush St.) | 312-642-3400 | www.luxbar.com

"Classic" American grub like burgers, salads and steaks offered at "reasonable" prices in "lively", "seriously hip" surrounds make this "neighborhood joint" a "great choice for the budget-conscious who don't want to sacrifice the see-and-be-seen atmosphere of the Gold Coast"; it's a "crazy noisy zoo" on weekends and during "big sport events", but service remains generally "prompt", so even snarkers saying there's "nothing d-lux" about it concede it's a "reliable" "pit stop", especially when "people-watching outdoors in the summer."

L. Woods Tap & Pine Lodge *American*   19 | 18 | 19 | $32

Lincolnwood | 7110 N. Lincoln Ave. (Kostner Ave.) | 847-677-3350 | www.lwoodsrestaurant.com

An "ersatz Wisconsin supper club", this "reasonably priced" Lincolnwood waystation is a "prototypical Lettuce Entertain You joint", delivering "gargantuan" portions of "consistently good" American fare, including "tasty barbecue", via "experienced and friendly" servers; the "casual" wood-paneled environs are bedecked with "a lot of fish and antlers", and those who say "nothing is going to blow your mind" are countered by "crowds" that suggest it's a "favorite of many."

Macello *Italian*   ▽ 25 | 22 | 22 | $31

West Loop | 1235 W. Lake St. (bet. Elizabeth St. & Racine Ave.) | 312-850-9870 | www.macellochicago.com

A "cool hidden gem", this West Loop Italian delivers "delicious" dishes via servers who seem "excited about the food and knowledgable on wines"; the "modern" decor exudes "warmth", and with affordable tabs devotees say you're in for a "meal that never disappoints."

	FOOD	DECOR	SERVICE	COST

Macku Sushi *Japanese*
25 | 21 | 23 | $46

Lincoln Park | 2239 N. Clybourn Ave. (bet. Greenview & Webster Aves.) | 773-880-8012 | www.mackusushi.com

So "fresh" are the "mind-blowing sashimi", "inventive sushi" and "amazing specials" at this "pricey but worth it" Lincoln Park Japanese that patrons wonder if there's "a fish market in the backyard"; "attentive" servers and a "trendy" yet "inviting" modern space also earn admiration from those who "cannot say enough" about it.

Magnolia Cafe M *American*
23 | 19 | 22 | $38

Uptown | 1224 W. Wilson Ave. (bet. Magnolia & Racine Aves.) | 773-728-8785 | www.magnoliacafeuptown.com

"Delicious" fare bolstered by a wine list that "works well with the menu" brings Uptowners to this "cozy" New American in a "small, but comfortable" candlelit room; service gets solid marks and prices are "fair", so it "makes for a fun escape" in an "underserved" part of town.

Mago *Mexican*
24 | 20 | 22 | $29

Arlington Heights | 115 W. Campbell St. (Vail Ave.) | 847-253-2222
Bolingbrook | 641 E. Boughton Rd. (Feather Sound Dr.) | 630-783-2222
NEW **South Barrington** | 100 W. Higgins Rd. (New Sutton Rd.) | 847-844-4400
www.magodining.com

"Definitely not your typical Mexican restaurant" enthuse fans of this "reasonably" priced Bolingbrook and Arlington Heights duo (with a newer South Barrington third) where "innovative" touches offer a "different spin" on standards ("even the tacos are interesting"); "bitchin' margaritas", "cool" Aztec-inflected decor and "excellent" service further leave devotees warning "keep it to yourself or we'll have to wait in long lines to get in."

NEW MAK: Modern Asian Kitchen *Asian*
- | - | - | I

Wicker Park | 1924 W. Division St. (bet. Damen & Wolcott Aves.) | 773-772-6251 | www.makrestaurant.com

A concise selection of affordable, updated Asian chow (wraps, bowls, salads) forms the menu at this fast-casual Wicker Parker; the wood plank storefront houses an open kitchen, small counter, handful of booths and propaganda-style posters.

Mama Milano *Italian/Pizza*
- | - | - | I

Old Town | 1419 N. Wells St. (bet. North Ave. & Schiller St.) | 312-787-3710 | www.mamamilano.com

Former old-school Italian Papa Milano's fathered this budget-friendly Old Town pizzeria offering classic pies and a handful of salads and sandwiches, all washed down by beer, wine and coffee drinks; its cozy, narrow space features vintage light fixtures, posters, rustic brickwork and a long communal dining bar with a TV.

Mana Food Bar *Eclectic/Vegetarian*
26 | 21 | 23 | $33

Wicker Park | 1742 W. Division St. (bet. Hermitage & Wood Sts.) | 773-342-1742 | www.manafoodbar.com

"Creatively prepared" Eclectic-vegetarian small plates are so "delicious" "you don't even realize you aren't eating meat" swear "discerning diners" of this no-reservations Wicker Park veggie "heaven"; service is "friendly" and prices are "reasonable" too, so the "only problem" is the "small" size of the "modern" wood-lined space, leading patrons to plead "please open in a bigger location."

Manny's Cafeteria & Delicatessen *Deli*   24 | 9 | 17 | $18

South Loop | 1141 S. Jefferson St. (bet. Grenshaw St. & Roosevelt Rd.) | 312-939-2855 🗷
Southwest Side | Midway Int't Airport | 5700 S. Cicero Ave., Concourse A (bet. 55th & 63rd Sts.) | 773-948-6300
www.mannysdeli.com

"Don't let the linoleum fool you" because "they don't make restaurants like this anymore" say fans of this "legit" South Loop "institution" (with a Midway sib) where "monstrous sandwiches", "hard-to-choose-from" steam trays and other deli "classics" ("talk about comfort food") are the path to "gastro heaven" – and an "awesome value for your money" too; the "sparse" "cafeteria-style" environs are full of "characters" who make "people-watching a highlight", and "old-school" (some say "rude") service is "part of the fun", so just make sure to "clear out your afternoon to take a big nap after imbibing."

Margie's Candies *American*   22 | 17 | 20 | $12

Bucktown | 1960 N. Western Ave. (Armitage Ave.) | 773-384-1035 ◐
Logan Square | 1813 W. Montrose Ave. (bet. Honroe St. & Ravenswood Ave.) | 773-348-0400
www.margiesfinecandies.com

"Treat yourself" to a "scoop of nostalgia" at these "old-timey" ice cream and candy "classics" serving up "amazing" splits and sundaes topped by hot fudge that's "not too sweet" and "not to rich" (but "so thick you need to cut it with a knife"), plus Traditional American fare, though most suggest "sticking to the desserts"; the circa-1921 Bucktown "institution" often has "lines around the block" so some try the Logan Square sequel, as both "hit the spot" and are "completely worth the time and money" for a "step back in time."

Marigold Ⓜ *Indian*   22 | 19 | 20 | M

Andersonville | 5413 N. Clark St. (bet. Balmoral & Rascher Aves.) | 773-989-4300 | www.marigoldrestaurant.com

After relocating from Uptown, this affordable Indian has new Andersonville digs, offering a similar menu of "modern Indian food", including dishes that provide an "interesting alternative" to the usual fare; craft beers, global wines and house cocktails make up the larger drink selection, and the space is more casual, with slightly lower tabs to match.

Market House on the Square *American*   - | - | - | M
(fka South Gate Cafe)

Lake Forest | 655 Forest Ave. (bet. Deerpath Rd. & Southgate) | 847-234-8800 | www.themarkethouse.com

This upscale Lake Forest American serves seasonal-focused dishes both classic and contemporary, along with specialty cocktails and wines by the quartino; the bi-level space is done up in wood and leather with lantern light fixtures, vintage local photography and fireplaces, and there's an outdoor dining area with all-weather wicker and granite furnishings.

Marmalade *American*   ▽ 25 | 18 | 21 | $18

North Center/St. Ben's | 1969 W. Montrose Ave. (Damen Ave.) | 773-883-9000 | www.marmaladechicago.com

"Every dish delivers" at this fairly "cheap" American BYO in "out-of-the-way" North Center offering an "extensive, imaginative" daytime menu of "decidedly upscale" "sweet and savory options"; "attentive" staffers tend to diners in a "bare-bones, but modern" milieu, and regulars warn that "long waits" on weekends will only increase "unless we can keep it quiet."

Masa Azul Ⓜ *Mexican*   - | - | - | M

Logan Square | 2901 W. Diversey Ave. (bet. Francisco Ave. & Richmond St.) | 773-687-0300 | www.masaazul.com

Modern Mexican is in (and Southwestern is out) at this Logan Square eatery where the revamped menu includes gourmet tacos and other updated classic dishes; a mood change in the airy, urban setting includes a new color scheme and lighting, while the concrete bar carries on with its monster tequila 'library' and craft cocktails (including some made with the lesser known Mexican spirit sotol).

🆕 Masaki Sushi *Japanese*   - | - | - | VE

Streeterville | Hilton Chicago Magnificent Mile | 990 N. Mies van der Rohe Way (Walton St.) | 312-280-9100 | www.masakichicago.com

The owners of Pelago bring this upscale Japanese and sushi specialist to the Streeterville Hilton, where high-priced, high-concept seasonal omakase menus are served alongside a serious wine, sake and tea list; the tiny, elegant space boasts a marble sushi bar, fine table appointments, imported art and bubble chandeliers, plus a hidden table for those seeking more privacy.

Mastro's Steakhouse ● *Steak*   26 | 23 | 24 | $77

River North | 520 N. Dearborn St. (Grand Ave.) | 312-521-5100 | www.mastrosrestaurants.com

Some of the "best steaks, period" keep this River North chophouse on the Chicago "food radar", as do its "massive" seafood towers and other "decadent" offerings; "professional" staffers are "there when you need them" in the "upscale" bi-level space with chandeliers and white linens, so it all adds up to a "premier" meal – with premier tabs to match.

Maude's Liquor Bar ●ⓏⓂ *French*   25 | 25 | 23 | $48

West Loop | 840 W. Randolph St. (bet. Green & Peoria Sts.) | 312-243-9712 | www.maudesliquorbar.com

"Cozy, yet totally hip", this moderately priced West Loop resto-lounge from Brendan Sodikoff (Au Cheval, Gilt Bar) does "delicious, understated classic French food" (think "buttery snails" and cassoulet) boosted by "inventive" house cocktails; toss in "dark", "romantic" digs and it's an "excellent date spot."

	FOOD	DECOR	SERVICE	COST

Maya Del Sol *Nuevo Latino*
23 | **22** | **22** | **$31**

Oak Park | 144 S. Oak Park Ave. (bet. Pleasant St. & South Blvd.) | 708-358-9800 | www.mayadelsol.com

"Creative fusion" fare and an "unbelievable drink menu" fuel a "festive, relaxed" atmosphere at this affordable Oak Park Nuevo Latino that's especially good for allergic eaters with its many dairy-, gluten- and meat-free offerings; service remains solid despite "constantly busy" environs and "the outdoor area is the place to be in the summer", so those complaining it's just "ok" are in the minority.

M Burger *Burgers*
18 | **8** | **17** | **$12**

Loop | Thompson Ctr. | 100 W. Randolph St. (Clark St.) | 312-578-1478
River North | 5 W. Ontario St. (State St.) | 312-428-3548
Streeterville | 161 E. Huron St. (bet. Michigan Ave. & St. Clair St.) | 312-254-8500
Gold Coast | Water Tower Pl. | 835 N. Michigan Ave. (bet. Chestnut & Pearson Sts.) | 312-867-1549
www.mburgerchicago.com

For "fast food, gourmet-style", this LEYE chow chain has some moaning "mmmm burger", declaring it "very good for what it is" – a "casual" sandwich supplier with "addicting fries" and "great shakes" at a "reasonable price"; eaters who were "expecting a lot more" due to the "hype" say it's "not the best burger in town, but it's not the worst either" and it helps "if you can handle the long wait and have a place to eat it" (some locations have a "few outdoor tables" in summer).

McCormick & Schmick's *Seafood*
19 | **19** | **20** | **$50**

Loop | 1 E. Wacker Dr. (bet. State St. & Wabash Ave.) | 312-923-7226
Gold Coast | 41 E. Chestnut St. (Wabash Ave.) | 312-397-9500
Rosemont | 5320 N. River Rd. (bet. Foster Ave. & Technology Blvd.) | 847-233-3776
Skokie | Westfield Old Orchard | 4999 Old Orchard Ctr. (Skokie Blvd.) | 847-763-9811
Oak Brook | 3001 Butterfield Rd. (bet. Meyers Rd. & Technology Dr.) | 630-571-3700
www.mccormickandschmicks.com

"Straightforward", "simple" seafood dishes, "fast" service and "comfortable" surrounds have many saying you "can't go wrong" at these "upscale but family-friendly" chain links; sure, a few sniff "been to one, been to all" and prices aren't cheap, but it's "convenient for business lunches" and still a "reliable" pick, especially at happy hour.

Meatheads *Burgers*
▽ **21** | **14** | **17** | **$11**

Roscoe Village | 3304 N. Western Ave. (bet. Barry & Belmont Aves.) | 773-525-5300 | www.meatheadsburgers.com

The small Illinois-based burger group gets a city outpost in Roscoe Village, where "tasty" Angus burgers are "made to order" so you can "customize" yours depending on what you "crave"; it also offers foot-long hot dogs, grilled cheese, milkshakes and fries three ways (original, Cajun or chili cheese) in a casual counter-service space with booths, banquettes, a condiment color scheme and local school football scores posted.

	FOOD	DECOR	SERVICE	COST

Mercadito ● *Mexican*

22 | 21 | 17 | $39

River North | 108 W. Kinzie St. (bet. Clark & La Salle Sts.) |
312-329-9555 | www.mercaditorestaurants.com
"Delicious", "schmancy tacos" and other "unique", "upscale" Mexican
dishes go with "killer" cocktails at this "popular River North hangout"; "beautiful people" are part of the "inviting" modern decor, so
despite service that's "somewhat compromised" when "noisy" and
crowded, it's a "cool" place just "to be seen."

Mercat a la Planxa *Spanish*

26 | 24 | 23 | $53

South Loop | Blackstone Hotel | 638 S. Michigan Ave. (Balbo Ave.) |
312-765-0524 | www.mercatchicago.com
Chef Jose Garces' "flavors meld beautifully" at this South Loop
Catalan in the Blackstone Hotel where his "true Barcelona-style tapas"
make for an "excellent" meal, especially when enjoyed with the "great
wines" and house cocktails; tabs aren't low, but the "open, modern
dining room" has a "tasteful" atmosphere, and service is "attentive."

NEW Mercer 113 ●🌣 *American*

- | - | - | E

River North | 113 W. Hubbard St. (bet. Clark & La Salle Sts.) |
312-595-0113 | www.merceronethirteen.com
Since its inception, the casual menu has been upgraded to include a
more upscale assortment of American supper club eats (snails, filet
mignon, Kobe burger) by Michael Lachowicz (Michael) at this River
North resto-lounge; signature craft cocktails remain a highlight amid
earthy-chic digs done up in wood and stone, trippy lighting, murals
of trees, mango-hued booths and a fireplace.

Merlo on Maple *Italian*

25 | 23 | 24 | $58

Gold Coast | 16 W. Maple St. (bet. Dearborn & State Sts.) |
312-335-8200 | www.merlochicago.com
"Consistently excellent" "authentic" cooking reminds of being "at a
house in Italy" at this Gold Coast Italian; it's not inexpensive, but
"attentive" staffers "know the menu well", and the "cozy" "candlelit"
space is just right for a "special night out."

NEW Merlo's Italian Restaurant *Italian*

- | - | - | M

Highland Park | 581 Roger Williams Ave. (bet. Pleasant & St. Johns Aves.) |
847-266-0600 | www.merlosrestaurant.com
Hearty, old-school Italian fare, including pastas (both regular and
gluten-free) and brick-oven pizzas, is the hook at this midrange
Highland Park eatery; the space is decorated with a blackbird theme
and has a convivial bar, plus it's conveniently located near Ravinia.

Mesón Sabika *Spanish*

25 | 23 | 23 | $37

Naperville | 1025 Aurora Ave. (bet. River Rd. & West St.) |
630-983-3000 | www.mesonsabika.com

Tapas Valencia *Spanish*

South Loop | 1530 S. State St. (bet. 15th & 16th Sts.) | 312-842-4444 |
www.tapasvalencia.com
The "amazing variety" of "flavorful", "well-prepared" Spanish tapas
"encourages sampling" at this "solid" Naperville and South Loop

duo tended by "cordial" servers; the suburban locale is set in a "charming old mansion" with an outdoor "garden paradise" for "dining under the stars", while the city post is smaller, and though the "cost can add up quickly", most agree they're still a "go-to."

Mexique ⓜ *Mexican* | 24 | 19 | 22 | $44 |

Noble Square | 1529 W. Chicago Ave. (bet. Armour St. & Ashland Ave.) | 312-850-0288 | www.mexiquechicago.com

For "inventive", "unexpected" fare boasting "flavors you won't taste anywhere else" fans swear by "personable" chef-owner Carlos Gaytan's "delicious" French-influenced Mexican cooking at this "lively", somewhat "out-of-the-way" Noble Square stop; "accommodating service" and a "clean, modern" setting also work in its favor, so bean-counters complaining of "high prices" are drowned out by fans insisting "you won't be disappointed."

NEW Mezcalina *Mexican* | - | - | - | M |

Loop | 333 E. Benton Pl. (Field Blvd.) | 312-240-5000 | www.mezcalina.com
Traditional Oaxacan dishes, Mexican fusion fare and 100-plus varieties of mezcal and tequila hit the table at this moderately priced Loop eatery that shares a space with the Mexican Black Coffee Gallery chain; colorful folk art and indigenous artists' murals grace the walls, while hand-lettered backs adorn the chairs, both inside and out in the seasonal patio area.

M Henry ⓜ *American* | 25 | 19 | 21 | $22 |

Andersonville | 5707 N. Clark St. (Hollywood Ave.) | 773-561-1600 | www.mhenry.net

M Henrietta ⓜ *American*

Edgewater | 1133 W. Granville Ave. (B'way) | 773-761-9700 | www.mhenrietta.com

You'll find a "different selection from the ordinary" at these daytime New Americans in Andersonville and Edgewater, where "enticing" sweet items and "interesting" savory choices make for "fabulous" breakfasts and brunches; "unless you get there early you'll probably have to wait", but affordable prices help, and "once you're seated the service is great."

NEW MH Fish House Ⓢⓜ *Seafood* | - | - | - | E |

Lake Forest | 670 N. Bank Ln. (bet. Deerpath Rd. & Southgate) | 847-234-8802 | www.mhfishhouse.com

Fresh fin fare in classic and creative preps and an entire wine selection available by the glass are the draws at this upscale Lake Forest fish house (little sib to Market House on the Square) set in the former Bank Lane Bistro space; the white-tablecloth setting has a romantic but unstuffy feel, while the year-round porch provides an added asset.

Mia Francesca *Italian* | 24 | 18 | 21 | $38 |

Lakeview | 3311 N. Clark St. (School St.) | 773-281-3310 | www.miafrancesca.com

After more than 20 years this "moderately priced" Lakeview Italian is "still at the top of its game" say fans saluting the "standout", "home-style" "comfort food", "expansive yet approachable wine list" and "professional" service; "tables are close together" in the "vibrant", "bustling" space, so it can get "loud" ("what? I can't hear you"), but adherents still "come back time and time again" for one of "the best all-around deals in town"; P.S. check out the "lovely" patio.

Michael Ⓜ *French*   26 | 22 | 25 | $70

Winnetka | 64 Green Bay Rd. (Winnetka Ave.) | 847-441-3100 | www.restaurantmichael.com

You can enjoy "always great" "classic" French fare "without the hassle of going into the city" at this "white-tablecloth" Winnetka dining room where chef-owner Michael Lachowicz turns out dishes strengthened by an "excellent use of spices and sauces"; "consistently great service" befits the fare, and though it's expensive, fans find the bills "reasonable" given the "fine quality."

Michael Jordan's Steak House ⏺ *Steak*   22 | 23 | 22 | $66

Streeterville | InterContinental Chicago | 505 N. Michigan Ave. (bet. Grand Ave. & Illinois St.) | 312-321-8823 | www.mjshchicago.com

"Warm", "helpful" staffers contribute to the "all-star performance" at this booth-enhanced dining room in Streeterville's InterContinental where supporters cheer a surprisingly "innovative menu for a steakhouse", deeming it "expensive but worth it for a special night out"; reticent refs, however, say "there are better options" in the city, though they concede it's still a "great stop for any fan of the Bulls or Jordan."

Milk & Honey Cafe *American*   22 | 18 | 19 | $15

Wicker Park | 1920 W. Division St. (bet. Damen & Wolcott Aves.) | 773-395-9434 | www.milkandhoneycafe.com

"Grab your morning paper and get a quick bite" at this counter-service Wicker Park American that "tempts" diners with a "simple" affordable menu of breakfast and lunch eats, like "outstanding housemade oatmeal" and "fresh" sandwiches; the "small" space can get "busy", but "friendly" staffers, a "chill vibe" and "welcoming atmosphere" all "encourage you to linger and work on your computer" – though if "noisy", "crowded" environs are "not your idea of a relaxing brunch, go before or after a rush" (or when "it's nice enough to sit outside").

NEW Milt's Barbecue for the Perplexed *BBQ/Kosher*   - | - | - | M

Lakeview | 3411 N. Broadway St. (Roscoe St.) | 773-661-6384 | www.miltsbbq.com

Pork-free barbecue is on offer at this kosher joint in Lakeview that plates house-smoked chow for lunch and dinner (it closes early on Fridays and isn't open on Saturday); decked out in green tiling and distressed wood, the space includes a communal bar, booths and banquettes, and all profits go to charity.

Mindy's Hot Chocolate Ⓜ *American*   24 | 21 | 21 | $33

Bucktown | 1747 N. Damen Ave. (Willow St.) | 773-489-1747 | www.hotchocolatechicago.com

"Mind-blowing" desserts – including "high-quality" hot chocolates that are "heaven" – might get top billing at Mindy Segal's Bucktown

American, but fans say the "upscale" comfort food is "really good" too; throw in "knowledgeable" service and affordable pricing, and it's no surprise the "small, intimate" space can get "kinda crowded."

Mirai Sushi *Japanese*

	25	20	22	$49

Wicker Park | 2020 W. Division St. (bet. Damen & Hoyne Aves.) | 773-862-8500 | www.miraisushi.com

Try it once and you will "return again and again" promise patrons of this "quality" Wicker Park Japanese delivering "excellent", "inventive" sushi plus other "flavorful preparations" to go along with the "snazzy sake, wine and cocktail options"; solid service and a "cool, trendy ambiance" make it a "good date spot", so if a few find tabs "steep", many don't notice, noting they could "eat here every day."

Miramar Bistro *French*

	▽ 17	18	19	$45

Highwood | 301 Waukegan Ave. (Temple Ave.) | 847-433-1078 | www.miramarbistro.com

Paris meets Havana at this somewhat costly Highwood bistro turning out "good" French standards alongside a few Cuban-accented dishes in banquette-enhanced digs with a "great bar" that helps make it a "fun place for drinks"; still, critcs remain unmoved, complaining of "tables on top of each other", "inconsistent" service and "hit-or-miss" fare, even as fans cite "fantastic" outdoor seating that "reminds of Paris."

Mity Nice *American*

	19	15	18	$27

Streeterville | Water Tower Pl. | 835 N. Michigan Ave. (bet. Chestnut & Pearson Sts.) | 312-335-4745 | www.mitynicechicago.com

"Comfort food to the max" is the draw of this "reasonably priced" American inside Streeterville's Water Tower Place mall, where the meal starts with a "cordial" welcome from servers and "buttery" popovers in lieu of a bread basket; while regulars regret the remodel from "woody lodge" to "contemporary coffee shop", others insist it's still a "reliable" "place to pause between shopping."

Mixteco Grill Ⓜ *Mexican*

	27	17	22	$30

Lakeview | 1601 W. Montrose Ave. (Ashland Ave.) | 773-868-1601 | www.mixtecogrill.com

"Interesting, flavorful" fare, including "excellent moles", is what it's about at this midpriced Lakeview Mexican that pairs its "delicious" dishes with a BYO policy ("what could be better?"); the colorful modest space is decorated with framed art, and since it's small, it can get "crowded" fast.

MK *American*

	27	25	26	$72

Near North | 868 N. Franklin St. (bet. Chestnut & Locust Sts.) | 312-482-9179 | www.mkchicago.com

Given the "inventive", "always changing" seasonal menu, "well-prepared" dishes and "excellent" wine list, regulars insist you "won't go wrong" at Michael Kornick's Near North New American; "professional" staffers work the "high-energy" space that's "elegant without being stuffy", so all in all it's a "special-occasion" "go-to" – with "special-occasion" tabs to match.

	FOOD	DECOR	SERVICE	COST

Mon Ami Gabi *French*
23 | 23 | 23 | $44

Lincoln Park | The Belden-Stratford | 2300 N. Lincoln Park W. (Belden Ave.) | 773-348-8886
Oak Brook | Oakbrook Center Mall | 260 Oakbrook Ctr. (Rte. 83) | 630-472-1900
www.monamigabi.com

"A little slice of France" in Chicagoland, this "reasonably priced" French duo offers "solid", "well-prepared" bistro fare via "attentive" service that "breaks the Gallic stereotype"; the outpost in Oak Brook's Center Mall is "delightful" during or "after a day of shopping", and the Lincoln Park locale "fits perfectly" in the "grand, old Parisian-styled" Belden-Stratford building.

NEW The Monarch ● *American*
- | - | - | M

Wicker Park | 1745 W. North Ave. (bet. Paulina & Wood Sts.) | 773-252-6053 | www.monarchchicago.com

The inventive New American menu includes bar bites and dinner options at this midpriced Wicker Park gastropub; a gleaming wood bar dispenses craft cocktails with tongue-in-cheek names inspired by American 'kings', while decor in the upscale tavern setting celebrates monarchs in various forms, from royalty to butterflies.

Monkey's Paw ● *Eclectic*
- | - | - | M

Lincoln Park | 2524 N. Southport Ave. (Lill Ave.) | 773-413-9314 | www.themonkeyspawchicago.com

Specializing in Eclectic farm-to-table grub, this midpriced Lincoln Park gastropub covers all of the comfort-food basics, from mac 'n' cheese to poutine, accompanied by a good list of craft beers and whiskey cocktails; the urban-rustic setting is lined in distressed vintage brick and features seats at the bar, window ledges or a 'library' room filled, appropriately, with vintage books and leather armchairs.

Montarra Ⓜ *American*
∇ 28 | 27 | 28 | $44

Algonquin | 1491 S. Randall Rd. (County Line Rd.) | 847-458-0505 | www.montarra.com

An "ultimate date place", this Algonquin New American is considered "worth a visit" for its "generally excellent", "beautifully presented" dishes matched by equally strong service; despite an "easily missable strip-mall" locale, its interior is modern with high ceilings, and prices are moderate.

Morsel *American*
- | - | - | M

Rogers Park | 1406 W. Morse Ave. (Glenwood Ave.) | 773-274-0700 | www.morselchicago.com

Across the street from the Rogers Park Morse El station, this midpriced American serves modern comfort fare, plus cocktails and weekly specials (e.g. all-you-can-eat mussels); the spacious setting has high ceilings and industrial touches, plus a full-service vintage bar.

Morton's The Steakhouse *Steak*
23 | 21 | 23 | $82

Loop | 65 E. Wacker Pl. (bet. Michigan & Wabash Aves.) | 312-201-0410
Gold Coast | Newberry Plaza | 1050 N. State St. (Maple St.) | 312-266-4820

(continued)

Morton's The Steakhouse

Rosemont | 9525 Bryn Mawr Ave. (River Rd.) | 847-678-5155
Northbrook | 699 Skokie Blvd. (Dundee Rd.) | 847-205-5111
Schaumburg | 1470 McConnor Pkwy. (bet. Golf & Meacham Rds.) | 847-413-8771
Naperville | 1751 Freedom Dr. (Diehl Rd.) | 630-577-1372
www.mortons.com

"Pack your extra stomach" (and "bring your expense account") to best "feast on meat" at this "king of steak" (with locations area-wide, including the "historic" State Street original) where "delicious, juicy" chops and "highly recommended" sides are served in "clubby" settings right out of *Mad Men* (some locales have been given modern renovations); while there's some debate as to whether it's "nothing short of spectacular" or "not quite on the same level" as its competitors, most agree it's an all-around "solid, consistent" pick.

Moto ⊠Ⓜ *Eclectic*   26 | 24 | 27 | $228

West Loop | 945 W. Fulton Mkt. (Sangamon St.) | 312-491-0058 | www.motorestaurant.com

"Molecular wow" sums up this minimalist West Loop Eclectic where chef-owner Homaro Cantu takes guests on a "true dining adventure" courtesy of an "inventive" multicourse tasting menu filled with "ingenious" dishes presented like "works of art"; sure, big-ticket prices are part of the experience, but "courteous" servers boost its "special-occasion" appeal.

NEW Mott Street ⊠Ⓜ *Asian*   - | - | - | M

Wicker Park | 1401 N. Ashland Ave. (Blackhawk St.) | 773-687-9977 | www.mottstreetchicago.com

Asian fusion sharing plates and seasonal craft cocktails are the draw at this midpriced Ruxbin spin-off in Wicker Park; the corner spot features a bright-red paint job, funky salvaged furniture and seating at the bar, communal tables and outdoors.

Mr. Beef ⊉ *Sandwiches*   24 | 7 | 14 | $11

River North | 666 N. Orleans St. (bet. Erie & Huron Sts.) | 312-337-8500 | www.mrbeefonorleans.com

"Loyal devotees" seeking "authentic" "Chicago street food done well" dig this "real-deal" River North "mecca" for its "damn good", "gut-filling" sandwiches at bargain prices; ok, some snark it "looks like it should be condemned" and say service seems to be "declining", but hey, you're "there to have a great Italian beef, not a dining experience"; P.S. cash-only and on weekends it reopens at 10:30 PM to serve late-night diners (till 4 AM Friday and 5 AM Saturday).

Mt. Everest Restaurant *Indian/Nepalese*   21 | 16 | 18 | $26

Evanston | 630 Church St. (bet. Chicago & Orrington Aves.) | 847-491-1069 | www.mteverestrestaurant.com

"Nicely prepared" Indian plates satisfy "all sort of palates" and the "flavorful" Nepali dishes are "an added attraction" at this "reasonably priced" Evanston eatery where devotees say "go with a group in order to sample many dishes" or try the "most excellent" lunch buffet "full of tasty choices"; "prompt" service makes up for unremarkable decor, and imbibers who feel the "bar selection leaves something to be desired" are advised to try the "don't-miss" beers.

NEW Municipal Bar & Dining Company ● *American*

| - | - | - | M |

River North | 216 W. Ohio St. (bet. Franklin & Wells Sts.) | 312-834-3409 | www.municipalchicago.com

There's a casual, studenty feel to this River North hipster sports bar serving a range of midpriced New American fare including an eclectic mix of apps plus salads, sandwiches, flatbreads and more; the trendy, dark setting, with unadorned tables and exposed-brick walls, includes a buzzing basement bar that stays open late.

NEW M Vie Ⓢ Ⓜ *American*

| - | - | - | M |

Noble Square | 1372 W. Grand Ave. (Noble St.) | 312-265-0159 | www.mviechicago.com

Traditional American fare with a Southern accent brings a comfort quotient to Noble Square at this casual-chic spot; inside has a honey onyx backlit bar featuring classic cocktails, and tabs are moderate.

Nabuki *Japanese*

| ▽ 24 | 22 | 21 | $46 |

Hinsdale | 18 E. First St. (bet. Garfield Ave. & Washington St.) | 630-654-8880 | www.nabukihinsdale.com

"Finally, city-quality sushi in the 'burbs" exult enthusiasts of this "high-end" Hinsdale Japanese, where "very solid", "elegant" eats are delivered by "involved" staffers amid "colorful" decor; some wish for less "pricey" tabs and "a little more legroom", but admit it's "worth a trip."

Nacional 27 Ⓢ *Nuevo Latino*

| 22 | 22 | 21 | $46 |

River North | 325 W. Huron St. (bet. Franklin & Orleans Sts.) | 312-664-2727 | www.n27chicago.com

"The flavors of South and Central America come alive" at this contemporary River North Nuevo Latino where "well-prepared" dishes are "great for sharing", servers "take the time to explain it all" and "you can dance the calories off after dinner" with music from DJs (Fridays and Saturdays); while fussers who "expected better" say "save your money", fans who "love" the "tasty" drinks and "lovely sidewalk patio" say it's a "reliable" choice "for something different."

Naf Naf Grill *Mediterranean/Mideastern*

| 22 | 16 | 18 | $13 |

NEW Loop | 309 W. Washington St. (Franklin St.) | 312-251-9000 Ⓢ
NEW Rosemont | 10433 Touhy (Chestnut St.) | 847-294-0700
Niles | 5716 W. Touhy Ave. (Austin Ave.) | 847-588-1500
Aurora | 4430 Fox Valley Center Dr. (bet. McCoy Dr. & New York St.) | 630-499-1700
Naperville | 1739 Freedom Dr. (bet. Diehl Rd. & Independence Ave.) | 630-904-7200
www.nafnafgrill.com

A "simple" menu of "solid, approachable" Middle Eastern–Mediterranean eats like falafel, kebabs and "pillow-soft" housemade pitas make for a "good change of pace" at this "fast-food" chainlet; ok, so the decor is "nonexistent", but no one's complaining about the "reasonable" prices.

Naha 🗷 American   26 | 23 | 25 | $74

River North | 500 N. Clark St. (Illinois St.) | 312-321-6242 | www.naha-chicago.com

Carrie Nahabedian has a "track record" of providing "consistently excellent", "high-quality" meals at this River North New American where many dishes feature "Mediterranean influences" and get a boost from "inventive" combinations of flavors; "top-line" service and "Zen-like decor" further justify the "pricey" tabs and also help cement its status as a "fine-dining favorite."

Namo Thai   - | - | - | I

North Center/St. Ben's | 3900 N. Lincoln Ave. (Byron St.) | 773-327-8818 | www.namothaicuisine.com

Modern Thai dishes like lobster pad Thai, tamarind lamb and softshell crab curry join the classics at this hip, affordable North Center BYO also serving an intriguing list of nonalcoholic beverages; a rustic-chic vibe is created by high ceilings with fans and ductwork, wood panels inscribed with encouraging Thai words and basket wall hangings and light fixtures.

Nando Milano Trattoria 🅼 Italian   - | - | - | M

Wicker Park | 2114 W. Division St. (bet. Hoyne Ave. & Leavitt St.) | 773-486-2636 | www.nandomilano.com

A concise menu of Italian fare, including housemade pastas and daily specials, is served at this midpriced Wicker Parker; reclaimed wood and exposed brick decorate the cozy, rustic space, and while it used to be BYO, it now has a full bar.

Native Foods Café Vegan   23 | 19 | 23 | $15

Loop | 218 S. Clark St. (Quincy St.) | 312-332-6332 🗷
Lakeview | 1023 W. Belmont Ave. (Kenmore Ave.) | 773-549-4904
Wicker Park | 1484 N. Milwaukee Ave. (Honore St.) | 773-489-8480
www.nativefoods.com

"Gorge yourself without the guilt" at this California-based chain, a "wholesome" "addition to Chicago's vegan" scene known for "creative" meatless fare that's both "flavorful and satisfying"; "enthusiasm" is the hallmark of the "personally invested staff", and digs are generally "pleasant" too.

Near Restaurant ●🗷🅼 Italian   - | - | - | M

Barrington | Barrington Commons | 108 Barrington Commons Court (bet. Hough Rd. & Main St.) | 847-382-1919 | www.near-restaurant.com

An Italian-born chef who has cooked at Schwa and Spiaggia is behind this Barrington Italian where passed-down family recipes are revived on a menu of shared plates, pastas and entrees; the setting is casual and modern with a granite bar and black-and-white photography, and they're open late for the area.

Nellcôte ● *American*
19 | 24 | 17 | $50

West Loop | 833 W. Randolph St. (Green St.) | 855-635-5268 |
www.nellcoterestaurant.com

You can "be seen" at this "chic, sexy" West Loop New American
where the "stunning" surrounds set the stage for upscale pizzas and
"pretty good" small plates from chef Jared Van Camp (Old Town
Social); "work-of-art" cocktails and "interesting" wines enhance its
"date-night" appeal while also taking the sting out of somewhat
spendy tabs and sometimes "noisy" weekend conditions.

NEW Nepal House *Indian/Nepalese*
- | - | - | M

South Loop | 1301 S. Michigan Ave. (13th St.) | 312-922-0601 |
www.nepalhouseonline.com

Momo (dumplings) and Thalis (combination plates) are among the
hard-to-find Nepalese offerings at this affordable South Loop spot
from the Chicago Curry House crowd that also does traditional Indian
fare like samosas, tikka masala and tandoori dishes; beverages run
from beer and wine to teas and lassi drinks in a warm setting with
white tablecloths, leather booths, framed artwork and Nepali
background music.

New England Seafood Company Fish Market *Seafood*
▽ 25 | 13 | 22 | $47

Lakeview | 3341 N. Lincoln Ave. (bet. Roscoe & School Sts.) |
773-871-3474 | www.neseafoodcompany.com

Lobster traps, netting and a fish tank set the tone at this "fast
and friendly" East Coast–style "seafood shack" inside a Lakeview
market where the fin fare is flown in daily and the moderately
priced menu features chowders, baked fish dinners, fried combos and sandwiches ("what a lobster roll!"); the tiny space is
BYO and counter-service only, and since it doesn't take reservations, you may want to "get there early."

New Rebozo *Mexican*
- | - | - | M

NEW River North | 46 E. Superior St. (bet. Rush St. & Wabash Ave.) |
312-202-9141
Oak Park | 1116 Madison St. (Harlem Ave.) | 708-445-0370 ⊠
www.newrebozo.com

You can get everything from tacos to more upscale, "original" dishes,
including "oh-my-god moles", at this casual Oak Park Mexican (with
a newer River North sequel); "amiable" staffers and affordable prices
are other reasons locals insist "you have to go."

Next Ⓜ *Eclectic*
29 | 26 | 29 | $175

West Loop | 953 W. Fulton Mkt. (bet. Morgan & Sangamon Sts.) |
312-226-0858 | www.nextrestaurant.com

Part "foodie dinner theater", part "culinary adventure", Grant Achatz's
West Loop Eclectic presents a "simply mind-blowing", often-changing
themed tasting menu prepared with an "unmatched" level of detail
and "impeccably presented" by an "exemplary", "professional" staff
that earns top Service honors in Chicago; the modern, high-style
space provides a fitting backdrop, and given the "stunningly good"

offerings, sky-high prices barely register – just note you'll need to score a "hard-to-get" online ticket in order to go.

Next Door Bistro ⓂＭ *American/Italian*   22 | 15 | 22 | $41

Northbrook | 250 Skokie Blvd. (bet. Dundee & Lake Cook Rds.) | 847-272-1491 | www.nextdoorbistro.com

"Regulars" head to this casual Northbrook Italian-American for an "extensive" menu of "delicious" fare ferried by "friendly, quick" servers; holdouts hint "preferred customers" often get better treatment, but "great prices" help take the edge off.

Niche ⓈＭ *American*   ▽ 26 | 25 | 27 | $62

Geneva | 14 S. Third St. (bet. James & State Sts.) | 630-262-1000 | www.nichegeneva.com

"Attentive", "personable" service, "wonderful" New American cuisine and a "stellar" selection of wines highlighting limited batch offerings add up to a "fine-dining" experience at this Geneva "must-try"; add in "relaxed, inviting" surroundings and it's a "great option for special-occasion or romantic dining" – just "fill your wallet" in preparation.

Nick's Fishmarket Ⓢ *Seafood*   24 | 22 | 23 | $60

Rosemont | O'Hare International Ctr. | 10275 W. Higgins Rd. (Mannheim Rd.) | 847-298-8200

Nick's Fishmarket Grill & Bar Ⓢ *Seafood*

River North | Merchandise Mart | 222 W. Merchandise Mart Plaza (bet. Orleans & Wells Sts.) | 312-621-0200
www.nicksfishmarketchicago.com

Diners "craving seafood" choose this duo for "fabulously fresh fish" and "choices galore"; the River North outpost has urban stylings and a blue-lit bar, while the Rosemont longtimer looks more "old-school", and though you'll "pay a lot" at both, solid service helps compensate.

Nightwood Ⓜ *American*   27 | 23 | 25 | $41

Pilsen | 2119 S. Halsted St. (21st St.) | 312-526-3385 | www.nightwoodrestaurant.com

You may find yourself "close to licking the plate" at this moderate Pilsen New American where chef Jason Vincent's "innovative", "well-prepared" dishes "celebrate" seasonal ingredients and are augmented by handcrafted cocktails made with housemade mixers and small-batch spirits; rustic exposed brick features in the "hip" digs, and there's a "nice outdoor patio" too.

90 Miles Cuban Cafe *Cuban*   23 | 18 | 21 | $19

Lakeview | 3101 N. Clybourn Ave. (Barry Ave.) | 773-248-2822
Logan Square | 2540 W. Armitage Ave. (Rockwell St.) | 773-227-2822
www.90milescubancafe.com

For "reliably good" Cuban , including some of the "best" ropa vieja around and pressed sandwiches that "rock hard", fans hit up these no-frills BYOs; Lakeview is tiny, while Logan Square is larger (and provides DIY sangria and mojito mixers if you bring the booze), and both have outdoor seats, generally "pleasant" staffers and low tabs.

Niu Japanese
Fusion Lounge *Asian*

24	22	21	$35

Streeterville | 332 E. Illinois St. (bet. Columbus Dr. & McClurg Ct.) | 312-527-2888 | www.niusushi.com
Diners are "psyched" by the "creative flavor combinations", "quality" sushi and "interesting" cocktails at this affordable Streeterville Asian; "friendly" staffers work the modern space, and the theater-adjacent location makes it a pick "before or after the movies."

NoMI Kitchen *American*

26	27	26	$72

Gold Coast | Park Hyatt Chicago | 800 N. Michigan Ave., 7th fl. (bet. Chicago Ave. & Pearson St.) | 312-239-4030 | www.parkchicago.hyatt.com
You can "relax and get away from the loudness of the city" at this "expensive" but "worth it" New American in the Gold Coast's Park Hyatt where local ingredients feature heavily on the "fantastic" menu, which includes "incredibly fresh" sushi too; the upscale-casual space with "beautiful views" overlooking Michigan Avenue and a "delightful" roof garden works well for "date night" or "business meetings", and an "excellent" staff adds to the appeal.

Noodles by Takashi
Yagihashi ●🗷 *Japanese*

▽ 22	14	19	$16

Loop | Macy's | 111 N. State St. (bet. Randolph & Washington Sts.) | 312-781-4483
This quick-serve Takashi spin-off at the upscale Macy's food court in the Loop is the "perfect" place to sample "delicious" Japanese ramen "without the high price"; the slim menu also includes a few other items, like fried rice and potstickers, and even if the nondescript shopping-mall setting isn't much, at least it guarantees "cheap" tabs.

Nookies *American*

20	14	20	$17

Edgewater | 1100 W. Bryn Mawr Ave. (Winthrop Ave.) | 773-516-4188
Old Town | 1746 N. Wells St. (bet. Eugenie St. & Lincoln Ave.) | 312-337-2454
Nookies Too *American*
Lincoln Park | 2114 N. Halsted St. (bet. Dickens & Webster Aves.) | 773-327-1400
Nookies Tree ● *American*
Lakeview | 3334 N. Halsted St. (Buckingham Pl.) | 773-248-9888 www.nookiesrestaurants.net
A "huge variety" of "classic" American "comfort food" keeps "everyone from twentysomethings to big families" "returning to sample more" at these "friendly" BYO "staples" famous for "monster" breakfasts and lunches at the "right prices"; they're especially popular on weekends, but "unpretentious" service ensures "long lines move quickly"; P.S. Lincoln Park and Lakeview are open 24 hours on

Fridays and Saturdays, while Old Town and Edgewater (which has a full bar) also serve dinner.

Noon-O-Kabab *Persian* | 24 | 19 | 20 | $26

Albany Park | 4661 N. Kedzie Ave. (Leland Ave.) | 773-279-8899 | www.noonokabab.com

"Grilled kebabs are the main attraction" at this Albany Park Persian, though it's "great for vegetarians as well", with Middle Eastern salads and other "satisfying" vittles offered at a "good price"; service can be "a tiny bit slow" when "busy", but is otherwise "warm" and "friendly" in the "cozy" space, so most ultimately qualify it "a true find."

Nori *Japanese* | ▽ 24 | 18 | 19 | $25

Lakeview | 954 W. Diversey Pkwy. (Sheffield Ave.) | 773-904-1000
Rogers Park | 1237 W. Devon Ave. (Magnolia Ave.) | 773-262-5216
Wicker Park | 1393 N. Milwaukee Ave. (Wood St.) | 773-292-9992
www.norichicago.com

"Delicious" and "creative rolls" including the "amazing dragon roll" top the menu at this "busy" Japanese threesome; if a few feel the "decor leaves much to be desired", "efficient" service helps distract, especially since BYO further lessens already "reasonable" tabs (though the full-service Lakeview branch has a corkage fee).

North Pond Ⓜ *American* | 26 | 27 | 25 | $74

Lincoln Park | 2610 N. Cannon Dr. (bet. Diversey & Fullerton Pkwys.) | 773-477-5845 | www.northpondrestaurant.com

Chef Bruce Sherman's "fabulously creative" seasonal cooking plus a "lovely", "romantic" location inside Lincoln Park and "excellent" views of North Pond are all a part of the "magical" experience at this "upscale" New American; "accommodating" service is another reason it's "perfect for a celebration" – and why it's easier to "get over the price."

Oak Tree Bakery & Restaurant *American* | 16 | 15 | 16 | $24

Gold Coast | Bloomingdale's Bldg. | 900 N. Michigan Ave. (bet. Delaware Pl. & Walton St.) | 312-751-1988 | www.oaktreechicago.com

An "oasis of quiet" since 1991, this midpriced Gold Coast American woos shoppers and "ladies who lunch" with "reliable" "comfort food" offered until 5 PM daily; "the seating is comfortable" too, so even if the "years have taken their toll", it's still a "pleasant stop" while "spending on the Magnificent Mile."

Oceanique Ⓩ *French/Seafood* | 25 | 20 | 24 | $69

Evanston | 505 Main St. (bet. Chicago & Hinman Aves.) | 847-864-3435 | www.oceanique.com

"Purveying foodie fare" since 1989, this "upscale" Evanston "fish mecca" still "dazzles" with "expertly prepared" New French dishes bolstered by an "exceptional" wine list; "fine service" (and "expensive" tabs) adds to the "first-class" feel, and those who say the decor could use "some improvement" will be cheered by a planned renovation (which will result in some menu changes too).

NEW Oiistar M *Japanese* 　　　－ | － | － | I

Wicker Park | 1385 N. Milwaukee Ave. (bet. Paulina & Wood Sts.) | 773-360-8791 | www.oiistar.com

Fusion-y, affordable ramens built on 18-hour broths are joined by Japanese snacks like steamed buns and tempura, plus draft brews, at this minimal modern Wicker Park noodle shop; projection-screen cartoons and clubby music entertain eaters amid birch walls, distressed wood benches and industrial ductwork.

NEW Old Fifth ⑤M *Eclectic* 　　　－ | － | － | M

Near West | 1027 W. Madison St. (bet. Aberdeen & Morgan Sts.) | 312-374-1672 | www.oldfifth.com

Chef-driven gastropub grub like thin-crust and double-decker pizza, beef and bacon sliders, hefeweizen hummus and loaded fries with cheddar and oxtail goes down well with an expansive whiskey list (including flights), brews and craft cocktails at this West Loop hang; the group-friendly wood and brick tavern setting has a casual vibe with sports on TVs and a small lounge area.

Old Jerusalem Restaurant *Mideastern* 　20 | 9 | 17 | $18

Old Town | 1411 N. Wells St. (bet. North Ave. & Schiller St.) | 312-944-0459 | www.oldjerusalemchicago.com

"Really basic, but well-made" Middle Eastern chow is "always a value" at this "reasonably priced" Old Town longtimer tended by "friendly" staffers; just "don't look up from your plate" because the "harsh lighting" "doesn't make your date look too good" warn diners who prefer outdoor seating or getting takeout.

Old Town Pour House ● *Pub Food* 　∇ 14 | 18 | 14 | $30

Old Town | 1419 N. Wells St. (bet. Burton Pl. & Schiller St.) | 312-477-2800 | www.oldtownpourhouse.com

An "incredible" beer list, consisting of a seemingly "endless" selection of tap brews, is the "focus" of this Old Town hang, though fans deem the upscale pub grub (pork belly, ahi tuna) "pretty solid" too; the digs also "sell the place", with "huge" TVs, front windows that open to sidewalk seating, a long bar and a grand staircase leading up to a loungey mezzanine.

Old Town Social ● *American* 　21 | 19 | 16 | $32

Old Town | 455 W. North Ave. (Cleveland Ave.) | 312-266-2277 | www.oldtownsocial.com

"Great for happy hours", "birthdays" or "big groups", this midpriced Old Town haunt turns out "tasty" and "original" New American fare, including "very good" charcuterie and a "delicious" brunch, bolstered by a "wide variety" of brews that make it a "beer lover's paradise"; the wood-accented "modern" digs have a "sick TV setup", and toward the end of the evening they "turn the lights down" and it "turns into more of a bar/lounge", especially on weekends when it can get "crazy packed."

	FOOD	DECOR	SERVICE	COST

NEW Oliver's Cafe Ⓜ *American/Eclectic* — | — | — | M

Bridgeport | 451 W. 31st St. (bet. Canal St. & Normal Ave.) | 312-791-1230 | www.oliverscafechicago.com

New American and Eclectic global fusion flavors issue from the kitchen of this midpriced Bridgeport bistro and BYO; the intimate interior glows with apricot walls and golden lighting, and the walls are dotted with artwork from the namesake chef-owner's personal collection.

Ombra *Italian* — | — | — | M

Andersonville | 5310 N. Clark St. (bet. Berwyn & Summerdale Aves.) | 773-506-8600 | www.barombra.com

Part of sibling restaurant Acre has been converted into this Andersonville cicchetti bar serving small Italian plates that are meant to be shared; as for the interior, expect a clever amalgamation of salvaged materials, like vintage newspaper wallpaper and leather jacket–covered seats, plus rustic wood accents and an aerial view of Florence suspended from the ceiling in panels.

NEW Oon *American* — | — | — | E

West Loop | 802 W. Randolph St. (Halsted St.) | 312-929-2555 | www.oonrestaurant.com

Matt Eversman (ex Saigon Sisters) crafts creative, upscale New American plates featuring Southeast Asian underpinnings (pho with foie gras, pork belly spring rolls) at this pricey West Loop entry; the casual space has big windows overlooking Randolph Street and vibrant abstract art, and the bar puts forth selections including sake cocktails.

Opart Thai House *Thai* 24 | 17 | 21 | $20

Lincoln Square | 4658 N. Western Ave. (Leland Ave.) | 773-989-8517
South Loop | 1906 S. State St. (Archer Ave.) | 312-567-9898
www.opartthai.com

"Authentically prepared dishes are aromatic and flavorful" at this Thai duo in Lincoln Square and the South Loop where "converts" also preach about the "nuanced spicing" and all around "delicious", "quality" fare; "decor is nothing to look at", but with "relatively inexpensive tabs" and solid service, loyalists still find it "hard to resist" and feel "lucky to live close" by; P.S. Lincoln Square is BYO.

Orange *Eclectic* 17 | 13 | 17 | $18

Lincoln Park | 2413 N. Clark St. (bet. Arlington Pl. & Fullerton Pkwy.) | 773-549-7833
Roscoe Village | 2011 W. Roscoe St. (bet. Damen & Seeley Aves.) | 773-248-0999
www.orangerestaurantchicago.com

"The creativity works" at these Eclectic "masters of breakfast" known for "tasty pancake flights", "funky, freakin' good" frushi (fruit sushi) and other "kooky" offerings (lunch is more "ordinary") served alongside the "gulpable" orange-infused coffee; occasionally "frantic" service and digs that "seem decorated with the leftovers from a low-rent basement" don't deter supporters who make it a "favorite non-high-end" option.

Original Gino's East *Pizza*   22 | 17 | 17 | $23

River North | 633 N. Wells St. (Ontario St.) | 312-988-4200 |
www.ginoseast.com
Streeterville | 162 E. Superior St. (bet. Fairbanks Ct. & Michigan Ave.) |
312-266-3337 | www.ginoseast.com
Lincoln Park | 2801 N. Lincoln Ave. (Racine Ave.) | 773-327-3737 |
www.ginoseastlakeview.com
O'Hare Area | 8725 W. Higgins Rd. (East River Rd.) |
773-444-2244 | www.ginosonhiggins.com
Libertyville | Cambridge Plaza | 820 S. Milwaukee Ave. (bet. Condell &
Valley Park Drs.) | 847-362-1300 | www.ginoseast.com
Barrington | 352 Kelsey Rd. (Northwest Hwy.) | 847-381-8300 |
www.ginoseast.com
Rolling Meadows | 1321 W. Golf Rd. (bet. Algonquin Rd. & Meijer Dr.) |
847-364-6644 | www.ginoseastrollingmeadows.com
St. Charles | Tin Cup Pass Shopping Ctr. | 1590 E. Main St. (Tyler Rd.) |
630-513-1311 | www.ginoseast.com
Wheaton | 315 W. Front St. (bet. West St. & Wheaton Ave.) |
630-588-1010 | www.ginoseast.com
In a city with the "best pizza in the solar system", this "reliable" pie
chain makes its mark with "true Chicago-style pizza" on "standout"
cornmeal crusts; service can veer from "helpful" and "attentive" to
a bit "lacking", and a few say it's just "ok", but many argue "there's
a reason" it's often "packed"; P.S. many locales feature graffitied
walls, so "remember to take a sharpie."

Osteria Via Stato *Italian*   23 | 19 | 21 | $40

River North | 620 N. State St. (Ontario St.) | 312-642-8450

Pizzeria Via Stato *Pizza*

River North | 620 N. State St. (Ontario St.) | 312-337-6634
www.osteriaviastato.com
"Well-presented", "consistently good" "Italian comfort food" available
à la carte or in a prix fixe "family-style" option draws diners to this
"lively" River North osteria in "pleasant", archway-enhanced environs, while "über-thin" pizza with "toppings to please kid and grown-
up tastes" alike makes for a "relaxing" meal at the adjacent pie parlor
(open for lunch too); service is "accommodating" and most have no
complaints about the tabs, so both will "easily satisfy a group."

Over Easy Café Ⓜ *American*   27 | 22 | 25 | $16

Ravenswood | 4943 N. Damen Ave. (bet. Ainslie & Argyle Sts.) |
773-506-2605 | www.overeasycafechicago.com
"Traditional and contemporary breakfast and brunch favorites" draw
'em in to this Ravenswood BYO, where the "wonderful" American
eats feature "interesting", "gourmet" twists; the "inviting" space is
small, and since it's "typically crowded on weekends" lines can be
"long", but luckily the "attentive" staff works "fast."

NEW Ovie Bar & Grill ◐ *American*   - | - | - | M

Loop | Ogilvie Transportation Ctr. | 120 N. Canal St. (bet. Randolph St. &
Washington Blvd.) | 312-902-1111 | www.oviebarandgrill.com
Ogilvie Station debuts another drinking and dining destination with
this self-referential spot where you can sample charcuterie and oys-

ters while imbibing craft cocktails and global wines, indulge in a full sit-down meal of midpriced New American cuisine or grab a quick sandwich to-go; smart neutral environs with industrial ductwork and white tablecloths create an upscale urban vibe, and the soundtrack comes courtesy of the rumbling Metra trains.

Owen & Engine ◐ *British* 24 | 23 | 24 | $32

Logan Square | 2700 N. Western Ave. (Schubert Ave.) | 773-235-2930 | www.owenandengine.com

The "outrageously good fish 'n' chips" and other "delicious" offerings are "some of the best high-concept pub food in town" say fans of this midpriced Logan Square Brit that also "makes a splash" with an "unmatched" selection of cask-conditioned and craft brews; "knowledgeable" staffers include some of the "friendliest, funnest bartenders" and the cozy wood-accented space has an upstairs area with a fireplace, so don't be surprised if it's "crazy crowded."

Oysy *Japanese* 22 | 20 | 20 | $32

River North | 50 E. Grand Ave. (bet. Rush St. & Wabash Ave.) | 312-670-6750
South Loop | 888 S. Michigan Ave. (9th St.) | 312-922-1127
www.oysysushi.com

"Quality sushi, sashimi and other Japanese fare" find favor at this "trendy" South Loop and River North twosome with "really pretty rolls, inventive combos" and "great lunch specials"; the "spare" "modern" space gets a boost from "polite" service, and with "reasonable prices", it's "highly recommended" "for a date or a group."

NEW Paladar *Cuban* - | - | - | M

Logan Square | 2252 N. Western Ave. (Belden Ave.) | 773-252-4747 | www.paladarchicago.com

Affordable Cuban cooking (small plates, pressed sandwiches and classic entrees) is paired with rum, rum and more rum (over 30 available) at this Bucktown haunt; the dark wood–enhanced storefront space has booth seating, communal tables and an outdoor patio, and family photos from the owner lend a warm, personal touch.

The Palm *Steak* 24 | 21 | 23 | $73

Loop | Swissôtel Chicago | 323 E. Wacker Dr. (Columbus Dr.) | 312-616-1000 | www.thepalm.com

"An old standby", this Loop link of the "old-fashioned" chophouse chain "continues to shine" with "soft, juicy filets", "huge lobsters" and other "consistently well-executed fare" delivered in "warm" surrounds enhanced by caricatures of local celebrities; "professional", "adult" service helps "make every meal an occasion", so regulars say bring your "expense account" and "eat like no one is watching."

Pappadeaux
Seafood Kitchen *Cajun/Seafood* 23 | 22 | 22 | $38

Westmont | 921 Pasquinelli Dr. (Oakmont Ln.) | 630-455-9846 | www.pappadeaux.com

"When you can't go to NOLA" head here suggest fans of this affordable Westmont seafood specialist where the "flavorful" dishes feature a "nice Cajun kick", "making you feel like being in the Big Easy"; "fast and friendly" service helps create a "positive vibe" in the spacious, wood-accented environs, and when it gets too "crowded" and "noisy", a seasonal patio provides an escape.

Paris Club ● *French* — 20 | 20 | 19 | $43

River North | 59 W. Hubbard St. (bet. Clark & Dearborn Sts.) | 312-595-0800 | www.parisclubchicago.com
A "chic" "urban" space "packed with beautiful young people" provides the backdrop for chef Jean Joho's "approachable", "well-executed" "bistro classics" at this "relatively affordable" River North Frenchie from the brothers Melman; a few critics call it "more club than Paris" and say "sightseeing" is the real "draw", but that apparently doesn't matter to most since it's "always jumping."

Park Grill *American* — 19 | 19 | 18 | $43

Loop | Millennium Park | 11 N. Michigan Ave. (bet. Madison & Washington Sts.) | 312-521-7275 | www.parkgrillchicago.com
"You can't beat the setting" at this Loop American in "gorgeous" Millennium Park where the "broad" menu of "remarkably good" fare gets a boost from "views of skaters at the rink" in winter and "people-watching" on the "delightful" patio in summer; service gets mixed marks ("attentive" vs. "spotty"), and critics who fault merely "decent" fare and "overpriced" tabs leave it to the "tourists", but plenty of pleased patrons note just being there "is a thrill."

NEW Park Tavern ● *American* — - | - | - | M

Rosemont | MB Financial Park at Rosemont | 5433 Park Pl. (bet. Balmoral & Bryn Mawr Aves.) | 847-349-5151 | www.parktavernrosemont.com
Near West | 1645 W. Jackson St. (Paulina St.) | 312-243-4276 | www.parktavernchicago.com
This gastropub duo serves creative, globally influenced New American bar food (house-smoked meats, tacos, sandwiches) plus craft cocktails and 40 brews with self-serve table taps; Near West has stonework and rustic surfaces, a big bar and a seasonal beer garden, and Rosemont has loads of TVs and a rooftop lounge.

NEW Parson's Chicken & Fish ● *American* — - | - | - | I

Logan Square | 2952 W. Armitage Ave. (bet. Humboldt Blvd. & Richmond St.) | 773-384-3333 | www.parsonschickenandfish.com
Not your basic fried food shack, this affordable Logan Square American from the Longman & Eagle crowd serves raw (sushi, oysters), fresh (salads, sandwiches) and fried fare (chicken and fish by the bucket) with crafty cocktails including a Negroni slush, canned beers and seasonal sodas; a '70s-inspired setting pumps out music of the era in a casual space with a vintage El Camino car and a large patio.

Parthenon *Greek* — 21 | 15 | 18 | $33

Greektown | 314 S. Halsted St. (bet. Jackson Blvd. & Van Buren St.) | 312-726-2407 | www.theparthenon.com
For a bit of "the Med translocated to Halsted", fans "take a crowd" to this circa-1968 Greektown "standard" to sup on "delicious" "tra-

ditional" Hellenic fare, including the "must-eat" "flaming" *saganaki* (cheese); "hustling" servers are "friendly", and you get "a lot for little money", so even if the decor doesn't rate highly, supporters say that's the price you pay for "soul."

Pasteur M *Vietnamese* ▽ 16 | 18 | 16 | $31

Edgewater | 5525 N. Broadway St. (bet. Bryn Mawr & Catalpa Aves.) | 773-728-4800 | www.pasteurrestaurantchicago.com

After a menu change (which may not be reflected in the Food score) fusion fare is out and straight Vietnamese is in at this Edgewater "gem" where the midpriced menu includes plenty of traditional dishes accompanied by exotic craft cocktails; the "comfortable" space features chic neutrals, white tablecloths, wicker and leather chairs, plush banquettes and gyroscope-inspired chandeliers.

Patron's Hacienda ● *Mexican/Steak* - | - | - | M

River North | 316 W. Erie St. (bet. Franklin & Orleans Sts.) | 312-642-2400 | www.patronschicago.com

Expect moderately priced Mexican meals and chophouse favorites (with options for vegetarians), signature margaritas and a massive tequila menu (including flights) at this River North arrival; the high-ceilinged, sports-barlike digs feature a kaleidoscope of color, funky furnishings, wall hangings, murals and multiple TVs.

Peacock Indian Restaurant *Indian* ▽ 18 | 15 | 17 | $25

Vernon Hills | Fashion Square Shopping Ctr. | 700 N. Milwaukee Ave. (Townline Rd.) | 847-816-3100 | www.peacockindianrestaurant.com

This Vernon Hills Indian has been turning out traditional tandoor dishes, curries and vegetarian options – along with chai, sweet or salty lassi drinks and selections from a full bar – since 1992; the affordable shopping-center spot serves family-style dinner and a generous lunch buffet, in a refined setting that's conversation-friendly.

The Peasantry M *American* - | - | - | M

Lincoln Park | 2723 N. Clark St. (bet. Diversey Pkwy. & Drummond Pl.) | 773-868-4888 | www.thepeasantry.com

The owner of Frank 'N' Dawgs goes slightly upscale with this 'elevated street food' concept in Lincoln Park serving inventive, globally influenced New American fare made with locally sourced ingredients; it's all washed down with microbrews and selections from a concise wine list, and enjoyed in a rustic-chic room with animal artwork, plenty of reclaimed wood and a handsome stone fireplace.

Pecking Order M *Chicken* - | - | - | I

Ravenswood | 4416 N. Clark St. (bet. Montrose & Sunnyside Aves.) | 773-907-9900 | www.peckingorderchicago.com

Chicken 'every which way' is the motto of this Ravenswood joint where birds come grilled, fried and roasted in flavors highlighting the owner's Filipino heritage, and there's an eclectic mix of sides plus shaved ice, beer, wine and boozy punches too; the cute storefront is decorated in primary colors and poultry statuary with communal tables, and prices are ultra-affordable.

Pegasus *Greek*

20 | 17 | 17 | $29

Greektown | 130 S. Halsted St. (bet. Adams & Monroe Sts.) |
312-226-4666 | www.pegasuschicago.com

Pegasus on the Fly ● *Greek*

Southwest Side | Midway Int'l Airport | 5700 S. Cicero Ave.
(bet. 55th & 63rd Sts.) | 773-581-1522 | www.pegasusonthefly.com
"Delicious" "Greek comfort food" has patrons saying "*opa!*" at this
"lively" yet "conversation-friendly" Greektowner (with a Midway
sib) "notable for its fabulous rooftop" "with impressive city views";
though "service varies between very good and just good", it's "less
rushed" than some of its neighbors, and that plus affordable tabs
help explain why it comes "recommended."

Pelago Ristorante *Italian*

27 | 25 | 25 | $78

Streeterville | Raffaello Hotel | 201 E. Delaware Pl.
(Mies van der Rohe Way) | 312-280-0700 |
www.pelagorestaurant.com
Set in Streeterville's Raffaello Hotel, this "lovely little find" turns out
"beautifully executed" modern Italian fare in a "serene" dining room
fit for a "cozy", "romantic" meal; "wonderful" service helps offset
the "pricey" tabs, and there's a terrace in season.

Penny's Noodle Shop *Asian*

20 | 13 | 18 | $17

Lakeview | 3400 N. Sheffield Ave. (Roscoe St.) | 773-281-8222 Ⓜ
Lincoln Park | 950 W. Diversey Pkwy. (bet. Mildred & Sheffield Aves.) |
773-281-8448
Wicker Park | 1542 N. Damen Ave. (North Ave.) | 773-394-0100 Ⓜ
Northfield | 320 Happ Rd. (Orchard Ln.) | 847-446-4747
Oak Park | 1130 Chicago Ave. (bet. Harlem Ave. & Marion St.) |
708-660-1300
www.pennysnoodleshop.com
A "favorite for a cheap eat", this Asian mini-chain offers "plentiful"
portions of "satisfying", "flavorful" fare – and "way more than just
noodles"; it may "lack ambiance" and is "not the most authentic"
option, but it's still a "reliable standby", especially appreciated for
"fast service when you're in a hurry"; P.S. the Lakeview and Northfield
locales are BYO.

Pensiero Ristorante 🅢Ⓜ *Italian*

▽ 21 | 20 | 18 | $50

Evanston | Margarita European Inn | 1566 Oak Ave. (Davis St.) |
847-475-7779 | www.pensieroitalian.com
Despite a series of chef changes at this resurrection of the former Va
Pensiero, this Italian in Evanston's Margarita European Inn maintains an "interesting menu" ("don't expect lasagna") paired with a
"wide-ranging" wine list; service is "attentive", and tabs are on
the expensive side.

Pequod's Pizzeria ● *Pizza*

24 | 14 | 19 | $19

Lincoln Park | 2207 Clybourn Ave. (bet. Greenview & Webster Aves.) |
773-327-1512 | www.pequodspizza.com
"What dreams are made of" effuse enthusiasts of the "salty, cheesy"
"caramelized crust" (a "revelation") that along with "sweet sauce"
makes this Lincoln Park pizza pub "stand out" in a crowded field;

"service is ok", the surrounds "divey" and there's "no ambiance", but really, "who cares" ask fans who wonder "why people waste time eating anything else."

Perennial Virant *American*   26 | 23 | 24 | $53

Lincoln Park | Hotel Lincoln | 1800 N. Lincoln Ave. (Clark St.) | 312-981-7070 | www.perennialvirant.com

Paul Virant (Vie) makes uses of "incredibly fresh" local ingredients in "delicious", "unfussy" dishes that are "interesting" "without being crazy" at this "light, airy" New American in Lincoln Park's Hotel Lincoln; "excellent" cocktails and "knowledgeable" service further explain why you can "count on a great meal", so though the bill's not cheap, it's still considered "reasonable."

Pete Miller's Seafood &   22 | 19 | 20 | $50
Prime Steak *Seafood/Steak*

Evanston | 1557 Sherman Ave. (bet. Davis & Grove Sts.) | 847-328-0399 ◗

Wheeling | 412 N. Milwaukee Ave. (bet. Mayer Ave. & Wolf Rd.) | 847-243-3700
www.petemillers.com

Loyalists who say these "high-end" suburban sibs are "surviving the onslaught of chain steakhouses with flying colors" cite their "prime" cuts, "delicious" seafood and "memorable sides" all served by an "engaged" staff; classy surrounds with dark-wood accents are livened by "fantastic live jazz" most nights.

Petterino's *American*   19 | 20 | 21 | $42

Loop | Goodman Theatre Bldg. | 150 N. Dearborn St. (Randolph St.) | 312-422-0150 | www.petterinos.com

Service "knows how to get you to the show on time" (and "valet is a huge plus") at this "swanky" Italian-tinged American that's "a must" for the Loop theater crowd with "dependably tasty" "Wisconsin supper club food" for a "reasonable price"; though some find the offerings "uninspired" and say it's "there to soak the tourists", it remains "popular", especially for its business lunch and Sunday brunch; P.S. "have a martini and dream about being a star" at the "unique" Monday night open mike.

Philly G's *Italian*   21 | 21 | 23 | $37

Vernon Hills | 1252 Rte. 45 E. (bet. Milwaukee Ave. & Town Center Rd.) | 847-634-1811 | www.phillygs.com

A "quaint" and "elegant country home setting" sets the stage for "dependably tasty" "authentic" fare at this Vernon Hills Italian run by "friendly folks" who make diners feel personally "invited to their house"; moderate tabs and a "pleasant" atmosphere further ensure it's a "family favorite."

Phil Stefani's 437 Rush ⌧ *Italian/Steak*   23 | 21 | 24 | $53

River North | 437 N. Rush St. (Hubbard St.) | 312-222-0101 | www.stefanirestaurants.com

A "can-do attitude" and "friendly" vibe pervade this "elegant" Italian steakhouse in River North where the staff treats diners like "old friends" while ferrying "homespun" dishes and "generous cuts of well-prepared meat"; black-and-white photos of the city decorate the "quintessential Chicago" space, and if it's too costly for some, regulars say "try lunch for better prices."

Phoenix *Chinese*　　23 | 11 | 15 | $26

Chinatown | 2131 S. Archer Ave., 2nd fl. (bet. Princeton & Wentworth Aves.) | 312-328-0848 | www.chinatownphoenix.com

"Yum, yum dim sum" chant diners at this "cheap" Chinatown "standby", a "popular" place to "stuff yourself" on "numerous" "authentic" offerings from the carts plus other "top-notch" Chinese dishes; sure, the "decor is pretty worn" and service can be "spotty", but loyalists insist it still "always works" for a "high-quality meal."

Pho 777 *Vietnamese*　　24 | 10 | 19 | $15

Uptown | 1065 W. Argyle St. (bet. Kenmore & Winthrop Aves.) | 773-561-9909

Set out on a "culinary adventure" at this BYO "hole-in-the-wall" Uptown "where your dollar goes amazingly far" with the "vast" Vietnamese menu of "flavorful" phos and other "authentic" basics; if the decor doesn't quite match, fans focus instead on the "awesomely bad" "Asian pop music" and "friendly" staff.

Piccolo Sogno *Italian*　　25 | 24 | 23 | $54

Near West | 464 N. Halsted St. (Grand Ave.) | 312-421-0077 | www.piccolosognorestaurant.com

Tony Priolo's "divine", "flavorful" fare is "impeccably prepared with fresh ingredients" and paired with a "very deep wine list" at this "authentic" Near West Italian; "elegant surroundings" include a "serene" garden featuring "twinkling lights and flowing vines", service is "lovely no matter how busy" and prices are "reasonable" given the "quality" – no wonder devotees dub it a "dream come true"; P.S. it has a River North sequel called Piccolo Sogno Due.

NEW Piccolo Sogno Due *Italian*　　- | - | - | M

River North | 340 N. Clark St. (bet. Kinzie St. & Wacker Dr.) | 312-822-0077 | www.piccolosognodue.com

Tony Priolo realizes another little dream with this River North sequel to the Near West original, offering an upscale Italian menu with a seafood slant; a lengthy Boot-centric wine list adds to the fine-dining feel in the airy modern dining room featuring white tablecloths and a massive mural, and there's riverside outdoor dining too.

Piece *Pizza*　　25 | 19 | 19 | $22

Wicker Park | 1927 W. North Ave. (Damen Ave.) | 773-772-4422 | www.piecechicago.com

"Don't let the appearance fool you" say fans of this Wicker Park pizzeria, because though the "sports bar" decor may "say pub grub", the "mouthwatering" thin-crust pizza is "high quality" with "infinitely customizable toppings" that "make it possible to get anything you might be craving"; the "crazy vast array of different beers" (including "excellent" ones brewed on-site) also "impresses" and service is "friendly", so though "it's a little loud", it's "worth braving the often lengthy wait"; P.S. there are "live bands and karaoke some nights – you decide if that's a benefit or liability."

Pierrot Gourmet *French*   22 | 20 | 20 | $28

River North | Peninsula Chicago | 108 E. Superior St. (bet. Michigan Ave. & Rush St.) | 312-573-6749 | www.peninsula.com

Francophiles get "whisked away to France" courtesy of "authentic" cooking, a "well-chosen" wine list and "warm farmhouse decor" at this "lovely Parisian bistro" inside River North's Peninsula Hotel; despite moderate tabs detractors deem it "overpriced" for what's on offer, but most still salute the "charmingly delightful" vibe that's further enhanced by seamless service.

Pine Yard *Chinese*   18 | 12 | 14 | $22

Evanston | 1033 Davis St. (Oak Ave.) | 847-475-4940 | www.pineyardrestaurant.com

"When you want some good old Chinese" this sprawling Evanston longtimer is a "dependable" choice, offering Mandarin-Sichuan specialties via service so "fast" plates arrive "before you've had one sip of drink"; decor is "cold" and some say it's "gone downhill", but "fair" prices help keep it a "multidecade favorite for takeout."

Pita Inn *Mediterranean/Mideastern*   23 | 11 | 17 | $12

Glenview | 9854 N. Milwaukee Ave. (bet. Central & Golf Rds.) | 847-759-9990
NEW **Mundelein** | 200 Oak Creek Plaza (Townline Rd.) | 847-566-8888
Skokie | 3910 Dempster St. (bet. Crawford & Hamlin Aves.) | 847-677-0211
Wheeling | 122 S. Elmhurst Rd. (Jenkins Ct.) | 847-808-7733
www.pita-inn.com

Diners willing to brave the "long lines" at these "bare-bones" North Suburban "madhouses" are rewarded with "huge portions" of "consistently delish" Mediterranean–Middle Eastern eats including "wonderfully smoky" baba ghanoush, "mouthwatering" shawarma and "some of the best falafel around"; with "extremely fast" service and "cheap" tabs to "fit everyone's budget", a "strong following" keeps them "deservedly packed."

Pizano's Pizza & Pasta *Italian/Pizza*   21 | 16 | 19 | $22

Loop | 61 E. Madison St. (bet. Michigan & Wabash Aves.) | 312-236-1777 ●
River North | 800 N. Dearborn St. (Chicago Ave.) | 312-335-8833 ●
Gold Coast | 864 N. State St. (bet. Chestnut St. & Delaware Pl.) | 312-751-1766 ●
Glenview | 1808 N. Waukegan Rd. (Chestnut Ave.) | 847-486-1777
www.pizanoschicago.com

"Stuff yourself silly" at these "credible joints" where enthusiasts taste its "Malnati heritage" in the "buttery, flaky" deep-dish pies offered alongside "tasty thin-crust (gasp!)" 'zas, plus "generous servings of homemade pasta" and other Italian standards; a few finger-waggers fuss "it doesn't stand out from the rest" and warn of "tables too close together", but most cheer "friendly" service, affordable tabs and say with one visit "you'll immediately understand why Chicago is known for its pizza"; P.S. River North is carryout only.

	FOOD	DECOR	SERVICE	COST

NEW Pizza House 1647 Ⓜ *Pizza*

Bucktown | 1647 W. Cortland St. (bet. Marshfield Ave. & Paulina St.) | 773-252-3500 | www.pizzahouse1647.com

No pie tops 12 inches (theory being so the center doesn't get soggy) at this Bucktown pizza parlor where thin-crust pies are topped with housemade ingredients and offered alongside salads, sandwiches and more; it's all consumed in a cozy, casual and kid-friendly setting with flat-screen TVs, and affordable tabs up the appeal.

Food: - | Decor: - | Service: - | Cost: I

Pizzeria da Nella Cucina Napoletana *Italian/Pizza*

Lincoln Park | 1443 W. Fullerton Ave. (bet. Greenview & Janssen Aves.) | 773-281-6600 | www.pizzeriadanella.com

Neapolitan pies are the specialty at Nella Grassano's midpriced Lincoln Park Italian, which also serves a full menu of fresh pastas, salads and desserts, plus Boot-based craft brews and affordable wines; the cozy-casual confines feature ochre walls, a blue ductwork ceiling and a granite bar, plus an open kitchen with a tile-adorned pizza oven and a sprawling brick-lined patio.

Food: - | Decor: - | Service: - | Cost: M

Pizzeria Due ◑ *Pizza*

River North | 619 N. Wabash Ave. (bet. Ohio & Ontario Sts.) | 312-943-2400 | www.pizzeriaunodue.com

Uno ◑ *Pizza*

River North | 29 E. Ohio St. (Wabash Ave.) | 312-321-1000 | www.unos.com

"Forsake all other Unos" order pie purists who declare these "world-famous" River North "originals" "about nine miles ahead of the chains around the country" thanks to "classic deep-dish" pizzas "laden with cheese and tomatoes" and balanced by "crispy", "pastrylike" crusts; sure, they're "not much for decor", but "out-of-town guests" appreciate the "old-time feel", and despite "long waits" (Due is "less crowded"), most agree "you have to go at least once."

Food: 22 | Decor: 15 | Service: 18 | Cost: $25

P.J. Clarke's ◑ *American*

Gold Coast | 1204 N. State Pkwy. (Division St.) | 312-664-1650 | www.pjclarkeschicago.com

This Gold Coast sports "saloon" is "known for its burgers" and other "consistent", "basic" American grub; critics say it's "nothing special", and the environs could use a "face-lift", but its "adult" atmosphere appeals, as do affordable tabs.

Food: 17 | Decor: 15 | Service: 17 | Cost: $26

Pleasant House Bakery ⓈⓂ *British*

Bridgeport | 964 W. 31st St. (Keeley St.) | 773-523-7437 | www.pleasanthousebakery.com

Savory British royal pies are among the offerings at this petite Bridgeport bakery/cafe also vending affordable farm-to-table lunch and dinner specials including burgers and fish 'n' chips, daily desserts, plus brunch and high tea on Sundays; you can BYO or enjoy its artisanal housemade sodas in a setting with an open kitchen, rustic wood and a blackboard menu.

Food: - | Decor: - | Service: - | Cost: I

	FOOD	DECOR	SERVICE	COST

🆕 Plzen ● *Eclectic*
- | - | - | I

Pilsen | 1519 W. 18th St. (bet. Ashland Ave. & Laflin St.) |
312-733-0248 | www.plzengastropub.com

Named for the Czech translation of the funky neighborhood, this
budget-friendly Pilsen Eclectic doles out locally sourced, globally inspired gastropub fare (think wild boar meatballs and burgers from a
Kuma's alum); it also offers artisanal cocktails and lots of craft beers
in a casual space decorated with colorful murals.

The Point ● Ⓜ *American*
- | - | - | I

West Loop | 401 N. Milwaukee Ave. (Kinzie St.) | 312-666-1600 |
www.pointbarchicago.com

Upgraded New American bar food (short rib nachos, polenta cakes,
truffle fries) pairs with craft brews, new and vintage-inspired cocktails and Julius Meinl coffee at this casual West Loop corner spot
named for its noteworthy angled building; its funky environs are outfitted with an elaborate parquet floor, leather banquettes, modern
art and sexy photomurals, and include a downstairs lounge.

🆕 Polanco Ⓜ *Mexican/Steak*
- | - | - | M

Logan Square | 2451 N. Milwaukee Ave. (Sacramento Ave.) |
773-227-9898 | www.polancochicago.com

This Logan Square Mexican has a steakhouse slant, serving steaks
with both French and Mexican sauces accompanied by classic and
Latin cocktails, craft beers and 50 tequilas; the casual space includes
a front patio and two bars, and tabs are moderate.

Pork Shoppe Ⓜ *BBQ*
▽ 20 | 13 | 20 | $15

Avondale | 2755 W. Belmont Ave. (bet. California & Washtenaw Aves.) |
773-961-7654 | www.porkshoppechicago.com

'Cue-lovers confess they'd "knock down old ladies and children"
for the "savory", "decadent" "pork belly pastrami" (a "can't-miss
item") served alongside other "serious" eats at this counter-service
Avondale BBQ joint; the minimalist storefront features butcher-
block communal tables and farm tools, and the "great prices and
customer service" are other marks in its favor.

Potbelly Sandwich Shop *Sandwiches*
18 | 13 | 17 | $11

Loop | One Illinois Ctr. | 111 E. Wacker Dr. (bet. Michigan &
Stetson Aves.) | 312-861-0013 🛇

Loop | 175 W. Jackson Blvd. (Financial Pl.) | 312-588-1150 🛇

Loop | 190 N. State St. (Lake St.) | 312-683-1234

Loop | 303 W. Madison St. (Franklin St.) | 312-346-1234

Loop | 55 W. Monroe St. (bet. Clark & Dearborn Sts.) |
312-577-0070 🛇

River North | 508 N. Clark St. (bet. Grand Ave. & Illinois St.) |
312-644-9131

River North | Shops at North Bridge | 520 N. Michigan Ave.
(bet. Grand Ave. & Ohio St.) | 312-644-1008

Lakeview | 3424 N. Southport Ave. (bet. Cornelia Ave. & Roscoe St.) |
773-289-1807

Lincoln Park | 1422 W. Webster Ave. (Clybourn Ave.) | 773-755-1234

(continued)

(continued)

Potbelly Sandwich Shop

Lincoln Park | 2264 N. Lincoln Ave. (bet. Orchard St. & Webster Ave.) | 773-528-1405

www.potbelly.com

Additional locations throughout the Chicago area

"So many sandwiches, so little time" muse champions of the "best damn" sammies "toasted fresh" at this "cheap", "reliable" homegrown chain where "tasty" salads, "don't-miss" milkshakes and "fresh baked cookies" also contribute to its "cult" following; frequent "live lunch-time music" and "friendly" staffers pep up the otherwise bare-bones surroundings, and though a few call the "cattle chute" experience "tedious", at least the "lines always move quickly."

Prairie Grass Cafe *American*   22 | 19 | 20 | $41

Northbrook | 601 Skokie Blvd. (bet. Dundee Rd. & Henrici Dr.) | 847-205-4433 | www.prairiegrasscafe.com

"Home cooking with flair and panache" comes courtesy of chef-owners Sarah Stegner and George Bumbaris at this "pleasant" Northbrook New American where "rethought" "comfort food" "draws on local ingredients"; the "comfortable" "mess hall"–like space gets "crowded" and "noisy at prime times", but guests generally find "the service and kitchen keep up", delivering a "good value for the quality."

Prasino *American*   22 | 21 | 19 | $31

NEW **Rosemont** | Fashion Outlet of Chicago | 5220 Fashion Outlet Way (bet. Emerson & Ruby Sts.)

Wicker Park | 1846 W. Division St. (Marion Ct.) | 312-878-1212

La Grange | 93 S. La Grange Rd. (Cossitt Ave.) | 708-469-7058

www.prasino.com

"Bold flavors" define the "extensive", "innovative" American menu at this midpriced duo in Wicker Park and suburban La Grange (with a newer Rosemont third), where the "green theme" ('prasino' is Greek for green) extends from the "locally sourced" ingredients and organic wines to the "modern", eco-friendly surroundings highlighting re-claimed materials; "friendly, polite" servers add to the "laid-back" vibe, and fans say it's an especially "fabulous" choice for breakfast.

Prosecco 🛐 *Italian*   24 | 23 | 24 | $56

River North | 710 N. Wells St. (bet. Huron & Superior Sts.) | 312-951-9500 | www.prosecco.us.com

A "complimentary taste of Prosecco" provides a fitting welcome to this "beautiful" and "romantic" River North Italian, a little "piece of Venice" boasting "authentic", "well-prepared" dishes that "aren't outrageously priced"; "warm", "professional" staffers offer "spot-on" wine recommendations, and though "busy" nights can be "noisy" with "tight seating", devotees revel in the "energetic vibe."

Prost! ☻ *German*   - | - | - | M

Lincoln Park | 2566 N. Lincoln Ave. (bet. Sheffield & Wrightwood Aves.) | 773-880-9900 | www.prostchicago.com

After a two-year hiatus, this expanded German gastrohaus in Lincoln Park is back, pairing modern chef-driven eats with two dozen tap brews (some served in a giant boot) from a beer-stein-bedecked bar; the straightforward setting is casual and warm, with rows of imported communal beer hall tables and many TVs, and prices are affordable.

Province 🅱 *American*   25 | 24 | 24 | $52

West Loop | 161 N. Jefferson St. (bet. Lake & Randolph Sts.) | 312-669-9900 | www.provincerestaurant.com

Chef-owner Randy Zweiban "uses Latin and Asian techniques" to "enhance locally sourced ingredients" with "bold and spicy flavors" at this somewhat pricey West Loop New American turning out "creative", "original" fare in "varying sizes of plates, from small to large"; the LEED-certified building offers an "open and airy yet intimate" setting and service is "friendly", so it works for both "a casual dinner or a special occasion."

The Publican   *American*   26 | 23 | 23 | $50

West Loop | 837 W. Fulton Mkt. (Green St.) | 312-733-9555 | www.thepublicanrestaurant.com

"Try everything" say fans of Paul Kahan's "inspired" West Loop New American, where the pork-centric menu allows for a "superb pigtastic experience" and includes other "well-prepared, full-of-flavor" share plates plus oysters too; "lots of craft beers" and "stiff" cocktails up the "cool" factor and the "huge communal tables" add group appeal, so even if it's "loud" and the bill can "add up quickly", it's still considered "all the rage (and rightfully so)."

Publican Quality Meats   *American*   27 | 19 | 23 | I

West Loop | 825 W. Fulton Mkt. (Green St.) | 312-445-8977 | www.publicanqualitymeats.com

"Card-carrying meat eaters" hail the house-cured charcuterie and "exceptional" sandwiches at Paul Kahan's West Loop market and cafe where the American menu also includes soups, salads and cheese plates plus beer and wine; the small white-tiled space is "popular" at lunch when many take it to go, and you can also visit the on-site butcher counter for "carry-out sausages" and more.

Public House ◑ *American*   18 | 19 | 17 | $30

River North | 400 N. State St. (Kinzie St.) | 312-265-1240 | www.publichousechicago.com

"Check out the table taps" at this midpriced River North drinking den, a "lively" American "sports bar" with a "lounge feel" where "upscale" pub grub, "tons of beers" and "plenty of TVs" for "watching the game" provide "hangout" appeal; those averse to "packed" conditions say it's "way better on weeknights" when a late-night menu is offered until 1 AM (2 AM on weekends).

Pump Room ◑ *American*   21 | 27 | 24 | $62

Gold Coast | Public Chicago | 1301 N. State Pkwy. (Goethe St.) | 312-229-6740 | www.pumproom.com

"As elegant" as the first "historic" iteration, but in a "new, edgy way", this high-end New American in the Gold Coast's Public Hotel offers "celebrated" chef Jean-Georges Vongerichten's "inventive", seasonally inspired fare lifted by a "robust wine list" and "thoughtful, precisely prepared" cocktails; sure, a few say it has "lost some charm" of the original, but most can still appreciate the "beautiful", "swanky" setting, where a "hoity-toity crowd" makes it a "favorite" for "people-watching."

Purple Pig ● *Mediterranean*　26 | 21 | 21 | $42

River North | 500 N. Michigan Ave. (Illinois St.) | 312-464-1744 | www.thepurplepigchicago.com

It's "always packed" at Jimmy Bannos Jr.'s "intimate" River North gastropub where the "interesting" Mediterranean menu is a "foodie adventure", full of "delicious", "mind-blowing" small plates including "unusual" "comfort zone"–busting choices you "won't see anywhere else"; "terrific" wines, "dynamite beers" and "friendly" staffers help fuel a "lively" scene, and while it's "easy to rack up a bill", it has all the makings for a "memorable" meal – if you can outlast the "long" wait (no reservations), that is.

Quartino ● *Italian*　22 | 19 | 21 | $32

River North | 626 N. State St. (Ontario St.) | 312-698-5000 | www.quartinochicago.com

"The more people in your party to share dishes, the better" at this "hip", "always crowded" River North Italian where "authentic", "way-above-average" "big and little bites" (including "wonderful house-cured meats"), "many wine options" by the carafe and "genuinely good" service "completely outweigh" the "astounding noise"; the "rustic" bi-level environs can get "tight", but prices are "so reasonable you can go back the next night" – and many do.

Quay ● *American*　19 | 22 | 19 | $42

Streeterville | 465 E. Illinois St. (bet. Lake Shore Dr. & McClurg Ct.) | 312-981-8400 | www.quaychicago.com

Three venues in one – a "sports bar, restaurant and lounge" – this Streeterville New American offers an "attractive", "group"-friendly setting for "well-prepared" meals, or just "cocktails and apps"; the staff does a solid job too, but a few would like more "competitive" drink pricing, and argue it's "trying to do too many things at once."

Quince Ⓜ *American*　25 | 22 | 25 | $62

Evanston | Homestead Hotel | 1625 Hinman Ave. (Davis St.) | 847-570-8400 | www.quincerestaurant.net

"Serious contemporary cuisine" full of "gourmet surprises" and "impeccable" service make this upscale New American in the "historic" Homestead Hotel one of "Evanston's finest"; sure, you may need an "expense account" to pay, but the "charming, romantic" atmosphere helps compensate.

NEW Rainbow Cuisine *Thai*　- | - | - | I

Lincoln Square | 4825 N. Western Ave. (Lawrence Ave.) | 773-754-7660 | www.orderrainbowcuisine.com

A former Spoon Thai chef is cooking up similar sustenance from scratch at this inexpensive Lincoln Square BYO also bearing bubble teas in a straightforward storefront setting; it's tiny with limited seating, making takeout and delivery popular options.

	FOOD	DECOR	SERVICE	COST

Ras Dashen *Ethiopian*
▽ **26** | **21** | **21** | **$25**

Edgewater | 5846 N. Broadway (bet. Ardmore & Rosedale Aves.) |
773-506-9601 | www.rasdashenchicago.com

"It's fun to eat with your hands" at this midpriced Edgewater Ethiopian,
the "real thing" for "well-spiced", "full-of-flavor" fare and "traditional" injera bread used as a "scooper"; "consistently gracious"
servers work the casual room decorated with paintings, so all in all
most "leave happy."

RA Sushi ❶ *Japanese*
18 | **18** | **16** | **$31**

Gold Coast | 1139 N. State St. (Elm St.) | 312-274-0011
Glenview | 2601 Aviator Ln. (Patriot Blvd.) | 847-510-1100
Lombard | Yorktown Ctr. | 310 Yorktown Shopping Ctr. (Fairfield Ave.) |
630-627-6800
www.rasushi.com

"Always buzzing" with a "mostly young crowd", this "trendy" sushi
chain provides "innovative" rolls and other bites "mixing traditional
and newer flavors"; despite its shortcomings on "authenticity", the
"party" atmosphere and "awesome" happy-hour "deals" that encourage "imbibing sake swiftly" are incentive enough for some.

Real Urban Barbecue *BBQ*
21 | **14** | **16** | **$19**

Highland Park | Port Clinton Square Shopping Ctr. | 610 Central Ave.
(2nd St.) | 224-770-4227
NEW **Vernon Hills** | Vernon Hills Town Ctr. | 1260 S. Milwaukee Ave.
(Greentree Pkwy.) | 847-613-1227
www.realurbanbbq.com

'Cue fans go "hog wild" for the "tangy" brisket at this "cafeteria-style"
Highland Park pit stop (with a Vernon Hills sequel) also offering "juicy"
pulled pork, "savory" sides "worth standing in line for" and other BBQ
standards; though a few cite "underwhelming" results and "wish for
table service at these prices", it still provides "refuge for those too
tired to drive into the city" for "porcine cuisine."

Red Door ❶ *Eclectic*
- | **-** | **-** | **M**

Bucktown | 2118 N. Damen Ave. (Charleston St.) | 773-697-7221 |
www.reddoorchicago.com

Fans say there's "something charming" about this Bucktown gastropub where the "huge", "phenomenal" beer garden provides a "tran-
quil" place to sample from the "solid beer list", craft cocktail menu
or group-friendly array of Eclectic small plates; the wood-trimmed
interior is roomy too, and prices won't break the bank.

NEW Red Square
- | **-** | **-** | **M**
Cafe Lounge *American/Russian*

Wicker Park | 1914 W. Division St. (bet. Damen & Wolcott Aves.) |
773-227-2284

Setting up shop in an old Wicker Park bathhouse, this spa/resto-bar
multitasker serves Russian-influenced small plates at moderate
prices, and sports a full bar pouring 20 plus Russian and Ukrainian
vodkas; saunas, steam baths and tanning booths are accessed by a
chip-embedded wristband you can also use to charge food and drinks.

| | FOOD | DECOR | SERVICE | COST |

Red Violet *Chinese*

| - | - | - | M |

River North | 121 W. Hubbard St. (LaSalle St.) | 312-828-0222 | www.redvioletchicago.com

Upscale, multiregional Chinese chow, paired with exotic cocktails, craft beers and a compact wine list, makes up the massive menu at this modern River North 200-seater; the bi-level, low-lit space offers a range of seating options, funky furnishings and cultural curios.

Reel Club *Seafood*
| 21 | 21 | 20 | $43 |

Oak Brook | Oakbrook Center Mall | 272 Oakbrook Ctr. (Harger Rd.) | 630-368-9400 | www.reel-club.com

"Worth hunting for" in the "sprawling" Oakbrook Center mall, this "elegant" Lettuce Entertain You seafooder nets props for "fine fish", "watchful service" and a wine list that "sparkles with variety"; the "modern" space holds a "sizable" bar, helping to accommodate the "hordes of wealthy shoppers" who make it a regular "go-to."

NEW The Refinery Ⓜ *American*
| - | - | - | E |

Old Town | 1209 N. Wells (Division St.) | 312-854-2970 | www.oldtownrefinery.com

As its name suggests, refined, upscale comfort food is the mission at this Old Town New American also dispensing decadent desserts and craft cocktails; the casual setting features vintage brick, industrial ductwork, banquette seating and a long bar.

NEW Reno ◑⇗ *American/Italian*

| - | - | - | M |

Logan Square | 2607 N. Milwaukee Ave. (Kedzie Ave.) | 773-697-4234 | www.renochicago.com

The Telegraph/Webster's Wine Bar team is behind this affordable Italian-American osteria in Logan Square serving wood-fired pizza and bagels, plus fresh pastas and sandwiches; the room has brick-lined walls, bare wood booths and tables (one communal) and a dual pastry/alcohol bar with fresh baked goods and a full bar.

NEW Restaurant
| - | - | - | M |

Beatrix *American/Coffeehouse*

Near North | Aloft Chicago City Ctr. | 515 N. Clark St. (Grand Ave.) | 312-284-1377 | www.beatrixchicago.com

Lettuce Entertain You is behind this combination dining destination, coffeehouse, wine and cocktail bar in River North's new Aloft Chicago City Center offering American eats all day long; the warm, airy digs have massive windows, wood beams, greenery and numerous seating options including lounge chairs, two bars and standard dining tables.

Retro Bistro Ⓜ *French*
| 25 | 18 | 23 | $45 |

Mt. Prospect | Mount Prospect Commons | 1746 W. Golf Rd. (Busse Rd.) | 847-439-2424 | www.retrobistro.com

The "high-quality" cooking "executed with creativity and care" "defies logic" say fans acknowledging the strip-mall setting of this "reasonably priced" Mount Prospect French and advising you to "get over it"; add in "charming" service and a "homey, welcoming" atmosphere and most concede it "wins us over every time."

NEW Revolución Steakhouse ◑ *Mexican/Steak*

`-` | `-` | `-` | M

Lakeview | 3443 N. Broadway (Stratford Pl.) | 773-661-9893 | www.revolucionchicago.com

This rustic, moderately priced Lakeview steakhouse pairs prime meats with Mexican flavors, plus ceviches, tacos and entrees, alongside a drink menu with margaritas, wine and craft beer (including the proprietary 5 Rabbit brew); the wood and brick rooms are decorated with Mexican Revolution artwork, a glass water wall behind the bar and clouds painted on the ceiling.

Revolution Brewing ◑ *American*

23 | 21 | 20 | $24

Logan Square | 2323 N. Milwaukee Ave. (bet. California & Fullerton Aves.) | 773-227-2739 | www.revbrew.com

Regulars say "the beer makes your toes curl" at this Logan Square American also vending "consistent", "inventive" bar bites "with class" including "surprisingly robust vegetarian" choices; set in a spacious restored space with tin ceilings and a fireplace, it's usually "packed", but "pleasant service in a sea of hipsters" keeps most happy.

Reza's *Mediterranean/Mideastern*

20 | 16 | 18 | $26

River North | 432 W. Ontario St. (bet. Kingsbury & Orleans Sts.) | 312-664-4500

Andersonville | 5255 N. Clark St. (Berwyn Ave.) | 773-561-1898

Oak Brook | 40 N. Tower Rd. (Butterfield Rd.) | 630-424-9900 www.rezasrestaurant.com

The saying "come hungry, leave happy applies" to this "steady" Med-Mideastern trio crow converts who insist you "can't go wrong" with "huge portions" of "reasonably good" Persian fare (also offered in buffet form); some feel the surroundings could use a "major refresh" and service can be inconsistent, but "if you're looking for quantity" and "great value" it "won't disappoint."

NEW Riccardo Enoteca *Italian*

`-` | `-` | `-` | M

Lincoln Park | 2116 N. Clark St. (bet. Dickens & Webster Aves.) | 773-549-5010 | www.riccardoenoteca.com

The owners of Riccardo Trattoria across the street are behind this atmospheric Lincoln Park wine bar where wood-oven pizza and Italian small plates are joined by a Boot-centric vino selection; the small space features polished wood and nautical photography, and tabs are affordable.

Riccardo Trattoria *Italian*

28 | 21 | 25 | $49

Lincoln Park | 2119 N. Clark St. (bet. Dickens & Webster Aves.) | 773-549-0038 | www.riccardotrattoria.com

It's "just like being in Italy" at this "cozy" Lincoln Park Italian that's "still one of the best after all these years" thanks to its "delicate", "simply wonderful" fare; service is "helpful" and the "relaxed" atmosphere is "romantic" enough for a date, and while it's not inexpensive, it's still deemed "reasonable" "given the quality"; P.S. when it's "hard to get in" you can try its newer enoteca sister across the street.

	FOOD	DECOR	SERVICE	COST

NEW Rickshaw Republic Ⓜ Asian — — — | I

Lincoln Park | 2312 N. Lincoln Ave. (bet. Belden Ave. & Halsted St.) | 773-697-4750 | www.rickshawrepublic.com

Rare Indonesian eats are on offer at this family-run Lincoln Park 'peddler' of authentic South East Asian street foods like satay, pangsit, pancakes, dumplings and noodles all at bargain prices (BYO helps too); distinctive background music and colorful masks and puppets help set the mood in the casual space, and free parking is a bonus.

Ricobene's ● Italian   24 | 14 | 20 | $12

Bridgeport | 252 W. 26th St. (Princeton Ave.) | 312-225-5555 | www.ricobenesfamoussteaks.com

Devotees "OMG" over the "huge" breaded steak sandwiches and pizza at this Italian-leaning Brideport counter-serve, where the wide-ranging menu also includes wings, BBQ and more; no-frills space may not stand out, but at least it works when you're "tight on money."

Riva Seafood   21 | 23 | 20 | $48

Streeterville | Navy Pier | 700 E. Grand Ave. (Streeter Dr.) | 312-644-7482 | www.rivanavypier.com

"Get a window seat" for "spectacular views of Lake Michigan and the Downtown skyline" at this "classy" seafooder on Streeterville's Navy Pier, where the "good to very good" fin fare satisfies for "long business lunches" and dining "before or after" the Shakespeare Theater; doubters warn you'll rub elbows with "tourists" and may encounter "rushed" service, but the "relaxing" vistas help compensate.

R.J. Grunts ● American   19 | 17 | 20 | $23

Lincoln Park | 2056 N. Lincoln Park W. (Dickens Ave.) | 773-929-5363 | www.rjgruntschicago.com

"Where it all began" for the Lettuce Entertain You "empire", this "moderately priced" Lincoln Park "institution" tended by "friendly" staffers is known for "huge" portions of American "comfort food", an "endless" salad bar (it "looks like a farmer's market") and "one of the best" weekend brunch buffets; photos of former staffers "paper the walls" of the "cramped" space, and a "cool, nostalgic" "hippie vibe" that "hasn't changed" since the '70s helps ensure it "stays popular."

RL American   24 | 26 | 24 | $55

Gold Coast | 115 E. Chicago Ave. (bet. Michigan Ave. & Rush St.) | 312-475-1100 | www.rlrestaurant.com

"Jackie O would be at home" at this "elegant" Gold Coast American, a Ralph Lauren production that "solidly delivers" with "delicious", "stylish" dishes in an "old-school" wood and leather space where you can "rub elbows with Chicago society"; if it's "expensive", that just makes it a "special event" kind of place.

NEW RM Champagne Salon ● American — — — | M

West Loop | 116 N. Green St. (bet. Randolph St. & Washington Blvd.) | 312-243-1199 | www.rmchampagnesalon.com

This Parisian partner to Nellcôte in the West Loop, tucked discreetly behind the mother ship, pops a wide-ranging collection of bubblies to complement a petite, midpriced menu with New American small plates, raw bar options and mini sweets; ornate furnishings include a marble fireplace, chandeliers and eclectic artwork on the walls.

Robinson's No. 1 Ribs *BBQ*　　18 | 9 | 12 | $20

Loop | Union Station | 225 S. Canal St. (bet. Adams St. & Jackson Blvd.) | 312-258-8477 | www.robinsonsribsunionstation.com
Lincoln Park | 655 W. Armitage Ave. (Orchard St.) | 312-337-1399 | www.ribs1.com
Oak Park | 940 Madison St. (bet. Clinton & Home Aves.) | 708-383-8452 | www.rib1.com

"Regulars" at these cost-conscious BBQ BYOs are "hooked" on ribs slathered with "out-of-this-world" sauce plus other "satisfying" plates; critics who say it's "coasting" have a bone to pick with sometimes "subpar" service and "sad" decor, adding that it's better for "carryout."

Rockit Bar & Grill ● *American*　　19 | 16 | 17 | $28

River North | 22 W. Hubbard St. (bet. Dearborn & State Sts.) | 312-645-6000 | www.rockitbarandgrill.com

Rockit Burger Bar ●Ⓜ *Burgers*

Wrigleyville | 3700 N. Clark St. (Waveland Ave.) | 773-645-4400 | www.rockitburgerbar.com

"Bring your entourage" for a "blast" at this "affordable" River North American and its burger-focused Wrigleyville sib scoring with "high-quality" "pub fare" and "efficient" service in "unpretentious" "sports bar" environs; if they're "too much of a scene" for some, others "dig the Bloody Mary bar" offered at the "above-par" weekend brunch and note the Wrigleyville outpost is "perfect" pre- or post-Cubs games.

Roditys ● *Greek*　　20 | 18 | 22 | $32

Greektown | 222 S. Halsted St. (bet. Adams St. & Jackson Blvd.) | 312-454-0800 | www.roditys.com

"Get your Greek fix" at this circa-1973 Greektowner that transports diners to the isles ("close your eyes and go to Greece") with the "just plain good" Hellenic fare; solid service, "moderate prices" and a "soothing" yet group-friendly atmosphere complete the picture.

Roka Akor *Japanese/Steak*　　24 | 25 | 22 | $66

River North | 456 N. Clark St. (Illinois St.) | 312-477-7652
NEW Skokie | 4999 Old Orchard Ctr. (Skokie Blvd.) | 847-329-7650 www.rokaakor.com

"Super-fresh" sushi and "delicious" meats from the robata grill are among the "above-par" offerings at this River North scenester steakhouse (with a newer Skokie sib); the modern setting is "group"-friendly, with ample "people-watching" opportunities, and though you'll pay a "premium", fans say the "quality" makes it "worth it."

Roots Handmade Pizza ● *American/Pizza*　　▽ 20 | 19 | 19 | $19

West Town | 1924 W. Chicago Ave. (Winchester Ave.) | 773-645-4949 | www.rootspizza.com

Piezani "welcome" this West Town pizzeria, cheering its "unique" scissor-cut pies that are "done to perfection" with Quad Cities–style malted crust and a "wonderful alternative to deep-dish"; affordable

American fare like salads and sausages extends the menu, and while a "massive" all-Midwestern beer list is considered alone "worth the visit", the "large" space and "comfortable booths" also make it appealing for "watching the game or just hanging out."

Rootstock Wine & Beer Bar 🌓 *American*

FOOD	DECOR	SERVICE	COST
23	20	20	$32

Humboldt Park | 954 N. California Ave. (Augusta Blvd.) | 773-292-1616 | www.rootstockbar.com

Admirers insist you'll "fall in love" with this approachable Humboldt Park boîte for its charcuterie, "beautiful" cheese plates and other "light, tasty" New American bites complemented by "diverse" wines by the glass and an "excellent" beer selection; it also promises a "casual" yet "cool living-room" vibe, so though a few voice concerns about the "sketchy" neighborhood, most agree "you won't be disappointed."

Rosal's Italian Kitchen ⊠ *Italian*

FOOD	DECOR	SERVICE	COST
26	17	25	$38

Little Italy/University Village | 1154 W. Taylor St. (Racine Ave.) | 312-243-2357 | www.rosals.com

Those who've "never had a bad meal" say some of "the best" Sicilian food around can be found at this Little Italy longtimer that continues to "impress" with its traditional fare; toss in strong service and affordable tabs and no one even brings up the small surrounds.

Rose Angelis Ⓜ *Italian*

FOOD	DECOR	SERVICE	COST
25	21	22	$31

Lincoln Park | 1314 W. Wrightwood Ave. (bet. Racine & Southport Aves.) | 773-296-0081 | www.roseangelis.com

"Enormous" portions of "delicious" "homemade" Italian fare offered at "beyond reasonable" tabs make this Lincoln Park vet a "favorite" while the "romantic", "cozy house" setting ensures it a "date destination"; add in "friendly" service and fans say it "never disappoints."

Rosebud *Italian*

FOOD	DECOR	SERVICE	COST
22	18	21	$41

Little Italy/University Village | 1500 W. Taylor St. (Laflin St.) | 312-942-1117

Rosebud Italian Specialties & Pizzeria *Italian*
Naperville | 22 E. Chicago Ave. (Washington St.) | 630-548-9800

Rosebud Old World Italian *Italian*
Schaumburg | 1370 Bank Dr. (Meacham Rd.) | 847-240-1414

Rosebud on Rush *Italian*
Streeterville | 720 N. Rush St. (Superior St.) | 312-266-6444

Rosebud Theater District ⊠ *Italian*
Loop | 3 First National Plaza | 70 W. Madison St. (bet. Clark & Dearborn Sts.) | 312-332-9500
www.rosebudrestaurants.com

"Popular with the tourists" but still "too good for locals to pass up", this "little-changed" Taylor Street "landmark" and its empire of metro-area eateries specializes in "huge portions" of "well-executed", "traditional" Italian and "thoughtful wine lists" presented by a "smart" crew; even if they're slightly "expensive", "loud" and "crowded to a fault", their "consistent" quality still wins kudos.

	FOOD	DECOR	SERVICE	COST

Rosebud Prime *Steak*
Loop | 1 S. Dearborn St. (Madison St.) | 312-384-1900

23 | 21 | 23 | $57

Rosebud Steakhouse *Steak*
Streeterville | 192 E. Walton St. (bet. Lake Shore Dr. & Michigan Ave.) | 312-397-1000

www.rosebudrestaurants.com

"In a city with great steaks", this Loop and Streeterville duo may be "overshadowed by glitzier" chophouses, but it still "really produces" with a "wide selection" of "top-quality" cuts set down by "old-school" staffers; an "elegant" setting and "pleasant" atmosphere lend "business-hangout" appeal, while softening expectedly "pricey" tabs.

Rosewood Restaurant & Banquets Steakhouse *Steak*

26 | 20 | 24 | $50

Rosemont | 9421 W. Higgins Rd. (bet. River Rd. & Willow Creek Dr.) | 847-696-9494 | www.rosewoodrestaurant.com

Though it may "look like the typical banquet facility", fans say the "prime meats" and "awesome sauces" "far exceed the first impression" at this "old-school" Rosemont chophouse; highly rated staffers and a "retro supper club" feel attract "business-lunchers", and if it's a "bit pricey", jet-setters claim there's "no better dining near O'Hare."

Roy's *Hawaiian*

▽ 24 | 20 | 23 | $51

River North | 720 N. State St. (Superior St.) | 312-787-7599 | www.roysrestaurant.com

It seems the "fish have leapt out of the ocean and onto the grill" at this River North rendition of the "upscale" "Hawaiian fusion" chain where dishes are "innovative but not fufu", "presentations are creative" and the "drinks are delectable"; further, the "relaxed" ambiance is "great for conversation" and service is "attentive" so most are left with "no complaints", except for the "pricey but oh-so-worth-it" tabs.

RPM Italian ● *Italian*

23 | 23 | 23 | $56

River North | 52 W. Illinois St. (Dearborn St.) | 312-222-1888 | www.rpmitalian.com

"Believe the hype" say fans of this "trendy" River North collaboration between "celebs" Giuliana and Bill Rancic and the Melmans, where "simple", "well-prepared" Italian dishes are dispensed by "attentive" staffers in "modern", "date"-friendly digs with two bars and banquettes; it's on the "pricey" side, and a few find it merely "average", but more would "go again", so don't be surprised when it's "crowded."

Ruby of Siam *Thai*

21 | 14 | 20 | $20

Loop | 170 W. Washington St. (bet. La Salle & Wells Sts.) | 312-609-0000 | www.rubyofsiam.com

Skokie | Skokie Fashion Sq. | 9420 Skokie Blvd. (Gross Point Rd.) | 847-675-7008 | www.rubyofsiamskokie.com

Siam Splendour *Thai*
Evanston | 1125 Emerson St. (Ridge Ave.) | 847-492-1008 | www.siamsplendourevanston.com

An "extensive" menu of "flavorful, satisfying" Thai "standards", including "plenty of vegetarian options", makes this "accommodating" city and suburban trio (Evanston is separately owned) a regular "go-to" for dine-in or carryout; "friendly" service helps compensate for "basic" "nondescript" digs, especially since the "price is right" (and even more "reasonable" at the BYO Loop and Skokie outposts).

Russell's Barbecue *BBQ*
21 | **12** | **16** | **$13**

Elmwood Park | 1621 N. Thatcher Ave. (North Ave.) | 708-453-7065 | www.russellsbarbecue.com

A "family favorite" since 1930, this "old-fashioned" Elmwood Park "tradition" "keeps people coming back" with its beef sandwiches and other "reasonably priced" BBQ specialties; service can be "spotty" and decor "isn't special", but it "brings back memories of childhood", so habitués still "drop in."

Russian Tea Time *Russian*
22 | **21** | **22** | **$40**

Loop | 77 E. Adams St. (bet. Michigan & Wabash Aves.) | 312-360-0000 | www.russianteatime.com

Convenient to the Art Institute and CSO, this "comfy", "old-world" Loop Russian proffers "boldly flavored" "dacha comfort food" and other "well-prepared" specialties via servers with "discretion and elan worthy of any haute Muscovite"; "exquisite teas" and "house-infused vodkas" round out the meal, though "prices on the high side" are part of the package.

Rustic House Ⓜ *American*
21 | **20** | **20** | **$48**

Lincoln Park | 1967 N. Halsted St. (Armitage Ave.) | 312-929-3227 | www.rustichousechicago.com

You may "dream about the rotisserie chicken" and other solid responsibly sourced meats at this "inviting" Lincoln Park American (sister to Gemini Bistro); farm-inspired decor and an "above-par" wine list keep it "warm and comfortable while still being upscale", and so many agree it's "fantastic without being overly fussy."

Ruth's Chris Steak House *Steak*
23 | **19** | **22** | **$68**

River North | 431 N. Dearborn St. (Hubbard St.) | 312-321-2725
Northbrook | Renaissance North Shore Hotel | 933 Skokie Blvd. (Sunset Ridge Rd.) | 847-498-6889
South Barrington | Arboretum Mall | 100 W. Higgins Rd. (Bartlett Rd.) | 847-551-3730
www.ruthschris.com

"Reliably excellent", these "civilized" triplets "honor" their "venerable" steakhouse franchise with "tender, flavorful" chops, "delicious" sides "large" enough to share and service that "could not be better"; so maybe it's "a bit corporate" and lacking "the character" of a local spot, but devotees insist the overall "consistent quality" still makes it "splurge"-worthy.

Ruxbin Ⓜ *Eclectic*
28 | **24** | **24** | **$45**

Noble Square | 851 N. Ashland Ave. (Pearson St.) | 312-624-8509 | www.ruxbinchicago.com

"Come early or be prepared to wait" at this Noble Square Eclectic, where Edward Kim puts together an "amazing" menu of "inventive", "high-end" "comfort food"; "small" digs lead to "crowded" conditions ("every inch of space is claimed"), and it doesn't accept reservations (except on Sundays), but service is "welcoming", and the BYO policy makes it an "incredible value"; P.S. don't forget to check out one of the "best bathrooms in the city."

Sabatino's ● *Italian* | 26 | 19 | 24 | $36 |

Irving Park | 4441 W. Irving Park Rd. (Kenneth Ave.) | 773-283-8331 | www.sabatinoschicago.com

"It does not get any more old school than this" attest admirers of this Old Irving Park "time machine" where you "get your money's worth" with "plentiful" portions of "delicious", "well-prepared" Italian "classics" served in "throwback" "supper club" surrounds"; "friendly" servers "done up" in white shirts and bow ties contribute to the "charm", but be warned it can be "crazy crowded" on weekends when there's piano music.

Sable Kitchen & Bar ● *American* | 23 | 22 | 22 | $47 |

River North | Hotel Palomar Chicago | 505 N. State St. (Illinois St.) | 312-755-9704 | www.sablechicago.com

"Inventive", "fun-to-share" American "small and medium bites" from former *Top Chef*-testant Heather Terhune "just click" at this River North hang in the Hotel Palomar where the "creative", "quality" cocktails "match the food" and fuel a "high-energy" bar scene; it's a "bit pricey" for some who find it "just ok" given the "hype", but the majority concludes "there's little room for disappointment here."

Sai Café *Japanese* | 27 | 17 | 23 | $37 |

Lincoln Park | 2010 N. Sheffield Ave. (Armitage Ave.) | 773-472-8080 | www.saicafe.com

There's "nothing crazy or too creative" because "it's all about the fish" at this "steady" Lincoln Park Japanese turning out "pristinely fresh", "spectacular" sushi and other "high-quality" fare via "efficient" servers; the "pleasant" enough decor doesn't inspire the same praise, but it still "can't be beat", especially given such "reasonable prices."

Saigon Sisters Ⓢ *Vietnamese* | 24 | 18 | 21 | $29 |

West Loop | 567 W. Lake St. (bet. Clinton & Jefferson Sts.) | 312-496-0090 | www.saigonsisters.com

"Banh mi me, baby!" implore "blown-away" boosters of this West Loop Vietnamese sister to the French Market stall where "interesting" fare boasting "bright flavors" tastes "upscale" but comes at "downscale prices"; "helpful" servers elevate the "basic" wood and steel space, but with limited seating, you may need to "get there in off hours" to snag a spot.

Saloon Steakhouse *Steak* | 22 | 18 | 21 | $53 |

Streeterville | Seneca Hotel | 200 E. Chestnut St. (Mies van der Rohe Way) | 312-280-5454 | www.saloonsteakhouse.com

A "hidden gem" in Streeterville's Seneca Hotel, this "clubby" "old Chicago steakhouse" matches the "solid" meat and seafood of some "famous-name" competitors, minus the "attitude" and "overcrowded tables"; as a "neighborhood hangout" it's "expensive", but carnivores contend it's still "a value for the dollar" considering the "quality."

Salpicón *Mexican*

24 | 21 | 22 | $52

Old Town | 1252 N. Wells St. (bet. Goethe & Scott Sts.) | 312-988-7811 | www.salpicon.com

A "standout", thanks to chef Priscila Satkoff's "command of regional cuisine", this Old Town Mexican "hits all the notes" with "inventively prepared" "authentic cuisine" paired with "tremendous margaritas", "tequilas galore" and an "outstanding wine list"; "helpful" staffers lend a "warm" feel in the "colorful" space, so somewhat costly tabs barely register for those deeming it an "all around winner."

Salsa 17 *Mexican*

21 | 21 | 21 | $32

Arlington Heights | 17 W. Campbell St. (bet. Dunton & Vail Aves.) | 847-590-1122 | www.salsa17.com

It's no wonder there's a "vibrant bar scene" since margaritas come in "virtually every flavor" at this "popular" Arlington Heights hacienda; it serves "savory", somewhat "upscale" Mexican food, including "terrific moles" and guacamole "made to order" at your table, and tabs are affordable.

San Soo Gab San ● *Korean*

25 | 10 | 14 | $25

Lincoln Square | 5247 N. Western Ave. (Foster Ave.) | 773-334-1589

A generous variety of "appetizing" small dishes pairs with an "excellent", "endless supply of cook-your-own-meats" at this Lincoln Square Korean BBQ overseen by a "speedy" crew; "the whole restaurant swims in smoke" and "your hair will smell for days", but budget-friendly tabs still help ensure regulars rate it "well worth it."

Santorini ● *Greek/Seafood*

22 | 19 | 20 | $41

Greektown | 800 W. Adams St. (Halsted St.) | 312-829-8820 | www.santorinichicago.com

From "great grilled octopus" and "expertly deboned" whole fish to other "hearty" Hellenic fare (both "traditional" and "modern"), "there's not a bum dish on the menu" assure aficionados of this Greektown seafooder; "lively" service and a "giant stone hearth" enhance the "casual" ambiance, and it's a strong "value" too – especially if you "go with a crowd" and order family-style.

Sapori Trattoria *Italian*

25 | 19 | 24 | $36

Lincoln Park | 2701 N. Halsted St. (Schubert Ave.) | 773-832-9999 | www.saporitrattoria.net

"Down-home" cooking is "guaranteed to delight" at this Lincoln Park Italian, a "small trattoria" where the food is "high quality", the "service always friendly" and the prices "fair"; sure, "decor could be better", but it's still "charming" – and there's "always a crowd."

Saranello's ● *Italian*

▽ 20 | 20 | 19 | $39

Wheeling | Westin Hotel | 601 N. Milwaukee Ave. (Wolf Rd.) | 847-777-6878 | www.saranellos.com

Cognoscenti croon about the "solid" fare ("love the meatballs") and rolling wine cart at this "reasonably priced" Lettuce Entertain You Italian in Wheeling's Westin Chicago North Shore; the "warm, welcoming" exposed-brick dining room further ups its allure.

NEW Sataza 🅱 *Indian*

— | — | — | I

Loop | Presidential Towers | 28 S. Clinton St. (bet. Madison & Monroe Sts.) | 312-655-8292 | www.sataza.com

The first location of a budding, bargain Indian eats concept comes to the Loop's Presidential Towers with a made-to-order, counter-serve setup; authentic ingredients are offered in wraps, rice bowls and salads with your pick of protein and house chutneys.

NEW Sauce & Bread Kitchen 🅼 *Eclectic/Sandwiches*

— | — | — | I

Edgewater | 6340 N. Clark St. (bet. Highland & Devon Aves.) | 773-216-5580 | www.sauceandbread.com

Merging two former food businesses (Co-Op Hot Sauce and Crumb) implied in the name, this Edgewater bakery/cafe offers a blackboard menu of sweets, sandwiches and Eclectic eats featuring housemade ingredients; the spare, hip setting has exposed brick, a map of the Midwest and a handful of seats; P.S. open Thursday–Sunday only.

The Savoy *American/Seafood*

— | — | — | M

Wicker Park | 1408 N. Milwaukee Ave. (bet. Evergreen & Wolcott Aves.) | 773-698-6925 | www.savoychicago.com

Seafood both raw and cooked plus a handful of fin-free apps, sides and mains come from an open kitchen at this Wicker Park New American set in a cozy dining room decorated with artwork from a local artist; a low-lit lounge in the back pours absinthe and cocktails, and there's a late-night menu offered too.

Sayat Nova *Armenian*

23 | 20 | 21 | $28

Streeterville | 157 E. Ohio St. (bet. Michigan Ave. & St. Clair St.) | 312-644-9159 | www.sayatnovachicago.com

"They have a way with lamb" and other "delicious" specialties at this "affordable" Streeterville Armenian, a "charming" "urban oasis" that's been feeding "Magnificent Mile shoppers" since 1969; atmospheric lantern lighting and mosaic alcoves lend a "gorgeous" touch, and while it's "not all that exotic" for everyone, it still works as a "change of pace" or just a "cozy" respite on those "cold Chicago nights."

Schwa 🅱🅼 *American*

28 | 15 | 23 | $143

Wicker Park | 1466 N. Ashland Ave. (Le Moyne St.) | 773-252-1466 | www.schwarestaurant.com

"Super high-end food without the attitude" describes Michael Carlson's "very small" Wicker Park BYO where a "hyper-creative", "well-executed" New American tasting menu is delivered by the chefs themselves; "less than minimalist" decor "fits the vibe", and it all adds up to a "singular dining experience", so even with spendy tabs, reservations are "nearly impossible to come by."

Scofflaw ❶ *Pub Food*

— | — | — | I

Logan Square | 3201 W. Armitage Ave. (bet. Kedzie & Sawyer Aves.) | 773-252-9700 | www.scofflawchicago.com

Expect a ramshackle farm-meets-parlor vibe – complete with tractor seat barstools, ornate settees and intimate nooks – at this Logan

Square drinking den, where a Longman & Eagle alum turns out gussied-up, pubby small plates; meanwhile, its tipples pay homage to gin, which appears in modern, carefully crafted cocktails, sipped before a roaring fireplace or in sweeping, semicircular booths.

| | FOOD | DECOR | SERVICE | COST |

Scoozi! *Italian* — 20 | 20 | 20 | $36

River North | 410 W. Huron St. (bet. Hudson Ave. & Sedgwick St.) | 312-943-5900 | www.leye.com

A "favorite" since "forever" (or 1986), this midpriced River North Italian is a Lettuce Entertain You stalwart for "homestyle" pastas and brick-oven pizzas (plus gluten-free offerings) delivered by "professional" staffers in a "huge" space where groups and families can "spread out"; so while it may offer "nothing daring", it's a "consistent" choice that keeps most "happy."

Seasons 52 *American* — 25 | 25 | 26 | $39

Schaumburg | 1770 E. Higgins Rd. (bet. Mall Dr. & Martingale Rd.) | 847-517-5252
Oak Brook | Oakbrook Center Shopping Mall | 3 Oakbrook Ctr. (Kingery Hwy.) | 630-571-4752
www.seasons52.com

At this "moderately priced", "über-healthy" chain the "creative" New American "concoctions" "change with the seasons" and weigh in at 475 calories or less, resulting in "incredible", "guilt-free dining"; "comfortable" upscale-casual environs and the "most attentive" servers further explain why it's "well patronized."

NEW Senza 🅂🅜 *American* — ▽ 28 | 23 | 26 | $78

Lakeview | 2873 N. Broadway (Surf St.) | 773-770-3527 | www.senzachicago.com

The "artfully presented" tasting menus are met with "oohs, aahs" and "groans of pleasure" at this "totally gluten-free" Lakeview New American where the "interesting" dishes highlight local ingredients; "warm, genuine" staffers watch over the the storefront space, and expensive tabs go hand in hand with the "fine-dining" experience; P.S. there's also a daytime bakery that offers coffee and treats.

Sepia *American* — 25 | 25 | 24 | $63

West Loop | 123 N. Jefferson St. (bet. Randolph & Washington Sts.) | 312-441-1920 | www.sepiachicago.com

Chef Andrew Zimmerman's "refined", "imaginative" New American dishes are equally matched by a "charming", "comfortable" dining room and "inviting" bar at this "sophisticated" West Loop "destination"; a "well-chosen" wine list and "polished" service up the appeal, and though it's "not inexpensive", for fans it's "the complete package."

1776 🅂 *American* — 25 | 20 | 23 | $43

Crystal Lake | 397 W. Virginia St./Rte. 14 (bet. Dole & McHenry Aves.) | 815-356-1776 | www.1776restaurant.com

Elk, boar, ostrich and bison are just some of the "unique" specials starring on the "excellent" and "interesting" New American menu at this "charming" Crystal Lake "jewel" also offering a "magnificent wine list" ("the owner, Andy, will help you choose"); "decor is lack-

ing, but who cares" say patriots who point to the "warm", "knowledgeable" staffers and moderate tabs, insisting "John Hancock,
Thomas Jefferson and the rest would be proud to dine here."

720 South Bar & Grill *American*   — | — | — | M

South Loop | Hilton Chicago | 720 S. Michigan Ave. (bet. Balbo Ave. &
8th St.) | 312-922-4400 | www.hilton.com

Seasonal American fare, including small plates, seafood and steaks,
plus updated dessert classics and creative breakfasts are what to
expect at this midpriced grill in the South Loop Hilton; the sophisticated setting combines various woods, fibers and natural stone
alongside white leather chairs, shimmery banquettes, drum light
fixtures and a wine storage room.

NEW Shaman 🖾 Ⓜ ⇪ *Mexican*   — | — | — | I

Ukrainian Village | 1438 W. Chicago Ave. (bet. Ashland Ave. &
Nobel St.) | 312-226-4175 | www.shamanchicago.com

The team behind Chilam Balam is behind this cash-only BYO in
Ukrainian Village serving an inexpensive mix of Mexican small
plates and some crossovers from its sibling's menu; the folksy room
has bright multicolored walls, and there's seasonal outdoor seating.

Shanghai Terrace 🖾 *Chinese*   26 | 28 | 26 | $69

River North | Peninsula Chicago | 108 E. Superior St., 4th fl.
(bet. Michigan Ave. & Rush St.) | 312-573-6744 |
www.chicago.peninsula.com

You'll feel "transported into another era" at this dining room in River
North's Peninsula Hotel, where "excellent", "upscale" Chinese fare
is served in an "exquisite" 1930s-styled room that "makes you feel
like you're in Shanghai" (and wins top Decor honors in Chicago);
"genuine" service and a "romantically lit" terrace provide further
enticements – just expect "premium" pricing.

Shaw's Crab House *Seafood*   25 | 21 | 23 | $53

River North | 21 E. Hubbard St. (bet. State St. & Wabash Ave.) |
312-527-2722

Schaumburg | 1900 E. Higgins Rd. (bet. Frontage & Woodfield Rds.) |
847-517-2722

www.shawscrabhouse.com

A "go-to if you want fish", this "bustling" River North "standby" and its
Schaumburg sequel deliver with "excellent", "well-prepared" dishes
including "top-notch" sushi and "fresh" oysters; service gets good
marks and the "retro", "old school"–style environs also please, and
if tabs are a little "steep", you can always "go casual in the bar area."

Shula's Steakhouse *Steak*   ▽ 22 | 18 | 22 | $77

Streeterville | Sheraton Chicago Hotel & Towers | 301 E. North Water St.
(bet. Columbus Dr. & New St.) | 312-670-0788

Itasca | Westin Chicago NW | 400 Park Blvd. (Thorndale Ave.) |
630-775-1499

www.donshula.com

"In a crowded field", "football nuts" befriend these Itasca and
Streeterville links of the national steakhouse chain, where memen-

FOOD | DECOR | SERVICE | COST

tos nod to the undefeated 1972 Miami Dolphins and "nice" servers "show cuts of meat" – including a behemoth porterhouse – tableside "before you order"; if some call the "caricature" concept ("menus on footballs?") a bit "goofy", swains support it, even despite Bears-leaning "regional partisanship."

NEW Siena Tavern ● *Italian* — | — | — | M

River North | 51 W. Kinzie St. (bet. Clark St. & Dearborn Pkwy.) | 312-595-1322 | www.sienatavern.com
Expect a "trendy, hip scene" at this expansive River North Italian from *Top Chef* alum Fabio Viviani, where midpriced fare like Neapolitan pies, housemade pastas and mozzarella-bar offerings are backed by Boot-centric wines and "tasty, addictive" cocktails; there are multiple seating areas including a central bar and lounge, and the rustic-meets-modern vibe is helped along by distressed wood, metalwork, textured walls and tufted leather.

Signature Room *American* 17 | 24 | 19 | $60

Streeterville | John Hancock Ctr. | 875 N. Michigan Ave. (bet. Chestnut St. & Delaware Pl.) | 312-787-9596 | www.signatureroom.com
It's all about the "spectacular" views – some of the "best in the city" – at this 95th-floor Streeterville New American perched atop the Hancock; sure, many find the "expensive" fare merely "ok" and say service can be "variable", but the "beautiful" scenery alone guarantees it's a "perfect special date place" and equally "cool" for a "couple of cocktails."

Silver Seafood ● *Chinese/Seafood* ▽ 27 | 11 | 18 | $22

Uptown | 4829 N. Broadway (Lawrence Ave.) | 773-784-0668 | www.silverseafoodrestaurant.com
"Terrific" Cantonese "comfort food" and seafood specialties are the hook at this affordable Uptown "favorite" where regulars recommend skipping the Americanized fare and trying "something different from the real Chinese menu"; the "simple setting" harkens "back to the '50s" and "service can vary", but "your taste buds will appreciate" the experience; P.S. open daily until 1 AM.

Simply It *Vietnamese* 21 | 14 | 19 | $19

Lincoln Park | 2269 N. Lincoln Ave. (Belden Ave.) | 773-248-0884 | www.simplyitrestaurant.com
An "extensive menu" of "authentic" Vietnamese dishes greets guests at this "reliable" Lincoln Park BYO "bargain"; if the decor lags behind, "attentive" service makes up for it, so most simply have a "lovely" meal.

Sixteen *American* 25 | 27 | 25 | $91

River North | Trump International Hotel & Tower | 401 N. Wabash Ave., 16th fl. (Kinzie St.) | 312-588-8030 | www.trumpchicagohotel.com
Floor-to-ceiling windows afford "awesome" city views at this "special-occasion" New American set on the 16th floor of River North's Trump International Hotel & Tower, where "fresh, seasonal ingredients" are

turned into "excellent" "works of art", offered in different tasting menus or à la carte; the upscale space manages to feel "intimate but expansive at the same time", and the "agreeable" staff helps take the sting out of "expensive" tabs.

Slurping Turtle ● *Japanese/Noodle Shop*   22 | 21 | 19 | $27

River North | 116 W. Hubbard St. (bet. Clark & La Salle Sts.) | 312-464-0466 | www.slurpingturtle.com

Diners can "slurp down" a "comforting bowl of steaming ramen" or "dive into" more adventurous "noshes" at chef Takashi Yagihashi's "hip" River North izakaya starring "casual Japanese food with modern flair"; if the service can seem a touch "iffy", fans instead focus on the "funky" ultramod decor, advising wafflers to just "do it" and go.

NEW Smalls Ⓢ Ⓜ *BBQ*   – | – | – | I

Avondale | 4009 N. Albany Ave. (Irving Park Rd.) | 312-857-4221 | www.smallschicago.com

House-smoked barbecue with funky modern condiments and buttermilk fried chicken star on the somewhat small menu at this budget-friendly Irving Park 'smoke shack & more'; it also serves breakfast and weekend brunch (but no booze) in diminutive counter-serve digs with a handful of seats.

Smith & Wollensky *Steak*   22 | 19 | 21 | $76

River North | 318 N. State St. (Kinzie St.) | 312-670-9900 | www.smithandwollensky.com

You can join the "business expense crowd" for "celebrity-watching" at this NYC transplant in River North, where "big-portioned", "cooked-as-ordered" "prime" meats are served in "happening" wood-accented digs; "helpful" staffers "take their responsibilities seriously" and the "lovely outdoor patio" offers "wonderful views", so dissenters dubbing it "underwhelming" are in the minority.

Smoke Daddy *BBQ*   22 | 14 | 17 | $24

Wicker Park | 1804 W. Division St. (bet. Honore & Wood Sts.) | 773-772-6656 | www.thesmokedaddy.com

Diners are enticed by the "meaty perfume in the air" at this Wicker Park "BBQ heaven" where "pretty good everything" includes "juicy and tender" ribs and an "awesome selection of sides"; "friendly" staffers mind the "no-frills" space, and though they don't take reservations, a recent expansion should "make crowds less of an issue."

Smoque BBQ Ⓜ *BBQ*   26 | 11 | 18 | $20

Irving Park | 3800 N. Pulaski Rd. (Grace St.) | 773-545-7427 | www.smoquebbq.com

"Still the best" in town (possibly "on the planet") say fans of this "laid-back" Old Irving Park "king of barbecue" offering "sublime" eats with an "addictive 'smoque' taste" including "outstanding" brisket and "delicious" ribs plus "very good" sides and "unbelievable" sauces; the "spartan" decor and "shared Formica tables are nothing to get excited about" and lines often "stretch out the door", but no matter since most agree it's "so freaking worth it", especially since BYO further makes its "value off the charts."

	FOOD	DECOR	SERVICE	COST

Socca *French/Italian*
| 22 | 20 | 21 | $39 |

Lakeview | 3301 N. Clark St. (Aldine Ave.) | 773-248-1155 | www.soccachicago.com

"Robust" French-Italian fare and "courteous" service shine at this "cozy" Lakeview bistro where the "specials are a highlight" and rates are "reasonable"; "versatile" enough for special occasions or "random nights", it's an overall "neighborhood fave."

Sola *American*
| 24 | 21 | 23 | $45 |

North Center/St. Ben's | 3868 N. Lincoln Ave. (Byron St.) | 773-327-3868 | www.sola-restaurant.com

"Say aloha to fresh, local flavors with an island twist" at chef-owner Carol Wallack's Hawaiian-inspired North Center New American that's "an eating experience to share" with "imaginative preparations" set down by "helpful" servers in "comfortable", contemporary digs; while quibblers claim it's "not particularly memorable", most insist it "rises above" the rest – and boasts a "gem of a brunch" on weekends.

South Branch Tavern Grille ⌧ *American*
| ▽ 20 | 19 | 16 | $27 |

Loop | 100 S. Wacker Dr. (Monroe St.) | 312-546-6177 | www.southbranchchicago.com

Whether for business lunches or "after-work drinks in the Loop", this New American fuels go-getters with a "vast", moderately priced menu and thoughtful beer list; solid service and an open, airy dining room further the year-round appeal, while scenic riverside seating makes it a "great venue in the summer"; P.S. weekdays only.

The Southern ●Ⓜ *Southern*
| 20 | 21 | 18 | $30 |

Wicker Park | 1840 W. North Ave. (bet. Honore St. & Wolcott Ave.) | 773-342-1840 | www.thesouthernchicago.com

"Winner winner, fried chicken dinner" chant cheerleaders who are "happy to be surrounded by Southern favorites" like "juicy, crisp" birds, "fluffy" biscuits and "gravy that will put your mama to shame" at this rustic Wicker Park hangout; artful cocktails and a "beautiful" rooftop deck (complete with cabanas) are reasons to linger.

Southport Grocery & Café *American*
| 23 | 17 | 20 | $20 |

Lakeview | 3552 N. Southport Ave. (bet. Addison St. & Cornelia Ave.) | 773-665-0100 | www.southportgrocery.com

"If you can climb over the strollers" and endure "long waits on weekends", you'll be rewarded with "creative", "consistently good" brunch/lunch fare delivered by "friendly" staffers at this midpriced Lakeview New American; perusing the "super-cool dry goods" passes time while queued for "limited seating" in the "small", "crowded" space, and regulars who "don't skip the cupcakes" warn you may need a "double workout" afterward.

South Water Kitchen *American*
| 14 | 15 | 16 | $32 |

Loop | Hotel Monaco | 225 N. Wabash Ave. (Wacker Pl.) | 312-236-9300 | www.southwaterkitchen.com

"Comfortable surroundings", "quick service" and "simple" American food draw "after-work" tipplers and a "mature", "pre-theater" crowd to this midpriced, "bistro-like" Loop eatery in the Hotel Monaco; if some find it "uninspired" all around, they concede the patio seating's an "upside."

Spacca Napoli Pizzeria M *Pizza*

27 | 19 | 22 | $25

Ravenswood | 1769 W. Sunnyside Ave. (bet. Hermitage & Ravenswood Aves.) | 773-878-2420 | www.spaccanapolipizzeria.com

You'll feel like you're "truly in Italy" at this affordable Ravenswood pizzeria where a "traditional, Naples-style" wood oven bakes "amazing" thin-crust Neopolitan pies; the casual space may lag a bit behind, but it's joined by a "wonderful" patio, and the staff is "friendly and efficient."

Spiaggia *Italian*

26 | 26 | 26 | $104

Gold Coast | One Magnificent Mile Bldg. | 980 N. Michigan Ave. (Oak St.) | 312-280-2750 | www.spiaggiarestaurant.com

"The place for a romantic evening" say fans of Tony Mantuano's Gold Coast Italian where "absolutely heavenly" fare is matched by an "elegant" dining room (jackets required) with a "nice view of the lake"; sure, it's "not for the faint of heart or light of wallet", but with "wonderful" service it has all the ingredients for a "special night."

Sprout M *American*

26 | 24 | 25 | $79

Lincoln Park | 1417 W. Fullerton Ave. (bet. Janssen & Southport Aves.) | 773-348-0706 | www.sproutrestaurant.com

Chef-"magician" Dale Levitski "excites taste buds" at his Lincoln Park New American, a "showplace for creative cuisine" with "innovative combinations", "clean flavors" and "outstanding tastes"; service is "warm and knowledgeable" and the stone-walled space "pleasant", which helps quiet those who find it "overpriced."

Stained Glass
Wine Bar Bistro *American*

24 | 21 | 23 | $55

Evanston | 1735 Benson Ave. (bet. Church & Clark Sts.) | 847-864-8600 | www.thestainedglass.com

At once "comfortable" and "classy", this "high-end" Evanston New American turns out "creative", "uniformly delicious" cuisine complemented by "an extraordinary wine selection" (including "imaginative flights"); you can "trust the advice" from "helpful servers" and prices are deemed "reasonable" given the "quality", so in sum, it's a "very returnable place"; P.S. its Cellar at The Stained Glass sibling is a more affordable option.

Standard Grill *American*

- | - | - | M

Westmont | Standard Market | 333 E. Ogden Ave. (Blackhawk Dr.) | 630-366-7040 | www.standardmarket.com

Set within the gleaming-white, barnlike Standard Market in Westmont, this sleek American uses artisanal, local ingredients in its affordable menu of salads, sandwiches, pizza and more; to drink are house cocktails, wine and beer (bottles from the bev section can be imbibed, corkage fee-free) plus an array of on-display, fruit-infused waters.

	FOOD	DECOR	SERVICE	COST

Stanley's Kitchen & Tap ❶ *American*   19 | 14 | 16 | $21

Lincoln Park | 1970 N. Lincoln Ave. (Sedgwick St.) | 312-642-0007 | www.stanleyskitchenandtap.com

Affordable American "comfort food" ("well-executed" fried chicken, "to-die-for" mac 'n' cheese) is a draw at this "casual" Lincoln Park "institution" that's "always a good time", especially when it morphs into a "lively" scene after dinner; meanwhile, reviewers who relish the brunch and its hangover-abating Bloody Mary bar call weekends the "best time to visit" for a "Southern fix."

Star of Siam *Thai*   20 | 18 | 19 | $21

River North | 11 E. Illinois St. (bet. State St. & Wabash Ave.) | 312-670-0100 | www.starofsiamchicago.com

It's "hard to find" given the area's "double-decker streets", but this "low-key" River North Thai is "worth the expedition" for "fragrant rice dishes" (with the "best peanut sauce around") and other picks from a "reliably decent" roster; "fast" service, "soothing" surrounds and overall "value" for lunch and takeout make it a "go-to" for folks who've "loved it for years."

State & Lake Chicago Tavern *American*   16 | 17 | 17 | $34

Loop | theWit Hotel | 201 N. State St. (Lake St.) | 312-239-9400 | www.stateandlakechicago.com

Not quite a "cookie-cutter hotel" hang, this "well-decorated", affordable Loop American offers a bit of a "respite" from the "aggressively hip theWit", coupling "tasty", locally sourced food with Midwestern beers and "good cocktails"; it's accommodating to "yuppies" after-work and the "pre- and post-theater" set, though too "pretentious" and "blah" for those who feel the dining's an "after-thought."

NEW Stetsons Modern   ▽ 24 | 22 | 24 | $58
Steak + Sushi *Steak*
(fka Stetson's Chop House)

Loop | Hyatt Regency | 151 E. Wacker Dr. (bet. Michigan & Stetson Aves.) | 312-239-4491 | www.stetsonschicago.com

The old-guard Stetson's Chop House in the Loop's Hyatt Regency has reconcepted into this updated steak and sushi hybrid as part of a big-bucks renovation; the menu covers raw fish and pricey meat cuts, while the striking space features glass-encased wine storage, embedded wall fireplaces and a lounge.

Storefront Company ❶Ⓜ *American*   - | - | - | E

Wicker Park | 1941 W. North Ave. (bet. Damen & Winchester Aves.) | 773-661-2609 | www.thestorefrontcompany.com

Acclaimed chef Bryan Moscatello (ex DC's Zola and Potenza) is cooking up modern American farm-to-table plates small and large in Wicker Park's famed Flat Iron Building, where patrons can have a moderately priced meal or full-blown expensive dining experience; seating options within the sleek digs include communal tables, a cozy dining room and a massive bar issuing updates on classic cocktails, and there's also a chef's open kitchen 'counter' showcasing four-course tasting menus.

	FOOD	DECOR	SERVICE	COST

Stout Barrel House & Galley *American* — | — | — | M
(fka Manor)

River North | 642 N. Clark St. (bet. Erie & Ontario Sts.) |
312-475-1390 | www.stoutchicago.com

The chef-driven gastropub fare at this sprawling River North tavern
can be enjoyed as a midpriced meal or a late-night snack (it's open
till 5 AM on Saturday); the rustic wood-and-brick setting includes a
central bar offering 20 rotating beers and cocktail pairings, a corner
fireplace and scattered TVs.

⒩⒠⒲ Suite 25 ● *S American* — | — | — | M

Logan Square | 2529 N. Milwaukee Ave., 2nd fl. (bet. Kedzie &
Sacramento Aves.) | 773-360-7478 | www.suite25chicago.com

South American bar food is in the spotlight at this hip, midpriced Logan
Square lair where lunch and dinner range from ceviche and a Peruvian
steak sandwich to stuffed burgers and empanadas; backlit by night,
the bar highlights an impressive global beer list complete with ciders
and large-format selections, while the scene encompasses 10 TVs,
a massive projection screen, booths and sofa seating.

Sullivan's Steakhouse *Steak* 24 | 21 | 21 | $61

River North | 415 N. Dearborn St. (Hubbard St.) | 312-527-3510
Lincolnshire | 250 Marriott Dr. (Milwaukee Ave.) | 847-883-0311
Naperville | 244 S. Main St. (bet. Chicago & Jackson Aves.) | 630-305-0230
www.sullivansteakhouse.com

"Sizzling steaks melt in your mouth" at this "high-end" chophouse
chain boasting "well-executed" presentations and a staff that's "always at the ready"; "dark, masculine" stylings and frequent live jazz
add to the "throwback atmosphere", and while a few feel it's not
quite "top tier", most are happy to shell out for "special occasions."

Sultan's Market *Mideastern* 21 | 13 | 16 | $11

Lincoln Park | 2521 N. Clark St. (bet. Deming & James Pls.) |
312-638-9151
Wicker Park | 2057 W. North Ave. (Hoyne Ave.) | 773-235-3072 ⊄
www.chicagofalafel.com

An "endless" salad bar "full of nowhere-else selections" is a draw at
this counter-service BYO duo in Lincoln Park and Wicker Park also
offering "fresh", "light" Middle Eastern fare like lentil soup and
falafel; service and decor may lag a bit behind, but with wallet-
friendly tabs (Wicker Park is cash-only), they're a "perfect lunch
place for every day."

⒩⒠⒲ Sumi Robata Bar *Japanese* — | — | — | M

River North | 702 N. Wells St. (bet. Huron & Superior Sts.) |
312-988-7864 | www.sumirobatabar.com

Robata and sashimi (but not sushi) are the specialties at this midpriced River North Japanese where former Japonais principal Gene
Kato serves up grilled meats, seafood and veggies with cocktails from
the downstairs Charcoal Bar plus a tight list of wines, beer and sake;
the digs are modern and minimalist (blond wood, marble and white accents), and you can sit at the robata bar to watch the chef work.

Sunda *Asian*

| 25 | 25 | 22 | $51 |

River North | 110 W. Illinois St. (bet. Clark & LaSalle Sts.) | 312-644-0500 | www.sundachicago.com

The "dressed-to-impress" set piles into this expensive River North hang for "excellent" sushi and other "amazeballs" Asian fusion fare plus "delicious" cocktails and a sake and wine list fit "for the most experienced drinkers"; service is generally "timely", and the "huge" modern space includes a "see-and-be-seen" bar area where "loud" conditions are just a part of the "trendy" atmosphere.

Sun Wah BBQ *Chinese*

| 25 | 11 | 16 | $24 |

Uptown | 5039 N. Broadway (bet. Argyle & Winona Sts.) | 773-769-1254 | www.sunwahbbq.com

"If you haven't had the duck dinner, you ain't living" ("don't forget to order ahead") insist regulars of this Uptown Chinese "favorite", where "it's hard to go wrong" when the other "authentic" dishes, especially the "Hong Kong–style BBQ" offerings, are so "chopstick licking good"; the atmosphere might be "nothing special" and when "it's packed, and that's often", service can be "hurried", but most agree "it's all worth it with cheap prices" – and of course "incredible food."

Superdawg Drive-In *Hot Dogs*

| 21 | 17 | 19 | $11 |

Northwest Side | 6363 N. Milwaukee Ave. (Devon Ave.) | 773-763-0660 ◗

Wheeling | 333 S. Milwaukee Ave. (Mors Ave.) | 847-459-1900 | www.superdawg.com

Car hops say "hiya" while handing out "Whoopercheesies", "crispy, light" fries and "juicy" Chicago-style dogs at this "classic" Northwest Side drive-in "legend" (a "must-see" for its rooftop mascots) and its "fantastic" spin-off in Wheeling; "steeped in tradition", it's the "ultimate" for many, and even skeptics say "try it once to check it off your bucket list."

🆕 Sushi Dokku ⓈⓂ *Japanese*

| - | - | - | M |

West Loop | 823 W. Randolph St. (Green St.) | 312-455-8238 | www.sushidokku.com

The team from the former Sushi Wabi returns to the West Loop with this midpriced Japanese, where raw fish, dressed nigiri, maki rolls and small plates are accompanied by adult beverages focusing on sake, whiskey, beer and wine; dark, mixed woods contribute to the minimal setting, and seating options include the sushi bar, tables and seasonal dining alfresco.

Sushi Naniwa *Japanese*

| ▽ 22 | 10 | 22 | $36 |

River North | 607 N. Wells St. (bet. Ohio & Ontario Sts.) | 312-255-8555 | www.sushinaniwa.com

Regulars have "no complaints" about this Japanese "go-to" in River North, with moderately priced, "fresh sushi rolls done well", "attentive" service and all-around "neighborhood-joint" appeal; though it has "zero atmosphere" compared to Bob San (its more upscale sib), the patio gives it a boost in the summer.

Sushi Para *Japanese*
| 19 | 11 | 15 | $24 |

Palatine | 1268 E. Dundee Rd. (Baldwin Ln.) | 847-202-9922 | www.sushiparachicago.com

Sushi Para D *Japanese*

Lincoln Park | 543 W. Diversey Pkwy. (bet. Hampden & Lehmann Cts.) | 773-248-1808 | www.sushiparachicago.com

Sushi Para II *Japanese*

Lincoln Park | 2256 N. Clark St. (bet. Belden & Grant Pls.) | 773-477-3219 | www.sushiparachicago.com

Sushi Para M *Japanese*

Bucktown | 1633 N. Milwaukee Ave. (bet. Damen & Wabansia Aves.) | 773-252-6828 | www.sushiparachicago.com

Sushi Sai *Japanese*

Loop | 123 N. Wacker Dr. (Randolph St.) | 312-332-8822 | www.sushisaionline.com

"Go hungry and order as much as you can" advise the initiated at this perennially "packed" Japanese mini-chain where the "quality", "all-you-can-eat" sushi "never stops" (a "long enough" à la carte menu is also offered); sure, there's "not much atmosphere" and service can be "indifferent", but devotees still insist the "bargain" is "hard to beat"; P.S. the Bucktown and Lincoln Park locations are BYO.

Sushisamba Rio ● *Japanese/S American*
| 20 | 23 | 18 | $51 |

River North | 504 N. Wells St. (Illinois St.) | 312-595-2300 | www.sushisamba.com

"Fashionista"-friendly digs (including a chic rooftop bar) set the stage for "inventive" sushi and "eclectic" Japanese–South American plates at this "trendy" River North "scene"; servers keep the "fun drinks" coming, so revelers overlook pricey tabs to soak in the "cool" vibe.

🆕 Sweet Baby Ray's Barbecue ● *BBQ*
| – | – | – | M |

Wrigleyville | 3478 N. Clark St. (Cornelia Ave.) | 773-975-7427 | www.sbrbbq.com

This midpriced BBQ mini-chain comes to Wrigleyville with its classic house-smoked barbecue with 17 sauce options, 100-plus bourbons and a wallboard of craft beers; the casual, meat-and-sauce-colored setting is home to several flat-screen TVs and an outdoor patio.

Sweet Maple Café *American*
| 26 | 16 | 21 | $20 |

Little Italy/University Village | 1339 W. Taylor St. (bet. Loomis & Racine Sts.) | 312-243-8908 | www.sweetmaplecafe.com

Regulars "recommend" this "tiny" Little Italy American given its "phenomenal", "down-home" daytime fare; toss in affordable tabs and solid service, and the only catch is that you may have to "wait in line" since the modest space is "not nearly as big as its popularity."

Swordfish *Japanese*
| ∇ 27 | 21 | 23 | $75 |

Batavia | 207 N. Randall Rd. (McKee St.) | 630-406-6463 | www.swordfishsushi.com

Some of the "best sushi in the Western 'burbs" can be found at this moderate Japanese offering an "interesting" menu of creative rolls and grilled dishes; modern decor and a solid staff increase the appeal.

	FOOD	DECOR	SERVICE	COST

NEW Table, Donkey & Stick *American/European*

	FOOD	DECOR	SERVICE	COST
	-	-	-	M

Logan Square | 2728 West Armitage Avenue (Fairfield Ave.) | 773-486-8525 | www.tabledonkeystick.com

Shin Thompson (of the former Bonsoiree) is back with this Alpine-inspired Logan Square restaurant named for a Grimm fairy tale where the midpriced New American menu of small and large plates features artisanal ingredients and mixed European influences; there's also small-production wines and beers from Austria and Bavaria, plus brandy and liqueur flights, all poured in a space decorated with wood, rustic tools and copper pots and home to an outdoor fire pit.

Table Fifty-two *American/Southern*

FOOD	DECOR	SERVICE	COST
25	23	24	$57

Gold Coast | 52 W. Elm St. (bet. Clark & Dearborn Sts.) | 312-573-4000 | www.tablefifty-two.com

For "Southern food done well", fans head to this pricey Gold Coast haunt where Art Smith prepares "comfort food" with a "refined flair" and "gourmet twist"; service is "on par" with the offerings, and the "tucked-away" carriage house setting has a "cozy", "homey feel."

Taco Joint Urban Taqueria & Cantina *Mexican*

FOOD	DECOR	SERVICE	COST
23	16	19	$20

Lincoln Park | 1969 N. Halsted St. (bet. Armitage Ave. & Willow St.) | 312-951-2457
NEW **Near North** | 158 W. Ontario St. (bet. LaSalle & Wells Sts.) | 312-337-8226 ◖
www.tacojoint.com

"Tantalizing" tacos with "interesting flavors" and other inexpensive Mexican street eats send "taste buds into a fury of joy" at this Lincoln Park sister to Zocalo (with a newer Near North brother); colorful cantina surrounds, "fast" service and a full bar including 50 agave tequilas make it a happy-hour natural, but meal-goers should be advised it doesn't take rezzies.

TAC Quick *Thai*

FOOD	DECOR	SERVICE	COST
26	16	18	$19

Wrigleyville | 3930 N. Sheridan Rd. (bet. Dakin St. & Irving Park Rd.) | 773-327-5253 | www.tacquick.net

For "out-of-the-ordinary Northern Thai dishes", go with the "secret menu, all the way" say seekers of "cheap eats, deliciously done" at this "authentic" Wrigleyville BYO; black-and-white decor, sidewalk seating and a "convenient location close to public transport" enhance the "way-better-than-average" experience.

Takashi Ⓜ *American/French*

FOOD	DECOR	SERVICE	COST
28	23	25	$66

Bucktown | 1952 N. Damen Ave. (Armitage Ave.) | 773-772-6170 | www.takashichicago.com

Fans are "blown away" by "true master" Takashi Yagihashi's "inspired", "soulful" New American–New French dishes at this Bucktown destination, where the "beautifully" presented Japanese-tinged dishes are set down by a "courteous" crew; the "cozy" space has an "understated upscale" vibe, and "pricey" tabs go hand in hand with the "fine-dining" experience.

	FOOD	DECOR	SERVICE	COST

NEW Takito Kitchen 🅂🅼 *Mexican* — | — | — | | I

Ukrainian Village | 2013 W. Division St. (Damen Ave.) |
773-687-9620 | www.takitokitchen.com

In Wicker Park's former Sabor Saveur space, this modern taqueria
features a Mexican–Nuevo Latino menu taking creative license with
seasonal, artisanal tacos (with numerous craft salsas) and sharing
plates, all paired with premium tequila, mescal and rum cocktails,
plus beer, wine, sangria and aguas frescas; the rustic-industrial space
houses a cement bar, open kitchen, handmade wood benches, street
art and vintage-inspired lighting.

Tallgrass 🅼 *French* — 27 | 25 | 27 | $82

Lockport | 1006 S. State St. (10th St.) | 815-838-5566 |
www.tallgrassrestaurant.com

The "fabulous" "old-school" French fare takes diners on "a trip back in
time" at this prix fixe–only Lockport "destination" where "surprising
innovations" elevate "classic" dishes; set in a "handsome, historic"
building, it "delivers a complete dining experience" with "knowledgeable, attentive" staffers and environs that are "elegant but not
stuffy", so many agree you "can't beat it for a world-class evening" –
even if "it'll take years before you can afford to return."

Tango Sur *Argentinean/Steak* — 24 | 18 | 19 | $31

Lakeview | 3763 N. Southport Ave. (Grace St.) | 773-477-5466 |
www.tangosur.net

"Serious meat lovers" appreciate that "flavorful steaks won't break
the bank" at this "authentic" Argentinean BYO in Lakeview where
"huge" servings of "delicious" beef with "flavorful sauces" come at
"surprisingly low prices"; some lament "long waits" and "crowded
weekends", but service that gets few complaints, a "candlelit" ambiance and outdoor seating help keep it "worth a stop."

Tank Noodle
Restaurant *Vietnamese* — 25 | 11 | 17 | $15
(aka Phò Xe Tång)

Uptown | 4953-55 N. Broadway (Argyle St.) | 773-878-2253 |
www.tank-noodle.com

"Hits" abound on the "book"-sized menu at this "popular"
Uptown Vietnamese where the "delicious", "authentic" offerings, including "delicate", "well-flavored" pho, compensate for
the modest, "hole-in-the-wall" setting; BYO makes the "super-
reasonable" tabs even more palatable, and service works "fast"
even when "busy."

Tank Sushi *Japanese* — 20 | 16 | 15 | $30

Lincoln Square | 4514 N. Lincoln Ave. (bet. Sunnyside & Wilson Aves.) |
773-769-2600 | www.tanksushi.com

Fans declare this "happening" Lincoln Square Japanese in simple,
modern digs a "destination for sushi and rolls"; though detractors
deem it "nothing memorable" and call out "spotty" service, bargain-
hunters can't resist the weekday lunch and weekend specials when
half-off maki offers "more bang for your buck."

	FOOD	DECOR	SERVICE	COST

Tanoshii *Japanese*
▽ 28 | 17 | 23 | $37

Andersonville | 5547 N. Clark St. (bet. Bryn Mawr Ave. & Gregory St.) | 773-878-6886

Chef-owner Mike Ham "takes pride and joy in his work and it shows" gush Andersonville groupies of the "spectacularly beautiful" sushi and other "custom-made creations" at this midpriced Japanese BYO; if the decor doesn't exactly inspire praise, "congenial, pleasant" service does, and most agree "you will not be disappointed."

Tapas Barcelona *Spanish*
20 | 18 | 19 | $29

Evanston | Northshore Hotel Retirement Home | 1615 Chicago Ave. (bet. Church & Davis Sts.) | 847-866-9900 | www.tapasbarcelona.com

"You can almost picture an Almodóvar scene playing out at the next table" at this "festive", "energetic" Evanston Spaniard where diners leave "happy and satisfied" thanks to "high-quality", "share-friendly" tapas (paella and pizza too) at moderate prices; servers are generally "attentive" and seating on the outdoor patio is "a dream."

Tapas Gitana Ⓜ *Spanish*
22 | 17 | 20 | $34

Lakeview | 3445 N. Halsted St. (bet. Cornelia Ave. & Roscoe St.) | 773-296-6046

Northfield | Northfield Village Ctr. | 310 Happ Rd. (Mt. Pleasant St.) | 847-784-9300
www.tapasgitana.com

"Variety" is the name of the game at this Northfield taparia and its Lakeview sequel where "classic Spanish ingredients" add an "authentic" touch to a "great selection" of "well-prepared" small plates and paellas; decor might be merely "passable" and service veers between "awesome" and "lacking", but "reasonably priced" wines and overall moderate tabs help make up for it.

Tasting Room ●Ⓢ *American*
▽ 18 | 18 | 20 | $54

West Loop | 1415 W. Randolph St. (Ogden Ave.) | 312-942-1313 | www.thetastingroomchicago.com

"Impressive" skyline views from the upstairs lounge and "endless wine options" are "the stars" at this "tastefully decorated" West Loop New American in a "warehouse space" complete with brickwork and overhead ducts; though doubters dub the small and large plates merely "decent" and "a tad overpriced", cushy couches and candlelight still make it a "good place to take a date."

Taverna 750 ● *Italian*
▽ 24 | 25 | 23 | $31

Wrigleyville | 750 W. Cornelia Ave. (Halsted St.) | 773-904-7466 | www.taverna750.com

"Tucked away on a Wrigleyville side street", this midpriced Italian proves itself a "solid choice", with "consistently very good" small plates, "tasty" cocktails and "personable" service; the brick-lined space and outdoor patio have a "trendy" vibe, especially during its "Sunday Funday" brunch (one of the "best in Boys Town"), and so it works perfectly "for groups of friends or an intimate date."

	FOOD	DECOR	SERVICE	COST

Tavern at the Park ☒ American
17 | 18 | 19 | $43

Loop | 130 E. Randolph St. (Beaubien Ct.) | 312-552-0070 | www.tavernatthepark.com

A Loop location complete with an "outdoor patio facing Millennium Park" helps make this "cozy" tri-level New American "a good option", especially since "many menu options" ensure "everyone will find something"; it's "reasonably priced" and service is generally "warm", so even those who find it merely "satisfactory" concede it's "convenient" for after-work drinks, "power lunches" and pre-event dinners.

Tavernita ◐ Spanish
▽ 21 | 21 | 19 | $49

River North | 151 W. Erie St. (bet. LaSalle & Wells Sts.) | 312-274-1111 | www.tavernita.com

"One of the liveliest places in town" is this upmarket River North Spaniard where Ryan Poli's "tasty" tapas feature "creative" "foodie flair" and get a boost from "top-echelon" cocktails; the spacious "group"-friendly setting with checked tile floors and globes of warm lighting attracts the "see-and-be-seen" set who barely notice the often "crowded" and "loud" conditions; P.S. the "small" companion pintxo bar, Barcito, offers a limited menu.

Tavern on Rush ◑ Steak
21 | 21 | 20 | $48

Gold Coast | 1031 N. Rush St. (Bellevue Pl.) | 312-664-9600 | www.tavernonrush.com

"See and be seen" at this "major" Gold Coast "hot spot" where the "solid" steakhouse fare comes with a side of "prime people-watching"; an "attractive" staff stays "cheerful even amid the chaos" and there's a "gorgeous" horseshoe bar, so despite somewhat "pricey" tabs it's "always crowded"; P.S. "in summer, the outdoor seating is the heartbeat of Chicago."

Taxim Greek
26 | 22 | 22 | $43

Wicker Park | 1558 N. Milwaukee Ave. (Damen Ave.) | 773-252-1558 | www.taximchicago.com

Diners who've gone once "daydream" about the "authentic" "carefully prepared" fare at this moderate Wicker Park Greek where the "flavorful" small and large plates are so "inventive", they're "unlike any other"; a "beautiful", "modern" space featuring archways and vaulted ceilings and "delightful" staffers further ensure it earns "must-try" status.

Telegraph
Wine Bar ◑ American
22 | 19 | 22 | $40

Logan Square | 2601 N. Milwaukee Ave. (bet. Kedzie Ave. & Logan Blvd.) | 773-292-9463 | www.telegraphwinebar.com

Oenophiles venture "off the beaten track" to this "warm and cozy" Logan Square wine bar offering "interesting" Euro-centric bottles backed by "inventive" New American small plates highlighting seasonal ingredients; "knowledgeable servers" elevate the "cool" rustic-chic space, and with moderate prices it has all the makings for an "awesome date place."

	FOOD	DECOR	SERVICE	COST

Tempo ●🚫 *Diner*
| | 19 | 13 | 18 | $20 |

Gold Coast | 6 E. Chestnut St. (State St.) | 312-943-4373
Eggs "almost as fluffy as the clouds over Lake Michigan" keep "loyal
devotees" coming to this 24/7 Gold Coast diner, a "favorite" for
breakfasts and "late-night" bites; though warnings include "30-minute
waits" on weekends and occasional "drunk, annoying" wee-hours
eaters, the "well-priced", "quality comfort food" wins over most;
P.S. it's cash-only and BYO is allowed until 10 PM, inside only.

Terzo Piano *Italian*
| | 22 | 25 | 22 | $48 |

Loop | The Art Institute of Chicago | 159 E. Monroe St.
(bet. Columbus Dr. & Michigan Ave.) | 312-443-8650 |
www.terzopianochicago.com
The "sublime setting" includes an "open", "minimalist" dining room
"bathed in light from huge windows" and a terrace featuring "knock-
out views" of the city skyline at this Loop Italian in the Modern Wing
of the Art Institute where chef Tony Mantuano (Spiaggia) delivers
"interesting" farm-to-table lunch fare (and dinner on Thursday); if
pickier diners deem it "overpriced" with "precious" portions, fans
point to "attentive" service and find it "reliable in all respects";
P.S. sandwiches and salads are offered at Piano Terra in the North
Garden during outdoor dining season.

NEW Tesori *Italian*
| | - | - | - | E |

Loop | 65 E. Adams St. (bet. Michigan & Wabash Aves.) |
312-786-9911 | www.tesorichicago.com
This luxe Loop Italian in the former Rhapsody space serves upscale
meals made with artisanal ingredients alongside craft beer, global
wines and seasonal cocktails; the chic urban environs adorned with
leather, wood and white tablecloths are illuminated by massive suspended fixtures and natural light from windows overlooking garden
seating, and its location near the Symphony Orchestra makes it convenient pre- or post-concert.

Texas de Brazil Churrascaria *Brazilian*
| | 24 | 24 | 24 | $55 |

Schaumburg | Woodfield Mall | 5 Woodfield Mall (bet. Frontage &
Meacham Rds.) | 847-413-1600 | www.texasdebrazil.com
"Bring your appetite" ("and maybe some Lipitor") in preparation
for a "meat overdose" at this all-you-can-eat Brazilian chain link in
Schaumburg where "attentive" gaucho waiters keep the "high-quality"
cuts coming and a "carnival" of flavors awaits at the "extensive" salad
bar; it's not cheap, so some plan to "munch until out of steam."

Thai Pastry *Thai*
| | ▽ 25 | 13 | 19 | $20 |

Uptown | 4925 N. Broadway (Rosemont Ave.) | 773-784-5399
Harwood Heights | 7350 W. Lawrence Ave. (Odell Ave.) | 708-867-8840
www.thaipastry.com
"Authentic" Thai "classics", including "wonderful" curries with "some
spice", are a "good value" at this "unpretentious" Uptowner with a
Harwood Heights sequel; service is "friendly", and though the neon
interior and nothing-special storefront earn middling marks, those
who don't want to dine in can get "prompt" delivery.

3rd Coast Cafe & Wine Bar ● *American*   18 | 15 | 18 | $20

Gold Coast | 1260 N. Dearborn Pkwy. (Goethe St.) | 312-649-0730 | www.3rdcoastcafe.com

A "quirky mix of college students and older couples" populates this "small" Gold Coast American where "basic" affordable eats make it a "go-to breakfast spot" and "nice place" for lunch or an "informal dinner"; a "helpful staff" furthers the "welcoming feel", so even those who find it merely "ordinary" concede it's "very convenient."

Three Aces ● *Italian*   22 | 17 | 20 | $28

Little Italy/University Village | 1321 W. Taylor St. (bet. Loomis & Throop Sts.) | 312-243-1577 | www.threeaceschicago.com

Though it may look like "Keith Richards' basement bar", this mid-priced "rockabilly gastropub" gives culinary nods to its Little Italy 'hood while swapping out the mixed nuts for grub that goes "way beyond normal bar fare"; service can be "varied", but with a "great beer selection" featuring many Midwestern brews, most barely notice.

III Forks   *American/Steak*   23 | 24 | 23 | $62

Loop | Village Market at Lakeshore East | 180 N. Field Blvd. (Park Dr.) | 312-938-4303 | www.3forks.com

A "gorgeous" Loop setting with floor-to-ceiling windows, fireplaces and "the coolest ever rooftop bar" complement the menu of "reliable" chops and "classic" American "standouts" at this "contemporary" Dallas-based addition to the "high-end" steakhouse scene; service is "professional" and "personable" too, leading even those "against chains" to say it's "a serious contender" (with prices to match).

Three Happiness ● *Chinese*   22 | 11 | 18 | $22

Chinatown | 209 W. Cermak Rd. (Wentworth Ave.) | 312-842-1964 | www.newthreehappiness.com

"One steamed, one fried, one vegetable: eat, repeat" chant champions of this "real-deal" "dim 'yum'" spot in Chinatown, where the affordable menu includes "choices, choices and more choices" of "authentic" Chinese "snack food"; despite decor that's "nothing special" and weekends that are "quite a scene", it "brings customers back for more"; P.S. it's not related to nearby New Three Happiness.

312 Chicago   *Italian*   21 | 20 | 21 | $42

Loop | Hotel Allegro | 136 N. LaSalle St. (Randolph St.) | 312-696-2420 | www.312chicago.com

Set in a "desirable" Loop location in the Hotel Allegro, this "busy" "white-tablecloth" Italian is "perfect for pre-theater dining" and "reliable" "business lunches" with "original" dishes and prices that won't break the bank; service can veer from "prompt" to a "little slow", and even if it's "not exceptional", it's also "never a bad meal."

Tiffin   *Indian*   ∇ 19 | 18 | 19 | $24

West Rogers Park | 2536 W. Devon Ave. (bet. Maplewood Ave. & Rockwell St.) | 773-338-2143 | www.tiffinrestaurant.com

The "reliably good" fare at this West Rogers Park Indian "tastes as if it came right from" the subcontinent with its "large portions" of "family favorites" such as chicken tikka masala and "succulent lamb chops" offered at prices "low enough not to complain"; "civilized" service, a "well-kept" setting and a "quite serviceable" lunch buffet round out the package.

Tin Fish *Seafood*　　24 | 21 | 21 | $40

Tinley Park | Cornerstone Ctr. | 18201 S. Harlem Ave. (183rd St.) | 708-532-0200 | www.tinfishrestaurant.com

Seafood is the "expected star" at this Tinley Parker where the "well-prepared" fare, including customizable "mix-and-match" options (you choose the preparation and sides), gets a boost from the "well-chosen wine list"; pictures of fish decorate the upscale-casual space, and with "helpful" staffers and "fair prices" don't be surprised if you "have to wait."

Toast *American*　　22 | 17 | 18 | $18

Lincoln Park | 746 W. Webster Ave. (bet. Burling & Halsted Sts.) | 773-935-5600
Bucktown | 2046 N. Damen Ave. (bet. Dickens & McLean Aves.) | 773-772-5600
www.toast-chicago.com

Go "healthy" or go "decadent" at these American "perfect little brunch spots" in Lincoln Park and Bucktown dishing out affordable, "inventive", "hangover-curing" breakfast and lunch fare daily; though some grouse about the "cramped" interiors and "long waits on weekends", service is "always competent" (if only "sometimes friendly").

Tocco *Italian*　　▽ 25 | 25 | 23 | $36

Bucktown | 1266 N. Milwaukee Ave. (bet. Ashland Ave. & Paulina St.) | 773-687-8895 | www.toccochicago.com

Diners visit this Bucktown Italian for "incredible pastas" and "Neapolitan-style" pizza with "appropriately blackened" crusts as "wafer-thin" as the upscale clientele; with a "mighty sleek" pink-and-white dining room and an accommodating staff, those in the know dub it "one of Chicago's best-kept secrets."

Todoroki Hibachi & Sushi *Japanese*　　- | - | - | M

Evanston | 526 Davis St. (bet. Chicago & Hinman Aves.) | 847-750-6565 | www.mytodoroki.com

Japanese steakhouse showmanship involving knives and flames constitute the 'turf' side of this midpriced Evanston BYO, while sushi both classic and creative (including all-you-can-eat options) comprises the 'surf'; the divided dining areas offer hibachi grill seating, a sushi bar, long leather banquettes and bare tables, as well as tatami rooms and modern artwork.

Tokio Pub ☒ *Japanese*　　- | - | - | M

Schaumburg | 1900 E. Higgins Rd. (Rte. 53) | 847-278-5181 | www.tokiopub.com

"Surprisingly edgy" and "hip" for its Schaumburg setting, this Japanese fusioner offers "inexpensive" plates and "interesting" cocktails delivered by "helpful" servers; the less-impressed carp about "subpar" sushi, suggesting it "needs a tune up."

	FOOD	DECOR	SERVICE	COST

Tom & Eddie's *Burgers* | 18 | 14 | 17 | $15 |

Deerfield | 740 Waukegan Rd. (bet. Deerfield Rd. & Osterman Ave.) | 847-948-5117
Vernon Hills | 1260 S. Milwaukee Ave. (Old Half Day Rd.) | 847-478-1019
Geneva | The Shops at Geneva Commons | 1042 Commons Dr. (bet. Bricher Rd. & Williamsburg Ave.) | 630-208-1351
Lombard | The Shops on Butterfield | 348 Yorktown Ctr. (bet. Butterfield Rd. & Highland Ave.) | 630-705-9850
NEW **Naperville** | 1516 N. Naper Blvd. (bet. Ogden & Ridgeland Aves.) | 630-324-0831
www.tomandeddies.com

"It's not your typical burger joint" say groupies of this northwest suburbs counter-service mini-chain turning out "inventive" burgers in "a wonderful variety" of options including turkey, ahi tuna and edamame patties, plus loads of topping and sauce choices too; though some deem the offerings "overrated" and "a bit pricey", a Coca-Cola Freestyle machine with some 125 flavor combos is a "cool touch."

NEW Tommy Knuckles | - | - | - | M |
Tavern & Lounge ● *American*

Lincoln Park | 433 W. Diversey Pkwy. (Pine Grove Ave.) | 773-248-3230 | www.tommyknucklesbar.com

American tavern eats are offered along with 50-plus beers and themed cocktails at this casual Lincoln Parker; retro basement bar furnishings are surrounded by brick walls lined with vintage posters of movie and music stars, and bills are affordable.

Top Notch Beefburger ⊠⏛ *Burgers* | ▽ 25 | 12 | 20 | $12 |

Far South Side | 2116 W. 95th St. (bet. Hamilton & Hoyne Aves.) | 773-445-7218

Since 1942 this "local gem" on the Far South Side has been slinging "mouthwatering" burgers (they grind their own meat daily), beef fat fries and "awesome" chocolate shakes; "prices are great" and service is solid, so fans say just "forget about the decor" and focus on the "hearty, homemade food" with a side of "tradition."

Topo Gigio Ristorante *Italian* | 24 | 19 | 22 | $38 |

Old Town | 1516 N. Wells St. (bet. North Ave. & Schiller St.) | 312-266-9355 | www.topogigiochicago.com

Diners "keep going back" to this "casual" Old Town "standout" for "pasta done perfectly" and other "authentic" "Italian favorites" at "moderate prices"; "charming" service also helps keep it a "popular" local hangout", especially in summer when the "lively" patio provides ample "people-watching."

Topolobampo ⊠Ⓜ *Mexican* | 28 | 24 | 26 | $70 |

River North | 445 N. Clark St. (Illinois St.) | 312-661-1434 | www.rickbayless.com

"Tops in its category", Rick Bayless' "world-class" River North destination ranks as a "magnificent experience", offering "wow"-worthy, "high-end" "nuevo" Mexican meals made up of "innovative", "flavorful" dishes plus "don't-miss" margaritas and "excellent" wines;

its "upper-crust" atmosphere ("totally different from Frontera next door") further explains the "premium" prices, while "welcoming, passionate" staffers are another reason to "keep going back" (if you can "snag a table").

Toro Sushi Ⓜ *Japanese*

26	14	19	$28

Lincoln Park | 2546 N. Clark St. (bet. Deming Pl. & Wrightwood Ave.) | 773-348-4877 | www.torosushi.biz

A "cult following" clamors for "talented" chef-owner Mitch Kim's "fresh", "imaginative" sushi at this "tiny", affordable Lincoln Park BYO; "you don't come for the ease of getting a table, the prompt service or the decor" but it's still a "favorite" of many, though it "pains" them to say so since "the wait is long enough already."

Tortas Frontera *Mexican*

▽ 23	10	17	$17

Loop | Urban Mkt. | 10 S. Dearborn St. (bet. Madison & Monroe Sts.) | 312-732-6505 | www.urbanmarketchicago.com 🏧
O'Hare Area | Terminal 1, Gate B10 | 10000 Bessie Coleman Dr. (Zemke Blvd.) | 773-686-6180 | www.rickbayless.com

Fans "do everything" they can to stop at these Mexican quick-serves, aka other "Rick Bayless success stories", in O'Hare and the Loop's Chase Tower, where "extremely flavorful" tortas (sandwiches), plus other solid fare including "fresh" juices, guacamole and breakfast items are like "a gift from god to the air traveler" (and worker).

🆕 Tortoise Club *American*

-	-	-	E

River North | Marina City | 350 N. State St. (bet. Kinzie St. & Wacker Dr.) | 312-755-1700 | www.tortoiseclub.com

This retro-styled River North fine-dining destination evokes the supper club era with a pricey American menu offering classics like steak tartare, wild pheasant pie and lobster Thermidor, plus brown spirits and classic cocktails; the occasion-worthy traditional setting is filled with posh furnishings, a grand piano and fireplace, and artwork featuring horses and Chicago celebs through the years.

Township ●💯 *Coffeehouse/Eclectic*

-	-	-	I

Logan Square | 2200 N. California Ave. (Palmer St.) | 773-384-1865 | www.townshipchicago.com

A "funky fusion" of restaurant, stage venue and coffee shop, this cash-only Logan Square lair serves casual Eclectic grub, including sandwiches and panini; beverages range from coffee drinks to 60 craft beers and specialty cocktails, which help the backstage room rock late with live music.

Tramonto's Steak & Seafood *Seafood/Steak*

▽ 22	23	20	$61

Wheeling | Westin Chicago North Shore | 601 N. Milwaukee Ave. (Wolf Rd.) | 847-777-6575 | www.westinnorthshore.com

Though namesake chef Rick Tramonto is no longer in-house, patrons promise this "haute" surf 'n' turfer at the Wheeling Westin remains "worth" the trek with its "gorgeous" waterfall wall–enhanced setting, "well-prepared steaks" and "sure-bet" fish dishes; though specials at "reasonable" prices have their fans, detractors deem it "overpriced" and the service "inconsistent" (sometimes "incredible", sometimes "spotty"), saying the experience "has declined in quality."

	FOOD	DECOR	SERVICE	COST

Trattoria D.O.C. *Italian*

20	17	20	$31

Evanston | 706 Main St. (bet. Custer & Sherman Aves.) | 847-475-1111 | www.trattoria-doc.com

Despite being "hidden" on a "quiet" street in Evanston, this "homey" Italian is "always busy" thanks to "reliable all-day dining" and a "friendly" staff; pasta fans praise the "fresh ingredients" and "inventive variations on familiar themes", while "moderate prices" and roomy digs make it a "great option for families" and other locals.

Trattoria Gianni Ⓜ *Italian*

20	17	21	$38

Lincoln Park | 1711 N. Halsted St. (bet. North Ave. & Willow St.) | 312-266-1976 | www.trattoriagianni.com

Located across the street from Lincoln Park's Steppenwolf theater, this Italian is a "good choice for pre- or post-theater dining" on "tasty, traditional" fare; service is "without pretension", and even if dissenters say that the atmosphere is "plain" and the menu "needs an overhaul", at least it's "not too expensive."

Trattoria No. 10 Ⓩ *Italian*

24	21	23	$47

Loop | 10 N. Dearborn St. (bet. Madison & Washington Sts.) | 312-984-1718 | www.trattoriaten.com

"Excellent" risotto, "dreamy" homemade ravioli and other "fantastico" dishes crafted with "quality ingredients" are on offer at this "charming" Loop Italian whose "underground location helps keep down outside noise"; "capable", "speedy" service suits it to business lunches or "pre- or post-theater" meals, and while it's not cheap, it's "not crazily priced" either.

Trattoria Roma *Italian*

23	20	21	$35

Old Town | 1535 N. Wells St. (bet. North Ave. & Schiller St.) | 312-664-7907 | www.trattoriaroma.com

"Fresh, homemade pastas" and other "simple and delicious" Italian fare is served in a "charming, old-world club atmosphere" at this Old Town trattoria; with "attentive" service and "affordable" prices it's clear why "lots of locals" call it their "favorite haunt."

Tre Kronor *Scandinavian*

24	19	22	$20

Albany Park | 3258 W. Foster Ave. (bet. Sawyer & Spaulding Aves.) | 773-267-9888 | www.trekronorrestaurant.com

"Herring worshipers" who "long for the old country" feast on "lovingly prepared" Scandinavian fare (breakfast is a particular "favorite") at this "value" Albany Park BYO; "elves dancing on the walls" and a "lovely patio" add to the "rustic charm", while service "makes you feel like family" – no wonder locals feel so "lucky."

NEW Trenchermen *American*

▽ 23	23	19	$54

Wicker Park | 2039 W. North Ave. (bet. Damen & Hoyne Aves.) | 773-661-1540 | www.trenchermen.com

The vintage Wicker Park bathhouse that once housed Spring has been transformed by the Sheerin brothers into this pricey New American celebration of all things excess, featuring "unusual but delicious" offerings with rich, forward-thinking flavor combinations and global accents; the bi-level, steampunk and art deco–inspired space houses two bars, antiques and terrariums, plus gargantuan stained-glass light fixtures dangling above suede banquettes.

NEW Tre Soldi *Italian/Pizza*

`- | - | - | E`

Streeterville | 212 E. Ohio St. (bet. Fairbanks Ct. & St Clair St.) | 312-664-0212 | www.tresoldichicago.com

Jack Weiss, the owner of Coco Pazzo, is behind this upscale Streeterville trattoria with a specialty in Roman thin-crust pizza and traditional cooking of the Lazio region (handcrafted pastas, roasted meats); the bar offers many wines by the glass, while decorative touches like columns, brick and artwork depicting Italian landmarks help set an Eternal City mood.

Troquet ● *French*

`- | - | - | I`

Ravenswood | 1834 W. Montrose Ave. (Wolcott St.) | 773-334-5664 | www.troquetchicago.com

The LM group's "cozy" corner tavern with a French accent offers an "inexpensive" menu of small plates (moules frites, quiche, fromage and charcuterie), sandwiches and entrees (pork belly, duck confit) paired with a handful of wines, Gallic cocktails and craft brews on tap; the welcoming, wood-on-wood room includes an open kitchen, a long bar with TVs and evocative black-and-white photography.

Tru ⌧ *French*

`27 | 27 | 28 | $150`

Streeterville | 676 N. St. Clair St. (bet. Erie & Huron Sts.) | 312-202-0001 | www.trurestaurant.com

When you want to "splurge and impress", fans suggest this Streeterville "fine-dining" destination that "hits all the high notes", from Anthony Martin's "artistic, creative and sublimely delicious" contemporary French tasting menus to the "thoughtfully paced flow of courses" overseen by a "personable" staff; the "elegant" art-filled dining room (jackets required) further ups the ante, and while the cost may make it a "once-in-a-lifetime" meal for some, at least it's a "truly special" one.

Tsukasa of Tokyo *Japanese*

`23 | 22 | 22 | $40`

Vernon Hills | 561 N. Milwaukee Ave. (Townline Rd) | 847-816-8770 | www.tsukasaoftokyo.com

Kids and adults "have a ball" watching the "friendly" chefs "flip their food" at this "top-notch" Vernon Hills teppanyaki that's an "entertaining" alternative to Japanese chain counterparts; while the hibachi fare "hits the spot", it can also "hit the pocketbook", though fans shrug it off as the price of "the show."

Tufano's Vernon Park Tap Ⓜ ⌐ *Italian*

`24 | 15 | 21 | $27`

Little Italy/University Village | 1073 W. Vernon Park Pl. (Carpenter St.) | 312-733-3393 | www.tufanosrestaurant.com

Open since 1930, this "fourth-generation family place" in University Village is a "casual" "Chicago classic", "attracting a loyal following" with "authentic Italian home cooking" delivered by servers with "gruff charm"; "checkered tablecloths" and a *Godfather* feel further make it a "true character place" – just be warned it's cash-only and doesn't accept reservations.

Turquoise *Turkish*
25 | 18 | 20 | $36

Roscoe Village | 2147 W. Roscoe St. (bet. Hamilton Ave. & Leavitt St.) | 773-549-3523 | www.turquoisedining.com

A "Turkish delight" say fans of the "flavorful", "exquisitely prepared" plates at this "value" Roscoe Villager with casual, white-tablecloth environs and a "low noise level" fit for "big groups" and "first dates" alike; there's also "pleasant sidewalk seating", so though service can be "slow" when it's "packed", it remains a "favorite local spot."

Tuscany *Italian*
22 | 20 | 22 | $40

Little Italy/University Village | 1014 W. Taylor St. (Miller St.) | 312-829-1990
Wheeling | 550 S. Milwaukee Ave. (Manchester Dr.) | 847-465-9988
Oak Brook | 1415 W. 22nd St. (Kingery Hwy.) | 630-990-1993 🗷
www.tuscanychicago.com

"Homestyle" Italian fare comes in "big portions" and is ferried by "experienced" servers at this trio from Phil Stefani (Riva, Tavern on Rush); fans say the trattoria setting is as suitable for a "special occasion" as for "more frequent dining", considering the "fair" prices.

Tweet ⊄ *American*
26 | 21 | 25 | $19

Uptown | 5020 N. Sheridan Rd. (Argyle St.) | 773-728-5576 | www.tweet.biz

"Awesomely good" breakfast and lunch eats come in "more-than-generous" portions at this cash-only Uptown New American, where the "extensive" menu includes many gluten-free choices and a "lot of options" for vegetarians too; "local art" decorates the walls of the small space, and though it gets "busy" on the weekends, "friendly", "efficient" servers keep things moving – and you can always "hunker down" with a "delicious" Bloody Mary if there's a wait.

25 Degrees *Burgers*
21 | 19 | 21 | $24

River North | 736 N. Clark St. (Superior St.) | 312-943-9700 | www.25degreesrestaurant.com

"Imaginative burgers", including a "build-your-own" option, are joined by sandwiches, sides, "adult milkshakes" and "refreshing" cocktails at this "casual", "modernistic" River North chain link; it may be "a little pricey" for what's on offer, but loyalists "love the atmosphere" and "bar scene" ("no place for old men"); P.S. outdoor tables are "lovely during the warm months."

Twin Anchors *BBQ*
22 | 15 | 19 | $29

Old Town | 1655 N. Sedgwick St. (Eugenie St.) | 312-266-1616 | www.twinanchorsribs.com

"Steeped in history", this midpriced Old Town barbecue "benchmark" and Sinatra favorite owes its long-standing popularity to "fall-off-the-bone" ribs and "lively" servers; the setting is either "dated or classic – depending on your POV", and while waits can be "brutally long", regulars insist it's "worth every minute"; P.S. no reservations.

	FOOD	DECOR	SERVICE	COST

Twisted Spoke ● *Pub Food* 20 | 17 | 17 | $21

Noble Square | 501 N. Ogden Ave. (Grand Ave.) | 312-666-1500 |
www.twistedspoke.com

Your "basic neighborhood biker bar", this Noble Square stop slings
solid burgers and other "quite filling" midpriced pub grub while
pouring "slammin' Bloody Marys"; the staff provides "service with
an edge" (while on some nights "X-rated TV screens" play), and
whether patrons call it "funky" and "casual" or just "a dump", most
agree "it's fun to try at least once."

NEW Two Ⓜ *American* - | - | - | M

West Town | 1132 W. Grand Ave. (May St.) | 312-624-8363 |
www.tworestaurantchicago.com

Sustainable Midwestern ingredients go into the ever-rotating, midpriced menu of small plates with a butcher's bent at this West Town
New American; it also offers microbrews, a huge wine list (with a
half-dozen on tap) and seasonal cocktails in a funky space filled with
vintage regional furnishings from libraries, hotels and barns, meat
art and a few communal tables.

2 Sparrows *American* 21 | 18 | 17 | $24

Lincoln Park | 553 W. Diversey Pkwy. (Lehmann Ct.) |
773-234-2320 | www.2sparrowschicago.com

"Inventive" and "delicious" breakfasts and lunches do it for those
who pack into this midpriced Lincoln Park New American, an especially popular choice for weekend brunch; exposed-wood walls give
the "bright" space a "rustic" feel, and while some say dishes can be
"hit-or-miss", they concede "when it's good, it's awesome."

NEW Umai *Japanese* - | - | - | M

Printer's Row | 730 S. Clark St. (bet. Harrison & Polk Sts.) |
312-986-8888 | www.umaichicago.com

Midpriced sushi and assorted Japanese standards (tempura, katsu,
udon, etc.) feature at this chic, modern Printer's Row joint; spacious
digs are done up in blond and dark wood with an oceanic mural that
adds a splash of color.

Uncle Bub's BBQ *BBQ* 21 | 15 | 19 | $18

Westmont | 132 S. Cass Ave. (Dallas St.) | 630-493-9000 |
www.unclebubs.com

"Tie on a bib and dig in" coach fans of this wallet-friendly "Southern
rib joint" in Westmont, where you order "awesome" "smoky BBQ"
from "efficient" servers at the counter before chowing down in a
"comfortably rustic setting"; it's all ultra-"casual" – so "when you
spill the sauce on yourself it won't matter."

Uncommon Ground ● *Coffeehouse/Eclectic* 22 | 20 | 20 | $29

Edgewater | 1401 W. Devon Ave. (Glenwood Ave.) | 773-465-9801
Lakeview | 3800 N. Clark St. (Grace St.) | 773-929-3680
www.uncommonground.com

With a "delicious" menu so local some produce comes from "their
own rooftop garden", these Eclectic "green" eateries in Edgewater

FOOD DECOR SERVICE COST

and Lakeview only seem "overpriced" "until you experience the quality of the ingredients"; while service varies, a "stellar beer selection" and "laid-back" ambiance are pluses – and "don't forget to check out the bands" (nightly at both locales).

Union Pizzeria *Pizza*   20 | 18 | 18 | $27

Evanston | 1245 Chicago Ave. (bet. Dempster & Hamilton Sts.) | 847-475-2400 | www.unionpizza.com

"Lovely" wood-fired pizzas and "interesting" small plates "perfect for sharing" provide "good value" at this "hip" Evanston pizzeria with solid service and an "airy, funky atmosphere"; what some call "loud and crowded" others dub "happy noise", but it's indisputably convenient before a show at Space, the "thriving" music venue that shares the building.

Union Sushi + Barbeque Bar *Japanese*   22 | 24 | 21 | $38

River North | 230 W. Erie St. (Franklin St.) | 312-662-4888 | www.eatatunion.com

"Clever ingredients", "unique rolls" and "creative items" from the robata grill set this midpriced River North Japanese "apart from the competition" while its "casual" but "upscale" "open space" bedecked with grafiitti and other urban stylings make it "very cool and trendy"; service gets solid marks and tabs are moderate, so even if sushi purists complain that "raw ingredients are hard to find", it remains a "popular" pick.

Urbanbelly M *Asian/Noodle Shop*   25 | 16 | 17 | $21

Logan Square | 3053 N. California Ave. (bet. Barry Ave. & Nelson St.) | 773-583-0500 | www.urbanbellychicago.com

"Interesting", "addictive" Asian fusion fare like "satisfying, belly-warming noodles" and "divine dumplings" are "elevated to a high level with quality, flavor and care" at "genius" chef-owner Bill Kim's counter-service Logan Square BYO; given "efficient" staffers and tabs "priced right" most "don't mind sitting at community tables" in the "unassuming", "hipster"-ish digs – and those who do simply "take it to go."

Vapiano *Italian/Pizza*   16 | 20 | 14 | $21

Lincoln Park | 2577 N. Clark St. (Wrightwood Ave.) | 773-904-7984 | www.vapianointernational.com

Boutique hotel atmosphere meets modern food court at this Lincoln Park link of the "semi-self-service" chain where multiple Italian-focused stations (pastas, pizzas, panini) give guests "lots of choices"; seating options include a plush red lounge and two modern dining areas, and while detractors dub it "just ok", others find it "reasonable, tasty and quick."

Vera M *Spanish*   ▽ 22 | 19 | 20 | $53

West Loop | 1023 W. Lake St. (Carpenter St.) | 312-243-9770 | www.verachicago.com

"High-quality" Spanish small plates form a "festival of flavor" at this spendy West Loop wine bar from a husband-and-wife team, where a "lively" yet intimate space with exposed brick and Edison bulb lighting helps create an appealing "environment for a night out"; "superb" staffers are a big plus, as is an ambitious sherry and global vino list (including some poured by tap).

Vermilion *Indian/Nuevo Latino*
23	21	20	$53

River North | 10 W. Hubbard St. (bet. Dearborn Pkwy. & State St.) | 312-527-4060 | www.thevermilionrestaurant.com
Indian and Latin flavors "pop" at this pricey River North "fusion concept" (with an NYC sib), where artfully presented "eclectic", "spicy" fare, "sophisticated" decor featuring fashion photography and "courteous" service combine; though a few find the "innovative" model to be "ill-conceived", most say it's an "appealing" food adventure."

Via Carducci *Italian*
21	18	20	$34

Lincoln Park | 1419 W. Fullerton Ave. (bet. Janssen & Southport Aves.) | 773-665-1981

Via Carducci La Sorella *Italian*
Wicker Park | 1928 W. Division St. (Winchester Ave.) | 773-252-2244
www.viacarducci-lasorella.com
Wicker Park and Lincoln Park locals swing by these midpriced "family places" for "authentic" Southern Italian standards including thin-crust pizza and rotini Santa Lucia (with sausage and tomato-cream sauce); unassuming "neighborhood" settings and "attentive, pleasant" service further prompt patrons to "recommend and return."

Viaggio ⌧Ⓜ *Italian*
▽			
24	17	21	$42

Near West | 1330 W. Madison St. (Odgen Ave.) | 312-829-3333 | www.viaggiochicago.com
Even mama "would have loved" this slightly spendy Near West Italian say loyalists who crave the "wonderful selection" of dishes including the signature pork chop Parmesan and "go-to" meatball salad ("yeah, you read right"); warm wood details and white tablecloths create a classy vibe, and "great service" helps it "feel like the place where everyone knows you."

Vie *American*
29	25	28	$69

Western Springs | 4471 Lawn Ave. (Burlington Ave.) | 708-246-2082 | www.vierestaurant.com
City dwellers say this Western Springs New American is "worth the travel" to the 'burbs for Paul Virant's "exceptional" New American cooking that showcases "the season's best" ingredients in "outstanding" "fine-dining" dishes; the space is "warm and inviting but still elegant", and "impeccable" service further justifies the spendy tabs.

The Village ❶ *Italian*
20	22	21	$34

Loop | Italian Vill. | 71 W. Monroe St., 2nd fl. (bet. Clark & Dearborn Sts.) | 312-332-7005 | www.italianvillage-chicago.com
"Twinkling lights" and "hidden booths" await at this "charming" "old-world" "standby", a part of the Capitanini family's "red-sauce Italian" trio in the Loop that's been "around forever" thanks to "dependable" "homestyle" food at affordable prices, a "mammoth" wine list and waiters who are "pros"; even those who find it "boring" concede it often "hits the spot."

	FOOD	DECOR	SERVICE	COST

Vincent ☒ American
Andersonville | 1475 W. Balmoral Ave. (bet. Clark St. & Glenwood Ave.) | 773-334-7168 | www.vincentchicago.com

The "different" "Dutch-inspired" New American menu includes some "incredible" choices at this "off-the-radar" Andersonville bistro offering hearty small and large plates plus mussels many ways (some of the "best in town"); the "cozy" space has a "warm" feel, and service scores highly.

23 | 21 | 24 | $39

Vinci ☒ Italian
Lincoln Park | 1732 N. Halsted St. (Willow St.) | 312-266-1199 | www.vincichicago.com

Theatergoers choose this "low-key", "fairly priced" Lincoln Park trattoria "near the Steppenwolf" for its "consistently well-prepared" "classic" Italian dishes delivered with "attentive, warm" service; regulars add the "pleasantness" of the villalike surroundings as another reason it's an "old reliable favorite."

20 | 19 | 21 | $41

Vito & Nick's ⌦ Pizza
Far South Side | 8433 S. Pulaski Rd. (84th Pl.) | 773-735-2050 | www.vitoandnick.com

"Thin crust rules" at this South Side pizza "icon" dishing out "awesome" pies that groupies grade some of the "best in Chicago"; "carpet on the walls" and "funky" decor "reminiscent of a grandmother's basement in the 1960s" is "so bad that it's good", and with "decent prices" and generally solid service, it's "packed every night of the week" (insiders keep it on "speed dial" for takeout too).

24 | 12 | 18 | $20

Vivere ☒ Italian
Loop | Italian Vill. | 71 W. Monroe St. (bet. Clark & Dearborn Sts.) | 312-332-4040 | www.italianvillage-chicago.com

Deemed the Italian Village's "fanciest" option, this Loop entry offers a "festive" baroque gold and velvet-trimmed dining room as a backdrop for "upscale", "quality" fare and a "comprehensive" wine list delivered by an "excellent" staff; true, it's "a little expensive", but then that's the price of "the good life."

23 | 23 | 23 | $50

Vivo ☒ Italian
West Loop | 838 W. Randolph St. (bet. Green & Peoria Sts.) | 312-733-3379 | www.vivo-chicago.com

"Still chic" after some 20 years, this "upscale" West Loop Italian offers "delicious" classics in "loft-ish, industrial" environs that are "a bit more exciting" than usual ("request the elevator shaft table" above the main floor for special occasions); add in "polite and prompt" service and regulars insist it "will never go out of style."

23 | 21 | 20 | $41

Volare ● Italian
Streeterville | 201 E. Grand Ave. (St. Clair St.) | 312-410-9900
Oakbrook Terrace | Oakbrook Towers | 1919 S. Meyers Rd. (Tower Rd.) | 630-495-0200
www.volarerestaurant.com

"It's always crowded, so come early" to these "red-gravy" Italians in Streeterville and Oakbrook Terrace dishing out "overall excellent"

23 | 19 | 21 | $39

heaps of "moderately priced" "homestyle cooking" with "accommo-dating", "family-friendly" service; despite "close-together" tables, "noise" and all, supporters "keep coming back"; P.S. outdoor seating is "perfect in summer."

NEW Vu Sua 🅂🅼 *Asian*

| - | - | - | M |

Lakeview | 2925 N. Halsted St. (Oakdale Ave.) | 773-360-8816 | www.vsuarestaurant.com

The team behind Macku Sushi presents upscale Vietnamese vittles with French underpinnings, mixed Asian influences and creative modern plate presentations in the former Lakeview home of Erwin; the space has been redone in a spare, sleek style with neutrals, booths and abstract gold light fixtures.

NEW Wâfel *Belgian*

| - | - | - | I |

West Town | 217 N. Clinton St. (Fulton St.) | 773-770-4894 | www.wafel.us

Classic Belgian waffles in the style of Brussels (thin and yeasty) and Liège (thick and sugary) with creative sweet and savory fillings are the draw at this wallet-friendly West Loop spot; you can go mobile with your handheld meal, or have a seat at one of the bare wood tables in the casual, modern Euro setting.

NEW Waffles *American*

| - | - | - | I |

South Loop | 1400 S. Michigan Ave. (14th St.) | 312-854-8572
Wrigleyville | 3617 N. Broadway (bet. Addison & Patterson Sts.) | 773-281-8440
www.waffleschicago.com

Gourmet Belgian waffles sweet and savory (e.g. green tea, chicken and bacon) are the draw along with build-your-own omelets, egg dishes and sandwiches at this daytime American duo in the South Loop and Wrigleyville; both have fairly basic settings with a modern cafe vibe – and casual prices to match.

Walnut Room *American*

| 18 | 25 | 19 | $31 |

Loop | Macy's | 111 N. State St. (bet. Randolph & Washington Sts.) | 312-781-3125 | www.visitmacyschicago.com

A "little piece of frozen history", this longtime Loop American in Macy's is set in "elegant" surrounds decorated with Russian Circassian walnut paneling and Austrian chandeliers that set the stage for traditional comfort food like chicken pot pie and lobster bisque brought by "old-time" Chicago servers; even if the offerings are "not exceptional", it's still a "classic", especially at the winter holidays when its "festive atmosphere" makes it a "Christmas mainstay."

Weber Grill *American*

| 21 | 18 | 20 | $36 |

River North | Hilton Garden Inn | 539 N. State St. (Grand Ave.) | 312-467-9696
Schaumburg | 1010 N. Meacham Rd. (American Ln.) | 847-413-0800
Lombard | 2331 Fountain Square Dr. (bet. Butterfield & Meyers Rds.) | 630-953-8880
www.webergrillrestaurant.com

"A step up from the backyard barbecue", this midpriced all-American trio features an "exhibition kitchen" concept where grill masters flip "reliably good" steaks, patties, pork ribs and more on giant Weber kettles; service is "friendly", and though eager eaters claim it's "always clogged with people", it's still "worth the trip."

Webster's Wine Bar ● *Eclectic*

18 | 19 | 20 | $35

Lincoln Park | 1480 W. Webster Ave. (bet. Ashland & Clybourn Aves.) | 773-868-0608 | www.websterwinebar.com

Oenophiles may come to this "cozy, romantic" Lincoln Park wine bar for the "killer" 500-bottle list (some 40 by the glass) and frequent tasting events tended by knowledgeable servers; the moderately priced menu of Eclectic small plates "is a pleasant surprise" too, further making it a "nice date place."

Wellfleet ⊠ *Seafood*

- | - | - | M

Albany Park | 4423 N. Elston Ave. (Montrose Ave.) | 773-283-7400 | www.fishguy.com

Longtime Albany Park seafood purveyor Bill Dugan has expanded his former temporary in-house restaurant to this petite BYO inside the Fish Guy Market serving a rotating menu of simply prepared fin-focused offerings plus New Haven–style pizzas; the rehabbed store features a stainless-steel dining counter set amid display cases and mounted game fish.

West Egg Cafe *Diner*

21 | 11 | 17 | $18

Near North | 620 N. Fairbanks Ct. (bet. Ohio & Ontario Sts.) | 312-280-8366

Bright and "bustling", this casual, "always crowded" Near North American diner offers "creative" egg creations, "fluffy" pancakes, sandwiches and other ultra-early eats that are a "must-have after a long night out"; "potentially long waits" come with the territory on weekends; P.S. closes at 3 PM.

Westminster Hot Dog ⊠ *Hot Dogs*

∇ 19 | 6 | 14 | $10

Loop | 11 N. Wells St. (Calhoun Pl.) | 312-445-9514 | www.westminsterhotdog.com

"High-end" hot dogs and specialty sausages (bison, anyone?) are "made fresh on the premises", and topped with "creative" extras like avocado ranch dressing and sundried-tomato pesto at this counter-service Loop lunch spot; though the cheap prices come with a "hole-in-the-wall" setting, the "deliciousness-to-convenience factor is a plus."

West Town Tavern ⊠ *American*

26 | 22 | 24 | $42

Noble Square | 1329 W. Chicago Ave. (Throop St.) | 312-666-6175 | www.westtowntavern.com

Situated in "up-and-coming" Noble Square, this "reliably splendid" American offers chef Susan Goss' "well-thought-out" "gourmet comfort food" "with a contemporary spin" in "welcoming" wood and brick-lined environs; with "value" tabs and a staff that "makes you feel like you're part of the family", it's "the rare place that can be both everyday and special occasion."

Wholly Frijoles 🅱 *Mexican* | 25 | 16 | 20 | $22 |

Lincolnwood | 3908 W. Touhy Ave. (Prairie Rd.) | 847-329-9810 | www.whollyfrijoles.net

It may have the "worst name in greater Chicago", but this "bargain"-priced Lincolnwood BYO "deserves the crowds" for its *magnifico* "mouthwatering" Mexican fare "prepared and presented with a gourmet hand"; service gets high marks too, so the only complaint is that its "small, tight" space means "getting in isn't easy."

Wiener's Circle ●🍴 *Hot Dogs* | 19 | 5 | 13 | $10 |

Lincoln Park | 2622 N. Clark St. (bet. Drummond Pl. & Wrightwood Ave.) | 773-477-7444 | www.wienercircle.net

In the wee hours, "manners get tossed out the window" at this cheap Lincoln Park hot dog "dive", where late-nighters line up for the legendarily "crude" "humor and abuse" dealt by "obscenity-screaming" cashiers when ordering the "satisfying" char-dogs and "sinfully crispy" fries; sober sorts may find the "sass" "an acquired taste."

Wildberry Pancakes & Cafe *American* | 23 | 20 | 22 | $18 |

Loop | 130 E. Randolph St. (bet. Beaubien Ct. & Stetson Ave.) | 312-938-9777

Libertyville | 1783 N. Milwaukee Ave. (Buckley Rd.) | 847-247-7777

Schaumburg | 1383 N. Meacham Rd. (McConnor Pkwy.) | 847-517-4000 www.wildberrycafe.com

"Get your day off to a great start" at this "slightly upscale" breakfast-and lunch-only pancake emporium with locations in the Loop and suburbs, where "solid" servers send out "huge", "reasonably priced" portions from an "amazingly big" American menu that has "more flair" than expected; it's "mobbed" on weekends, so "be prepared to wait."

Wildfire *Steak* | 23 | 21 | 22 | $44 |

River North | 159 W. Erie St. (bet. La Salle Dr. & Wells St.) | 312-787-9000

Lincolnshire | 235 Parkway Dr. (Milwaukee Ave.) | 847-279-7900

Glenview | 1300 Patriot Blvd. (Lake Ave.) | 847-657-6363

Schaumburg | 1250 E. Higgins Rd. (bet. Meacham Rd. & National Pkwy.) | 847-995-0100

Oak Brook | Oakbrook Center Mall | 232 Oakbrook Ctr. (Kingery Hwy.) | 630-586-9000 www.wildfirerestaurant.com

"Another Melman success story", this steakhouse mini-chain in River North and the suburbs "runs like a well-oiled machine" with "lots of choices", "consistently quality" dishes, "professional" service and "bustling, but still relaxing dining rooms"; if tabs aren't exactly low, it's still "not quite as expensive" as some others in its category.

Wildfish *Japanese* | 20 | 19 | 19 | $37 |

Deerfield | Deerfield Commons Shopping Ctr. | 730 Waukegan Rd. (bet. Deerfield Rd. & Osterman Ave.) | 847-317-9453

Arlington Heights | Arlington Town Sq. | 60 S. Arlington Heights Rd. (bet. Northwest Hwy. & Sigwalt St.) | 847-870-8260 www.wildfishsushi.com

"Fresh" specialty rolls in "creative" combinations please both sushi lovers and more "occidental palates" at this midpriced Japanese duo in Arlington Heights and Deerfield; service can be "pleasant" or just "adequate" in the modern setting, but friends say it's "worth a drop in."

Wilmette Chop House ⬛Ⓜ *Steak* | - | - | - | E |

Wilmette | 1162 Wilmette Ave. (bet. Central & Lake Aves.) | 847-278-2462 | www.wilmettechophouse.com

Classic steaks, seafood, sides and cocktails are offered at this Wilmette redo of Bluette; new owners have transformed the intimate space into a softly lit, upscale setting done up in chocolate and vanilla colors with paisley wall panels and modern art.

Wishbone *Southern* | 20 | 17 | 19 | $20 |

Roscoe Village | 3300 N. Lincoln Ave. (School St.) | 773-549-2663
West Loop | 1001 W. Washington Blvd. (Morgan St.) | 312-850-2663
www.wishbonechicago.com

Serving "Southern vittles" "with a smile", this "affordable" "down-home" duo also puts a Cajun "spin on breakfast"; the settings are "relaxed" and feature a "spacious patio" in the West Loop and an art-filled interior in Roscoe Village, and though the service can sometimes seem "harried" due to "noisy kids" and "hideous lines for Sunday brunch", it remains a "longtime favorite."

NEW Wood ● *American* | - | - | - | M |

Lakeview | 3335 N. Halsted St. (Buckingham Pl.) | 773-935-9663 | www.woodchicago.com

Named for its wood-burning oven, this Boys Town New American specializes in small plates, housemade flatbreads and cheese/charcuterie paired with barrel-aged brown spirits and cocktails both contemporary and classic; the spare, modern setting features a bar with funky glass tile backing, massive wraparound banquettes and lots of people-watching windows; P.S. Belgian frites with a dozen dipping sauces are available late-night at their Backwoods pickup window (enter on Buckingham).

Xoco ⬛Ⓜ *Mexican* | 27 | 16 | 18 | $19 |

River North | 449 N. Clark St. (Illinois St.) | 312-334-3688 | www.rickbayless.com

You'll get "fantastic" Mexican "street eats" with the "usual [Rick] Bayless upgrades" at this River North counter-serve where grub like "tremendous" tortas, "amazing" churros and "incredible" breakfast items succeed in offering "fast food without compromising quality"; the "small" space can have "long lines" (and be a "mob scene" at lunch), and the ordering process can be "kind of weird", but all is forgiven considering the "affordable" tabs.

Yolk *Diner* | 22 | 17 | 20 | $17 |

River North | 747 N. Wells St. (bet. Chicago Ave. & Superior St.) | 312-787-2277
Streeterville | 355 E. Ohio St. (McClurg Ct.) | 312-822-9655
South Loop | 1120 S. Michigan Ave. (11th St.) | 312-789-9655
www.eatyolk.com

"Enormous portions" of "gorgeous" pancakes and "perfectly done" eggs make for a "filling breakfast" or "outstanding brunch" (they also serve lunch) at this "bright and sunny" daytime diner trio; even "efficient and friendly" service can't tame lengthy "weekend waits", but fans assure "people are waiting for a reason."

Yoshi's Café 🅼 *French/Japanese*

26	21	25	$51

Lakeview | 3257 N. Halsted St. (Aldine Ave.) | 773-248-6160 | www.yoshiscafe.com

Still a "remarkably good standby" after more than 30 years, chef-owner Yoshi Katsumura's Lakeview destination provides a "top-shelf experience", from the "consistently delicious" and "creative" French-Japanese fusion cuisine down to the "A+" service; inside is "unpretentious, warm and inviting", and prices are in keeping with the "high-quality" experience.

Yusho *Japanese*

▽ 26	20	22	$46

Avondale | 2853 N. Kedzie Ave. (bet. Diversey Ave. & George St.) | 773-904-8558 | www.yusho-chicago.com

Cheg Matthias Merges "rocks" at this "cool" Avondale Japanese where there's "no gimmicks", just "well-prepared" street eats bursting with "incredible" "complex" flavors plus craft beers, sake and "delicious" cocktails too; "friendly" staffers keep watch over the casual storefront setting, and if it's not cheap, it's still a "great place to hang out and just drink and eat until your heart is content."

Yu's Mandarin Restaurant *Chinese/Korean*

24	17	20	$22

Schaumburg | 200 E. Golf Rd. (Wilkening Rd.) | 847-882-5340 | www.yusrestaurant.com

Fans say this Schaumburg longtimer "can't be beat" for "really flipping tasty" Chinese and Korean eats, especially since "value" prices and "pleasant" service are part of the mix; you can view the "experienced wok cooks" through glass windows into the open kitchen, and regulars suggest you go "when you can watch the noodles being made" (Friday–Saturday at 8 PM).

Yuzu Sushi & Robata Grill *Japanese*

-	-	-	I

East Village | 1715 W. Chicago Ave. (bet. Hermitage Ave. & Paulina St.) | 312-666-4100 | www.yuzuchicago.com

Sushi, small plates and robata-grilled items are "fresh" and affordable at this "awesome" BYO East Villager from a Sushi Wabi vet; 100-year-old reclaimed wood and walls lined with *manga* (Japanese comic-strip art) warm up the industrial decor, and if it "takes awhile" for the "friendly" staff to deliver the goods, admirers attest it's "worth the wait."

Zaleski & Horvath MarketCafe *Deli*

▽ 24	14	20	$12

Hyde Park | 1323 E. 57th St. (bet. Kenwood & Kimbark Aves.) | 773-538-7372
Kenwood | 1126 E. 47th St. (bet. Greenwood & Woodlawn Aves.) | 773-538-7372
www.zhmarketcafe.com

Fans find an "oasis of deliciousness" at these "feel-good" counter-service delis in Kenwood and Hyde Park offering up "fabulous sandwiches" and more; "local ownership that supports the neighborhood" is a further draw, and noshers can also peruse the "interesting, eclectic" products including "locally sourced, artisanal discoveries" in the adjoining "specialty markets."

Zapatista *Mexican*   18 | 18 | 18 | $28

South Loop | 1307 S. Wabash Ave. (13th St.) | 312-435-1307
Northbrook | 992 Willow Rd. (Three Lakes Dr.) | 847-559-0939
Naperville | 1703 Freedom Dr. (Diehl Rd.) | 630-904-1703
www.zapatistamexicangrill.com

"They really bust the piñata" at this midpriced Mexican trio where the fajitas are "sizzling" and "the tequilas are many"; the colorfully rustic settings have optional patio dining, and though sticklers call out "forgettable" fare, "extreme" noise and spotty service, the majority applauds the "upscale approach."

Zed 451 ◐ *Eclectic/Steak*   22 | 24 | 22 | $52

River North | 739 N. Clark St. (bet. Chicago Ave. & Superior St.) | 312-266-6691 | www.zed451.com

Anyone "looking for an indulgence in meat" will find it at this Eclectic steakhouse in River North where the pricey all-you-can-eat option includes "prodigious amounts" of "well-prepared" beef, seafood, chicken and more (you can go à la carte too) plus a "standout" salad bar; the "huge", "group"-friendly space has an "upscale" vibe, and the rooftop bar is a prime place to sample from the "interesting" cocktail and wine menu.

Zia's Trattoria *Italian*   22 | 18 | 20 | $38

Edison Park | 6699 N. Northwest Hwy. (Oliphant Ave.) | 773-775-0808 | www.ziaschicago.com

"Solid", "pretty authentic" Italian dishes, "warm" service and a "cozy", "relaxed" atmosphere keep people coming to this *bellissimo* Edison Park "find"; the environs are "nothing fancy" but it is "kid-friendly", and even those who grouse about "crowded" tables and "noisy" patrons call it a "good value."

Zocalo *Mexican*   21 | 22 | 21 | $36

River North | 358 W. Ontario St. (Orleans St.) | 312-302-9977 | www.zocalochicago.com

A "sophisticated" "modern flair" takes the "traditional" Mexican cooking "up a notch" at this "affordable" River Norther also winning fans with a "wonderful tequila selection" and some of the "best" margaritas; "friendly" service contributes to a "lively", "unpretentious" vibe in the warm, wood-accented space so it's a "reliable favorite."

INDEXES

LOCATION MAPS

Special Features

Listings cover the best in each category and include names, locations and Food ratings. Multi-location restaurants' features may vary by branch.

BREAKFAST

(See also Hotel Dining)

Ann Sather | **multi.**	21
Bagel | **multi.**	20
Bite | **Ukrainian Vill**	22
Bongo Room | **multi.**	24
Café Selmarie | **Lincoln Sq**	21
Chicago Diner | **Lakeview**	24
NEW Ferris/Jack | **Near North**	-
Flo | **Noble Sq**	20
Ina's | **W Loop**	22
Julius Meinl | **Lakeview**	21
Kitsch'n | **Roscoe Vill**	20
Lou Mitchell's | **Loop**	24
Lula | **Logan Sq**	26
Manny's | **multi.**	24
M Henry/Henrietta | **Andersonville**	25
Milk/Honey | **Wicker Pk**	22
Nookies | **multi.**	20
Over Easy | **Ravenswood**	27
Phoenix | **Chinatown**	23
NEW Rest. Beatrix | **Near North**	-
Tempo | **Gold Coast**	19
Toast | **multi.**	22
Tre Kronor | **Albany Pk**	24
Uncommon Ground | **Lakeview**	22
Wishbone | **multi.**	20
Yolk | **S Loop**	22

BRUNCH

Ann Sather | **Andersonville**	21
Bakin'/Eggs | **Lakeview**	20
Big Jones | **Andersonville**	24
Bite | **Ukrainian Vill**	22
Bongo Room | **multi.**	24
Bristol | **Bucktown**	25
Feast | **Bucktown**	21

Flo | **Noble Sq**	20
Frontera Grill | **River N**	27
Gage | **Loop**	23
Hearty | **Lakeview**	21
Heaven/Seven | **multi.**	22
Hot Chocolate | **Bucktown**	24
NEW Howells/Hood | **Streeterville**	-
Kitsch'n | **Roscoe Vill**	20
Lobby | **River N**	25
Mercadito | **River N**	22
M Henry/Henrietta | **Andersonville**	25
Milk/Honey | **Wicker Pk**	22
Nightwood | **Pilsen**	27
NoMI Kitchen | **Gold Coast**	26
North Pond | **Lincoln Pk**	26
Orange | **multi.**	17
Over Easy | **Ravenswood**	27
Prairie Grass | **Northbrook**	22
Publican | **W Loop**	26
RL | **Gold Coast**	24
Salpicón | **Old Town**	24
Sixteen | **River N**	25
Sweet Maple | **Little Italy/University Vill**	26
Toast | **multi.**	22
Uncommon Ground | **multi.**	22
Wishbone | **multi.**	20
Yoshi's Café | **Lakeview**	26

BUFFET

(Check availability)

Andies | **Andersonville**	20
Aurelio's Pizza | **multi.**	21
Chicago Curry | **S Loop**	20
Chief O'Neill's | **NW Side**	18
Clubhouse | **Oak Brook**	22
Cumin | **Wicker Pk**	24
Curry Hut | **Highwood**	19

Dining Room/Kendall | **Near W**	23
Edwardo's Pizza | **Oak Pk**	19
Fogo de Chão | **River N**	24
Gaylord Indian | **multi.**	22
India House | **multi.**	22
Indian Garden | **Streeterville**	20
Karyn's | **Lincoln Pk**	19
Las Tablas | **Lakeview**	23
Lobby | **River N**	25
Mesón Sabika/Tapas Valencia | **Naperville**	25
Mt. Everest | **Evanston**	21
Reza's | **multi.**	20
R.J. Grunts | **Lincoln Pk**	19
Robinson's Ribs | **Oak Pk**	18
Ruby/Siam | **multi.**	21
Shaw's Crab | **multi.**	25
Signature Room | **Streeterville**	17
Sixteen | **River N**	25
Stanley's | **Lincoln Pk**	19
Tiffin | **W Rogers Pk**	19
Zed 451 | **River N**	22

BUSINESS DINING

Ai Sushi | **River N**	21
Alinea | **Lincoln Pk**	29
Allium | **Gold Coast**	23
Amuse | **Loop**	-
Aria | **Loop**	23
NEW Artisan Table | **Naperville**	-
Atwood Cafe | **Loop**	22
Balsan | **Gold Coast**	23
NEW Bavette's | **River N**	24
Benny's Chop | **River N**	25
Blackbird | **W Loop**	27
NEW Boarding Hse. | **River N**	22
NEW Bobby's | **Deerfield**	17
Boka | **Lincoln Pk**	26
Bombay Spice Grill | **River N**	22
Brasserie by LM | **S Loop**	18
Brazzaz | **River N**	22
NEW Brindille | **River N**	-
Café/Architectes | **Gold Coast**	24

Cape Cod | **Streeterville**	22
Capital Grille | **multi.**	24
Carlucci | **Rosemont**	22
Carmichael's | **W Loop**	20
Catch 35 | **multi.**	23
Chez Moi | **Lincoln Pk**	-
Chicago Chop | **River N**	23
Chicago Cut | **River N**	26
Chicago Prime | **Schaumburg**	25
NEW Chuck's | **Loop**	-
Clubhouse | **Oak Brook**	22
Coco Pazzo | **River N**	25
NEW Cottage/Dixie | **Homewood**	-
David Burke Prime | **River N**	25
Deca | **Streeterville**	21
NEW Del Frisco's | **Gold Coast**	27
Devon Seafood | **multi.**	21
Ditka's | **multi.**	22
EJ's Pl. | **Skokie**	20
NEW Embeya | **W Loop**	22
Epic Rest. | **River N**	20
Erie Cafe | **River N**	22
Everest | **Loop**	27
Filini | **Loop**	22
Fleming's | **multi.**	20
Florentine | **Loop**	20
Fogo de Chão | **River N**	24
Fulton's | **River N**	18
Gene/Georgetti | **River N**	25
Gibsons | **multi.**	26
NEW Grace | **W Loop**	29
Grill/Alley | **Streeterville**	20
Harry Caray's | **multi.**	22
Henri | **Loop**	27
Hugo's | **multi.**	24
Inovasi | **Lake Bluff**	25
Japonais | **River N**	24
Joe's Sea/Steak | **River N**	27
NEW J. Rocco | **River N**	-
NEW Kabocha | **W Loop**	-
Karma | **Mundelein**	23
Keefer's | **River N**	25

Kinzie Chop | **River N**	24	
Lawry's | **River N**	23	
Le Colonial | **Gold Coast**	23	
Les Nomades | **Streeterville**	28	
NEW Little Market | **Gold Coast**	-	
Lloyd's Chicago | **Loop**	16	
NEW LM Bistro | **River N**	-	
Lobby | **River N**	25	
NEW Local | **Gold Coast**	-	
Lockwood | **Loop**	23	
L2O | **Lincoln Pk**	26	
NEW Masaki | **Streeterville**	-	
Mastro's Steak | **River N**	26	
McCormick/Schmick | **multi.**	19	
Mercat | **S Loop**	26	
NEW MH Fish | **Lake Forest**	-	
Michael | **Winnetka**	26	
Michael Jordan's | **Streeterville**	22	
MK | **Near North**	27	
Morton's | **multi.**	23	
Naha | **River N**	26	
Next | **W Loop**	29	
Nick's Fish | **multi.**	24	
NoMI Kitchen | **Gold Coast**	26	
NEW Ovie B&G | **Loop**	-	
Palm | **Loop**	24	
NEW Park Tavern | **Rosemont**	-	
Patron's Hacienda | **River N**	-	
Pelago | **Streeterville**	27	
Perennial Virant | **Lincoln Pk**	26	
Phil Stefani's | **River N**	23	
Piccolo Sogno | **Near W**	25	
NEW Piccolo Sogno Due | **River N**	-	
Prasino | **La Grange**	22	
Province | **W Loop**	25	
Pump Room | **Gold Coast**	21	
Quince | **Evanston**	25	
NEW Revolución | **Lakeview**	-	
RL | **Gold Coast**	24	
Roka Akor | **River N**	24	

Rosewood | **Rosemont**	26
Roy's | **River N**	24
Ruth's Chris | **multi.**	23
Sable | **River N**	23
Saloon Steak | **Streeterville**	22
Saranello's | **Wheeling**	20
Sepia | **W Loop**	25
720 South B&G | **S Loop**	-
Shanghai Terrace | **River N**	26
Shaw's Crab | **multi.**	25
NEW Siena Tavern | **River N**	-
Sixteen | **River N**	25
Smith/Wollensky | **River N**	22
South Branch | **Loop**	20
Spiaggia | **Gold Coast**	26
NEW Stetsons | **Loop**	24
Sullivan's Steak | **multi.**	24
Takashi | **Bucktown**	28
Tallgrass | **Lockport**	27
NEW Tesori | **Loop**	-
III Forks | **Loop**	23
312 Chicago | **Loop**	21
Topolobampo | **River N**	28
NEW Tortoise Club | **River N**	-
Trattoria No. 10 | **Loop**	24
Tru | **Streeterville**	27
Vivere | **Loop**	23
Weber Grill | **River N**	21
Wilmette Chop | **Wilmette**	-

BYO

NEW Ahjoomah's | **Chinatown**	-
Al Dente | **NW Side**	23
NEW Andy's | **Lakeview**	26
Anna's Asian | **W Loop**	-
Ann Sather | **multi.**	21
Apart Pizza Co. | **multi.**	25
Art of Pizza | **Lakeview**	23
Bacchanalia | **SW Side**	22
BadHappy | **River N**	-
Bagel | **Lakeview**	20
Belly Shack | **Humboldt Pk**	25
Bento Box | **Bucktown**	27

Birchwood | **Wicker Pk**	23
Birrieria Zaragoza | **SW Side**	27
NEW Bistro Dre | **Lakeview**	-
Bite | **Ukrainian Vill**	22
NEW Bub City | **River N**	-
Burger Point | **S Loop**	-
Butcher/Burger | **Lincoln Pk**	25
Butterfly | **multi.**	20
Cemitas Puebla | **Humboldt Pk**	24
NEW Chez Simo | **Lincoln Sq**	-
Chilam Balam | **Lakeview**	25
Chilapan | **Logan Sq**	25
City Farms Mkt. | **Lakeview**	-
Coast/South Coast | **Bucktown**	24
Crisp | **Lakeview**	24
Dawali | **Lincoln Pk**	23
Dimo's Pizza | **Lakeview**	22
NEW Duran | **W Loop**	-
Eggy's | **Streeterville**	-
EL Ideas | **Pilsen**	28
Epic Burger | **multi.**	19
NEW Flour/Stone | **Streeterville**	-
Franks 'N' Dawgs | **Lincoln Pk**	25
Giordano's | **Hyde Pk**	22
Goosefoot | **Lincoln Sq**	29
NEW Hamachi | **W Rogers Pk**	-
Han 202 | **Bridgeport**	25
NEW Haute/Dog | **Wicker Pk**	-
HB Home Bistro | **Lakeview**	25
Hema's | **multi.**	22
Honey 1 BBQ | **Bucktown**	21
Irazu | **Bucktown**	23
Jam | **Logan Sq**	22
Jin Thai | **Edgewater**	-
Joy's Noodles | **Lakeview**	22
Joy Yee's | **multi.**	20
Karyn's | **Lincoln Pk**	19
NEW LM Bistro | **River N**	-
Los Nopales | **Lincoln Sq**	23
NEW L'Patron | **Logan Sq**	-
NEW MAK | **Wicker Pk**	-
Marmalade | **North Ctr/St. Ben's**	25
M Henry/Henrietta | **multi.**	25
Mixteco Grill | **Lakeview**	27
Mr. Beef | **River N**	24
Namo | **North Ctr/St. Ben's**	-
90 Miles | **multi.**	23
Nookies | **multi.**	20
NEW Oliver's | **Bridgeport**	-
Opart Thai | **Lincoln Sq**	24
Original Gino's | **Lincoln Pk**	22
Over Easy | **Ravenswood**	27
Penny's | **multi.**	20
Pho 777 | **Uptown**	24
Pleasant House | **Bridgeport**	-
Red Violet | **River N**	-
NEW Rickshaw | **Lincoln Pk**	-
Robinson's Ribs | **multi.**	18
Ruby/Siam | **multi.**	21
Ruxbin | **Noble Sq**	28
Salsa 17 | **Arlington Hts**	21
NEW Sauce/Bread | **Edgewater**	-
Schwa | **Wicker Pk**	28
Shaman | **Ukrainian Vill**	-
Simply It | **Lincoln Pk**	21
Smoque BBQ | **Old Irving Pk**	26
Sultan's Market | **multi.**	21
Sushi Para/Sai | **multi.**	19
TAC Quick | **Wrigleyville**	26
Tango Sur | **Lakeview**	24
Tank Noodle | **Uptown**	25
Tanoshii | **Andersonville**	28
Tempo | **Gold Coast**	19
Thai Pastry | **multi.**	25
Todoroki Hibachi | **Evanston**	-
Toro Sushi | **Lincoln Pk**	26
Tre Kronor | **Albany Pk**	24
Urbanbelly | **Logan Sq**	25
Waffles | **multi.**	-
Wellfleet | **Albany Pk**	-
Wholly Frijoles | **Lincolnwood**	25
Wildberry Pancakes | **Loop**	23

Yolk	**multi.**	22
Yuzu Sushi	**E Vill**	-

CELEBRITY CHEFS

Grant Achatz
Alinea	**Lincoln Pk**	29
Aviary	**W Loop**	26
Next	**W Loop**	29

Rodelio Aglibot
NEW e+o	**Mt. Prospect**	-

Rick Bayless
Frontera Fresco	**multi.**	24
Frontera Grill	**River N**	27
Topolobampo	**River N**	28
Tortas Frontera	**multi.**	23
Xoco	**River N**	27

Graham Elliot Bowles
NEW g.e.b.	**W Loop**	-
Graham Elliot	**River N**	24
Grahamwich	**River N**	19

George Bumbaris, Sarah Stegner
Prairie Grass	**Northbrook**	22

Homaro Cantu
Ing	**W Loop**	23
Moto	**W Loop**	26

Michael Carlson
Schwa	**Wicker Pk**	28

Curtis Duffy
NEW Grace	**W Loop**	29

Stephanie Izard
Girl/The Goat	**W Loop**	27
NEW Little Goat Bread	**W Loop**	-
NEW Little Goat Diner	**W Loop**	22

Jean Joho
Everest	**Loop**	27
Paris Club	**River N**	20

Paul Kahan
Avec	**W Loop**	28
Big Star	**Wicker Pk**	26
Blackbird	**W Loop**	27
Publican	**W Loop**	26
Publican Meats	**W Loop**	26

Michael Kornick
Ada St.	**Bucktown**	24
DMK Burger Bar	**multi.**	22
Fish Bar	**Lakeview**	24
MK	**Near North**	27

Dale Levitski
Frog n Snail	**Lakeview**	20
Sprout	**Lincoln Pk**	26

Roland Liccioni
Les Nomades	**Streeterville**	28

Tony Mantuano
Bar Toma	**Gold Coast**	17
Café Spiaggia	**Gold Coast**	25
Spiaggia	**Gold Coast**	26
Terzo Piano	**Loop**	22

Carrie Nahabedian
NEW Brindille	**River N**	-
Naha	**River N**	26

Brendan Sodikoff
Au Cheval	**W Loop**	25
NEW Bavette's	**River N**	24
Gilt Bar	**River N**	25
Maude's Liquor	**W Loop**	25

Paul Virant
Perennial Virant	**Lincoln Pk**	26
Vie	**W Springs**	29

Fabio Viviani
NEW Siena Tavern	**River N**	-

Jean-Georges Vongerichten
Pump Room	**Gold Coast**	21

Takashi Yagihashi
Noodles/Yagihashi	**Loop**	22
Slurping Turtle	**River N**	22
Takashi	**Bucktown**	28

CHILD-FRIENDLY
(Alternatives to the usual fast-food places; * children's menu available)
American Girl	**Streeterville**	13
Ann Sather*	**multi.**	21
Antico Posto*	**Oak Brook**	23
Artopolis	**Greektown**	21
Athena	**Greektown**	19
Aurelio's Pizza*	**multi.**	21

Bagel*	multi.	20
Bakin'/Eggs*	Lakeview	20
Bandera*	Streeterville	23
Berghoff	O'Hare Area	19
Big Bowl*	multi.	20
Bob Chinn's*	Wheeling	23
Bricks	Lincoln Pk	23
Cafecito	Loop	24
Café Selmarie*	Lincoln Sq	21
Carson's*	River N	21
Chicago Pizza	Lincoln Pk	25
NEW Crosby's Kit.*	Lakeview	19
Davis St. Fish*	Evanston	19
NEW Duran	W Loop	–
Edwardo's Pizza*	multi.	19
Eleven City*	S Loop	19
NEW Fat Rice	Logan Sq	–
Five Guys	multi.	17
Foodlife/ease*	Streeterville	19
Gale St. Inn*	Jefferson Pk	21
Greek Islands*	multi.	22
Hackney's*	multi.	18
Harry Caray's*	multi.	22
Heaven/Seven*	multi.	22
Hot Doug's	Avondale	27
Ina's	W Loop	22
NEW Isabel's	Lincoln Pk	–
Jake Melnick's*	Gold Coast	19
Jerry's*	Wicker Pk	20
John's Pl.*	Lincoln Pk	17
Joy Yee's	Chinatown	20
Kitsch'n*	Roscoe Vill	20
Lawry's*	River N	23
NEW Little Goat Diner*	W Loop	22
Lou Malnati's*	multi.	25
Lou Mitchell's*	Loop	24
LuLu's	Evanston	21
Manny's*	SW Side	24
Margie's	Bucktown	22
Milk/Honey*	Wicker Pk	22
Mity Nice*	Streeterville	19
Nookies*	multi.	20

Oak Tree	Gold Coast	16
Orange*	multi.	17
Original Gino's*	multi.	22
Pegasus	SW Side	20
Phoenix	Chinatown	23
Pita Inn	multi.	23
NEW Pizza Hse. 1647	Bucktown	–
Pizzeria Due/Uno*	River N	22
Potbelly	multi.	18
R.J. Grunts*	Lincoln Pk	19
Robinson's Ribs*	multi.	18
Roditys	Greektown	20
Russell's*	Elmwood Pk	21
Sapori Trattoria	Lincoln Pk	25
Scoozi!*	River N	20
Smoque BBQ*	Old Irving Pk	26
Southport*	Lakeview	23
Stanley's*	Lincoln Pk	19
Sweet Maple	Little Italy/University Vill	26
Tempo	Gold Coast	19
3rd Coast Cafe	Gold Coast	18
Three Happiness	Chinatown	22
Toast*	multi.	22
Trattoria D.O.C.	Evanston	20
Tufano's	Little Italy/University Vill	24
Twin Anchors*	Old Town	22
Uncommon Ground*	Lakeview	22
NEW Wâfel	W Town	–
Walnut Room*	Loop	18
Weber Grill*	multi.	21
Wishbone*	multi.	20
Yolk*	multi.	22
Yu's Mandarin	Schaumburg	24

DINING ALONE

(Other than hotels and places with counter service)

Al's Beef	Roscoe Vill	22
Ann Sather	multi.	21
Artopolis	Greektown	21
Avec	W Loop	28

Bagel	**multi.**	20
Banh Mi/Co.	**Lakeview**	-
Bar Toma	**Gold Coast**	17
Big Bowl	**multi.**	20
Bin	**River N**	21
Bistrot Zinc	**Gold Coast**	21
Bite	**Ukrainian Vill**	22
Blind Faith	**Evanston**	20
Bridge Bar Chicago	**River N**	-
Café Selmarie	**Lincoln Sq**	21
Chicago Chop	**River N**	23
Chicago Diner	**Lakeview**	24
Chief O'Neill's	**NW Side**	18
Davis St. Fish	**Evanston**	19
DMK Burger Bar	**multi.**	22
Eleven City	**S Loop**	19
Epic Burger	**multi.**	19
Franks 'N' Dawgs	**Lincoln Pk**	25
Fred's	**Gold Coast**	20
Goose Island	**multi.**	17
Grafton Pub/Grill	**Lincoln Sq**	22
GT Fish/Oyster	**River N**	25
Half Shell	**Lakeview**	22
Harry Caray's	**multi.**	22
Heaven/Seven	**multi.**	22
Hopleaf	**Andersonville**	24
Hubbard Inn	**River N**	20
Joy Yee's	**multi.**	20
Kinzie Chop	**River N**	24
Koi	**Evanston**	17
Lou Mitchell's	**Loop**	24
Lula	**Logan Sq**	26
McCormick/Schmick	**multi.**	19
Mirai Sushi	**Wicker Pk**	25
Oak Tree	**Gold Coast**	16
Old Jerusalem	**Old Town**	20
Oysy	**multi.**	22
Reza's	**multi.**	20
Shaw's Crab	**multi.**	25
Tanoshii	**Andersonville**	28
Toast	**multi.**	22
Toro Sushi	**Lincoln Pk**	26

ENTERTAINMENT

(Call for types and times of performances)

Catch 35	**Loop**	23
Chicago Chop	**River N**	23
Chicago Prime	**Schaumburg**	25
Chief O'Neill's	**NW Side**	18
Edelweiss	**Norridge**	22
Geja's	**Lincoln Pk**	22
Lobby	**River N**	25
Mesón Sabika/Tapas Valencia	**Naperville**	25
Nacional 27	**River N**	22
Philly G's	**Vernon Hills**	21
Sabatino's	**Old Irving Pk**	26
Sayat Nova	**Streeterville**	23
Shaw's Crab	**River N**	25
Signature Room	**Streeterville**	17
Smoke Daddy	**Wicker Pk**	22
Sullivan's Steak	**multi.**	24
Tapas Gitana	**Northfield**	22
Uncommon Ground	**Lakeview**	22

FIREPLACES

Adelle's	**Wheaton**	26
Ai Sushi	**River N**	21
Andies	**Andersonville**	20
Ann Sather	**Lakeview**	21
Bistrot Margot	**Old Town**	22
Blokes/Birds	**Lakeview**	18
Brio	**Lombard**	-
NEW Cantina Pasadita	**Avondale**	-
Carson's	**Deerfield**	21
Chicago Prime	**Schaumburg**	25
Chief O'Neill's	**NW Side**	18
Courtright's	**Willow Spgs**	27
NEW Crosby's Kit.	**Lakeview**	19
Dee's	**Lincoln Pk**	19
Devon Seafood	**River N**	21
Edelweiss	**Norridge**	22
EJ's Pl.	**Skokie**	20
Erie Cafe	**River N**	22
Estate Ultra Bar	**River W**	-
Feast	**Bucktown**	21

Francesca's | **Forest Pk** 22

NEW freestyle | **River N** -

Froggy's | **Highwood** 25

Frontier | **Noble Sq** 22

Gage | **Loop** 23

Gene/Georgetti | **River N** 25

Grafton Pub/Grill | **Lincoln Sq** 22

Inovasi | **Lake Bluff** 25

Japonais | **River N** 24

Jerry's | **Wicker Pk** 20

Jerry's Restaurant | **Winnetka** 22

John's Pl. | **Lincoln Pk** 17

Keefer's | **River N** 25

Koi | **Evanston** 17

La Madia | **River N** 23

Les Nomades | **Streeterville** 28

Le Vichyssois | **Lakemoor** 25

Lovells | **Lake Forest** 22

Milk/Honey | **Wicker Pk** 22

North Pond | **Lincoln Pk** 26

Owen/Engine | **Logan Sq** 24

Oysy | **S Loop** 22

Park Grill | **Loop** 19

Pelago | **Streeterville** 27

Penny's | **multi.** 20

Pensiero | **Evanston** 21

Quartino | **River N** 22

Quince | **Evanston** 25

RL | **Gold Coast** 24

Robinson's Ribs | **Lincoln Pk** 18

Rockit | **Wrigleyville** 19

Rustic Hse. | **Lincoln Pk** 21

Ruth's Chris | **Northbrook** 23

Sai Café | **Lincoln Pk** 27

Santorini | **Greektown** 22

Sola | **North Ctr/St. Ben's** 24

Sullivan's Steak | **Lincolnshire** 24

Sunda | **River N** 25

Swordfish | **Batavia** 27

Tallgrass | **Lockport** 27

III Forks | **Loop** 23

NEW Tortoise Club | **River N** -

Trattoria Gianni | **Lincoln Pk** 20

Uncommon Ground | **multi.** 22

Vie | **W Springs** 29

Weber Grill | **multi.** 21

Webster's | **Lincoln Pk** 18

HISTORIC PLACES

(Year opened; * building)

1800 | Chief O'Neill's* | **NW Side** 18

1847 | Mesón Sabika/Tapas
Valencia* | **Naperville** 25

1870 | Depot Nuevo* | **Wilmette** 18

1880 | Bourgeois Pig* | **Lincoln Pk** 20

1880 | West Town* | **Noble Sq** 26

1881 | Twin Anchors* | **Old Town** 22

1887 | Merlo* | **Gold Coast** 25

1890 | Lawry's* | **River N** 23

1890 | Pizzeria Due/Uno* |
River N 22

1890 | Sapori Trattoria* |
Lincoln Pk 25

1890 | Sepia* | **W Loop** 25

1890 | Webster's* | **Lincoln Pk** 18

1892 | Francesca's* | **Naperville** 22

1897 | Tallgrass* | **Lockport** 27

1898 | Berghoff | **Loop** 19

1900 | Vivo* | **W Loop** 23

1905 | Carnivale* | **W Loop** 21

1905 | Chicago Firehouse* |
S Loop 22

1906 | Masa Azul* | **Logan Sq** -

1907 | Bistro Voltaire* |
Near North 22

1907 | Walnut Room | **Loop** 18

1910 | Hackney's* | **Print's Row** 18

1912 | Eleven City* | **S Loop** 19

1920 | Chef's Station* | **Evanston** 24

1920 | Crosby's Kit.* |
Lakeview 19

1920 | Dining Room/Kendall* |
Near W 23

1920 | 3rd Coast Cafe* |
Gold Coast 18

1921 | Margie's | **Bucktown** 22

1922 | Del Rio* | **Highwood** 20

1923 | Lou Mitchell's | **Loop** 24

1927 | David Burke Prime* | **River N** 25

1927 | Village* | **Loop** 20

1927 | Vivere* | **Loop** 23

1930 | Russell's | **Elmwood Pk** 21

1930 | Tufano's* | **Little Italy/University Vill** 24

1932 | Fontano's | **Hinsdale** 27

1933 | Bruna's | **SW Side** 23

1933 | Cape Cod | **Streeterville** 22

1934 | Billy Goat | **River N** 16

1935 | FatDuck* | **Forest Pk** 20

1938 | Al's Beef | **Niles** 22

1939 | Hackney's | **multi.** 18

1940 | Due Lire* | **Lincoln Sq** 23

1940 | Township* | **Logan Sq** -

1941 | Gene/Georgetti | **River N** 25

1942 | Home Run Inn | **SW Side** 24

1942 | Manny's | **S Loop** 24

1942 | Top Notch | **Far S Side** 25

1946 | Ricobene's | **Bridgeport** 24

1948 | Superdawg | **NW Side** 21

1950 | Gene/Jude's | **O'Hare Area** 24

1955 | Kaufman's | **Skokie** 23

1955 | Pizzeria Due/Uno | **River N** 22

1959 | Aurelio's Pizza | **multi.** 21

1961 | Artist's Cafe | **Loop** 15

1961 | Butch McGuire's | **Near North** 18

HOTEL DINING

Aloft Chicago City Ctr.
NEW Rest. Beatrix | **Near North** -

Blackstone Hotel
Mercat | **S Loop** 26

Chicago Marriott Naperville
NEW Artisan Table | **Naperville** -

Club Quarters Wacker at Michigan
Bacino's | **Loop** 21

Dana Hotel & Spa
NEW freestyle | **River N** -

Doubletree Libertyville
Karma | **Mundelein** 23

Doubletree O'Hare
Gibsons | **Rosemont** 26

Drake Hotel
Cape Cod | **Streeterville** 22

Essex Inn
Brasserie by LM | **S Loop** 18

Fairmont Chicago Hotel
Aria | **Loop** 23

Four Seasons Hotel Chicago
Allium | **Gold Coast** 23

Hard Rock Hotel
NEW Chuck's | **Loop** -

Hilton Chicago
720 South B&G | **S Loop** -

Hilton Chicago Mag. Mile
NEW Masaki | **Streeterville** -

Hilton Garden Inn
Weber Grill | **River N** 21

Hilton Suites Chicago/Mag. Mile
NEW Local | **Gold Coast** -

Holiday Inn Chicago Downtown
Aurelio's Pizza | **Loop** 21

Homestead Hotel
Quince | **Evanston** 25

Hotel Allegro
312 Chicago | **Loop** 21

Hotel Burnham
Atwood Cafe | **Loop** 22

Hotel Felix
NEW LM Bistro | **River N** -

Hotel Lincoln
Perennial Virant | **Lincoln Pk** 26

Hotel Monaco
South Water | **Loop** 14

Hotel Palomar
Sable | **River N** 23

Hyatt Regency
NEW Stetsons | **Loop** 24

InterContinental Chicago
Michael Jordan's | **Streeterville** 22

James Chicago Hotel
David Burke Prime | **River N** 25

JW Marriott Chicago
Florentine | **Loop** 20

Margarita European Inn
Pensiero | **Evanston** 21

MileNorth
NEW Ferris/Jack | **Near North** −

Palmer House Hilton
Lockwood | **Loop** 23

Park Hyatt Chicago
NoMI Kitchen | **Gold Coast** 26

Peninsula Chicago
Lobby | **River N** 25
Pierrot Gourmet | **River N** 22
Shanghai Terrace | **River N** 26

Public Chicago
Pump Room | **Gold Coast** 21

Radisson Blu Aqua Hotel
Filini | **Loop** 22

Raffaello Hotel
Pelago | **Streeterville** 27

Renaissance North Shore Hotel
Ruth's Chris | **Northbrook** 23

Ritz-Carlton Chicago
Deca | **Streeterville** 21

Rivers Casino
Hugo's | **Des Plaines** 24

Seneca Hotel
Francesca's | **Streeterville** 22
Saloon Steak | **Streeterville** 22

Sheraton Chicago Hotel
Shula's Steak | **Streeterville** 22

The Shoreham
Caffe Rom | **Loop** 22

Sofitel Chicago Water Tower
Café/Architectes | **Gold Coast** 24

Swissôtel Chicago
Amuse | **Loop** −
Palm | **Loop** 24

The Talbott Hotel
NEW Little Market | **Gold Coast** −

Tremont Hotel
Ditka's | **Gold Coast** 22

Trump Int'l Hotel
Sixteen | **River N** 25

Waldorf-Astoria Chicago
Balsan | **Gold Coast** 23

Westin Chicago North Shore
Tramonto's | **Wheeling** 22

Westin Chicago NW
Shula's Steak | **Itasca** 22

Westin Lombard
Harry Caray's | **Lombard** 22

Westin Michigan Ave.
Grill/Alley | **Streeterville** 20

Westin River North
Kamehachi | **River N** 22

The Wit Hotel
State/Lake | **Loop** 16

JACKET REQUIRED

Les Nomades | **Streeterville** 28
Spiaggia | **Gold Coast** 26
Tru | **Streeterville** 27

LATE DINING

(Weekday closing hour)
Al's Beef | 12 AM, varies | **multi.** 22
NEW American Junkie | varies | −
River N
Anthem | varies | **Ukrainian Vill** 18
Artopolis | 12 AM | **Greektown** 21
Au Cheval | 1:30 AM | **W Loop** 25
Avec | 12 AM | **W Loop** 28
Bangers/Lace | 2 AM | **Wicker Pk** 20
Barrelhouse Flat | varies | −
Lincoln Pk
Bedford | varies | **Wicker Pk** 17
Beer Bistro | varies | **multi.** 17
Bricks | varies | **North Ctr/St. Ben's** 23
Big Star | 2 AM | **Wicker Pk** 26
Bijan's | 3:30 AM | **River N** 20
Billy Goat | varies | **River N** 16

NEW Billy Sunday | 2 AM | **Logan Sq** — ┘

Bite | varies | **Ukrainian Vill** 22┘

NEW BlackFinn | varies | **Mt. Prospect** — ┘

Blokes/Birds | 2 AM | **Lakeview** 18┘

Bluebird | varies | **Bucktown** 22┘

NEW Boarding Hse. | varies | **River N** 22┘

NEW Bodega | varies | **Lincoln Pk** — ┘

Branch 27 | varies | **Noble Sq** 19┘

NEW Brasserie 54/LM | 12 AM | **Andersonville** — ┘

Bridge House | varies | **River N** 18┘

NEW Bub City | varies | **River N** — ┘

Bullhead Cantina | varies | **Humboldt Pk** — ┘

Butch McGuire's | varies | **Near North** 18┘

Café Iberico | 11:30 PM | **River N** 22┘

NEW Cantina Pasadita | varies | **Avondale** — ┘

NEW Carriage Hse. | 12 AM | **Wicker Pk** 21┘

NEW Central Standard | varies | **River N** — ┘

NEW Centro Rist. | varies | **Near North** — ┘

Chicago Cut | 2 AM | **River N** 26┘

Chief O'Neill's | 1 AM | **NW Side** 18┘

Coast/South Coast | 12 AM | **Bucktown** 24┘

Dimo's Pizza | varies | **Lakeview** 22┘

DiSotto | varies | **Streeterville** 23┘

DMK Burger Bar | 12 AM | **Lakeview** 22┘

NEW Dryhop | 2 AM | **Lakeview** — ┘

Duke/Perth | varies | **Lakeview** 20┘

NEW El Hefe | 2 AM | **Near North** — ┘

Estate Ultra Bar | varies | **River W** — ┘

Farmhouse | varies | **Near North** 23┘

FatDuck | varies | **Forest Pk** 20┘

NEW Fat Sandwich | varies | **Lincoln Pk** — ┘

NEW Ferris/Jack | varies | **Near North** — ┘

Fifty/50 | 1 AM | **Wicker Pk** 18┘

Fireside | varies | **Andersonville** 20┘

Fountainhead | 1:30 AM | **Ravenswood** 20┘

NEW freestyle | 2 AM | **River N** — ┘

Frontier | varies | **Noble Sq** 22┘

Gage | varies | **Loop** 23┘

NEW g.e.b. | 12 AM | **W Loop** — ┘

Gene/Jude's | varies | **O'Hare Area** 24┘

Gibsons | varies | **multi.** 26┘

Gilt Bar | 12 AM | **River N** 25┘

NEW Gino's East | varies | **Printer's Row** — ┘

Giordano's | varies | **SW Side** 22┘

Glenview House | varies | **Glenview** 19┘

Grafton Pub/Grill | varies | **Lincoln Sq** 22┘

Harry Caray's | 12 AM | **River N** 22┘

Heartland | varies | **Rogers Pk** 17┘

Homestead | varies | **Ukrainian Vill** — ┘

Hop Häus | varies | **Rogers Pk** 20┘

NEW Howells/Hood | 12 AM | **Streeterville** — ┘

Hub 51 | 12 AM | **River N** 20┘

Hugo's | varies | **multi.** 24┘

Itto Sushi | 12 AM | **Lincoln Pk** 25┘

Jake Melnick's | 1 AM | **Gold Coast** 19┘

NEW Jellyfish | varies | **River N** — ┘

Kamehachi | varies | **Old Town** 22┘

Kuma's | varies | **multi.** 27┘

Lady Gregory's | varies | **Andersonville** 20┘

NEW Lao Ma La | 2 AM | **Chinatown** — ┘

Lao Sze Chuan/You Ju | varies | **multi.** 24┘

NEW La Sirena | 2 AM | **W Loop** 24┘

NEW Little Goat Bread | 2 AM | **W Loop** — ┘

NEW Little Goat Diner | 2 AM | 22
    W Loop

NEW Local | 2 AM | **Gold Coast** -

Longman/Eagle | 1 AM | 27
    Logan Sq

Lucky's | varies | **multi.** 18

Luxbar | 1:30 AM | **Gold Coast** 19

Margie's | varies | **Bucktown** 22

Mastro's Steak | varies | **River N** 26

Maude's Liquor | 2 AM | **W Loop** 25

Mercadito | varies | **River N** 22

NEW Mercer 113 | varies | -
    River N

Michael Jordan's | 2 AM | 22
    Streeterville

NEW Monarch | varies | -
    Wicker Pk

Monkey's Paw | varies | -
    Lincoln Pk

NEW Municipal | varies | -
    River N

Near Restaurant | varies | -
    Barrington

Nellcôte | varies | **W Loop** 19

Noodles/Yagihashi | 3 AM | 22
    Loop

Nookies | 12 AM | **Lakeview** 20

NEW Old Fifth | varies | **Near W** -

Old Town Pour Hse. | 2 AM | 14
    Old Town

Old Town Social | 1:30 AM | 21
    Old Town

NEW Ovie B&G | 12 AM | **Loop** -

Owen/Engine | 2 AM | **Logan Sq** 24

Paris Club | varies | **River N** 20

NEW Park Tavern | varies | **multi.** -

NEW Parson's | 2 AM | -
    Logan Sq

Patron's Hacienda | varies | -
    River N

Pegasus | varies | **SW Side** 20

Pequod's | varies | **Lincoln Pk** 24

Pete Miller's | varies | **Evanston** 22

Pizano's | varies | **multi.** 21

Pizzeria Due/Uno | varies | 22
    River N

P.J. Clarke's | 2 AM | **Gold Coast** 17

NEW Plzen | varies | **Pilsen** -

Point | varies | **W Loop** -

Prost! | 2 AM | **Lincoln Pk** -

Public House | 1 AM | **River N** 18

Pump Room | varies | **Gold Coast** 21

Purple Pig | 12 AM | **River N** 26

Quartino | 1 AM | **River N** 22

Quay | varies | **Streeterville** 19

RA Sushi | varies | **multi.** 18

Red Door | 12 AM | **Bucktown** -

NEW Reno | varies | **Logan Sq** -

NEW Rest. Beatrix | 12 AM | -
    Near North

NEW Revolución | varies | -
    Lakeview

Revolution Brewing | 12 AM | 23
    Logan Sq

Ricobene's | varies | **Bridgeport** 24

R.J. Grunts | varies | **Lincoln Pk** 19

NEW RM Champagne | varies | -
    W Loop

Rockit | 1:30 AM | **River N** 19

Roditys | 12 AM | **Greektown** 20

Roots Pizza | 2 AM | **W Town** 20

Rootstock | 1 AM | **Humboldt Pk** 23

RPM Italian | varies | **River N** 23

Sable | varies | **River N** 23

San Soo Gab San | 24 hrs. | 25
    Lincoln Sq

Santorini | 12 AM | **Greektown** 22

Saranello's | varies | **Wheeling** 20

Scofflaw | varies | **Logan Sq** -

NEW Siena Tavern | varies | -
    River N

Silver | 1 AM | **Uptown** 27

Slurping Turtle | varies | **River N** 22

Southern | varies | **Wicker Pk** 20

Stanley's | varies | **Lincoln Pk** 19

Storefront Co. | 2 AM | **Wicker Pk** -

NEW Suite 25 | varies | **Logan Sq** -

Superdawg | varies | **NW Side** 21

SushiSamba | 1 AM | **River N** 20

NEW Sweet Baby Ray's | 2 AM | –
Wrigleyville

Taco Joint | 12 AM | **Near North** 23

Tasting Room | varies | **W Loop** 18

Taverna 750 | varies | 24
Wrigleyville

Tavernita | varies | **River N** 21

Tavern/Rush | 12 AM | 21
Gold Coast

Telegraph | varies | **Logan Sq** 22

Tempo | 24 hrs. | **Gold Coast** 19

3rd Coast Cafe | 12 AM | 18
Gold Coast

Three Aces | varies | 22
Little Italy/University Vill

Three Happiness | 6 AM | 22
Chinatown

NEW Tommy Knuckles | varies | –
Lincoln Pk

Township | 2 AM | **Logan Sq** –

Troquet | varies | **Ravenswood** –

Twisted Spoke | 1 AM | **Noble Sq** 20

Uncommon Ground | varies | 22
multi.

Village | 11:30 PM | **Loop** 20

Volare | varies | **multi.** 23

Webster's | 12:30 AM | 18
Lincoln Pk

Wiener's Circle | 4 AM | 19
Lincoln Pk

NEW Wood | varies | **Lakeview** –

Zed 451 | varies | **River N** 22

MEET FOR A DRINK

Acre | **Andersonville** 20

Ada St. | **Bucktown** 24

Adobo | **Old Town** 20

NEW American Junkie | **River N** –

Arrow/Ogden | **W Loop** –

Au Cheval | **W Loop** 25

Balena | **Lincoln Pk** 24

Bandera | **Streeterville** 23

Bangers/Lace | **Wicker Pk** 20

NEW Bar Pastoral | **Lakeview** –

Barrelhouse Flat | **Lincoln Pk** –

Bar Toma | **Gold Coast** 17

NEW Bavette's | **River N** 24

Bedford | **Wicker Pk** 17

NEW Belly Q | **W Loop** 22

Benny's Chop | **River N** 25

NEW Billy Sunday | **Logan Sq** –

Blokes/Birds | **Lakeview** 18

NEW Boarding Hse. | **River N** 22

Boka | **Lincoln Pk** 26

Bridge Bar Chicago | **River N** –

Bridge House | **River N** 18

Bristol | **Bucktown** 25

Café/Architectes | **Gold Coast** 24

Carnivale | **W Loop** 21

Catch 35 | **multi.** 23

Cellar/Stained Glass | **Evanston** 22

NEW Centro Rist. | **Near North** –

Chicago Cut | **River N** 26

Cité | **Streeterville** 19

NEW City Winery | **W Loop** 16

Club Lucky | **Bucktown** 21

NEW Cottage/Dixie | **Homewood** –

NEW Del Frisco's | **Gold Coast** 27

Devon Seafood | **Oakbrook Terr** 21

Ditka's | **multi.** 22

NEW Embeya | **W Loop** 22

Epic Rest. | **River N** 20

Estate Ultra Bar | **River W** –

NEW Found | **Evanston** –

Fred's | **Gold Coast** 20

NEW freestyle | **River N** –

Fulton's | **River N** 18

Gage | **Loop** 23

Gibsons | **multi.** 26

Gilt Bar | **River N** 25

Girl/The Goat | **W Loop** 27

Goose Island | **multi.** 17

Graham Elliot | **River N** 24

Henri | **Loop** 27

Hopleaf | **Andersonville** 24

NEW Howells/Hood | **Streeterville**	_
Hubbard Inn | **River N**	20
Hub 51 | **River N**	20
Hugo's | **multi.**	24
Japonais | **River N**	24
Joe's Sea/Steak | **River N**	27
Keefer's | **River N**	25
NEW La Grande Vie | **Streeterville**	_
NEW Lao 18 | **River N**	_
NEW La Sirena | **W Loop**	24
Le Colonial | **Gold Coast**	23
NEW Little Market | **Gold Coast**	_
Lockwood | **Loop**	23
Longman/Eagle | **Logan Sq**	27
Lula | **Logan Sq**	26
Luxbar | **Gold Coast**	19
Market House | **Lake Forest**	_
Masa Azul | **Logan Sq**	_
Mastro's Steak | **River N**	26
Maude's Liquor | **W Loop**	25
Mercadito | **River N**	22
NEW Mercer 113 | **River N**	_
NEW Mezcalina | **Loop**	_
Michael Jordan's | **Streeterville**	22
MK | **Near North**	27
NEW Monarch | **Wicker Pk**	_
NEW Municipal | **River N**	_
Nacional 27 | **River N**	22
Nellcôte | **W Loop**	19
NoMI Kitchen | **Gold Coast**	26
Old Town Pour Hse. | **Old Town**	14
Old Town Social | **Old Town**	21
NEW Oliver's | **Bridgeport**	_
Owen/Engine | **Logan Sq**	24
Paris Club | **River N**	20
Patron's Hacienda | **River N**	_
Perennial Virant | **Lincoln Pk**	26
NEW Piccolo Sogno Due | **River N**	_
Prosecco | **River N**	24
Prost! | **Lincoln Pk**	_
Publican | **W Loop**	26
Public House | **River N**	18
Pump Room | **Gold Coast**	21
Quartino | **River N**	22
Quay | **Streeterville**	19
NEW Red Square | **Wicker Pk**	_
NEW Rest. Beatrix | **Near North**	_
NEW Revolución | **Lakeview**	_
Revolution Brewing | **Logan Sq**	23
NEW Riccardo Eno. | **Lincoln Pk**	_
RL | **Gold Coast**	24
NEW RM Champagne | **W Loop**	_
Roka Akor | **River N**	24
Rosebud Prime/Steak | **Streeterville**	23
Scofflaw | **Logan Sq**	_
Sepia | **W Loop**	25
Shaw's Crab | **multi.**	25
Signature Room | **Streeterville**	17
Sixteen | **River N**	25
Smith/Wollensky | **River N**	22
Southern | **Wicker Pk**	20
Stained Glass | **Evanston**	24
NEW Stetsons | **Loop**	24
Storefront Co. | **Wicker Pk**	_
Stout Barrel Hse. | **River N**	_
NEW Suite 25 | **Logan Sq**	_
Sullivan's Steak | **River N**	24
Sunda | **River N**	25
SushiSamba | **River N**	20
Tasting Room | **W Loop**	18
Taverna 750 | **Wrigleyville**	24
Tavernita | **River N**	21
Tavern/Rush | **Gold Coast**	21
Telegraph | **Logan Sq**	22
NEW Tesori | **Loop**	_
Three Aces | **Little Italy/University Vill**	22
III Forks | **Loop**	23
312 Chicago | **Loop**	21
NEW Tortoise Club | **River N**	_
NEW Trenchermen | **Wicker Pk**	23
Troquet | **Ravenswood**	_

Union Sushi + BBQ | **River N**	22
Vera | **W Loop**	22
Webster's | **Lincoln Pk**	18

MICROBREWERIES

NEW Dryhop | **Lakeview**	-
Goose Island | **multi.**	17
Piece | **Wicker Pk**	25
Revolution Brewing | **Logan Sq**	23

NEWCOMERS

Ahjoomah's | **Chinatown**	-
American Junkie | **River N**	-
Andy's | **Lakeview**	26
Artisan Table | **Naperville**	-
Avenue | **Wilmette**	-
¡Ay Chiwowa! | **River N**	-
Bar Pastoral | **Lakeview**	-
Bavette's | **River N**	24
Belly Q | **W Loop**	22
Benjamin Tapas | **Highland Pk**	-
Billy Sunday | **Logan Sq**	-
Bistro Dre | **Lakeview**	-
BlackFinn | **Mt. Prospect**	-
Boarding Hse. | **River N**	22
Bobby's | **Deerfield**	17
Bodega | **Lincoln Pk**	-
Brasserie 54/LM | **Andersonville**	-
Brindille | **River N**	-
Bub City | **River N**	-
Cantina Pasadita | **Avondale**	-
Carriage Hse. | **Wicker Pk**	21
Central Standard | **River N**	-
Centro Rist. | **Near North**	-
Chez Simo | **Lincoln Sq**	-
Chuck's | **Loop**	-
City Winery | **W Loop**	16
Copper Hse. | **North Ctr/St. Ben's**	-
Cottage/Dixie | **Homewood**	-
County BBQ | **Little Italy/University Vill**	-
Covo Gyro | **Wicker Pk**	-
Crosby's Kit. | **Lakeview**	19
Dak Korean | **Edgewater**	-
Da Lobsta | **Gold Coast**	-
Del Frisco's | **Gold Coast**	27
Dryhop | **Lakeview**	-
Duran | **W Loop**	-
e+o | **Mt. Prospect**	-
8,000 Miles | **Roselle**	-
El Hefe | **Near North**	-
Elizabeth | **Lincoln Sq**	-
Embeya | **W Loop**	22
Endgrain | **Roscoe Vill**	-
En Hakkore | **Bucktown**	-
Enso | **Bucktown**	-
Fat Rice | **Logan Sq**	-
Fat Sandwich | **Lincoln Pk**	-
Fatty's | **multi.**	-
Ferris/Jack | **Near North**	-
Flour/Stone | **Streeterville**	-
Found | **Evanston**	-
freestyle | **River N**	-
Gari Sushi | **E Vill**	-
Gather | **Lincoln Sq**	-
g.e.b. | **W Loop**	-
Gino's East | **Printer's Row**	-
Glunz Tavern | **Old Town**	-
Grace | **W Loop**	29
Grass Fed | **Bucktown**	-
Guildhall | **Glencoe**	-
Hamachi | **W Rogers Pk**	-
Harvest Room | **Palos Hts**	-
Hash Hse. | **Gold Coast**	21
Haute/Dog | **Wicker Pk**	-
Himmel's | **Lincoln Sq**	-
Howells/Hood | **Streeterville**	-
Isabel's | **Lincoln Pk**	-
Jellyfish | **River N**	-
J. Rocco | **River N**	-
Juno | **Lincoln Pk**	-
Kabocha | **W Loop**	-
Kai Zan | **Humboldt Pk**	-
Kizin Creole | **W Rogers Pk**	-
La Grande Vie | **Streeterville**	-

Lao 18	River N	—
Lao Ma La	Chinatown	—
Lao Yunnan	Chinatown	—
La Sirena	W Loop	24
Leadbelly	NW Side	—
Little Goat Bread	W Loop	—
Little Goat Diner	W Loop	22
Little Market	Gold Coast	—
LM Bistro	River N	—
Local	Gold Coast	—
Local Root	Streeterville	—
L'Patron	Logan Sq	—
MAK	Wicker Pk	—
Masaki	Streeterville	—
Mercer 113	River N	—
Merlo's	Highland Pk	—
Mezcalina	Loop	—
MH Fish	Lake Forest	—
Milt's BBQ	Lakeview	—
Monarch	Wicker Pk	—
Mott Street	Wicker Pk	—
Municipal	River N	—
M Vie	Noble Sq	—
Nepal House	S Loop	—
Oiistar	Wicker Pk	—
Old Fifth	Near W	—
Oliver's	Bridgeport	—
Oon	W Loop	—
Ovie B&G	Loop	—
Paladar	Logan Sq	—
Park Tavern	multi.	—
Parson's	Logan Sq	—
Piccolo Sogno Due	River N	—
Pizza Hse. 1647	Bucktown	—
Pleasant House	Bridgeport	—
Plzen	Pilsen	—
Polanco	Logan Sq	—
Rainbow Cuisine	Lincoln Sq	—
Red Square	Wicker Pk	—
Refinery	Old Town	—
Reno	Logan Sq	—
Rest. Beatrix	Near North	—
Revolución	Lakeview	—
Riccardo Eno.	Lincoln Pk	—
Rickshaw	Lincoln Pk	—
RM Champagne	W Loop	—
Sataza	Loop	—
Sauce/Bread	Edgewater	—
Senza	Lakeview	28
Shaman	Ukrainian Vill	—
Siena Tavern	River N	—
Smalls	Avondale	—
Stetsons	Loop	24
Suite 25	Logan Sq	—
Sumi Robata	River N	—
Sushi Dokku	W Loop	—
Sweet Baby Ray's	Wrigleyville	—
Table, Donkey/Stick	Logan Sq	—
Takito	Ukrainian Vill	—
Tesori	Loop	—
Tommy Knuckles	Lincoln Pk	—
Tortoise Club	River N	—
Trenchermen	Wicker Pk	23
Tre Soldi	Streeterville	—
Two	W Town	—
Umai	Printer's Row	—
Vu Sua	Lakeview	—
Wâfel	W Town	—
Wood	Lakeview	—

OUTDOOR DINING

Big Jones	Andersonville	24
Big Star	Wicker Pk	26
Bistro Campagne	Lincoln Sq	25
Blackbird	W Loop	27
Boka	Lincoln Pk	26
Carmine's	Gold Coast	21
Chez Joël	Little Italy/University Vill	24
David Burke Prime	River N	25
Dinotto	Old Town	21
Estate Ultra Bar	River W	—
Henri	Loop	27
NEW Howells/Hood	Streeterville	—

Japonais | **River N**	24
Keefer's | **River N**	25
Longman/Eagle | **Logan Sq**	27
Lula | **Logan Sq**	26
Mercadito | **River N**	22
Mercat | **S Loop**	26
Mesón Sabika/Tapas Valencia | **multi.**	25
Mia Francesca | **Lakeview**	24
Miramar | **Highwood**	17
Naha | **River N**	26
Nightwood | **Pilsen**	27
NoMI Kitchen | **Gold Coast**	26
Oceanique | **Evanston**	25
Paris Club | **River N**	20
Park Grill | **Loop**	19
NEW Parson's | **Logan Sq**	-
Pegasus | **Greektown**	20
Pelago | **Streeterville**	27
Pensiero | **Evanston**	21
Piccolo Sogno | **Near W**	25
Pizzeria Due/Uno | **River N**	22
Purple Pig | **River N**	26
Rosebud | **Streeterville**	22
Salpicón | **Old Town**	24
Shanghai Terrace | **River N**	26
Sixteen | **River N**	25
NEW Table, Donkey/Stick | **Logan Sq**	-
NEW Tesori | **Loop**	-
Topo Gigio | **Old Town**	24
Zed 451 | **River N**	22

PEOPLE-WATCHING

Ada St. | **Bucktown**	24
Allium | **Gold Coast**	23
Au Cheval | **W Loop**	25
Avec | **W Loop**	28
NEW ¡Ay Chiwowa! | **River N**	-
Balena | **Lincoln Pk**	24
Balsan | **Gold Coast**	23
Barrelhouse Flat | **Lincoln Pk**	-
Bar Toma | **Gold Coast**	17

NEW Bavette's | **River N**	24
Bedford | **Wicker Pk**	17
NEW Belly Q | **W Loop**	22
Benny's Chop | **River N**	25
Big Star | **Wicker Pk**	26
Bistronomic | **Gold Coast**	23
Blackbird | **W Loop**	27
NEW Boarding Hse. | **River N**	22
Boka | **Lincoln Pk**	26
Bristol | **Bucktown**	25
NEW Bub City | **River N**	-
Carmine's | **Gold Coast**	21
Carnivale | **W Loop**	21
NEW Carriage Hse. | **Wicker Pk**	21
NEW Centro Rist. | **Near North**	-
Chicago Chop | **River N**	23
Chicago Cut | **River N**	26
NEW Del Frisco's | **Gold Coast**	27
NEW Embeya | **W Loop**	22
Estate Ultra Bar | **River W**	-
NEW Ferris/Jack | **Near North**	-
NEW Found | **Evanston**	-
Fred's | **Gold Coast**	20
NEW freestyle | **River N**	-
Gage | **Loop**	23
Gene/Georgetti | **River N**	25
Gibsons | **multi.**	26
Gilt Bar | **River N**	25
Girl/The Goat | **W Loop**	27
NEW Grace | **W Loop**	29
Graham Elliot | **River N**	24
GT Fish/Oyster | **River N**	25
Harry Caray's | **multi.**	22
Henri | **Loop**	27
NEW Howells/Hood | **Streeterville**	-
Hubbard Inn | **River N**	20
Hub 51 | **River N**	20
Hugo's | **multi.**	24
Japonais | **River N**	24
Joe's Sea/Steak | **River N**	27
Keefer's | **River N**	25
Kuma's | **Avondale**	27

NEW La Sirena | **W Loop**	24	Aviary | **W Loop**	26
Le Colonial | **Gold Coast**	23	NEW Bavette's | **River N**	24
NEW Little Goat Bread | **W Loop**	–	Benny's Chop | **River N**	25
Longman/Eagle | **Logan Sq**	27	Blackbird | **W Loop**	27
Manny's | **S Loop**	24	NEW Boarding Hse. | **River N**	22
Mastro's Steak | **River N**	26	Capital Grille | **Streeterville**	24
Maude's Liquor | **W Loop**	25	Chicago Chop | **River N**	23
Mercadito | **River N**	22	Chicago Cut | **River N**	26
Mercat | **S Loop**	26	Coco Pazzo | **River N**	25
Miramar | **Highwood**	17	David Burke Prime | **River N**	25
MK | **Near North**	27	NEW Del Frisco's | **Gold Coast**	27
NEW Monarch | **Wicker Pk**	–	Epic Rest. | **River N**	20
Nellcôte | **W Loop**	19	Everest | **Loop**	27
Next | **W Loop**	29	Fred's | **Gold Coast**	20
NoMI Kitchen | **Gold Coast**	26	Gene/Georgetti | **River N**	25
Old Town Social | **Old Town**	21	Gibsons | **multi.**	26
NEW Oliver's | **Bridgeport**	–	Girl/The Goat | **W Loop**	27
Paris Club | **River N**	20	NEW Grace | **W Loop**	29
Perennial Virant | **Lincoln Pk**	26	GT Fish/Oyster | **River N**	25
Publican | **W Loop**	26	Hugo's | **multi.**	24
Pump Room | **Gold Coast**	21	Joe's Sea/Steak | **River N**	27
Purple Pig | **River N**	26	Keefer's | **River N**	25
Quartino | **River N**	22	Les Nomades | **Streeterville**	28
NEW RM Champagne | **W Loop**	–	NEW Little Goat Bread | **W Loop**	–
Roka Akor | **River N**	24	L2O | **Lincoln Pk**	26
Rosebud | **multi.**	22	Mastro's Steak | **River N**	26
Rosebud Prime/Steak | **Streeterville**	23	MK | **Near North**	27
		Morton's | **multi.**	23
Sixteen | **River N**	25	Naha | **River N**	26
Slurping Turtle | **River N**	22	Nellcôte | **W Loop**	19
Sunda | **River N**	25	Next | **W Loop**	29
SushiSamba | **River N**	20	NoMI Kitchen | **Gold Coast**	26
Tavernita | **River N**	21	NEW Piccolo Sogno Due | **River N**	–
Tavern/Rush | **Gold Coast**	21		
Three Aces | **Little Italy/University Vill**	22	Pump Room | **Gold Coast**	21
		RL | **Gold Coast**	24
III Forks | **Loop**	23	Rosebud | **Little Italy/University Vill**	22
NEW Trenchermen | **Wicker Pk**	23	Rosebud Prime/Steak | **multi.**	23
Urbanbelly | **Logan Sq**	25	Sixteen | **River N**	25
POWER SCENES		Slurping Turtle | **River N**	22
Alinea | **Lincoln Pk**	29	Smith/Wollensky | **River N**	22
Allium | **Gold Coast**	23	Spiaggia | **Gold Coast**	26

NEW Tesori | **Loop**	-
III Forks | **Loop**	23
Topolobampo | **River N**	28
NEW Tortoise Club | **River N**	-
NEW Trenchermen | **Wicker Pk**	23
Tru | **Streeterville**	27

PRIX FIXE MENUS

(Call for prices and times)

Alinea | **Lincoln Pk**	29
Arun's | **NW Side**	27
Courtright's | **Willow Spgs**	27
EL Ideas | **Pilsen**	28
Everest | **Loop**	27
Goosefoot | **Lincoln Sq**	29
Green Zebra | **Noble Sq**	27
Les Nomades | **Streeterville**	28
L2O | **Lincoln Pk**	26
MK | **Near North**	27
Moto | **W Loop**	26
Next | **W Loop**	29
North Pond | **Lincoln Pk**	26
Oceanique | **Evanston**	25
Roy's | **River N**	24
Schwa | **Wicker Pk**	28
Sixteen | **River N**	25
Spiaggia | **Gold Coast**	26
Tallgrass | **Lockport**	27
Topolobampo | **River N**	28
Tru | **Streeterville**	27

QUICK BITES

Al's Beef | **multi.**	22
Antique Taco | **Wicker Pk**	23
Artist's Cafe | **multi.**	15
Art of Pizza | **Lakeview**	23
Artopolis | **Greektown**	21
BadHappy | **River N**	-
Bagel | **multi.**	20
Baker/Nosh | **Uptown**	-
Bakin'/Eggs | **Lakeview**	20
Ba Le | **multi.**	23
Banh Mi/Co. | **multi.**	-
Barrio | **Lakeview**	-

Belly Shack | **Humboldt Pk**	25
Berghoff | **O'Hare Area**	19
Big/Little's | **Near North**	25
Big Bowl | **multi.**	20
Big Star | **Wicker Pk**	26
Bijan's | **River N**	20
Billy Goat | **multi.**	16
Bin | **River N**	21
Birchwood | **Wicker Pk**	23
Birrieria Zaragoza | **SW Side**	27
Bourgeois Pig | **Lincoln Pk**	20
Burger Bar | **Lincoln Pk**	22
Burger Joint | **River N**	16
Burger Point | **S Loop**	-
Butcher/Burger | **Lincoln Pk**	25
Café Selmarie | **Lincoln Sq**	21
Cemitas Puebla | **Humboldt Pk**	24
Chicago Pizza | **Lincoln Pk**	25
City Farms Mkt. | **Lakeview**	-
Convito | **Wilmette**	20
NEW Covo Gyro | **Wicker Pk**	-
Crisp | **Lakeview**	24
NEW Dak Korean | **Edgewater**	-
NEW Da Lobsta | **Gold Coast**	-
Deca | **Streeterville**	21
Del Seoul | **Lakeview**	23
Dimo's Pizza | **Lakeview**	22
Edzo's | **multi.**	26
Eleven City | **S Loop**	19
NEW Enso | **Bucktown**	-
Epic Burger | **multi.**	19
Epic Rest. | **River N**	20
NEW Fat Sandwich | **Lincoln Pk**	-
NEW Fatty's | **multi.**	-
Fat Willy's | **Logan Sq**	20
Five Guys | **multi.**	17
Fontano's | **multi.**	27
Foodlife/ease | **Streeterville**	19
Frankie's | **Gold Coast**	18
Franks 'N' Dawgs | **Lincoln Pk**	25
Gene/Jude's | **O'Hare Area**	24
Hannah's Bretzel | **multi.**	23

NEW Haute/Dog | **Wicker Pk**	-‌
Honey 1 BBQ | **Bucktown**	21
Indie Burger | **Lakeview**	-‌
Jerry's | **Wicker Pk**	20
Julius Meinl | **multi.**	21
Kaufman's | **Skokie**	23
Labriola Bakery | **Oak Brook**	24
La Lagartija | **W Loop**	-‌
Lillie's Q | **Bucktown**	22
NEW Little Goat Bread | **W Loop**	-‌
NEW L'Patron | **Logan Sq**	-‌
Manny's | **multi.**	24
M Burger | **multi.**	18
Meatheads | **Roscoe Vill**	21
Mr. Beef | **River N**	24
Naf Naf | **multi.**	22
Native Foods | **multi.**	23
90 Miles | **Logan Sq**	23
Noodles/Yagihashi | **Loop**	22
Noon-O-Kabab | **Albany Pk**	24
Old Jerusalem | **Old Town**	20
Pegasus | **SW Side**	20
Penny's | **multi.**	20
Pierrot Gourmet | **River N**	22
Pork Shoppe | **Avondale**	20
Potbelly | **multi.**	18
Quartino | **River N**	22
Real Urban BBQ | **multi.**	21
Rootstock | **Humboldt Pk**	23
Russell's | **Elmwood Pk**	21
NEW Sataza | **Loop**	-‌
Seasons 52 | **Oak Brook**	25
State/Lake | **Loop**	16
Superdawg | **NW Side**	21
Taco Joint | **Lincoln Pk**	23
Tasting Room | **W Loop**	18
Tempo | **Gold Coast**	19
Tom & Eddie's | **multi.**	18
Top Notch | **Far S Side**	25
NEW Tortoise Club | **River N**	-‌
Township | **Logan Sq**	-‌
Uncle Bub's BBQ | **Westmont**	21

Uncommon Ground | **Lakeview**	22
Urbanbelly | **Logan Sq**	25
Vapiano | **Lincoln Pk**	16
NEW Wâfel | **W Town**	-‌
Webster's | **Lincoln Pk**	18
Westminster | **Loop**	19
Wiener's Circle | **Lincoln Pk**	19
Zaleski/Horvath | **Kenwood**	24

QUIET CONVERSATION

Akai Hana | **Wilmette**	21
Aria | **Loop**	23
Arun's | **NW Side**	27
A Tavola | **Ukrainian Vill**	26
Autre Monde | **Berwyn**	26
Barrington Country | **Barrington**	24
Basil Leaf | **Lincoln Pk**	19
Benny's Chop | **River N**	25
Bistro Bordeaux | **Evanston**	23
Briciola | **Ukrainian Vill**	-‌
Café/Architectes | **Gold Coast**	24
Café Selmarie | **Lincoln Sq**	21
Café Spiaggia | **Gold Coast**	25
Cape Cod | **Streeterville**	22
Chalkboard | **Lakeview**	23
Chef's Station | **Evanston**	24
Chicago Prime | **Schaumburg**	25
Cité | **Streeterville**	19
City Farms Mkt. | **Lakeview**	-‌
NEW Cottage/Dixie | **Homewood**	-‌
D & J Bistro | **Lake Zurich**	24
Eggy's | **Streeterville**	-‌
Everest | **Loop**	27
Filini | **Loop**	22
Gaetano's | **Forest Pk**	27
Gaylord Indian | **multi.**	22
Goosefoot | **Lincoln Sq**	29
NEW Grace | **W Loop**	29
Henri | **Loop**	27
Inovasi | **Lake Bluff**	25
Itto Sushi | **Lincoln Pk**	25
Jilly's | **Evanston**	21

La Crêperie	**Lakeview**	21
La Gondola	**Lakeview**	20
La Petite Folie	**Hyde Pk**	25
Lawry's	**River N**	23
Les Nomades	**Streeterville**	28
Le Vichyssois	**Lakemoor**	25
Lovells	**Lake Forest**	22
L2O	**Lincoln Pk**	26
Market House	**Lake Forest**	-
Merlo	**Gold Coast**	25
NEW MH Fish	**Lake Forest**	-
North Pond	**Lincoln Pk**	26
Oceanique	**Evanston**	25
NEW Ovie B&G	**Loop**	-
Pensiero	**Evanston**	21
Pierrot Gourmet	**River N**	22
Quince	**Evanston**	25
Red Door	**Bucktown**	-
RL	**Gold Coast**	24
Russian Tea	**Loop**	22
1776	**Crystal Lake**	25
Shanghai Terrace	**River N**	26
Signature Room	**Streeterville**	17
South Water	**Loop**	14
Spiaggia	**Gold Coast**	26
Standard Grill	**Westmont**	-
Table Fifty-two	**Gold Coast**	25
Tallgrass	**Lockport**	27
Tasting Room	**W Loop**	18
Tru	**Streeterville**	27
Vera	**W Loop**	22
Village	**Loop**	20
Vinci	**Lincoln Pk**	20
Vivere	**Loop**	23
Wilmette Chop	**Wilmette**	-

RAW BARS

Balsan	**Gold Coast**	23
Benny's Chop	**River N**	25
Bob Chinn's	**Wheeling**	23
Cape Cod	**Streeterville**	22
Davis St. Fish	**Evanston**	19
Deca	**Streeterville**	21

NEW freestyle	**River N**	-
Frontier	**Noble Sq**	22
GT Fish/Oyster	**River N**	25
Henri	**Loop**	27
NEW Kabocha	**W Loop**	-
Niu	**Streeterville**	24
Quay	**Streeterville**	19
Shaw's Crab	**multi.**	25
Tavernita	**River N**	21
Tin Fish	**Tinley Park**	24

ROMANTIC PLACES

Ada St.	**Bucktown**	24
Arami	**W Town**	27
A Tavola	**Ukrainian Vill**	26
Autre Monde	**Berwyn**	26
Balsan	**Gold Coast**	23
Barrelhouse Flat	**Lincoln Pk**	-
Barrington Country	**Barrington**	24
Bar Toma	**Gold Coast**	17
NEW Bavette's	**River N**	24
Bedford	**Wicker Pk**	17
NEW Billy Sunday	**Logan Sq**	-
Bistro Campagne	**Lincoln Sq**	25
NEW Boarding Hse.	**River N**	22
NEW Bobby's	**Deerfield**	17
Boka	**Lincoln Pk**	26
NEW Brindille	**River N**	-
Café Absinthe	**Bucktown**	21
NEW Carriage Hse.	**Wicker Pk**	21
Chez Joël	**Little Italy/University Vill**	24
Chez Moi	**Lincoln Pk**	-
Cité	**Streeterville**	19
Coco Pazzo	**River N**	25
NEW Cottage/Dixie	**Homewood**	-
Courtright's	**Willow Spgs**	27
DiSotto	**Streeterville**	23
Eduardo's Enoteca	**Gold Coast**	23
NEW Elizabeth	**Lincoln Sq**	-
Epic Rest.	**River N**	20
Estate Ultra Bar	**River W**	-
Everest	**Loop**	27

Filini | **Loop**	22
Geja's | **Lincoln Pk**	22
Gilt Bar | **River N**	25
NEW Grace | **W Loop**	29
Henri | **Loop**	27
Japonais | **River N**	24
NEW La Grande Vie | **Streeterville**	─
Le Colonial | **Gold Coast**	23
Les Nomades | **Streeterville**	28
L2O | **Lincoln Pk**	26
Macello | **W Loop**	25
Market House | **Lake Forest**	─
NEW Masaki | **Streeterville**	─
Maude's Liquor | **W Loop**	25
NEW Mercer 113 | **River N**	─
Merlo | **Gold Coast**	25
MK | **Near North**	27
Nacional 27 | **River N**	22
Naha | **River N**	26
Nellcôte | **W Loop**	19
Next | **W Loop**	29
NoMI Kitchen | **Gold Coast**	26
North Pond | **Lincoln Pk**	26
Oceanique | **Evanston**	25
NEW Oliver's | **Bridgeport**	─
Paris Club | **River N**	20
Pelago | **Streeterville**	27
Pensiero | **Evanston**	21
Perennial Virant | **Lincoln Pk**	26
Piccolo Sogno | **Near W**	25
NEW Piccolo Sogno Due | **River N**	─
Prosecco | **River N**	24
Pump Room | **Gold Coast**	21
Purple Pig | **River N**	26
Quay | **Streeterville**	19
NEW Riccardo Eno. | **Lincoln Pk**	─
Riccardo Trat. | **Lincoln Pk**	28
RL | **Gold Coast**	24
NEW RM Champagne | **W Loop**	─
Roka Akor | **River N**	24
RPM Italian | **River N**	23
Sepia | **W Loop**	25

Shanghai Terrace | **River N**	26
Signature Room | **Streeterville**	17
Sixteen | **River N**	25
Sunda | **River N**	25
Table Fifty-two | **Gold Coast**	25
Tallgrass | **Lockport**	27
Tasting Room | **W Loop**	18
Taverna 750 | **Wrigleyville**	24
Taxim | **Wicker Pk**	26
Telegraph | **Logan Sq**	22
NEW Tortoise Club | **River N**	─
Tru | **Streeterville**	27
Vie | **W Springs**	29
Vinci | **Lincoln Pk**	20
Vivo | **W Loop**	23
Webster's | **Lincoln Pk**	18

SENIOR APPEAL

Andies | **Lakeview**	20
Ann Sather | **multi.**	21
A Tavola | **Ukrainian Vill**	26
Bacchanalia | **SW Side**	22
Bagel | **multi.**	20
Barrington Country | **Barrington**	24
Berghoff | **Loop**	19
Bistro Bordeaux | **Evanston**	23
Bob Chinn's | **Wheeling**	23
Bruna's | **SW Side**	23
Calo Ristorante | **Andersonville**	21
Cape Cod | **Streeterville**	22
Carson's | **multi.**	21
Courtright's | **Willow Spgs**	27
Davis St. Fish | **Evanston**	19
Del Rio | **Highwood**	20
Edelweiss | **Norridge**	22
EJ's Pl. | **Skokie**	20
Francesco's | **Northbrook**	22
Froggy's | **Highwood**	25
Gale St. Inn | **Jefferson Pk**	21
Hackney's | **multi.**	18
Jilly's | **Evanston**	21
Kiki's Bistro | **Near North**	25
La Gondola | **Lakeview**	20

La Petite Folie	**Hyde Pk**	25
Lawry's	**River N**	23
Les Nomades	**Streeterville**	28
Le Vichyssois	**Lakemoor**	25
Lou Mitchell's	**Loop**	24
Lovells	**Lake Forest**	22
L. Woods Tap	**Lincolnwood**	19
Market House	**Lake Forest**	–
Next Door	**Northbrook**	22
Nick's Fish	**Rosemont**	24
Oak Tree	**Gold Coast**	16
Parthenon	**Greektown**	21
Pegasus	**Greektown**	20
Rosebud	**Loop**	22
Russell's	**Elmwood Pk**	21
Russian Tea	**Loop**	22
Sabatino's	**Old Irving Pk**	26
1776	**Crystal Lake**	25
Tallgrass	**Lockport**	27
Tre Kronor	**Albany Pk**	24
Tufano's	**Little Italy/University Vill**	24
Village	**Loop**	20

SINGLES SCENES

Adobo	**Old Town**	20
Arrow/Ogden	**W Loop**	–
NEW ¡Ay Chiwowa!	**River N**	–
Balena	**Lincoln Pk**	24
Barrelhouse Flat	**Lincoln Pk**	–
NEW Bub City	**River N**	–
Café Iberico	**River N**	22
Carnivale	**W Loop**	21
Clubhouse	**Oak Brook**	22
NEW Del Frisco's	**Gold Coast**	27
Ditka's	**Gold Coast**	22
Estate Ultra Bar	**River W**	–
Gibsons	**multi.**	26
Gilt Bar	**River N**	25
Hubbard Inn	**River N**	20
Hub 51	**River N**	20
Hugo's	**multi.**	24
Japonais	**River N**	24

Lady Gregory's	**Andersonville**	20
Luxbar	**Gold Coast**	19
Mercadito	**River N**	22
Old Town Social	**Old Town**	21
Paris Club	**River N**	20
NEW Park Tavern	**multi.**	–
P.J. Clarke's	**Gold Coast**	17
Public House	**River N**	18
Rockit	**River N**	19
RPM Italian	**River N**	23
Scoozi!	**River N**	20
Stanley's	**Lincoln Pk**	19
Sullivan's Steak	**multi.**	24
Sunda	**River N**	25
SushiSamba	**River N**	20
Tavernita	**River N**	21
Tavern/Rush	**Gold Coast**	21
Zaleski/Horvath	**Kenwood**	24

SPECIAL OCCASIONS

Alinea	**Lincoln Pk**	29
Arun's	**NW Side**	27
Aviary	**W Loop**	26
Benny's Chop	**River N**	25
Blackbird	**W Loop**	27
NEW Boarding Hse.	**River N**	22
Brazzaz	**River N**	22
NEW Brindille	**River N**	–
NEW Cottage/Dixie	**Homewood**	–
Courtright's	**Willow Spgs**	27
Dan McGee	**Frankfort**	26
NEW Del Frisco's	**Gold Coast**	27
EL Ideas	**Pilsen**	28
Epic Rest.	**River N**	20
Everest	**Loop**	27
Gibsons	**multi.**	26
Goosefoot	**Lincoln Sq**	29
NEW Grace	**W Loop**	29
Henri	**Loop**	27
Ing	**W Loop**	23
NEW Kabocha	**W Loop**	–
Lawry's	**River N**	23
Lovells	**Lake Forest**	22

L2O | **Lincoln Pk** _26_
NEW Masaki | **Streeterville** _－_
Mastro's Steak | **River N** _26_
NEW MH Fish | **Lake Forest** _－_
Michael | **Winnetka** _26_
Michael Jordan's | **Streeterville** _22_
Morton's | **multi.** _23_
Moto | **W Loop** _26_
Next | **W Loop** _29_
Niche | **Geneva** _26_
NoMI Kitchen | **Gold Coast** _26_
NEW Ovie B&G | **Loop** _－_
Palm | **Loop** _24_
NEW Piccolo Sogno Due | **River N** _－_
Pump Room | **Gold Coast** _21_
Quay | **Streeterville** _19_
Quince | **Evanston** _25_
Roy's | **River N** _24_
Schwa | **Wicker Pk** _28_
Shaw's Crab | **multi.** _25_
Sixteen | **River N** _25_
Spiaggia | **Gold Coast** _26_
NEW Stetsons | **Loop** _24_
Takashi | **Bucktown** _28_
Topolobampo | **River N** _28_
NEW Tortoise Club | **River N** _－_
Tramonto's | **Wheeling** _22_
Tru | **Streeterville** _27_
Vie | **W Springs** _29_
Wilmette Chop | **Wilmette** _－_

TEEN APPEAL

Al's Beef | **multi.** _22_
Ann Sather | **multi.** _21_
Art of Pizza | **Lakeview** _23_
Aurelio's Pizza | **multi.** _21_
Bacino's | **multi.** _21_
Ba Le | **multi.** _23_
Bandera | **Streeterville** _23_
Big Bowl | **multi.** _20_
Bob Chinn's | **Wheeling** _23_
Burger Bar | **Lincoln Pk** _22_
Calo Ristorante | **Andersonville** _21_

Chicago Pizza | **Lincoln Pk** _25_
Dimo's Pizza | **Lakeview** _22_
DMK Burger Bar | **Lakeview** _22_
Edwardo's Pizza | **multi.** _19_
Edzo's | **Evanston** _26_
Epic Burger | **multi.** _19_
Five Guys | **Rogers Pk** _17_
Gene/Jude's | **O'Hare Area** _24_
Giordano's | **multi.** _22_
Hannah's Bretzel | **Loop** _23_
Harry Caray's | **multi.** _22_
Heaven/Seven | **multi.** _22_
Home Run Inn | **multi.** _24_
Hot Doug's | **Avondale** _27_
Joy Yee's | **multi.** _20_
Lou Malnati's | **multi.** _25_
LuLu's | **Evanston** _21_
L. Woods Tap | **Lincolnwood** _19_
Margie's | **multi.** _22_
Nookies | **multi.** _20_
Original Gino's | **multi.** _22_
Penny's | **multi.** _20_
Pizzeria Due/Uno | **River N** _22_
Potbelly | **multi.** _18_
R.J. Grunts | **Lincoln Pk** _19_
Robinson's Ribs | **multi.** _18_
Russell's | **Elmwood Pk** _21_
Stanley's | **Lincoln Pk** _19_
Superdawg | **NW Side** _21_
Tempo | **Gold Coast** _19_
Toast | **multi.** _22_
Wiener's Circle | **Lincoln Pk** _19_
Wishbone | **multi.** _20_

TRENDY

Ada St. | **Bucktown** _24_
Antique Taco | **Wicker Pk** _23_
Arami | **W Town** _27_
Au Cheval | **W Loop** _25_
Avec | **W Loop** _28_
NEW ¡Ay Chiwowa! | **River N** _－_
Balena | **Lincoln Pk** _24_
Barrelhouse Flat | **Lincoln Pk** _－_

🆕 Bavette's | **River N**	24	
Bedford | **Wicker Pk**	17	
🆕 Belly Q | **W Loop**	22	
Belly Shack | **Humboldt Pk**	25	
Big Star | **Wicker Pk**	26	
Blackbird | **W Loop**	27	
🆕 Boarding Hse. | **River N**	22	
Boka | **Lincoln Pk**	26	
Bristol | **Bucktown**	25	
Estate Ultra Bar | **River W**	–	
🆕 Fat Rice | **Logan Sq**	–	
🆕 Found | **Evanston**	–	
Fred's | **Gold Coast**	20	
🆕 freestyle | **River N**	–	
Gemini | **Lincoln Pk**	21	
Gilt Bar | **River N**	25	
Girl/The Goat | **W Loop**	27	
Graham Elliot | **River N**	24	
GT Fish/Oyster | **River N**	25	
Hot Chocolate | **Bucktown**	24	
Hot Doug's | **Avondale**	27	
Hub 51 | **River N**	20	
Lao You Ju | **Chinatown**	24	
🆕 La Sirena | **W Loop**	24	
🆕 Little Goat Bread | **W Loop**	–	
Longman/Eagle | **Logan Sq**	27	
Maude's Liquor | **W Loop**	25	
Mercadito | **River N**	22	
🆕 Mercer 113 | **River N**	–	
MK | **Near North**	27	
🆕 Monarch | **Wicker Pk**	–	
Nellcôte | **W Loop**	19	
Nightwood | **Pilsen**	27	
Old Town Social | **Old Town**	21	
🆕 Oliver's | **Bridgeport**	–	
Paris Club | **River N**	20	
🆕 Piccolo Sogno Due | **River N**	–	
Publican | **W Loop**	26	
Pump Room | **Gold Coast**	21	
Quartino | **River N**	22	
Revolution Brewing | **Logan Sq**	23	
Roka Akor | **multi.**	24	

Roots Pizza | **W Town**	20	
Rootstock | **Humboldt Pk**	23	
RPM Italian | **River N**	23	
Ruxbin | **Noble Sq**	28	
Sable | **River N**	23	
Scofflaw | **Logan Sq**	–	
Sepia | **W Loop**	25	
Shaman | **Ukrainian Vill**	–	
Slurping Turtle | **River N**	22	
🆕 Sumi Robata | **River N**	–	
Sunda | **River N**	25	
SushiSamba | **River N**	20	
Tavernita | **River N**	21	
🆕 Trenchermen | **Wicker Pk**	23	
Union Sushi + BBQ | **River N**	22	
Urbanbelly | **Logan Sq**	25	
Vera | **W Loop**	22	
Xoco | **River N**	27	
Yusho | **Avondale**	26	

VIEWS

Balsan | **Gold Coast**	23	
Bridge Bar Chicago | **River N**	–	
Bridge House | **River N**	18	
Chicago Cut | **River N**	26	
Courtright's | **Willow Spgs**	27	
Deca | **Streeterville**	21	
Dining Room/Kendall | **Near W**	23	
Epic Rest. | **River N**	20	
Everest | **Loop**	27	
Fulton's | **River N**	18	
La Tasca | **Arlington Hts**	21	
Lobby | **River N**	25	
Mercat | **S Loop**	26	
NoMI Kitchen | **Gold Coast**	26	
North Pond | **Lincoln Pk**	26	
Park Grill | **Loop**	19	
Quay | **Streeterville**	19	
Riva | **Streeterville**	21	
Shanghai Terrace | **River N**	26	
Signature Room | **Streeterville**	17	
Sixteen | **River N**	25	
Spiaggia | **Gold Coast**	26	

Tavern/Rush | **Gold Coast**	21
lll Forks | **Loop**	23
Zed 451 | **River N**	22

WINE BARS

Autre Monde | **Berwyn**	26
Avec | **W Loop**	28
Bacino's | **multi.**	21
Bar Toma | **Gold Coast**	17
Basil Leaf | **Lincoln Pk**	19
Bella Via | **Highland Pk**	20
Bin | **River N**	21
Bistronomic | **Gold Coast**	23
Bistrot Zinc | **Gold Coast**	21
NEW Boarding Hse. | **River N**	22
NEW Bobby's | **Deerfield**	17
Bread & Wine | **Old Irving Pk**	20
Broadway Cellars | **Edgewater**	22
Bruna's | **SW Side**	23
NEW Bub City | **River N**	–
NEW Chuck's | **Loop**	–
Cyrano's | **River N**	19
Davanti | **Little Italy/University Vill**	26
Devon Seafood | **River N**	21
DiSotto | **Streeterville**	23
Fleming's | **Lincolnshire**	20
Flight | **Glenview**	22
Jake Melnick's | **Gold Coast**	19
NEW Jellyfish | **River N**	–
Jin Ju | **Andersonville**	24
Libertad | **Skokie**	25
NEW Little Goat Bread | **W Loop**	–
NEW Local | **Gold Coast**	–
Mago | **multi.**	24
NEW MH Fish | **Lake Forest**	–
NEW Ovie B&G | **Loop**	–
Quartino | **River N**	22
Rootstock | **Humboldt Pk**	23
Rustic Hse. | **Lincoln Pk**	21
Saloon Steak | **Streeterville**	22
Signature Room | **Streeterville**	17

South Water | **Loop**	14
Stained Glass | **Evanston**	24
Tasting Room | **W Loop**	18
Telegraph | **Logan Sq**	22
3rd Coast Cafe | **Gold Coast**	18
lll Forks | **Loop**	23
NEW Tortoise Club | **River N**	–
Vera | **W Loop**	22
Walnut Room | **Loop**	18
Webster's | **Lincoln Pk**	18
Yu's Mandarin | **Schaumburg**	24

WINNING WINE LISTS

Acadia | **S Loop**	27
Ada St. | **Bucktown**	24
Alinea | **Lincoln Pk**	29
Arun's | **NW Side**	27
Avec | **W Loop**	28
Balena | **Lincoln Pk**	24
Benny's Chop | **River N**	25
Bin | **River N**	21
Blackbird | **W Loop**	27
NEW Boarding Hse. | **River N**	22
Boka | **Lincoln Pk**	26
NEW Brindille | **River N**	–
Chicago Cut | **River N**	26
Coco Pazzo | **River N**	25
Courtright's | **Willow Spgs**	27
David Burke Prime | **River N**	25
NEW Del Frisco's | **Gold Coast**	27
Del Rio | **Highwood**	20
Epic Rest. | **River N**	20
Everest | **Loop**	27
Filini | **Loop**	22
Fleming's | **multi.**	20
Geja's | **Lincoln Pk**	22
Gibsons | **multi.**	26
NEW Grace | **W Loop**	29
Graham Elliot | **River N**	24
Green Zebra | **Noble Sq**	27
Henri | **Loop**	27
Hugo's | **multi.**	24
Joe's Sea/Steak | **River N**	27

Keefer's | **River N**	25
Les Nomades | **Streeterville**	28
Lockwood | **Loop**	23
L2O | **Lincoln Pk**	26
Michael | **Winnetka**	26
MK | **Near North**	27
Morton's | **multi.**	23
Moto | **W Loop**	26
Naha | **River N**	26
Next | **W Loop**	29
Niche | **Geneva**	26
NoMI Kitchen | **Gold Coast**	26
North Pond | **Lincoln Pk**	26
Oceanique | **Evanston**	25
Pelago | **Streeterville**	27
Perennial Virant | **Lincoln Pk**	26
Piccolo Sogno | **Near W**	25
NEW Piccolo Sogno Due | **River N**	-
Prosecco | **River N**	24
Publican | **W Loop**	26
Purple Pig | **River N**	26

Ruth's Chris | **multi.**	23
Salpicón | **Old Town**	24
Sepia | **W Loop**	25
1776 | **Crystal Lake**	25
NEW Siena Tavern | **River N**	-
Signature Room | **Streeterville**	17
Sixteen | **River N**	25
Spiaggia | **Gold Coast**	26
Sprout | **Lincoln Pk**	26
Sunda | **River N**	25
Takashi | **Bucktown**	28
Tallgrass | **Lockport**	27
Tasting Room | **W Loop**	18
III Forks | **Loop**	23
Topolobampo | **River N**	28
Tru | **Streeterville**	27
NEW Two | **W Town**	-
Vera | **W Loop**	22
Vivere | **Loop**	23
Webster's | **Lincoln Pk**	18
West Town | **Noble Sq**	26

Cuisines

Includes names, locations and Food ratings.

AMERICAN

Abigail's | **Highland Pk**	24
Acadia | **S Loop**	27
Acre | **Andersonville**	20
Ada St. | **Bucktown**	24
Adelle's | **Wheaton**	26
Al Dente | **NW Side**	23
Alinea | **Lincoln Pk**	29
Allium | **Gold Coast**	23
American Girl | **Streeterville**	13
Amuse | **Loop**	–
Ann Sather | **multi.**	21
Anthem | **Ukrainian Vill**	18
Aquitaine | **Lincoln Pk**	21
NEW Artisan Table | **Naperville**	–
Athenian Room | **Lincoln Pk**	22
Atwood Cafe | **Loop**	22
Au Cheval | **W Loop**	25
Bakin'/Eggs | **Lakeview**	20
Bandera | **Streeterville**	23
Bangers/Lace | **Wicker Pk**	20
NEW Bar Pastoral | **Lakeview**	–
Barrelhouse Flat | **Lincoln Pk**	–
NEW Bavette's | **River N**	24
Bedford | **Wicker Pk**	17
Beer Bistro | **multi.**	17
Berghoff | **O'Hare Area**	19
Bijan's | **River N**	20
Billy Goat | **multi.**	16
NEW Billy Sunday | **Logan Sq**	–
Bin | **River N**	21
NEW Bistro Dre | **Lakeview**	–
Bite | **Ukrainian Vill**	22
Blackbird | **W Loop**	27
NEW BlackFinn | **Mt. Prospect**	–
Bluebird | **Bucktown**	22
Bluegrass | **Highland Pk**	21
NEW Boarding Hse. | **River N**	22
NEW Bobby's | **Deerfield**	17
Boka | **Lincoln Pk**	26

Bongo Room | **multi.**	24
Branch 27 | **Noble Sq**	19
Bread & Wine | **Old Irving Pk**	20
Bridge Bar Chicago | **River N**	–
Bridge House | **River N**	18
Bristol | **Bucktown**	25
Broadway Cellars | **Edgewater**	22
Browntrout | **North Ctr/St. Ben's**	24
Brunch | **River N**	16
Butch McGuire's | **Near North**	18
Café Absinthe | **Bucktown**	21
Café Selmarie | **Lincoln Sq**	21
Ceres' Table | **Uptown**	24
Chalkboard | **Lakeview**	23
Chef's Station | **Evanston**	24
Chicago Firehouse | **S Loop**	22
NEW Chuck's | **Loop**	–
Cité | **Streeterville**	19
City Farms Mkt. | **Lakeview**	–
City Tavern | **S Loop**	16
Clubhouse | **Oak Brook**	22
Cooper's Hawk | **multi.**	21
NEW Copper Hse. | **North Ctr/St. Ben's**	–
Courtright's | **Willow Spgs**	27
NEW Crosby's Kit. | **Lakeview**	19
Dan McGee | **Frankfort**	26
David Burke Prime | **River N**	25
Dining Room/Kendall | **Near W**	23
Ditka's | **multi.**	22
DMK Burger Bar | **Lakeview**	22
NEW Dryhop | **Lakeview**	–
NEW e+o | **Mt. Prospect**	–
Eduardo's Enoteca | **Gold Coast**	23
Eggy's | **Streeterville**	–
EL Ideas | **Pilsen**	28
NEW Elizabeth | **Lincoln Sq**	–
NEW Endgrain | **Roscoe Vill**	–
Epic Rest. | **River N**	20
Estate Ultra Bar | **River W**	–

CUISINES

Restaurant	Rating
Exchequer | **Loop**	20
Farmhouse | **multi.**	23
FatDuck | **Forest Pk**	20
NEW Fatty's | **Lincoln Pk**	-
Feast | **Bucktown**	21
NEW Ferris/Jack | **Near North**	-
Fifty/50 | **Wicker Pk**	18
Fireside | **Andersonville**	20
Florentine | **Loop**	20
NEW Found | **Evanston**	-
Fountainhead | **Ravenswood**	20
Fred's | **Gold Coast**	20
NEW freestyle | **River N**	-
Frog n Snail | **Lakeview**	20
Frontier | **Noble Sq**	22
Gage | **Loop**	23
Gale St. Inn | **Jefferson Pk**	21
NEW Gather | **Lincoln Sq**	-
NEW g.e.b. | **W Loop**	-
Gemini | **Lincoln Pk**	21
Gilt Bar | **River N**	25
Girl/The Goat | **W Loop**	27
Glenn's Diner | **Ravenswood**	24
Glenview House | **Glenview**	19
Glunz Tavern | **Old Town**	-
Goosefoot | **Lincoln Sq**	29
NEW Grace | **W Loop**	29
Graham Elliot | **River N**	24
Grange Hall | **W Loop**	22
Grill/Alley | **Streeterville**	20
NEW Guildhall | **Glencoe**	-
Harry Caray's | **River N**	20
Harry Caray's | **SW Side**	22
NEW Harvest Room | **Palos Hts**	-
NEW Hash Hse. | **Gold Coast**	21
NEW Haute/Dog | **Wicker Pk**	-
HB Home Bistro | **Lakeview**	25
Hearty | **Lakeview**	21
Henri | **Loop**	27
Homestead | **Ukrainian Vill**	-
Hot Chocolate | **Bucktown**	24
NEW Howells/Hood | **Streeterville**	-
Ina's | **W Loop**	22
Ing | **W Loop**	23
Inovasi | **Lake Bluff**	25
Jack's/Halsted | **Lakeview**	17
J. Alexander's | **Oak Brook**	20
Jam | **Logan Sq**	22
Jane's | **Bucktown**	21
Jerry's Restaurant | **Winnetka**	22
Jilly's | **Evanston**	21
John's Pl. | **multi.**	17
Karyn's/Green | **Greektown**	24
Lady Gregory's | **Andersonville**	20
NEW La Grande Vie | **Streeterville**	-
Lawry's | **River N**	23
NEW Little Market | **Gold Coast**	-
Lloyd's Chicago | **Loop**	16
Lobby | **River N**	25
NEW Local | **Gold Coast**	-
NEW Local Root | **Streeterville**	-
Lockwood | **Loop**	23
Longman/Eagle | **Logan Sq**	27
Lou Mitchell's | **Loop**	24
Lovells | **Lake Forest**	22
Lucky's | **Pilsen**	18
Luxbar | **Gold Coast**	19
L. Woods Tap | **Lincolnwood**	19
Magnolia Cafe | **Uptown**	23
Margie's | **multi.**	22
Market House | **Lake Forest**	-
Marmalade | **North Ctr/St. Ben's**	25
NEW Mercer 113 | **River N**	-
M Henry/Henrietta | **multi.**	25
NEW MH Fish | **Lake Forest**	-
Milk/Honey | **Wicker Pk**	22
Mity Nice | **Streeterville**	19
MK | **Near North**	27
NEW Monarch | **Wicker Pk**	-
Montarra | **Algonquin**	28
MorseL | **Rogers Pk**	-
NEW Municipal | **River N**	-
NEW M Vie | **Noble Sq**	-
Naha | **River N**	26

Nellcôte | **W Loop**	19
Next Door | **Northbrook**	22
Niche | **Geneva**	26
Nightwood | **Pilsen**	27
NoMI Kitchen | **Gold Coast**	26
Nookies | **multi.**	20
North Pond | **Lincoln Pk**	26
Oak Tree | **Gold Coast**	16
Old Town Pour Hse. | **Old Town**	14
Old Town Social | **Old Town**	21
NEW Oliver's | **Bridgeport**	–
NEW Oon | **W Loop**	–
Over Easy | **Ravenswood**	27
NEW Ovie B&G | **Loop**	–
Park Grill | **Loop**	19
NEW Park Tavern | **multi.**	–
Peasantry | **Lincoln Pk**	–
Perennial Virant | **Lincoln Pk**	26
Petterino's | **Loop**	19
P.J. Clarke's | **Gold Coast**	17
Point | **W Loop**	–
Prairie Grass | **Northbrook**	22
Prasino | **multi.**	22
Province | **W Loop**	25
Publican | **W Loop**	26
Publican Meats | **W Loop**	26
Public House | **River N**	18
Pump Room | **Gold Coast**	21
Quay | **Streeterville**	19
Quince | **Evanston**	25
Red Door | **Bucktown**	–
NEW Red Square | **Wicker Pk**	–
NEW Refinery | **Old Town**	–
NEW Reno | **Logan Sq**	–
NEW Rest. Beatrix | **Near North**	–
Revolution Brewing | **Logan Sq**	23
R.J. Grunts | **Lincoln Pk**	19
RL | **Gold Coast**	24
NEW RM Champagne | **W Loop**	–
Rockit | **multi.**	19
Roots Pizza | **W Town**	20
Rootstock | **Humboldt Pk**	23

Rustic Hse. | **Lincoln Pk**	21
Ruxbin | **Noble Sq**	28
Sable | **River N**	23
Savoy | **Wicker Pk**	–
Schwa | **Wicker Pk**	28
Scofflaw | **Logan Sq**	–
Seasons 52 | **multi.**	25
NEW Senza | **Lakeview**	28
Sepia | **W Loop**	25
1776 | **Crystal Lake**	25
720 South B&G | **S Loop**	–
Signature Room | **Streeterville**	17
Sixteen | **River N**	25
Sola | **North Ctr/St. Ben's**	24
South Branch | **Loop**	20
Southport | **Lakeview**	23
South Water | **Loop**	14
Sprout | **Lincoln Pk**	26
Stained Glass | **Evanston**	24
Standard Grill | **Westmont**	–
Stanley's | **Lincoln Pk**	19
State/Lake | **Loop**	16
Storefront Co. | **Wicker Pk**	–
Stout Barrel Hse. | **River N**	–
Sweet Maple |	26
Little Italy/University Vill	
NEW Table, Donkey/Stick |	–
Logan Sq	
Table Fifty-two | **Gold Coast**	25
Takashi | **Bucktown**	28
Tasting Room | **W Loop**	18
Tavern/Park | **Loop**	17
Tavern/Rush | **Gold Coast**	21
Telegraph | **Logan Sq**	22
3rd Coast Cafe | **Gold Coast**	18
III Forks | **Loop**	23
Toast | **multi.**	22
NEW Tommy Knuckles |	–
Lincoln Pk	
NEW Tortoise Club | **River N**	–
NEW Trenchermen | **Wicker Pk**	23
Tweet | **Uptown**	26
Twisted Spoke | **Noble Sq**	20

CUISINES

NEW Two | **W Town**	—
2 Sparrows | **Lincoln Pk**	21
Uncommon Ground | **multi.**	22
Union Pizza | **Evanston**	20
Vie | **W Springs**	29
Vincent | **Andersonville**	23
Waffles | **multi.**	—
Walnut Room | **Loop**	18
Weber Grill | **multi.**	21
West Town | **Noble Sq**	26
Wildberry Pancakes | **multi.**	23
Wildfire | **multi.**	23
NEW Wood | **Lakeview**	—

ARGENTINEAN

Tango Sur | **Lakeview**	24

ARMENIAN

Sayat Nova | **Streeterville**	23

ASIAN

Anna's Asian | **W Loop**	—
NEW Belly Q | **W Loop**	22
Belly Shack | **Humboldt Pk**	25
Bento Box | **Bucktown**	27
NEW Embeya | **W Loop**	22
Han 202 | **Bridgeport**	25
NEW Jellyfish | **River N**	—
Joy Yee's | **multi.**	20
Karma | **Mundelein**	23
Koi | **Evanston**	17
NEW MAK | **Wicker Pk**	—
NEW Mott Street | **Wicker Pk**	—
Niu | **Streeterville**	24
NEW Oon | **W Loop**	—
Sunda | **River N**	25
Township | **Logan Sq**	—

AUSTRIAN

Julius Meinl | **multi.**	21

BAKERIES

Baker/Nosh | **Uptown**	—
NEW Endgrain | **Roscoe Vill**	—

Kaufman's | **Skokie**	23
NEW Little Goat Bread | **W Loop**	—
Southport | **Lakeview**	23

BARBECUE

NEW Belly Q | **W Loop**	22
Bricks | **multi.**	23
NEW Bub City | **River N**	—
Carson's | **multi.**	21
Chicago Q | **Gold Coast**	21
Fat Willy's | **Logan Sq**	20
Hecky's | **Evanston**	21
Honey 1 BBQ | **Bucktown**	21
Lillie's Q | **multi.**	22
L. Woods Tap | **Lincolnwood**	19
NEW Milt's BBQ | **Lakeview**	—
Pork Shoppe | **Avondale**	20
Real Urban BBQ | **multi.**	21
Robinson's Ribs | **multi.**	18
Russell's | **Elmwood Pk**	21
NEW Smalls | **Avondale**	—
Smoke Daddy | **Wicker Pk**	22
Smoque BBQ | **Old Irving Pk**	26
NEW Sweet Baby Ray's | **Wrigleyville**	—
Twin Anchors | **Old Town**	22
Uncle Bub's BBQ | **Westmont**	21
Weber Grill | **multi.**	21

BELGIAN

Hopleaf | **Andersonville**	24
NEW Wâfel | **W Town**	—

BRAZILIAN

Brazzaz | **River N**	22
Fogo de Chão | **River N**	24
NEW La Sirena | **W Loop**	24
SushiSamba | **River N**	20
Texas de Brazil | **Schaumburg**	24

BRITISH

Blokes/Birds | **Lakeview**	18
Owen/Engine | **Logan Sq**	24
Pleasant House | **Bridgeport**	—

BURGERS

Abigail's | **Highland Pk**	24
Acadia | **S Loop**	27
Anthem | **Ukrainian Vill**	18
Athenian Room | **Lincoln Pk**	22
Au Cheval | **W Loop**	25
Big/Little's | **Near North**	25
Big Jones | **Andersonville**	24
Billy Goat | **multi.**	16
Bin | **River N**	21
Bread & Wine | **Old Irving Pk**	20
Burger Bar | **Lincoln Pk**	22
Burger Joint | **River N**	16
Burger Point | **S Loop**	-
Butcher/Burger | **Lincoln Pk**	25
Café/Architectes | **Gold Coast**	24
DMK Burger Bar | **multi.**	22
Edzo's | **multi.**	26
Epic Burger | **multi.**	19
Farmhouse | **Near North**	23
NEW Fatty's | **multi.**	-
Five Guys | **multi.**	17
Frog n Snail | **Lakeview**	20
Gage | **Loop**	23
Gemini | **Lincoln Pk**	21
Grange Hall | **W Loop**	22
Hackney's | **multi.**	18
Hamburger Mary's | **Andersonville**	19
Hop Häus | **Rogers Pk**	20
Hot Chocolate | **Bucktown**	24
Hugo's | **multi.**	24
Indie Burger | **Lakeview**	-
Kuma's | **multi.**	27
M Burger | **multi.**	18
Meatheads | **Roscoe Vill**	21
Nightwood | **Pilsen**	27
NoMI Kitchen | **Gold Coast**	26
Old Town Social | **Old Town**	21
Owen/Engine | **Logan Sq**	24
Paris Club | **River N**	20
P.J. Clarke's | **Gold Coast**	17
Revolution Brewing | **Logan Sq**	23

R.J. Grunts | **Lincoln Pk**	19
Rockit | **Wrigleyville**	19
Rosebud Prime/Steak | **Loop**	23
Superdawg | **multi.**	21
Three Aces | **Little Italy/University Vill**	22
Tom & Eddie's | **multi.**	18
Top Notch | **Far S Side**	25
NEW Tortoise Club | **River N**	-
25 Degrees | **River N**	21
Twisted Spoke | **Noble Sq**	20
Wiener's Circle | **Lincoln Pk**	19

CAJUN

Dixie | **Evanston**	20
Heaven/Seven | **multi.**	22
Pappadeaux | **Westmont**	23
Wishbone | **multi.**	20

CHICKEN

NEW Dak Korean | **Edgewater**	-
NEW Parson's | **Logan Sq**	-
Pecking Order | **Ravenswood**	-

CHINESE

(* dim sum specialist)

Big Bowl | **multi.**	20
Chens | **Wrigleyville**	20
Dee's | **Lincoln Pk**	19
NEW 8,000 Miles | **Roselle**	-
Emperor's Choice | **Chinatown**	22
Hai Yen | **Uptown**	25
Lao Beijing | **multi.**	24
Lao Hunan | **Chinatown**	25
NEW Lao Ma La | **Chinatown**	-
NEW Lao Yunnan | **Chinatown**	-
LuLu's* | **Evanston**	21
Phoenix* | **Chinatown**	23
Pine Yard | **Evanston**	18
Red Violet | **River N**	-
Shanghai Terrace | **River N**	26
Silver | **Uptown**	27
Sun Wah BBQ | **Uptown**	25
Three Happiness* | **Chinatown**	22
Yu's Mandarin | **Schaumburg**	24

COFFEEHOUSES

Artist's Cafe | S Loop	15
Berghoff | O'Hare Area	19
Bourgeois Pig | Lincoln Pk	20
Cafecito | Loop	24
Café Selmarie | Lincoln Sq	21
Caffe Rom | Loop	22
Julius Meinl | multi.	21
NEW Rest. Beatrix | Near North	-
Township | Logan Sq	-
Uncommon Ground | multi.	22

COLOMBIAN

La Parrilla | NW Side	-
Las Tablas | multi.	23

CONTINENTAL

Hubbard Inn | River N	20

COSTA RICAN

Irazu | Bucktown	23

CREOLE

Heaven/Seven | multi.	22
NEW Kizin Creole | W Rogers Pk	-
Pappadeaux | Westmont	23

CRÊPES

La Crêperie | Lakeview	21

CUBAN

Cafecito | Loop	24
Cafe Laguardia | Bucktown	19
90 Miles | multi.	23
NEW Paladar | Logan Sq	-

DELIS

Bagel | multi.	20
Eleven City | S Loop	19
Kaufman's | Skokie	23
Lucky's | multi.	18
Manny's | multi.	24
Zaleski/Horvath | multi.	24

DINER

Artist's Cafe | multi.	15
Bakin'/Eggs | Lakeview	20
Chicago Diner | multi.	24
Eggy's | Streeterville	-
Eleven City | S Loop	19
Glenn's Diner | Ravenswood	24
NEW Isabel's | Lincoln Pk	-
NEW Little Goat Diner | W Loop	22
Lou Mitchell's | Loop	24
Manny's | multi.	24
Milk/Honey | Wicker Pk	22
Nookies | Lakeview	20
Tempo | Gold Coast	19
West Egg | Near North	21
Yolk | multi.	22

ECLECTIC

Aviary | W Loop	26
BadHappy | River N	-
Cellar/Stained Glass | Evanston	22
NEW Cottage/Dixie | Homewood	-
Deleece | Lakeview	21
NEW En Hakkore | Bucktown	-
NEW Fat Rice | Logan Sq	-
Flight | Glenview	22
Foodlife/ease | Streeterville	19
Han 202 | Bridgeport	25
Heartland | Rogers Pk	17
Hub 51 | River N	20
Jane's | Bucktown	21
Kitsch'n | Roscoe Vill	20
Lula | Logan Sq	26
Mana | Wicker Pk	26
Monkey's Paw | Lincoln Pk	-
Moto | W Loop	26
Next | W Loop	29
NEW Old Fifth | Near W	-
NEW Oliver's | Bridgeport	-
Orange | multi.	17
Peasantry | Lincoln Pk	-
Pecking Order | Ravenswood	-
NEW Plzen | Pilsen	-
Red Door | Bucktown	-
Ruxbin | Noble Sq	28

NEW Sauce/Bread | **Edgewater**	-⌐
Sixteen | **River N**	25
Tavernita | **River N**	21
Township | **Logan Sq**	-⌐
Uncommon Ground | **multi.**	22
Webster's | **Lincoln Pk**	18
Zed 451 | **River N**	22

ETHIOPIAN

Demera | **Uptown**	20
Ethiopian Diamond | **multi.**	22
Ras Dashen | **Edgewater**	26

EUROPEAN

Autre Monde | **Berwyn**	26
Balsan | **Gold Coast**	23
NEW City Winery | **W Loop**	16
NEW Dryhop | **Lakeview**	-⌐
NEW Duran | **W Loop**	-⌐
Gage | **Loop**	23
Goosefoot | **Lincoln Sq**	29
NEW Himmel's | **Lincoln Sq**	-⌐
Vincent | **Andersonville**	23

FILIPINO

Coobah | **Lakeview**	23
Pecking Order | **Ravenswood**	-⌐

FONDUE

Geja's | **Lincoln Pk**	22

FRENCH

Aquitaine | **Lincoln Pk**	21
Ba Le | **Loop**	23
Bistronomic | **Gold Coast**	23
NEW Brindille | **River N**	-⌐
Café Absinthe | **Bucktown**	21
Café/Architectes | **Gold Coast**	24
Convito | **Wilmette**	20
Crêperie St-Germain | **Evanston**	-⌐
Cyrano's | **River N**	19
Deca | **Streeterville**	21
Dining Room/Kendall | **Near W**	23
Everest | **Loop**	27

Froggy's | **Highwood**	25
Frog n Snail | **Lakeview**	20
Glunz Tavern | **Old Town**	-⌐
Jilly's | **Evanston**	21
La Petite Folie | **Hyde Pk**	25
Les Nomades | **Streeterville**	28
Le Vichyssois | **Lakemoor**	25
Maude's Liquor | **W Loop**	25
Mexique | **Noble Sq**	24
Michael | **Winnetka**	26
Oceanique | **Evanston**	25
Paris Club | **River N**	20
NEW RM Champagne | **W Loop**	-⌐
NEW Table, Donkey/Stick | **Logan Sq**	-⌐
Takashi | **Bucktown**	28
Tallgrass | **Lockport**	27
Troquet | **Ravenswood**	-⌐
Tru | **Streeterville**	27
Yoshi's Café | **Lakeview**	26

FRENCH (BISTRO)

Barrington Country | **Barrington**	24
Bistro Bordeaux | **Evanston**	23
Bistro Campagne | **Lincoln Sq**	25
Bistrot Margot | **Old Town**	22
Bistrot Zinc | **Gold Coast**	21
Bistro Voltaire | **Near North**	22
Cafe Central | **Highland Pk**	22
Café Touché | **Edison Pk**	23
Chez Joël | **Little Italy/University Vill**	24
Chez Moi | **Lincoln Pk**	-⌐
NEW Chez Simo | **Lincoln Sq**	-⌐
D & J Bistro | **Lake Zurich**	24
Kiki's Bistro | **Near North**	25
Koda | **Far S Side**	23
La Crêperie | **Lakeview**	21
La Sardine | **W Loop**	24
Le Bouchon | **Bucktown**	23
NEW LM Bistro | **River N**	-⌐
Miramar | **Highwood**	17
Mon Ami Gabi | **multi.**	23

Pierrot Gourmet | **River N**	22
Retro Bistro | **Mt. Prospect**	25
Socca | **Lakeview**	22

FRENCH (BRASSERIE)

Brasserie by LM | **S Loop**	18
NEW Brasserie 54/LM | **Andersonville**	-

GASTROPUB

Bangers/Lace | Amer. | **Wicker Pk**	20
NEW Billy Sunday | Amer. | **Logan Sq**	-
Blokes/Birds | British | **Lakeview**	18
Branch 27 | Amer. | **Noble Sq**	19
Bristol | Amer. | **Bucktown**	25
NEW Dryhop | Euro. | **Lakeview**	-
Fountainhead | Eclectic | **Ravenswood**	20
Frontier | Amer. | **Noble Sq**	22
Gage | Amer. | **Loop**	23
Gilt Bar | Amer. | **River N**	25
Hopleaf | Belgian | **Andersonville**	24
Longman/Eagle | Amer. | **Logan Sq**	27
Monkey's Paw | Eclectic | **Lincoln Pk**	-
NEW Municipal | Amer. | **River N**	-
NEW Old Fifth | Eclectic | **Near W**	-
Old Town Pour Hse. | Amer. | **Old Town**	14
Owen/Engine | British | **Logan Sq**	24
Publican | Amer. | **W Loop**	26
Public House | Amer. | **River N**	18
Purple Pig | Med. | **River N**	26
Red Door | Eclectic | **Bucktown**	-
Revolution Brewing | Amer. | **Logan Sq**	23
Stout Barrel Hse. | Amer. | **River N**	-
Three Aces | Italian | **Little Italy/University Vill**	22
Troquet | French | **Ravenswood**	-

GERMAN

Berghoff | **Loop**	19
Edelweiss | **Norridge**	22
Prost! | **Lincoln Pk**	-

GREEK

Artopolis | **Greektown**	21
Athena | **Greektown**	19
Athenian Room | **Lincoln Pk**	22
Avli | **Winnetka**	22
NEW Covo Gyro | **Wicker Pk**	-
Greek Islands | **multi.**	22
Parthenon | **Greektown**	21
Pegasus | **multi.**	20
Roditys | **Greektown**	20
Santorini | **Greektown**	22
Taxim | **Wicker Pk**	26

HAITIAN

NEW Kizin Creole | **W Rogers Pk**	-

HAWAIIAN

Roy's | **River N**	24

HOT DOGS

Al's Beef | **multi.**	22
Five Guys | **multi.**	17
Franks 'N' Dawgs | **Lincoln Pk**	25
Gene/Jude's | **O'Hare Area**	24
Glunz Tavern | **Old Town**	-
NEW Haute/Dog | **Wicker Pk**	-
Hot Doug's | **Avondale**	27
Superdawg | **multi.**	21
Westminster | **Loop**	19
Wiener's Circle | **Lincoln Pk**	19

ICE CREAM PARLORS

Margie's | **multi.**	22

INDIAN

Bombay Spice Grill | **River N**	22
Chicago Curry | **S Loop**	20
Cumin | **Wicker Pk**	24
Curry Hut | **Highwood**	19
Gaylord Indian | **multi.**	22

Hema's | **multi.**	22
India House | **multi.**	22
Indian Garden | **Streeterville**	20
Marigold | **Andersonville**	22
Mt. Everest | **Evanston**	21
NEW Nepal House | **S Loop**	–
Peacock | **Vernon Hills**	18
NEW Sataza | **Loop**	–
Tiffin | **W Rogers Pk**	19

INDONESIAN

NEW Rickshaw | **Lincoln Pk**	–

IRISH

Chief O'Neill's | **NW Side**	18
Lady Gregory's | **Andersonville**	20

ITALIAN

(N=Northern; S=Southern)

Al's Beef | **Wicker Pk**	22
Angelina | S | **Lakeview**	23
Anna Maria | **Ravenswood**	20
Anteprima | **Andersonville**	26
Antico Posto | **Oak Brook**	23
A Tavola | N | **Ukrainian Vill**	26
Aurelio's Pizza | **multi.**	21
Bacchanalia | **SW Side**	22
Bacino's | **multi.**	21
Balena | **Lincoln Pk**	24
Bar Toma | **Gold Coast**	17
Basil Leaf | **Lincoln Pk**	19
Bella Notte | S | **Noble Sq**	23
Bella Via | **Highland Pk**	20
Briciola | **Ukrainian Vill**	–
Brio | N | **Lombard**	–
Bruna's | **SW Side**	23
Cafe Lucci | **Glenview**	24
Café Spiaggia | **Gold Coast**	25
Caffe Rom | **Loop**	22
Calo Ristorante | **Andersonville**	21
Campagnola | **Evanston**	24
Carlos/Carlos | N | **Arlington Hts**	25
Carlucci | N | **Rosemont**	22
Carmine's | **Gold Coast**	21

NEW Centro Rist. | **Near North**	–
Club Lucky | **Bucktown**	21
Coco Pazzo | N | **River N**	25
Coco Pazzo Café | **Streeterville**	22
Convito | **Wilmette**	20
Davanti | **multi.**	26
Del Rio | **Highwood**	20
Dinotto | **Old Town**	21
DiSotto | **Streeterville**	23
Due Lire | **Lincoln Sq**	23
Eduardo's Enoteca | **Gold Coast**	23
EJ's Pl. | **Skokie**	20
Erie Cafe | **River N**	22
Filini | **Loop**	22
Florentine | **Loop**	20
Francesca's | **multi.**	22
Francesco's | **Northbrook**	22
Frankie's | **Gold Coast**	18
Gaetano's | **Forest Pk**	27
Gioco | **S Loop**	22
Harry Caray's | **multi.**	22
NEW Isabel's | **Lincoln Pk**	–
NEW J. Rocco | S | **River N**	–
La Bocca/Verità | **Lincoln Sq**	22
Labriola Bakery | **Oak Brook**	24
La Gondola | **Lakeview**	20
La Madia | **River N**	23
La Scarola | **River W**	26
Macello | **W Loop**	25
Mama Milano | S | **Old Town**	–
Merlo | N | **Gold Coast**	25
NEW Merlo's | **Highland Pk**	–
Mia Francesca | **Lakeview**	24
Nando Milano | **Wicker Pk**	–
Near Restaurant | **Barrington**	–
Next Door | **Northbrook**	22
Ombra | **Andersonville**	–
Osteria/Pizzeria Via Stato | **River N**	23
Pelago | **Streeterville**	27
Pensiero | **Evanston**	21
Petterino's | **Loop**	19
Philly G's | **Vernon Hills**	21

Phil Stefani's | **River N**	23
Piccolo Sogno | **Near W**	25
NEW Piccolo Sogno Due | **River N**	-
Pizano's | **multi.**	21
Pizzeria da Nella | **Lincoln Pk**	-
Prosecco | **River N**	24
Quartino | **River N**	22
NEW Reno | **Logan Sq**	-
NEW Riccardo Eno. | **Lincoln Pk**	-
Riccardo Trat. | N | **Lincoln Pk**	28
Ricobene's | **Bridgeport**	24
Rosal's | S | **Little Italy/University Vill**	26
Rose Angelis | **Lincoln Pk**	25
Rosebud | **multi.**	22
RPM Italian | **River N**	23
Sabatino's | **Old Irving Pk**	26
Sapori Trattoria | **Lincoln Pk**	25
Saranello's | **Wheeling**	20
Scoozi! | **River N**	20
NEW Siena Tavern | **River N**	-
Socca | **Lakeview**	22
Spacca Napoli | **Ravenswood**	27
Spiaggia | **Gold Coast**	26
Taverna 750 | **Wrigleyville**	24
Terzo Piano | **Loop**	22
NEW Tesori | **Loop**	-
Three Aces | **Little Italy/University Vill**	22
312 Chicago | **Loop**	21
Tocco | **Bucktown**	25
Topo Gigio | **Old Town**	24
Trattoria D.O.C. | **Evanston**	20
Trattoria Gianni | **Lincoln Pk**	20
Trattoria No. 10 | **Loop**	24
Trattoria Roma | **Old Town**	23
NEW Tre Soldi | S | **Streeterville**	-
Tufano's | S | **Little Italy/University Vill**	24
Tuscany | N | **multi.**	22
Vapiano | **Lincoln Pk**	16
Via Carducci | S | **multi.**	21
Viaggio | **Near W**	24

Village | **Loop**	20
Vinci | **Lincoln Pk**	20
Vito & Nick's | **Far S Side**	24
Vivere | **Loop**	23
Vivo | **W Loop**	23
Volare | **multi.**	23
Zia's Trattoria | **Edison Pk**	22

JAPANESE
(* sushi specialist)

Agami* | **Uptown**	24
Ai Sushi* | **River N**	21
Akai Hana* | **Wilmette**	21
Arami* | **W Town**	27
Aria* | **Loop**	23
Bob San* | **Wicker Pk**	23
Butterfly* | **multi.**	20
Chens* | **Wrigleyville**	20
Coast/South Coast* | **multi.**	24
Dee's* | **Lincoln Pk**	19
NEW 8,000 Miles | **Roselle**	-
NEW Enso | **Bucktown**	-
NEW Gari Sushi* | **E Vill**	-
Gyu-Kaku | **Streeterville**	23
NEW Hamachi* | **W Rogers Pk**	-
Indie Cafe* | **Edgewater**	24
Itto Sushi* | **Lincoln Pk**	25
Japonais* | **River N**	24
Joy Yee's* | **Chinatown**	20
NEW Juno* | **Lincoln Pk**	-
NEW Kabocha | **W Loop**	-
NEW Kai Zan | **Humboldt Pk**	-
Kamehachi* | **multi.**	22
Katsu* | **NW Side**	29
Kuni's* | **Evanston**	23
Macku Sushi* | **Lincoln Pk**	25
NEW Masaki* | **Streeterville**	-
Mirai Sushi* | **Wicker Pk**	25
Nabuki | **Hinsdale**	24
Noodles/Yagihashi | **Loop**	22
Nori | **multi.**	24
NEW Oiistar | **Wicker Pk**	-
Oysy* | **multi.**	22

RA Sushi* | **multi.**	18
Roka Akor* | **multi.**	24
Sai Café* | **Lincoln Pk**	27
Slurping Turtle | **River N**	22
NEW Stetsons* | **Loop**	24
NEW Sumi Robata | **River N**	-
NEW Sushi Dokku | **W Loop**	-
Sushi Naniwa* | **River N**	22
Sushi Para/Sai* | **multi.**	19
SushiSamba | **River N**	20
Swordfish* | **Batavia**	27
Tank Sushi* | **Lincoln Sq**	20
Tanoshii | **Andersonville**	28
Todoroki Hibachi | **Evanston**	-
Tokio Pub | **Schaumburg**	-
Toro Sushi | **Lincoln Pk**	26
Tsukasa of Tokyo | **Vernon Hills**	23
NEW Umai* | **Printer's Row**	-
Union Sushi + BBQ* | **River N**	22
Wildfish* | **multi.**	20
Yoshi's Café | **Lakeview**	26
Yusho | **Avondale**	26
Yuzu Sushi | **E Vill**	-

KOREAN

(* barbecue specialist)

NEW Ahjoomah's | **Chinatown**	-
Crisp | **Lakeview**	24
NEW Dak Korean | **Edgewater**	-
Del Seoul | **Lakeview**	23
NEW En Hakkore | **Bucktown**	-
Jin Ju | **Andersonville**	24
San Soo Gab San* | **Lincoln Sq**	25
Yu's Mandarin | **Schaumburg**	24

KOSHER/ KOSHER-STYLE

NEW Hamachi | **W Rogers Pk**	-
NEW Milt's BBQ | **Lakeview**	-

LEBANESE

Old Jerusalem | **Old Town**	20

MALAYSIAN

NEW Rickshaw | **Lincoln Pk**	-

MEDITERRANEAN

Ada St. | **Bucktown**	24
Andies | **multi.**	20
Artopolis | **Greektown**	21
Autre Monde | **Berwyn**	26
Avec | **W Loop**	28
Caravan | **Uptown**	-
NEW City Winery | **W Loop**	16
NEW Covo Gyro | **Wicker Pk**	-
Dawali | **multi.**	23
Naf Naf | **multi.**	22
Pita Inn | **multi.**	23
Purple Pig | **River N**	26
Reza's | **multi.**	20
NEW Tesori | **Loop**	-

MEXICAN

Adobo | **Old Town**	20
Antique Taco | **Wicker Pk**	23
A Toda Madre | **Geneva**	-
Barrio | **Lakeview**	-
Bien Trucha | **Geneva**	29
Big Star | **Wicker Pk**	26
Birrieria Zaragoza | **SW Side**	27
NEW Bodega | **Lincoln Pk**	-
Bullhead Cantina | **Humboldt Pk**	-
Cafe Laguardia | **Bucktown**	19
Cantina Laredo | **River N**	18
NEW Cantina Pasadita | **Avondale**	-
Cemitas Puebla | **Humboldt Pk**	24
Chilam Balam | **Lakeview**	25
Chilapan | **Logan Sq**	25
De Cero | **W Loop**	20
NEW El Hefe | **Near North**	-
Frontera Fresco | **multi.**	24
Frontera Grill | **River N**	27
La Casa/Isaac | **multi.**	20
La Lagartija | **W Loop**	-
Los Nopales | **Lincoln Sq**	23
NEW L'Patron | **Logan Sq**	-
Lupita's | **Evanston**	20
Mago | **multi.**	24

CUISINES

Masa Azul | **Logan Sq**	–
Mercadito | **River N**	22
Mexique | **Noble Sq**	24
NEW Mezcalina | **Loop**	–
Mixteco Grill | **Lakeview**	27
New Rebozo | **multi.**	–
Patron's Hacienda | **River N**	–
NEW Polanco | **Logan Sq**	–
NEW Revolución | **Lakeview**	–
Salpicón | **Old Town**	24
Salsa 17 | **Arlington Hts**	21
Shaman | **Ukrainian Vill**	–
Taco Joint | **multi.**	23
NEW Takito | **Ukrainian Vill**	–
Topolobampo | **River N**	28
Tortas Frontera | **multi.**	23
Wholly Frijoles | **Lincolnwood**	25
Xoco | **River N**	27
Zapatista | **multi.**	18
Zocalo | **River N**	21

MIDDLE EASTERN

Alhambra | **W Loop**	17
Andies | **multi.**	20
Caravan | **Uptown**	–
Dawali | **multi.**	23
Naf Naf | **multi.**	22
Pita Inn | **multi.**	23
Reza's | **multi.**	20
Sultan's Market | **multi.**	21

NEPALESE

Chicago Curry | **S Loop**	20
Cumin | **Wicker Pk**	24
Curry Hut | **Highwood**	19
Mt. Everest | **Evanston**	21
NEW Nepal House | **S Loop**	–

NOODLE SHOPS

NEW Andy's | **Lakeview**	26
Arami | **W Town**	27
Big Bowl | **multi.**	20
Hai Yen | **Uptown**	25
Joy Yee's | **S Loop**	20

Le Colonial | **Gold Coast**	23
LuLu's | **Evanston**	21
Noodles/Yagihashi | **Loop**	22
NEW Oiistar | **Wicker Pk**	–
Pasteur | **Edgewater**	16
Penny's | **multi.**	20
Pho 777 | **Uptown**	24
Saigon Sisters | **W Loop**	24
Simply It | **Lincoln Pk**	21
Slurping Turtle | **River N**	22
Tank Noodle | **Uptown**	25
Three Happiness | **Chinatown**	22
Urbanbelly | **Logan Sq**	25
Yu's Mandarin | **Schaumburg**	24

NUEVO LATINO

Belly Shack | **Humboldt Pk**	25
Carnivale | **W Loop**	21
Coobah | **Lakeview**	23
Depot Nuevo | **Wilmette**	18
Libertad | **Skokie**	25
Maya Del Sol | **Oak Pk**	23
Nacional 27 | **River N**	22

PERSIAN

Noon-O-Kabab | **Albany Pk**	24

PIZZA

Apart Pizza Co. | **multi.**	25
Art of Pizza | **Lakeview**	23
Aurelio's Pizza | **multi.**	21
Bacino's | **multi.**	21
Bar Toma | **Gold Coast**	17
Bricks | **multi.**	23
Chicago Pizza | **Lincoln Pk**	25
Coalfire Pizza | **Noble Sq**	24
Dimo's Pizza | **Lakeview**	22
Edwardo's Pizza | **multi.**	19
Exchequer | **Loop**	20
NEW Flour/Stone | **Streeterville**	–
Frankie's | **Gold Coast**	18
NEW Gino's East | **Printer's Row**	–
Giordano's | **multi.**	22
NEW Himmel's | **Lincoln Sq**	–

Home Run Inn | **multi.**	24
La Gondola | **Lakeview**	20
La Madia | **River N**	23
Lou Malnati's | **multi.**	25
Mama Milano | **Old Town**	-
Original Gino's | **multi.**	22
Osteria/Pizzeria Via Stato | **River N**	23
Pequod's | **Lincoln Pk**	24
Piece | **Wicker Pk**	25
Pizano's | **multi.**	21
NEW Pizza Hse. 1647 | **Bucktown**	-
Pizzeria da Nella | **Lincoln Pk**	-
Pizzeria Due/Uno | **River N**	22
Quartino | **River N**	22
NEW Riccardo Eno. | **Lincoln Pk**	-
Roots Pizza | **W Town**	20
Spacca Napoli | **Ravenswood**	27
NEW Tre Soldi | **Streeterville**	-
Union Pizza | **Evanston**	20
Vapiano | **Lincoln Pk**	16
Vito & Nick's | **Far S Side**	24

PUB FOOD

Anthem | **Ukrainian Vill**	18
Arrow/Ogden | **W Loop**	-
Bangers/Lace | **Wicker Pk**	20
Beer Bistro | **multi.**	17
Billy Goat | **multi.**	16
Duke/Perth | **Lakeview**	20
Goose Island | **multi.**	17
Grafton Pub/Grill | **Lincoln Sq**	22
Jake Melnick's | **Gold Coast**	19
Old Town Pour Hse. | **Old Town**	14
Old Town Social | **Old Town**	21
Scofflaw | **Logan Sq**	-
South Branch | **Loop**	20
Twisted Spoke | **Noble Sq**	20

RUSSIAN

NEW Red Square | **Wicker Pk**	-
Russian Tea | **Loop**	22

SANDWICHES

(See also Delis)

Al's Beef | **multi.**	22
Bagel | **multi.**	20
Baker/Nosh | **Uptown**	-
Ba Le | **multi.**	23
Banh Mi/Co. | **multi.**	-
Berghoff | **Loop**	19
Big/Little's | **Near North**	25
Birchwood | **Wicker Pk**	23
Bourgeois Pig | **Lincoln Pk**	20
Brunch | **River N**	16
Cafecito | **Loop**	24
Cemitas Puebla | **Humboldt Pk**	24
City Farms Mkt. | **Lakeview**	-
NEW Covo Gyro | **Wicker Pk**	-
Del Seoul | **Lakeview**	23
NEW Duran | **W Loop**	-
Epic Burger | **River N**	19
NEW Fat Sandwich | **Lincoln Pk**	-
Five Guys | **S Loop**	17
Fontano's | **multi.**	27
Giordano's | **multi.**	22
Grahamwich | **River N**	19
Hannah's Bretzel | **multi.**	23
Jerry's | **Wicker Pk**	20
NEW Little Goat Bread | **W Loop**	-
NEW Local Root | **Streeterville**	-
Lucky's | **multi.**	18
Mr. Beef | **River N**	24
Pita Inn | **multi.**	23
Potbelly | **multi.**	18
Publican Meats | **W Loop**	26
Ricobene's | **Bridgeport**	24
Superdawg | **multi.**	21
Tortas Frontera | **Loop**	23
NEW Wâfel | **W Town**	-

SCANDINAVIAN

Tre Kronor | **Albany Pk**	24

CUISINES

SCOTTISH

Duke/Perth | **Lakeview** 20

SEAFOOD

Acadia | **S Loop** 27
Big/Little's | **Near North** 25
Bob Chinn's | **Wheeling** 23
Cape Cod | **Streeterville** 22
Catch 35 | **multi.** 23
🆕 Da Lobsta | **Gold Coast** –
Davis St. Fish | **Evanston** 19
Devon Seafood | **multi.** 21
Fireside | **Andersonville** 20
Fish Bar | **Lakeview** 24
Fulton's | **River N** 18
Glenn's Diner | **Ravenswood** 24
GT Fish/Oyster | **River N** 25
Half Shell | **Lakeview** 22
Hugo's | **multi.** 24
Joe's Sea/Steak | **River N** 27
Keefer's | **River N** 25
L2O | **Lincoln Pk** 26
McCormick/Schmick | **multi.** 19
🆕 MH Fish | **Lake Forest** –
New England Sea | **Lakeview** 25
Nick's Fish | **multi.** 24
Oceanique | **Evanston** 25
Pappadeaux | **Westmont** 23
Pelago | **Streeterville** 27
Pete Miller's | **multi.** 22
Reel Club | **Oak Brook** 21
Riva | **Streeterville** 21
Santorini | **Greektown** 22
Savoy | **Wicker Pk** –
Shaw's Crab | **multi.** 25
Silver | **Uptown** 27
Tin Fish | **Tinley Park** 24
Tramonto's | **Wheeling** 22
Wellfleet | **Albany Pk** –

SMALL PLATES

(See also Spanish tapas specialist)
Ada St. | Amer./Med. | **Bucktown** 24
Avec | Med. | **W Loop** 28

Aviary | Eclectic | **W Loop** 26
Barrelhouse Flat | Amer. | –
    Lincoln Pk
Bluebird | Amer. | **Bucktown** 22
Boka | Amer. | **Lincoln Pk** 26
Browntrout | Amer. | 24
    North Ctr/St. Ben's
Cellar/Stained Glass | Eclectic | 22
    Evanston
Cyrano's | French | **River N** 19
Davanti | Italian | 26
    Little Italy/University Vill
DiSotto | Italian | **Streeterville** 23
Flight | Eclectic | **Glenview** 22
Girl/The Goat | Amer. | **W Loop** 27
Green Zebra | Veg. | **Noble Sq** 27
Lao You Ju | Chinese | 24
    Chinatown
Libertad | Nuevo Latino | **Skokie** 25
Ombra | Italian | **Andersonville** –
Purple Pig | Med. | **River N** 26
Rootstock | Amer. | **Humboldt Pk** 23
Sable | Amer. | **River N** 23
Tavernita | Latin | **River N** 21
Taxim | Greek | **Wicker Pk** 26
Telegraph | Amer. | **Logan Sq** 22
Webster's | Eclectic | **Lincoln Pk** 18
Yusho | Japanese | **Avondale** 26

SOUTH AMERICAN

🆕 Suite 25 | **Logan Sq** –

SOUTHERN

Big Jones | **Andersonville** 24
🆕 Carriage Hse. | **Wicker Pk** 21
Dixie | **Evanston** 20
Lillie's Q | **multi.** 22
Southern | **Wicker Pk** 20
Table Fifty-two | **Gold Coast** 25
Wishbone | **multi.** 20

SOUTHWESTERN

Bandera | **Streeterville** 23
Flo | **Noble Sq** 20

SPANISH

(* tapas specialist)

NEW Benjamin Tapas* | Highland Pk	-
Cafe Ba-Ba-Reeba!* | Lincoln Pk	22
Café Iberico* | River N	22
Emilio's Tapas* | multi.	23
La Tasca* | Arlington Hts	21
Mercat | S Loop	26
Mesón Sabika/Tapas Valencia* | multi.	25
Tapas Barcelona* | Evanston	20
Tapas Gitana* | multi.	22
Tavernita* | River N	21
Vera | W Loop	22

STEAKHOUSES

NEW Bavette's | River N	24
Benny's Chop | River N	25
Brazzaz | River N	22
Capital Grille | multi.	24
Carmichael's | W Loop	20
Chicago Chop | River N	23
Chicago Cut | River N	26
Chicago Prime | Schaumburg	25
David Burke Prime | River N	25
NEW Del Frisco's | Gold Coast	27
Devon Seafood | Oakbrook Terr	21
Ditka's | multi.	22
EJ's Pl. | Skokie	20
Erie Cafe | River N	22
Fleming's | multi.	20
Fogo de Chão | River N	24
Fulton's | River N	18
Gene/Georgetti | River N	25
Gibsons | multi.	26
NEW Grass Fed | Bucktown	-
Grill/Alley | Streeterville	20
Harry Caray's | multi.	22
Hugo's | multi.	24
Joe's Sea/Steak | River N	27
Keefer's | River N	25
Kinzie Chop | River N	24
La Parrilla | NW Side	-

Las Tablas | multi.	23
Lawry's | River N	23
Mastro's Steak | River N	26
Michael Jordan's | Streeterville	22
Morton's | multi.	23
Palm | Loop	24
Patron's Hacienda | River N	-
Pete Miller's | multi.	22
Phil Stefani's | River N	23
NEW Polanco | Logan Sq	-
Reel Club | Oak Brook	21
NEW Revolución | Lakeview	-
Riva | Streeterville	21
Roka Akor | multi.	24
Rosebud Prime/Steak | multi.	23
Rosewood | Rosemont	26
Ruth's Chris | multi.	23
Saloon Steak | Streeterville	22
NEW Sauce/Bread | Edgewater	-
Shula's Steak | multi.	22
Smith/Wollensky | River N	22
NEW Stetsons | Loop	24
Sullivan's Steak | multi.	24
Tango Sur | Lakeview	24
Tavern/Rush | Gold Coast	21
Texas de Brazil | Schaumburg	24
III Forks | Loop	23
Tramonto's | Wheeling	22
Wildfire | multi.	23
Wilmette Chop | Wilmette	-

SWEDISH

Ann Sather | multi.	21

THAI

NEW Andy's | Lakeview	26
Arun's | NW Side	27
Big Bowl | multi.	20
Butterfly | multi.	20
Cozy Noodles | Lakeview	21
Indie Cafe | Edgewater	24
Jin Thai | Edgewater	-
Joy's Noodles | Lakeview	22

CUISINES

Namo | **North Ctr/St. Ben's** __-__

Opart Thai | **multi.** __24__

NEW Rainbow Cuisine |
  Lincoln Sq __-__

Ruby/Siam | **multi.** __21__

Star/Siam | **River N** __20__

TAC Quick | **Wrigleyville** __26__

Thai Pastry | **multi.** __25__

TURKISH

Turquoise | **Roscoe Vill** __25__

VEGETARIAN

(* vegan)

Andies | **multi.** __20__

NEW Bistro Dre | **Lakeview** __-__

Blind Faith* | **Evanston** __20__

Chicago Diner | **multi.** __24__

Green Zebra | **Noble Sq** __27__

Heartland* | **Rogers Pk** __17__

Hema's | **multi.** __22__

Karyn's* | **multi.** __19__

Karyn's/Green* | **Greektown** __24__

Mana | **Wicker Pk** __26__

Native Foods* | **multi.** __23__

Tiffin | **W Rogers Pk** __19__

VIETNAMESE

Ba Le | **multi.** __23__

Banh Mi/Co. | **multi.** __-__

Hai Yen | **Uptown** __25__

Le Colonial | **Gold Coast** __23__

Pasteur | **Edgewater** __16__

Pho 777 | **Uptown** __24__

Saigon Sisters | **W Loop** __24__

Simply It | **Lincoln Pk** __21__

Tank Noodle | **Uptown** __25__

Locations

Includes names, cuisines and Food ratings.

City North

ANDERSONVILLE/EDGEWATER

Acre	*Amer.*	20
Andies	*Med./Mideast*	20
Ann Sather	*Amer./Swedish*	21
Anteprima	*Italian*	26
Apart Pizza Co.	*Pizza*	25
Big Jones	*Southern*	24
Bongo Room	*Amer.*	24
NEW Brasserie 54/LM	*French*	–
Broadway Cellars	*Amer.*	22
Calo Ristorante	*Italian*	21
NEW Dak Korean	*Korean*	–
Ethiopian Diamond	*Ethiopian*	22
Fireside	*Amer.*	20
Francesca's	*Italian*	22
Hamburger Mary's	*Burgers*	19
Hopleaf	*Belgian*	24
Indie Cafe	*Japanese/Thai*	24
Jin Ju	*Korean*	24
Jin Thai	*Thai*	–
Lady Gregory's	*Amer./Irish*	20
Marigold	*Indian*	22
M Henry/Henrietta	*Amer.*	25
Nookies	*Amer.*	20
Ombra	*Italian*	–
Pasteur	*Viet.*	16
Ras Dashen	*Ethiopian*	26
Reza's	*Med./Mideast.*	20
NEW Sauce/Bread	*Eclectic/Sandwiches*	–
Tanoshii	*Japanese*	28
Uncommon Ground	*Coffee/Eclectic*	22
Vincent	*Amer.*	23

GOLD COAST

Allium	*Amer.*	23
Balsan	*Euro.*	23
Bar Toma	*Italian/Pizza*	17
Big Bowl	*Asian*	20
Bistronomic	*French*	23
Bistrot Zinc	*French*	21
Café/Architectes	*French*	24
Café Spiaggia	*Italian*	25
Carmine's	*Italian*	21
Chicago Q	*BBQ*	21
NEW Da Lobsta	*Seafood*	–
NEW Del Frisco's	*Steak*	27
Ditka's	*Steak*	22
Eduardo's Enoteca	*Italian*	23
Edwardo's Pizza	*Pizza*	19
Epic Burger	*Burgers*	19
Frankie's	*Italian/Pizza*	18
Fred's	*Amer.*	20
Gaylord Indian	*Indian*	22
Gibsons	*Steak*	26
NEW Hash Hse.	*Amer.*	21
Hugo's	*Seafood/Steak*	24
Jake Melnick's	*Pub*	19
Le Colonial	*Viet.*	23
NEW Little Market	*Amer.*	–
NEW Local	*Amer.*	–
Luxbar	*Amer.*	19
M Burger	*Burgers*	18
McCormick/Schmick	*Seafood*	19
Merlo	*Italian*	25
Morton's	*Steak*	23
NoMI Kitchen	*Amer.*	26
Oak Tree	*Amer.*	16
Pizano's	*Italian/Pizza*	21
P.J. Clarke's	*Amer.*	17
Pump Room	*Amer.*	21
RA Sushi	*Japanese*	18
RL	*Amer.*	24
Spiaggia	*Italian*	26
Table Fifty-two	*Amer./Southern*	25
Tavern/Rush	*Steak*	21
Tempo	*Diner*	19
3rd Coast Cafe	*Amer.*	18

LOCATIONS

LAKEVIEW/ WRIGLEYVILLE

Al's Beef	*Sandwiches*	22
Andies	*Med./Mideast*	20
NEW Andy's	*Thai*	26
Angelina	*Italian*	23
Ann Sather	*Amer./Swedish*	21
Art of Pizza	*Pizza*	23
Bagel	*Deli*	20
Bakin'/Eggs	*Amer.*	20
Banh Mi/Co.	*Sandwiches/Viet.*	-
NEW Bar Pastoral	*Amer.*	-
Barrio	*Mex.*	-
NEW Bistro Dre	*Amer./Veg.*	-
Blokes/Birds	*British*	18
Chalkboard	*Amer.*	23
Chens	*Asian*	20
Chicago Diner	*Diner/Veg.*	24
Chilam Balam	*Mex.*	25
City Farms Mkt.	*Sandwiches*	-
Coobah	*Filipino/Nuevo Latino*	23
Cozy Noodles	*Thai*	21
Crisp	*Korean*	24
NEW Crosby's Kit.	*Amer.*	19
Deleece	*Eclectic*	21
Del Seoul	*Korean*	23
Dimo's Pizza	*Pizza*	22
DMK Burger Bar	*Burgers*	22
NEW Dryhop	*Euro.*	-
Duke/Perth	*Scottish*	20
Fish Bar	*Seafood*	24
Frog n Snail	*Amer./French*	20
Giordano's	*Pizza*	22
Goose Island	*Pub*	17
Half Shell	*Seafood*	22
HB Home Bistro	*Amer.*	25
Hearty	*Amer.*	21
Indie Burger	*Burgers*	-
Jack's/Halsted	*Amer.*	17
Joy's Noodles	*Thai*	22
Joy Yee's	*Asian*	20
Julius Meinl	*Austrian*	21
Kuma's	*Burgers*	27

La Crêperie	*Crêpes/French*	21
La Gondola	*Italian*	20
Las Tablas	*Colombian/Steak*	23
Lucky's	*Deli/Sandwiches*	18
Mia Francesca	*Italian*	24
NEW Milt's BBQ	*BBQ/Kosher*	-
Mixteco Grill	*Mex.*	27
Native Foods	*Vegan*	23
New England Sea	*Seafood*	25
90 Miles	*Cuban*	23
Nookies	*Amer.*	20
Nori	*Japanese*	24
Penny's	*Asian*	20
Potbelly	*Sandwiches*	18
NEW Revolución	*Mex./Steak*	-
Rockit	*Burgers*	19
NEW Senza	*Amer.*	28
Socca	*French/Italian*	22
Southport	*Amer.*	23
NEW Sweet Baby Ray's	*BBQ*	-
TAC Quick	*Thai*	26
Tango Sur	*Argent./Steak*	24
Tapas Gitana	*Spanish*	22
Taverna 750	*Italian*	24
Uncommon Ground	*Coffee/Eclectic*	22
NEW Vu Sua	*Asian*	-
Waffles	*Amer.*	-
NEW Wood	*Amer.*	-
Yoshi's Café	*French/Japanese*	26

LINCOLN PARK

Alinea	*Amer.*	29
Aquitaine	*Amer./French*	21
Athenian Room	*Amer./Greek*	22
Bacino's	*Italian*	21
Balena	*Italian*	24
Barrelhouse Flat	*Amer.*	-
Basil Leaf	*Italian*	19
Beer Bistro	*Amer./Pub*	17
NEW Bodega	*Mex.*	-
Boka	*Amer.*	26
Bourgeois Pig	*Coffee/Sandwiches*	20

Bricks | *BBQ/Pizza*	23
Burger Bar | *Burgers*	22
Butcher/Burger | *Burgers*	25
Cafe Ba-Ba-Reeba! | *Spanish*	22
Chez Moi | *French*	–
Chicago Pizza | *Pizza*	25
Dawali | *Med./Mideast.*	23
Dee's | *Asian*	19
Edwardo's Pizza | *Pizza*	19
Edzo's | *Burgers*	26
Eleven Lincoln Park | *Diner*	19
Epic Burger | *Burgers*	19
NEW Fat Sandwich | *Sandwiches*	–
NEW Fatty's | *Burgers*	–
Five Guys | *Burgers / Hot Dogs*	17
Franks 'N' Dawgs | *Hot Dogs*	25
Geja's | *Fondue*	22
Gemini | *Amer.*	21
Goose Island | *Pub*	17
Hema's | *Indian*	22
NEW Isabel's | *Diner/Italian*	–
Itto Sushi | *Japanese*	25
J. Alexander's | *Amer.*	20
John's Pl. | *Amer.*	17
NEW Juno | *Japanese*	–
Karyn's | *Vegan/Veg.*	19
Lou Malnati's | *Pizza*	25
L2O | *Seafood*	26
Macku Sushi | *Japanese*	25
Mon Ami Gabi | *French*	23
Monkey's Paw | *Eclectic*	–
Nookies | *Amer.*	20
North Pond | *Amer.*	26
Orange | *Eclectic*	17
Original Gino's | *Pizza*	22
Peasantry | *Amer.*	–
Penny's | *Asian*	20
Pequod's | *Pizza*	24
Perennial Virant | *Amer.*	26
Pizzeria da Nella | *Italian/Pizza*	–
Potbelly | *Sandwiches*	18
Prost! | *German*	–

NEW Riccardo Eno. | *Italian*	–
Riccardo Trat. | *Italian*	28
NEW Rickshaw | *Asian*	–
R.J. Grunts | *Amer.*	19
Robinson's Ribs | *BBQ*	18
Rose Angelis | *Italian*	25
Rustic Hse. | *Amer.*	21
Sai Café | *Japanese*	27
Sapori Trattoria | *Italian*	25
Simply It | *Viet.*	21
Sprout | *Amer.*	26
Stanley's | *Amer.*	19
Sultan's Market | *Mideast.*	21
Sushi Para/Sai | *Japanese*	19
Taco Joint | *Mex.*	23
Toast | *Amer.*	22
NEW Tommy Knuckles | *Amer.*	–
Toro Sushi | *Japanese*	26
Trattoria Gianni | *Italian*	20
2 Sparrows | *Amer.*	21
Vapiano | *Italian/Pizza*	16
Via Carducci | *Italian*	21
Vinci | *Italian*	20
Webster's | *Eclectic*	18
Wiener's Circle | *Hot Dogs*	19

LINCOLN SQUARE/ UPTOWN

Agami | *Japanese*	24
Baker/Nosh | *Bakery/Sandwiches*	–
Ba Le | *Sandwiches/Viet.*	23
Bistro Campagne | *French*	25
Café Selmarie | *Amer.*	21
Caravan | *Med./Mideast.*	–
Ceres' Table | *Amer.*	24
NEW Chez Simo | *French*	–
Demera | *Ethiopian*	20
Due Lire | *Italian*	23
NEW Elizabeth | *Amer.*	–
NEW Gather | *Amer.*	–
Goosefoot | *Amer.*	29
Grafton Pub/Grill | *Pub*	22
Hai Yen | *Viet.*	25

LOCATIONS

NEW Himmel's	*Euro./Pizza*	-
Julius Meinl	*Austrian*	21
La Bocca/Verità	*Italian*	22
Los Nopales	*Mex.*	23
Magnolia Cafe	*Amer.*	23
Opart Thai	*Thai*	24
Pho 777	*Viet.*	24
NEW Rainbow Cuisine	*Thai*	-
San Soo Gab San	*Korean*	25
Silver	*Chinese/Seafood*	27
Sun Wah BBQ	*Chinese*	25
Tank Noodle	*Viet.*	25
Tank Sushi	*Japanese*	20
Thai Pastry	*Thai*	25
Tweet	*Amer.*	26

NEAR NORTH

Big/Little's	*Seafood*	25
Bistro Voltaire	*French*	22
Butch McGuire's	*Amer.*	18
NEW Centro Rist.	*Italian*	-
NEW El Hefe	*Mex.*	-
Farmhouse	*Amer.*	23
NEW Ferris/Jack	*Amer.*	-
Fleming's	*Steak*	20
Kiki's Bistro	*French*	25
MK	*Amer.*	27
NEW Rest. Beatrix	*Amer./Coffee*	-
Taco Joint	*Mex.*	23
West Egg	*Diner*	21

NORTH CENTER/ ST. BEN'S

Bricks	*BBQ/Pizza*	23
Browntrout	*Amer.*	24
NEW Copper Hse.	*Amer.*	-
Marmalade	*Amer.*	25
Namo	*Thai*	-
Sola	*Amer.*	24

OLD TOWN

Adobo	*Mex.*	20
Bistrot Margot	*French*	22
Dinotto	*Italian*	21

Glunz Tavern	*Hot Dogs*	-
Kamehachi	*Japanese*	22
Mama Milano	*Italian/Pizza*	-
Nookies	*Amer.*	20
Old Jerusalem	*Mideast.*	20
Old Town Pour Hse.	*Pub*	14
Old Town Social	*Amer.*	21
NEW Refinery	*Amer.*	-
Salpicón	*Mex.*	24
Topo Gigio	*Italian*	24
Trattoria Roma	*Italian*	23
Twin Anchors	*BBQ*	22

ROGERS PARK/ WEST ROGERS PARK

Ethiopian Diamond	*Ethiopian*	22
Five Guys	*Burgers / Hot Dogs*	17
NEW Hamachi	*Japanese/Kosher*	-
Heartland	*Eclectic/Veg.*	17
Hema's	*Indian*	22
Hop Häus	*Burgers*	20
NEW Kizin Creole	*Creole/Haitian*	-
MorseL	*Amer.*	-
Nori	*Japanese*	24
Tiffin	*Indian*	19

Downtown

LOOP

Al's Beef	*Sandwiches*	22
Amuse	*Amer.*	-
Aria	*Asian*	23
Artist's Cafe	*Coffee/Diner*	15
Atwood Cafe	*Amer.*	22
Aurelio's Pizza	*Pizza*	21
Bacino's	*Italian*	21
Ba Le	*Sandwiches/Viet.*	23
Berghoff	*German*	19
Billy Goat	*Burgers*	16
Cafecito	*Coffee/Cuban*	24
Caffe Rom	*Coffee*	22
Catch 35	*Seafood*	23
NEW Chuck's	*Amer.*	-

Epic Burger	*Burgers*	19
Everest	*French*	27
Exchequer	*Amer.*	20
Filini	*Italian*	22
Florentine	*Italian*	20
Fontano's	*Sandwiches*	27
Frontera Fresco	*Mex.*	24
Gage	*Amer.*	23
Giordano's	*Pizza*	22
Hannah's Bretzel	*Sandwiches*	23
Heaven/Seven	*Cajun/Creole*	22
Henri	*Amer.*	27
Kamehachi	*Japanese*	22
Lloyd's Chicago	*Amer.*	16
Lockwood	*Amer.*	23
Lou Mitchell's	*Diner*	24
M Burger	*Burgers*	18
McCormick/Schmick	*Seafood*	19
NEW Mezcalina	*Mex.*	-
Morton's	*Steak*	23
Naf Naf	*Med./Mideast.*	22
Native Foods	*Vegan*	23
Noodles/Yagihashi	*Japanese*	22
NEW Ovie B&G	*Amer.*	-
Palm	*Steak*	24
Park Grill	*Amer.*	19
Petterino's	*Amer.*	19
Pizano's	*Italian/Pizza*	21
Potbelly	*Sandwiches*	18
Robinson's Ribs	*BBQ*	18
Rosebud	*Italian*	22
Rosebud Prime/Steak	*Steak*	23
Ruby/Siam	*Thai*	21
Russian Tea	*Russian*	22
NEW Sataza	*Indian*	-
South Branch	*Amer.*	20
South Water	*Amer.*	14
State/Lake	*Amer.*	16
NEW Stetsons	*Steak*	24
Sushi Para/Sai	*Japanese*	19
Tavern/Park	*Amer.*	17
Terzo Piano	*Italian*	22

NEW Tesori	*Italian*	-
III Forks	*Amer./Steak*	23
312 Chicago	*Italian*	21
Tortas Frontera	*Mex.*	23
Trattoria No. 10	*Italian*	24
Village	*Italian*	20
Vivere	*Italian*	23
Walnut Room	*Amer.*	18
Westminster	*Hot Dogs*	19
Wildberry Pancakes	*Amer.*	23

RIVER NORTH

Ai Sushi	*Japanese*	21
Al's Beef	*Sandwiches*	22
NEW American Junkie	*Amer.*	-
NEW ¡Ay Chiwowa!	*Mex.*	-
BadHappy	*Eclectic*	-
NEW Bavette's	*Amer./Steak*	24
Benny's Chop	*Steak*	25
Big Bowl	*Asian*	20
Bijan's	*Amer.*	20
Billy Goat	*Burgers*	16
Bin	*Amer.*	21
NEW Boarding Hse.	*Amer.*	22
Bombay Spice Grill	*Indian*	22
Brazzaz	*Brazilian/Steak*	22
Bridge Bar Chicago	*Amer.*	-
Bridge House	*Amer.*	18
NEW Brindille	*French*	-
Brunch	*Amer./Sandwiches*	16
NEW Bub City	*BBQ*	-
Burger Joint	*Burgers*	16
Café Iberico	*Spanish*	22
Cantina Laredo	*Mex.*	18
Carson's	*BBQ*	21
NEW Central Standard	*Amer./Eclectic*	-
Chicago Chop	*Steak*	23
Chicago Cut	*Steak*	26
Coco Pazzo	*Italian*	25
Cyrano's	*French*	19
David Burke Prime	*Steak*	25
Devon Seafood	*Seafood*	21

Epic Burger | *Burgers*	19
Epic Rest. | *Amer.*	20
Erie Cafe | *Steak*	22
Fogo de Chão | *Brazilian/Steak*	24
NEW freestyle | *Amer.*	-
Frontera Grill | *Mex.*	27
Fulton's | *Seafood/Steak*	18
Gene/Georgetti | *Steak*	25
Gilt Bar | *Amer.*	25
Giordano's | *Pizza*	22
Graham Elliot | *Amer.*	24
Grahamwich | *Sandwiches*	19
GT Fish/Oyster | *Seafood*	25
Hannah's Bretzel | *Sandwiches*	23
Harry Caray's | *Italian/Steak*	22
Harry Caray's | *Amer.*	20
Heaven/Seven | *Cajun/Creole*	22
Hubbard Inn | *Continental*	20
Hub 51 | *Amer./Eclectic*	20
India House | *Indian*	22
Japonais | *Japanese*	24
NEW Jellyfish | *Asian*	-
Joe's Sea/Steak | *Seafood/Steak*	27
NEW J. Rocco | *Italian*	-
Kamehachi | *Japanese*	22
Karyn's | *Vegan/Veg.*	19
Keefer's | *Steak*	25
Kinzie Chop | *Steak*	24
La Madia | *Italian/Pizza*	23
NEW Lao 18 | *Chinese*	-
Lawry's | *Amer./Steak*	23
NEW LM Bistro | *French*	-
Lobby | *Amer.*	25
Lou Malnati's | *Pizza*	25
Mastro's Steak | *Steak*	26
M Burger | *Burgers*	18
Mercadito | *Mex.*	22
NEW Mercer 113 | *Amer.*	-
Mr. Beef | *Sandwiches*	24
NEW Municipal | *Amer.*	-
Nacional 27 | *Nuevo Latino*	22
Naha | *Amer.*	26
New Rebozo | *Mex.*	-
Nick's Fish | *Seafood*	24
Original Gino's | *Pizza*	22
Osteria/Pizzeria Via Stato | *Italian/Pizza*	23
Oysy | *Japanese*	22
Paris Club | *French*	20
Patron's Hacienda | *Mex./Steak*	-
Phil Stefani's | *Italian/Steak*	23
NEW Piccolo Sogno Due | *Italian*	-
Pierrot Gourmet | *French*	22
Pizano's | *Italian/Pizza*	21
Pizzeria Due/Uno | *Pizza*	22
Potbelly | *Sandwiches*	18
Prosecco | *Italian*	24
Public House | *Amer.*	18
Purple Pig | *Med.*	26
Quartino | *Italian*	22
Red Violet | *Chinese*	-
Reza's | *Med./Mideast.*	20
Rockit | *Amer.*	19
Roka Akor | *Japanese/Steak*	24
Roy's | *Hawaiian*	24
RPM Italian | *Italian*	23
Ruth's Chris | *Steak*	23
Sable | *Amer.*	23
Scoozi! | *Italian*	20
Shanghai Terrace | *Chinese*	26
Shaw's Crab | *Seafood*	25
NEW Siena Tavern | *Italian*	-
Sixteen | *Amer.*	25
Slurping Turtle | *Japanese/Noodle Shop*	22
Smith/Wollensky | *Steak*	22
Star/Siam | *Thai*	20
Stout Barrel Hse. | *Amer.*	-
Sullivan's Steak | *Steak*	24
NEW Sumi Robata | *Japanese*	-
Sunda | *Asian*	25
Sushi Naniwa | *Japanese*	22
SushiSamba | *Japanese/S Amer.*	20
Tavernita | *Spanish*	21

Topolobampo | *Mex.*   28

LOCATIONS

Red Door	*Eclectic*	–
Sushi Para/Sai	*Japanese*	19
Takashi	*Amer./French*	28
Toast	*Amer.*	22
Tocco	*Italian*	25

EDISON PARK/ O'HARE AREA

Berghoff	*Coffee*	19
Big Bowl	*Asian*	20
Billy Goat	*Burgers*	16
Café Touché	*French*	23
Capital Grille	*Steak*	24
Carlucci	*Italian*	22
Fleming's	*Steak*	20
Gene/Jude's	*Hot Dogs*	24
Gibsons	*Steak*	26
Harry Caray's	*Italian/Steak*	22
Hugo's	*Seafood/Steak*	24
McCormick/Schmick	*Seafood*	19
Morton's	*Steak*	23
Naf Naf	*Med./Mideast.*	22
Nick's Fish	*Seafood*	24
Original Gino's	*Pizza*	22
NEW Park Tavern	*Amer.*	–
Prasino	*Amer.*	22
Rosewood	*Steak*	26
Sullivan's Steak	*Steak*	24
Tortas Frontera	*Mex.*	23
Wildfire	*Steak*	23
Zia's Trattoria	*Italian*	22

HUMBOLDT PARK

Belly Shack	*Asian*	25
Bullhead Cantina	*Mex.*	–
Cemitas Puebla	*Mex.*	24
NEW Kai Zan	*Japanese*	–
Rootstock	*Amer.*	23

IRVING PARK

Bread & Wine	*Amer.*	20
Sabatino's	*Italian*	26
Smoque BBQ	*BBQ*	26

LOGAN SQUARE

NEW Billy Sunday	*Amer.*	–
Chicago Diner	*Diner/Veg.*	24
Chilapan	*Mex.*	25
NEW Fat Rice	*Eclectic*	–
Fat Willy's	*BBQ*	20
Giordano's	*Pizza*	22
Jam	*Amer.*	22
Longman/Eagle	*Amer.*	27
NEW L'Patron	*Mex.*	–
Lula	*Eclectic*	26
Margie's	*Amer.*	22
Masa Azul	*Mex.*	–
90 Miles	*Cuban*	23
Owen/Engine	*British*	24
NEW Paladar	*Cuban*	–
NEW Parson's	*Amer.*	–
NEW Polanco	*Mex./Steak*	–
NEW Reno	*Amer./Italian*	–
Revolution Brewing	*Amer.*	23
Scofflaw	*Pub*	–
NEW Suite 25	*S Amer.*	–
NEW Table, Donkey/Stick	*Amer./Euro.*	–
Telegraph	*Amer.*	22
Township	*Coffee/Eclectic*	–
Urbanbelly	*Asian/Noodle Shop*	25

NORTHWEST SIDE/ RAVENSWOOD

Al Dente	*Amer.*	23
Anna Maria	*Italian*	20
Apart Pizza Co.	*Pizza*	25
Arun's	*Thai*	27
Chief O'Neill's	*Irish*	18
Dawali	*Med./Mideast.*	23
Fountainhead	*Amer.*	20
Gale St. Inn	*Amer.*	21
Giordano's	*Pizza*	22
Glenn's Diner	*Diner*	24
Julius Meinl	*Austrian*	21
Katsu	*Japanese*	29
La Parrilla	*Colombian/Steak*	–

Las Tablas	*Colombian/Steak*	23
NEW Leadbelly	*Burgers*	–
Noon-O-Kabab	*Persian*	24
Over Easy	*Amer.*	27
Pecking Order	*Chicken*	–
Spacca Napoli	*Pizza*	27
Superdawg	*Hot Dogs*	21
Tre Kronor	*Scan.*	24
Troquet	*French*	–
Wellfleet	*Seafood*	–

ROSCOE VILLAGE

Al's Beef	*Sandwiches*	22
Banh Mi/Co.	*Sandwiches/Viet.*	–
NEW Endgrain	*Amer./Bakery*	–
John's Pl.	*Amer.*	17
Kitsch'n	*Eclectic*	20
Meatheads	*Burgers*	21
Orange	*Eclectic*	17
Turquoise	*Turkish*	25
Wishbone	*Southern*	20

WICKER PARK

Al's Beef	*Sandwiches*	22
Antique Taco	*Mex.*	23
Bangers/Lace	*Pub*	20
Bedford	*Amer.*	17
Big Star	*Mex.*	26
Birchwood	*Sandwiches*	23
Bob San	*Japanese*	23
Bongo Room	*Amer.*	24
NEW Carriage Hse.	*Southern*	21
NEW Covo Gyro	*Greek/Sandwiches*	–
Cumin	*Indian/Nepalese*	24
Fifty/50	*Amer.*	18
Francesca's	*Italian*	22
NEW Haute/Dog	*Hot Dogs*	–
Jerry's	*Sandwiches*	20
NEW MAK	*Asian*	–
Mana	*Eclectic/Veg.*	26
Milk/Honey	*Amer.*	22
Mirai Sushi	*Japanese*	25

NEW Monarch	*Amer.*	–
NEW Mott Street	*Asian*	–
Nando Milano	*Italian*	–
Native Foods	*Vegan*	23
Nori	*Japanese*	24
NEW Oiistar	*Japanese*	–
Penny's	*Asian*	20
Piece	*Pizza*	25
Prasino	*Amer.*	22
NEW Red Square	*Amer./Russian*	–
Savoy	*Amer./Seafood*	–
Schwa	*Amer.*	28
Smoke Daddy	*BBQ*	22
Southern	*Southern*	20
Storefront Co.	*Amer.*	–
Sultan's Market	*Mideast.*	21
Taxim	*Greek*	26
NEW Trenchermen	*Amer.*	23
Via Carducci	*Italian*	21

City South

BEVERLY

Fontano's	*Sandwiches*	27

BRIDGEPORT

Han 202	*Asian*	25
NEW Oliver's	*Amer./Eclectic*	–
Pleasant House	*British*	–
Ricobene's	*Italian*	24

CHINATOWN

NEW Ahjoomah's	*Korean*	–
Al's Beef	*Sandwiches*	22
Ba Le	*Sandwiches/Viet.*	23
Emperor's Choice	*Chinese*	22
Joy Yee's	*Asian*	20
Lao Beijing	*Chinese*	24
Lao Hunan	*Chinese*	25
NEW Lao Ma La	*Chinese*	–
NEW Lao Yunnan	*Chinese*	–
Phoenix	*Chinese*	23
Three Happiness	*Chinese*	22

FAR SOUTH SIDE

Koda	*French*	23
Lou Malnati's	*Pizza*	25
Top Notch	*Burgers*	25
Vito & Nick's	*Pizza*	24

HYDE PARK/KENWOOD

Edwardo's Pizza	*Pizza*	19
Five Guys	*Burgers / Hot Dogs*	17
Giordano's	*Pizza*	22
La Petite Folie	*French*	25
Zaleski/Horvath	*Deli*	24

NEAR SOUTH SIDE

Epic Burger	*Burgers*	19

PILSEN

EL Ideas	*Amer.*	28
Lucky's	*Deli/Sandwiches*	18
Nightwood	*Amer.*	27
NEW Plzen	*Eclectic*	-

PRINTER'S ROW

NEW Gino's East	*Pizza*	-
Hackney's	*Burgers*	18
NEW Umai	*Japanese*	-

SOUTH LOOP

Acadia	*Amer./Seafood*	27
Artist's Cafe	*Coffee/Diner*	15
Bongo Room	*Amer.*	24
Brasserie by LM	*French*	18
Burger Point	*Burgers*	-
Chicago Curry	*Indian/Nepalese*	20
Chicago Firehouse	*Amer.*	22
City Tavern	*Amer.*	16
Eleven City	*Diner*	19
Five Guys	*Burgers / Hot Dogs*	17
Gioco	*Italian*	22
Joy Yee's	*Asian*	20
Manny's	*Deli*	24
Mercat	*Spanish*	26
Mesón Sabika/Tapas Valencia	*Spanish*	25
NEW Nepal House	*Indian/Nepalese*	-

Opart Thai	*Thai*	24
Oysy	*Japanese*	22
720 South B&G	*Amer.*	-
Coast/South Coast	*Japanese*	24
Waffles	*Amer.*	-
Yolk	*Diner*	22
Zapatista	*Mex.*	18

SOUTHWEST SIDE

Bacchanalia	*Italian*	22
Birrieria Zaragoza	*Mex.*	27
Bruna's	*Italian*	23
Giordano's	*Pizza*	22
Harry Caray's	*Amer.*	22
Home Run Inn	*Pizza*	24
Manny's	*Deli*	24
Pegasus	*Greek*	20

City West

EAST VILLAGE

NEW Gari Sushi	*Japanese*	-
Yuzu Sushi	*Japanese*	-

GREEKTOWN

Artopolis	*Greek/Med.*	21
Athena	*Greek*	19
Giordano's	*Pizza*	22
Greek Islands	*Greek*	22
Karyn's/Green	*Amer./Vegan*	24
Parthenon	*Greek*	21
Pegasus	*Greek*	20
Roditys	*Greek*	20
Santorini	*Greek/Seafood*	22

LITTLE ITALY/ UNIVERSITY VILLAGE

Al's Beef	*Sandwiches*	22
Chez Joël	*French*	24
NEW County BBQ	*BBQ*	-
Davanti	*Italian*	26
Fontano's	*Sandwiches*	27
Francesca's	*Italian*	22
Rosal's	*Italian*	26
Rosebud	*Italian*	22

Sweet Maple	*Amer.*	26
Three Aces	*Italian*	22
Tufano's	*Italian*	24
Tuscany	*Italian*	22

NEAR WEST

Dining Room/Kendall	*French*	23
NEW Old Fifth	*Eclectic*	-
NEW Park Tavern	*Amer.*	-
Piccolo Sogno	*Italian*	25
Viaggio	*Italian*	24

NOBLE SQUARE

Bella Notte	*Italian*	23
Branch 27	*Amer.*	19
Butterfly	*Japanese/Thai*	20
Coalfire Pizza	*Pizza*	24
Flo	*SW*	20
Frontier	*Amer.*	22
Green Zebra	*Veg.*	27
Mexique	*Mex.*	24
NEW M Vie	*Amer.*	-
Ruxbin	*Eclectic*	28
Twisted Spoke	*Pub*	20
West Town	*Amer.*	26

RIVER WEST

Estate Ultra Bar	*Amer.*	-
La Scarola	*Italian*	26

UKRAINIAN VILLAGE

Anthem	*Pub*	18
A Tavola	*Italian*	26
Bite	*Amer.*	22
Briciola	*Italian*	-
Homestead	*Amer.*	-
Shaman	*Mex.*	-
NEW Takito	*Mex.*	-

WEST LOOP

Alhambra	*Mideast.*	17
Anna's Asian	*Asian*	-
Arrow/Ogden	*Pub*	-
Au Cheval	*Amer.*	25
Avec	*Med.*	28

Aviary	*Eclectic*	26
Bacino's	*Italian*	21
Beer Bistro	*Amer./Pub*	17
NEW Belly Q	*Asian/BBQ*	22
Billy Goat	*Burgers*	16
Blackbird	*Amer.*	27
Butterfly	*Japanese/Thai*	20
Carmichael's	*Steak*	20
Carnivale	*Nuevo Latino*	21
NEW City Winery	*Med.*	16
De Cero	*Mex.*	20
NEW Duran	*Euro./Sandwiches*	-
NEW Embeya	*Asian*	22
NEW g.e.b.	*Amer.*	-
Girl/The Goat	*Amer.*	27
NEW Grace	*Amer.*	29
Grange Hall	*Amer./Burgers*	22
Hannah's Bretzel	*Sandwiches*	23
Ina's	*Amer.*	22
Ing	*Amer.*	23
NEW Kabocha	*Japanese*	-
La Lagartija	*Mex.*	-
La Sardine	*French*	24
NEW La Sirena	*S Amer.*	24
Lillie's Q	*BBQ/Southern*	22
NEW Little Goat Bread	*Bakery/Sandwiches*	-
NEW Little Goat Diner	*Diner*	22
Macello	*Italian*	25
Maude's Liquor	*French*	25
Moto	*Eclectic*	26
Nellcôte	*Amer.*	19
Next	*Eclectic*	29
NEW Oon	*Amer.*	-
Point	*Amer.*	-
Province	*Amer.*	25
Publican	*Amer.*	26
Publican Meats	*Amer.*	26
NEW RM Champagne	*Amer.*	-
Saigon Sisters	*Viet.*	24
Sepia	*Amer.*	25
NEW Sushi Dokku	*Japanese*	-
Tasting Room	*Amer.*	18

LOCATIONS

Vera	*Spanish*	22
Vivo	*Italian*	23
Wishbone	*Southern*	20

WEST TOWN

Arami	*Japanese*	27
Butterfly	*Japanese/Thai*	20
Roots Pizza	*Amer./Pizza*	20
NEW Two	*Amer.*	-
NEW Wâfel	*Belgian*	-

Suburbs

SUBURBAN NORTH

Abigail's	*Amer.*	24
Akai Hana	*Japanese*	21
NEW Avenue	*Amer.*	-
Avli	*Greek*	22
Bagel	*Deli*	20
Bella Via	*Italian*	20
NEW Benjamin Tapas	*Spanish*	-
Bistro Bordeaux	*French*	23
Blind Faith	*Veg.*	20
Bluegrass	*Amer.*	21
NEW Bobby's	*Amer.*	17
Bob Chinn's	*Seafood*	23
Cafe Central	*French*	22
Cafe Lucci	*Italian*	24
Campagnola	*Italian*	24
Carson's	*BBQ*	21
Cellar/Stained Glass	*Eclectic*	22
Chef's Station	*Amer.*	24
Coast/South Coast	*Japanese*	24
Convito	*French/Italian*	20
Cooper's Hawk	*Amer.*	21
Crêperie St-Germain	*French*	-
Curry Hut	*Indian/Nepalese*	19
Davis St. Fish	*Seafood*	19
Del Rio	*Italian*	20
Depot Nuevo	*Nuevo Latino*	18
Dixie	*Cajun/Southern*	20
Edwardo's Pizza	*Pizza*	19
Edzo's	*Burgers*	26
EJ's Pl.	*Italian/Steak*	20

Epic Burger	*Burgers*	19
Farmhouse	*Amer.*	23
NEW Fatty's	*Burgers*	-
Five Guys	*Burgers / Hot Dogs*	17
Flight	*Eclectic*	22
NEW Found	*Amer.*	-
Francesca's	*Italian*	22
Francesco's	*Italian*	22
Froggy's	*French*	25
Frontera Fresco	*Mex.*	24
Glenview House	*Amer.*	19
NEW Guildhall	*Amer.*	-
Hackney's	*Burgers*	18
Hecky's	*BBQ*	21
La Casa/Isaac	*Mex.*	20
J. Alexander's	*Amer.*	20
Jerry's Restaurant	*Amer.*	22
Jilly's	*Amer./French*	21
Joy Yee's	*Asian*	20
Kamehachi	*Japanese*	22
Karma	*Asian*	23
Kaufman's	*Bakery/Deli*	23
Koi	*Asian*	17
Kuni's	*Japanese*	23
Libertad	*Nuevo Latino*	25
Lou Malnati's	*Pizza*	25
Lovells	*Amer.*	22
LuLu's	*Asian*	21
Lupita's	*Mex.*	20
L. Woods Tap	*Amer.*	19
Market House	*Amer.*	-
McCormick/Schmick	*Seafood*	19
NEW Merlo's	*Italian*	-
NEW MH Fish	*Seafood*	-
Michael	*French*	26
Miramar	*French*	17
Morton's	*Steak*	23
Mt. Everest	*Indian/Nepalese*	21
Next Door	*Amer./Italian*	22
Oceanique	*French/Seafood*	25
Original Gino's	*Pizza*	22
Peacock	*Indian*	18

Penny's	Asian	20	Cooper's Hawk	Amer.	21
Pensiero	Italian	21	D & J Bistro	French	24
Pete Miller's	Seafood/Steak	22	**NEW** e+o	Amer.	-
Philly G's	Italian	21	Edelweiss	German	22
Pine Yard	Chinese	18	**NEW** 8,000 Miles	Chinese/Japanese	-
Pita Inn	Med./Mideast.	23	Five Guys	Burgers / Hot Dogs	17
Pizano's	Italian/Pizza	21	Gaylord Indian	Indian	22
Prairie Grass	Amer.	22	Hackney's	Burgers	18
Quince	Amer.	25	Home Run Inn	Pizza	24
RA Sushi	Japanese	18	India House	Indian	22
Real Urban BBQ	BBQ	21	Inovasi	Amer.	25
Roka Akor	Japanese/Steak	24	La Tasca	Spanish	21
Ruby/Siam	Thai	21	Le Vichyssois	French	25
Ruth's Chris	Steak	23	Lou Malnati's	Pizza	25
Saranello's	Italian	20	Mago	Mex.	24
Stained Glass	Amer.	24	Montarra	Amer.	28
Superdawg	Hot Dogs	21	Morton's	Steak	23
Tapas Barcelona	Spanish	20	Naf Naf	Med./Mideast.	22
Tapas Gitana	Spanish	22	Near Restaurant	Italian	-
Todoroki Hibachi	Japanese	-	Original Gino's	Pizza	22
Tom & Eddie's	Burgers	18	Retro Bistro	French	25
Tramonto's	Seafood/Steak	22	Rosebud	Italian	22
Trattoria D.O.C.	Italian	20	Ruth's Chris	Steak	23
Tsukasa of Tokyo	Japanese	23	Salsa 17	Mex.	21
Tuscany	Italian	22	Seasons 52	Amer.	25
Union Pizza	Pizza	20	1776	Amer.	25
Wholly Frijoles	Mex.	25	Shaw's Crab	Seafood	25
Wildberry Pancakes	Amer.	23	Shula's Steak	Steak	22
Wildfire	Steak	23	Sushi Para/Sai	Japanese	19
Wildfish	Japanese	20	Texas de Brazil	Brazilian	24
Wilmette Chop	Steak	-	Thai Pastry	Thai	25
Zapatista	Mex.	18	Tokio Pub	Japanese	-
		Weber Grill	Amer.	21

L
O
C
A
T
I
O
N
S

SUBURBAN NW

Al's Beef	Sandwiches	22
Aurelio's Pizza	Pizza	21
Barrington Country	French	24
Big Bowl	Asian	20
Billy Goat	Burgers	16
NEW BlackFinn	Amer.	-
Carlos/Carlos	Italian	25
Chicago Prime	Steak	25

Wildberry Pancakes	Amer.	23
Wildfire	Steak	23
Wildfish	Japanese	20
Yu's Mandarin	Chinese/Korean	24

SUBURBAN SOUTH

Aurelio's Pizza	Pizza	21
NEW Cottage/Dixie	Amer./Eclectic	-

SUBURBAN SW

Al's Beef	*Sandwiches*	22
Aurelio's Pizza	*Pizza*	21
Cooper's Hawk	*Amer.*	21
Courtright's	*Amer.*	27
Dan McGee	*Amer.*	26
Hackney's	*Burgers*	18
NEW Harvest Room	*Amer.*	-
Tallgrass	*French*	27
Tin Fish	*Seafood*	24

SUBURBAN WEST

Adelle's	*Amer.*	26
Antico Posto	*Italian*	23
NEW Artisan Table	*Amer.*	-
A Toda Madre	*Mex.*	-
Aurelio's Pizza	*Pizza*	21
Autre Monde	*Med.*	26
Bacino's	*Italian*	21
Bien Trucha	*Mex.*	29
Brio	*Italian*	-
Capital Grille	*Steak*	24
Catch 35	*Seafood*	23
Clubhouse	*Amer.*	22
Cooper's Hawk	*Amer.*	21
Davanti	*Italian*	26
Devon Seafood	*Seafood/Steak*	21
Ditka's	*Steak*	22
DMK Burger Bar	*Burgers*	22
Edwardo's Pizza	*Pizza*	19
Emilio's Tapas	*Spanish*	23
FatDuck	*Amer.*	20
Five Guys	*Burgers / Hot Dogs*	17
Fontano's	*Sandwiches*	27
Francesca's	*Italian*	22
Gaetano's	*Italian*	27
Gibsons	*Steak*	26
Greek Islands	*Greek*	22
Harry Caray's	*Italian/Steak*	22
Heaven/Seven	*Cajun/Creole*	22
Home Run Inn	*Pizza*	24

Hugo's	*Seafood/Steak*	24
J. Alexander's	*Amer.*	20
Joy Yee's	*Asian*	20
Labriola Bakery	*Italian/Pizza*	24
Lao Beijing	*Chinese*	24
Lou Malnati's	*Pizza*	25
Mago	*Mex.*	24
Maya Del Sol	*Nuevo Latino*	23
McCormick/Schmick	*Seafood*	19
Mesón Sabika/Tapas Valencia	*Spanish*	25
Mon Ami Gabi	*French*	23
Morton's	*Steak*	23
Nabuki	*Japanese*	24
Naf Naf	*Med./Mideast.*	22
New Rebozo	*Mex.*	-
Niche	*Amer.*	26
Original Gino's	*Pizza*	22
Pappadeaux	*Cajun/Seafood*	23
Penny's	*Asian*	20
Prasino	*Amer.*	22
RA Sushi	*Japanese*	18
Reel Club	*Seafood*	21
Reza's	*Med./Mideast.*	20
Robinson's Ribs	*BBQ*	18
Rosebud	*Italian*	22
Russell's	*BBQ*	21
Seasons 52	*Amer.*	25
Standard Grill	*Amer.*	-
Sullivan's Steak	*Steak*	24
Swordfish	*Japanese*	27
Tom & Eddie's	*Burgers*	18
Tuscany	*Italian*	22
Uncle Bub's BBQ	*BBQ*	21
Vie	*Amer.*	29
Volare	*Italian*	23
Weber Grill	*Amer.*	21
Wildfire	*Steak*	23
Zapatista	*Mex.*	18

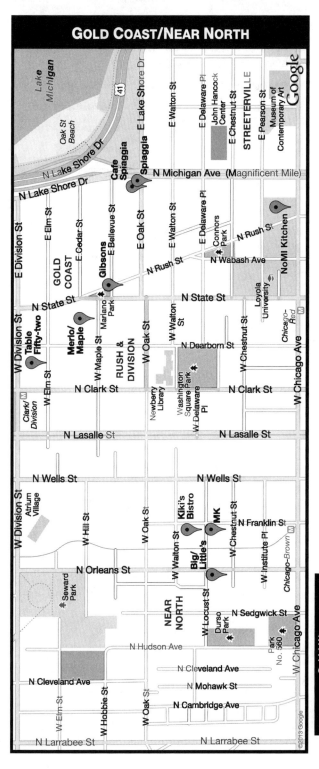

GOLD COAST/NEAR NORTH

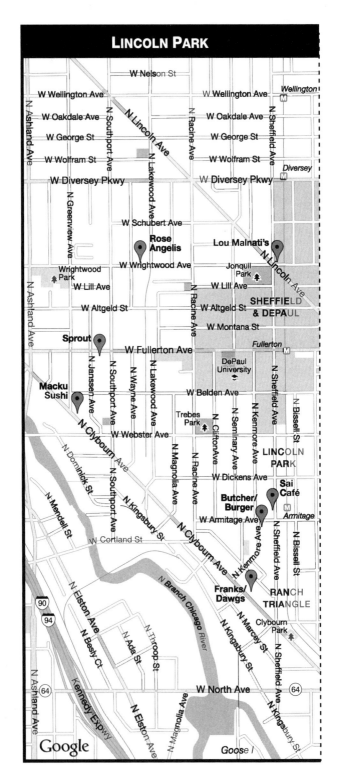

LINCOLN PARK

W Nelson St

W Wellington Ave
W Wellington Ave
Wellington

N Ashland Ave

W Oakdale Ave
N Southport Ave
N Lincoln Ave
N Racine Ave
W Oakdale Ave
N Sheffield Ave

W George St
W George St

W Wolfram St
W Wolfram St

W Diversey Pkwy
N Lakewood Ave
W Diversey Pkwy
Diversey

N Greenview Ave

W Schubert Ave

Rose Angelis
Lou Malnati's

W Wrightwood Ave
Jonquil Park
N Lincoln Ave

Wrightwood Park

W Lill Ave
W Lill Ave

N Racine Ave

W Altgeld St
W Altgeld St
SHEFFIELD & DEPAUL

W Montana St

Sprout
W Fullerton Ave
Fullerton

N Janssen Ave
N Southport Ave
N Wayne Ave
N Lakewood Ave

DePaul University
N Sheffield Ave

Macku Sushi
W Belden Ave

N Clybourn Ave
Trebes Park
N Clifton Ave
N Seminary Ave
N Kenmore Ave
N Bissell St

W Webster Ave

N Dominick St
N Magnolia Ave
N Racine Ave

W Dickens Ave
LINCOLN PARK

N Mendell St
Sai Café

N Southport Ave
N Kingsbury Ave
Butcher/ Burger
W Armitage Ave
Armitage

N Kenmore Ave
N Sheffield Ave
N Bissell St

W Cortland St

N Clybourn Ave
N Branch Chicago River
Franks/ Dawgs
RANCH TRIANGLE

90
94

N Elston Ave
N Besly Ct
N Kingsbury St
N Marcey St
Clybourn Park
N Sheffield Ave

N Dominick St
N Ada St
N Throop St

W North Ave
64
64

N Ashland Ave
Kennedy Expwy
N Elston Ave
N Magnolia Ave
Goose I

Google

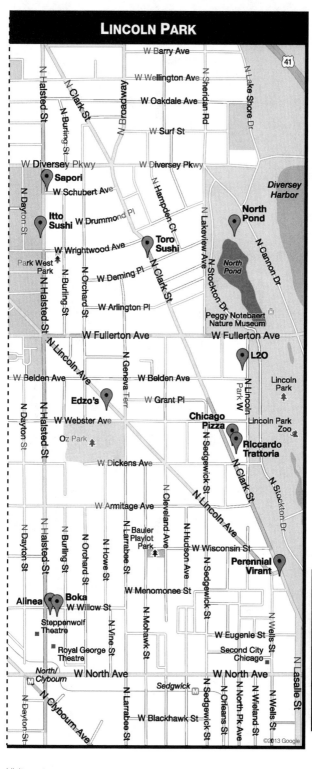

LINCOLN PARK

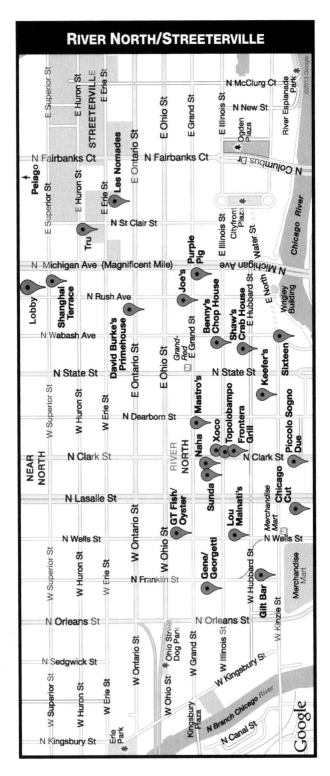

©2013 Google

STREETERVILLE

E Superior St

E Huron St

E Erie St

N McClurg Ct

River Esplanade Park

N New St

E Ohio St

E Grand St

E Illinois St

Ogden Plaza

N Fairbanks Ct

Les Nomades

E Ontario St

N Fairbanks Ct

N Columbus Dr

Pelago

E Superior St

E Huron St

E Erie St

N St Clair St

E Illinois St

Cityfront Plaza

Chicago River

Tru

E Illinois St

Water St

N Michigan Ave (Magnificent Mile)

N Michigan Ave

Purple Pig

Wrigley Building

Lobby

Shanghai Terrace

N Rush Ave

Joe's

Benny's Chop House

Shaw's Crab House

E Hubbard St

E North

Sixteen

N Wabash Ave

David Burke's Primehouse

E Ontario St

E Ohio St

Grand-Red

E Grand St

N State St

Keefer's

Sixteen

N State St

E Ohio St

Mastro's

N Dearborn St

Topolobampo

Xoco

Frontera Grill

Piccolo Sogno Due

NEAR NORTH

W Superior St

W Huron St

W Erie St

N Clark St

Naha

N Clark St

RIVER NORTH

N Lasalle St

Sunda

GT Fish/Oyster

Chicago Cut

Merchandise Mart

Merchandise Mart

W Ontario St

W Ohio St

Lou Malnati's

N Wells St

N Wells St

W Superior St

W Huron St

W Erie St

Gene/Georgetti

N Franklin St

W Hubbard St

Glit Bar

W Kinzie St

N Orleans St

N Orleans St

W Illinois St

W Kingsbury St

Merchandise Mart

N Sedgwick St

Ohio Street Dog Park

W Grand St

W Kingsbury St

Kingsbury Plaza

N Branch Chicago River

N Canal St

W Superior St

W Huron St

W Erie St

N Ontario St

Erie Park

N Kingsbury St

Google

Visit zagat.com

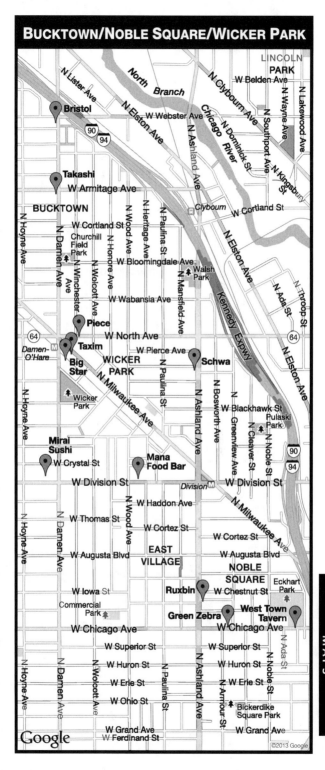

BUCKTOWN/NOBLE SQUARE/WICKER PARK

LINCOLN
PARK

W Belden Ave

Bristol

Takashi

W Armitage Ave

BUCKTOWN

Clybourn

W Cortland St
Churchill
Field
Park

W Bloomingdale Ave

Walsh
Park

W Wabansia Ave

Piece

W North Ave

Taxim

W Pierce Ave

Schwa

Big
Star

WICKER
PARK

Damen-
O'Hare

Wicker
Park

W Blackhawk St

Pulaski
Park

Mirai
Sushi

W Crystal St

Mana
Food Bar

W Division St

Division

W Division St

W Haddon Ave

W Thomas St

W Cortez St

W Cortez St

W Augusta Blvd

EAST
VILLAGE

W Augusta Blvd

NOBLE
SQUARE

Eckhart
Park

W Iowa St

Commercial
Park

Ruxbin

W Chestnut St

West Town
Tavern

Green Zebra

W Chicago Ave

W Chicago Ave

W Superior St

W Superior St

W Huron St

W Huron St

W Erie St

W Erie St

W Ohio St

Bickerdike
Square Park

W Grand Ave
W Ferdinand St

W Grand Ave

Google

©2013 Google

MAPS

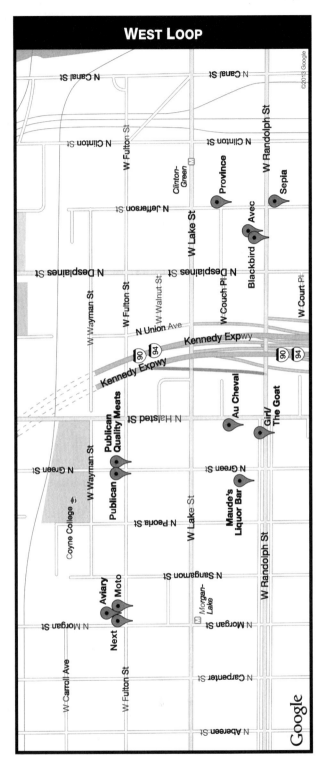